Insurance Theory and Practice

This book provides a comprehensive overview of the theory, functioning, management and legal background of the insurance industry. Written in accessible, non-technical style, *Insurance Theory and Practice* begins with an examination of the insurance concept, its guiding principles and legal rules before moving on to an analysis of the market, its players and their roles and relationships.

The model is the UK insurance market which is globally recognized and forms the basis of the insurance system in a range of countries in the Middle East, Africa and the Caribbean as well as Australia and Canada. *Insurance Theory and Practice* covers the underlying ideas behind insurance transactions, together with the legal and financial principles that permit these concepts to function in the real world.

Key issues considered include:

- the role of the constituent parts of the insurance market
- the operation of both life and general insurers with special reference to the operation of the Lloyd's market
- the nature and function of reinsurers, brokers and loss adjusters
- the influence of government, both in terms of market regulation and consumer protection
- alternatives to the established private sector insurers, such as government schemes, Islamic insurance and alternative risk financing

By illustrating the theoretical and technical aspects with case studies and discussions of current issues, Rob Thoyts successfully introduces the reader to the fundamentals of insurance in a clear and accessible fashion. This book is a concise and invaluable source of information on the theory and practice of insurance for undergraduate students of business and economics.

Rob Thoyts is Senior Lecturer at London Guildhall University, and also lectures at the Chartered Insurance Institute and the Institute of Risk Management.

Insurance Theory and Practice

Rob Thoyts

Routledge
Taylor & Francis Group

LONDON AND NEW YORK

First published 2010
by Routledge
2 Park Square, Milton Park, Abingdon, Oxon, OX14 4RN

Simultaneously published in the USA and Canada
by Routledge
711 Third Avenue, New York, NY 10017

Routledge is an imprint of the Taylor & Francis Group

Typeset in Times New Roman by Glyph International Ltd.

British Library Cataloguing in Publication Data
A catalogue record for this book is available from the British Library

Library of Congress Cataloging in Publication Data
Thoyts, Rob, 1964–
Insurance theory and practice / by Rob Thoyts.
    p. cm.
Includes bibliographical references and index.
1. Insurance. I. Title.
HG8051.T53 2010
368–dc22

2009049056

ISBN 13: 978–0–415–55904–1 (hbk)
ISBN 13: 978–0–415–55905–8 (pbk)
ISBN 13: 978–0–203–85059–6 (ebk)

Contents

List of figures vii
List of tables viii
List of UK and British Statutes ix
List of cases xii
Acknowledgments and Further Reading xiv

Introduction 1

1 Insurance as a risk transfer mechanism 4

2 Fundamental legal principles of insurance 24

3 The insurance contract 64

4 Financial and accounting principles 81

5 The structure and regulation of the UK insurance market 101

6 Lloyd's of London 136

7 Reinsurance 164

8 Insurance intermediaries 185

9 Claims handling 203

10 Life assurance 213

11 Pensions 225

12 Policyholder and third party protection 241

13   Alternative insurance systems   265

14   The role of insurance in risk management   286

     Appendix I The major classes of personal lines insurance   305
     Appendix II The major classes of commercial insurance   311
     Index   322

Figures

1.1	The classification of risk	6
1.2	The insurance concept	10
1.3	Traditional model of pure risk premium	14
1.4	Insurance as a risk-spreading mechanism	19
2.1	Insurance law and the insurance concept	26
4.1	Pattern of payments	83
4.2	Normal distribution	85
4.3	Lloyd's combined ratio by market sector	86
5.1	The structure of the UK insurance market	103
5.2	Risks to an insurer's solvency	118
5.3	The capital requirements for insurers	122
5.4	The ARROW process	127
6.1	Capital and premium flows in the Lloyd's market	140
6.2	Lloyd's capital base	142
6.3	Lloyd's losses, 1988–1992	150
6.4	Global non-life premium growth, 1980–1992	151
6.5	The LMX spiral	155
6.6	Source of Lloyd's capital	161
6.7	Lloyd's profit or loss, 1988–2008	162
7.1	How reinsurance risks are spread	168
7.2	A reinsurance pool	172
7.3	Types of reinsurance policy	173
7.4	The structure of a surplus reinsurance policy	175
7.5	The structure of an excess of loss reinsurance policy	177
7.6	The structure of a catastrophe excess of loss reinsurance policy	179
10.1	An illustrative mortality curve	214
10.2	The level premium concept	215
12.1	The FSCS levy funding arrangements	247
12.2	MIB levy, 2003–2009	264
14.1	The three pillars of risk management	287
14.2	The Heinrich triangle	288
14.3	The objectives of risk control	291
14.4	The source of finance for fundamental risks	302
14.5	The alternative means of financing fundamental risk	303

Tables

1.1	Insurability of risks and perils	18
4.1	Premium investment returns	89
4.2	Profit and loss account for Xanadu General plc	93
4.3	Balance sheet for Xanadu General plc	95
5.1	Reasons for company failure	128
6.1	Average annual losses, 1973–1992	152
6.2	Global catastrophes, 1988–1992	152
6.3	Equitas liabilities and assets in the run off	158
7.1	Surplus treaty example	175
7.2	Cost of global catastrophes	183
11.1	Replies to survey questions on pensions	235
11.2	Annuity rates for a single male aged 65 (no widow's pension)	237
11.3	Pension provision, all adults, 2005/06	238
13.1	Non-life insurance expenditure as a percentage of GDP, 2008	280
13.2	Non-life insurance expenditure as a percentage of GDP, Islamic countries, 2008	281
14.1	Risk financing – anticipated response to risk	294

UK and British Statutes

Assurance Companies Act 1909	30, 111
Assurance Companies Act 1946	112
Civil Partnerships Act 2004	30, 32
Companies Act 1862	102, 106
Companies Act 1967	112
Companies Act 1985	259
Competition Act 1998	197
Contract (Rights of Third Parties) Act 1999	169, 259
Criminal Damage Act 1971	312
Criminal Injuries to Properties (Compensation) Act 1971	270
Criminal Damage (Compensation) (Northern Ireland) Order 1977	270
Employers Liability (Compulsory Insurance) Act 1969	316
Employers Liability (Compulsory Insurance) Regulations 1971	205, 316
Employers Liability Insurance Companies Act 1907	111
Finance Act 1984	216
Financial Services Act 1986	58, 188, 195–196, 230, 248
Financial Services & Markets Act 2000	30, 113, 117–118, 188, 196, 241–242, 245, 253–254, 305
Fire Prevention (Metropolis) Act 1774	45
Fraud Act 2006	206
Industrial Assurance Act 1923	112
Insolvency Act 1986	169
Insurance Brokers Registration Act 1977	194–196
Insurance Companies Act 1982	113–117, 129, 148, 196, 241–242
Insurance Companies Amendment Act 1973	28, 218
Joint Stock Companies Act 1844	102
Life Assurance Act 1774	28–32, 38, 42, 137, 218–219
Life Assurance Act 1870	111–112
Limited Liability Act 1855	102
Limited Liability Partnership Act 2000	141

Lloyd's Act 1871   137, 144
Lloyd's Act 1982   148, 159
Married Women's Property Act 1882   219
Marine Insurance Act 1745   28, 107
Marine Insurance Act 1788   29
Marine Insurance Act 1906   28–29, 33, 38,
                                                            69, 107, 192–193
Marine Insurance (Gambling) Policies Act 1909   28
Misrepresentation Act 1967   58
Pensions Act 1995   232
Pensions Act 2004   238
Pensions Act 2007   239
Pensions Act 2008   239
Policies of Assurances Act 1867   219
Policyholder Protection Act 1975   242–245
Policyholder Protection Act 1997   244–245
Rehabilitation of Offenders Act 1974   35–36
Riot (Damages) Act 1886   48–49
Road Safety Act 2006   263
Road Traffic Act 1930   259, 305
Road Traffic Act 1988   259–260, 305–306
Sex Discrimination Act 1975   229
Sex Discrimination Act 1975 (Amendment of Legislation)
        Regulations 2008   229
Social Security Act 1986   227–228
Social Security Pensions Act 1975   226
Theft Act 1968   74
Third Parties (Rights Against Insurers) Act 1930   258–259
Unfair Contract Terms Act 1977   55–56, 75, 113

EU Directives

Accounting Directive 91/674   91–93
Consolidated Life Directive 2002/83   117–119, 122
Financial Groups Directive 2002/87   118
Gender Directive 2004 2004/113   229
Insurance Mediation Directive 2002/92   197–198
1st Life Insurance Directive 79/267   113
1st Motor Directive 72/166   305
2nd Motor Directive 84/5   260, 306
3rd Motor Directive 90/232   306
4th Motor Directive 2000/26   262–263, 306
5th Motor Directive 2005/14   306
1st Non Life Insurance Directive 73/239   113–115, 118
3rd Non Life Insurance Directive 92/49   244
Reinsurance Directive 2005/68   118

Other Legislation

Insurance Contracts Act 1984 (Australia)   254
National Flood Insurance Act 1968 (USA)   268–269
Flood Disaster Protection Act 1973 (USA)   268
Terrorism Reinsurance Insurance Act 2002 (USA)   271

Cases cited

Adams v Lindsall (1818) EWHC K.B. J59   65

Agapitos v Agnew (The Aegon) (2002) Q.B 556   207

Arbuthnot & Others v Feltrim (1995) 2 A.C. 145   156

Bank of Nova Scotia v Hellenic Mutual War Risk Association
    (The Good Luck) (1991) 1 A.C 233   36, 70

Banque Financiere de la Cite v Westgate Insurance (1991) 2 A.C 249   38, 56

Brotherton v Aseguradora Colseguros (2003) 2 All E.R (Comm) 298   36

Carter v Boehm (1766) 3 Burr 1905   32, 38

Castellain v Preston (1883) L.R. 11 Q.B.D. 380 CA   27, 42, 48

Commercial Union v Hayden (1977) Q.B 804   54

Container Transport International v Oceanus Mutual Underwriting
    Association (1984) 1 Lloyd's Rep. 476, CA (Civ Div)   34, 59

Dalby v India & London Life Assurance (1854) 15 C.B.364   31, 42, 163, 218

Dawsons Ltd v Bonnin (1922) 2 A.C. 413   70

De Hahn v Hartley (1786) 1 T.R 343   68

De Maurier (Jewels) Ltd v Bastion Insurance (1967) 2 Lloyd's Rep. 550   71

Deeny & Others v Gooda Walker (1994) 2 A.C 145   156

Drake Insurance v Provident Insurance (2003) EWCA Civ. 1834   35, 53

Economides v Commercial Union (1997) 3 All E.R. 636   33–34, 36

Elcock v Thomson (1949) 2 K.B 755   45

Equitable Life v Hyman (2000) 3 W.L.R 529, HL   129, 234

Ewer v National Employers Mutual (1937) 2 All E.R 193, KBD   206

Fraser v BN Furman (Productions) Ltd (1967) 1 W.L.R. 898   205

Galloway v Guardian Royal Exchange (1999) Lloyd's Rep I.R 209, CA   207

General Accident v Cronk (1901) 17 T.L.R 233   65

General Assurance Society v Chandermull Jain (1966) A.I.R. S.C. 1644   73

Glafki Shipping Co v Pinos Shipping Co "The Maira" (1986)
    2 Lloyd's Rep. 12, HL   44

Godsall v Boldero (1807) 9 East 72   31

Gray v Barr (1971) 2 Q.B. 554   204

Griffiths v Fleming (1909) 1 K.B 805, CA   30

Halford v Kymer (1830) 10 B & C 724   30

Hardy v Motor Insurers' Bureau (1964) 2 Q.B 745   205

Harris v Society of Lloyds (2008) EWHC 1433 (Comm)   160

Harse v Pearl Life Assurance Co (1904) 1 K.B 558, CA   30

Hebdon v West (1863) 3 B & S 579   30

Henderson & Others v Merrett Syndicates (1995) 2 A.C 145   156
Inversiones Manria SA v Sphere Drake Insurance (The Dora)
   (1989) 1 Lloyd's Rep. 69   36
Jaffrey & Others v Lloyds (2002) EWHC Civ 1101   159–160
Joel v Law Union (1908) 2 K.B 863, CA   36
Kennedy v Smith (1976) S.L.T 110   70
Lawrence v Accidental Insurance Co Ltd (1881) L.R. 7 Q.B.D. 216   40
Legal & General v Drake Ins (1991) 1 All E.R 283   52
Leppard v Excess Insurance (1979) 1 W.L.R 512   44–45
Leyland Shipping Co Ltd v Norwich Union Fire Insurance Society
   (1918) A.C. 350, HL   39–41
Lister v Romford Ice and Cold Storage Ltd (1957) A.C. 555   49
Macaura v Northern Assurance (1925) A.C. 619, HL   27
March Cabaret Club v London Assurance (1975) 1 Lloyd's Rep. 169, QBD   36
Mark Rowlands Ltd v Berni Inns Ltd (1986) Q.B. 211   29
Marsden v City & County Insurance (1865) L.R. 1 C.P. 232   40
Morris v Ford Motor Co (1973) Q.B. 792   49
Newsholme Bros v Road Transport & General Ins (1929) 2 K.B. 356   187–188
North British & Mercantile Ins Co v London, Liverpool & Globe Ins Co
   (1877) L.R. 5 Ch. D. 569, CA   52
Pan Atlantic Ins Co Ltd v Pine Top Ins Co Ltd (1994) 3 All E.R. 581, HL   35, 55, 62
Pawsey v Scottish Union & National (1907) The Times 17.10.07   39
Petrofina Ltd v Magnaload Ltd (1984) Q.B. 127   49
Printpak v AGF Ins (1999) 1 All E.R. (Comm) 466   73
Provincial Ins v Morgan (1933) A.C. 240   69
R v Financial Ombudsman Service Ltd ex parte IFG Financial Services Ltd
   (2005) EWHC 1153   257
R v Insurance Ombudsman Bureau ex parte Aegon Life (1994) L.R.L.R 101   257
Reynolds and Anderson v Phoenix Assurance Co Ltd (1978) 2 Lloyd's
   Rep. 440, QBD   36, 44–45
Rozanes v Bowen (1928) 32 Ll. L. Rep. 98, CA   33
Rust v Abbey Life (1979) 2 Lloyd's Rep. 334, CA   65
Sadler's Co v Badcock (1743) 2 Atk. 554   27, 29
Samual & Co v Duras (1924) A.C. 431   39
Simcock v Scottish Imperial Insurance Co (1902) 10 S.L.T 286, OH   30
Siu Yin Kwan v Eastern Insurance Co (1994) 2 A.C. 199   29
Society of Lloyd's v Henderson (2007) All E.R. (D) 446   160
Society of Lloyd's v Levy & Others (2004) All E.R. (D) 566   160
Sofi v Prudential Assurance (1993) 2 Lloyd's Rep. 559   204
Sprung v Royal Insurance (1997) C.L.C 70   209
Stone v Reliance Mutual Ins (1972) 1 Lloyd's Rep. 469, CA (Civ Div)   188
Strive Shipping Corporation and Royal Bank of Scotland plc v Hellenic Mutual
   War Risks Association (The Grecia Express) (2002) EWHC 203   36
Sun Fire Office v Hart (1889) L.R 14 App. Cas. 98, PC (Wind)   73
Wainwright v Bland (1835) 1 Moo. & R. 481   30
Woolcott v Sun Alliance (1978) 1 W.L.R. 493   35–36
Young v Sun Alliance (1977) 1 W.L.R. 104   75

Acknowledgments and Further Reading

When I joined London Guildhall University (now London Metropolitan University) in 1998 to teach risk and insurance, my teaching was handicapped by the lack of a good general text book covering the subject of insurance from the UK perspective. Plenty of excellent specialist texts were available but these covered one aspect of insurance or one particular market sector. There were several basic introductory texts which were fine as a starting point, but were not really at a level suitable for undergraduates or insurance managers of the future. This book is my attempt to fill the gap by covering the subject in sufficient breadth, whilst at the same time considering the issues in more depth than would be the case with a basic introductory text.

I am however only too conscious that there is only so much ground that I can cover with a text of this nature. Whilst writing I was constantly aware that in producing an introductory text, I was leaving much of the detail of the story untold. Readers, who wish to explore some of the topics introduced in this book in greater depth, may wish to look into some of the following works.

As an introduction to the area of risk, Peter Bernstein's much praised *Against the Gods* is required reading, whilst for an examination of how we as human beings respond to risk John Adam's economically titled *Risk* is a useful guide. Although the numerous American texts not unreasonably concentrate on US insurance practice, useful general comment can be found in many. Rejda's perennial favourite *Principles of risk management* and Baranoff's more recent *Risk management & insurance* are two worthy examples.

During the writing of this book, I was greatly indebted to John Birds' long established *Modern Insurance Law* who considers this aspect in much greater depth. Malcolm Clarke's *Policies and perceptions of insurance law in the twenty-first century* provides some interesting additional comment to the straightforward reporting of the law. Kiln & Kiln's *Reinsurance in practice* considers this part of insurance from a practitioner's viewpoint and Bawcutt's *Captive insurance companies* is another long running specialist work. Those with an interest in the less salubrious period of Lloyd's history might want to turn to Raphael's somewhat journalistic *Ultimate risk*.

Of course for a technical consideration of the many and varied classes of insurance, the Chartered Insurance Institute produce a range of titles to support their professional examinations.

I owe a thousand thanks to team at Routledge for their help and support in bringing this project to fruition. Of course behind many authors is a long suffering wife and for Anna's patience and forbearance I offer my gratitude and my love.

Finally, this book is dedicated to the various managers who have helped me so much during my insurance career both as a broker and an academic (and without whom this book might never have been written), managers such as Laurie Cannell and Derek Geldart at Frizzells, Allan Broadbent at Alexander & Alexander and Fred Smith at London Guildhall University. You might not always appreciate a good manager when you have one, but you certainly notice when you do not.

Rob Thoyts
May 2010

Introduction

The origins of insurance are so indistinct that uncertainty exists as to when the practice first began. Suffice to say that informal risk sharing has probably been going on for thousands of years. The development of modern insurance is much more recent, beginning in the sixteenth century, but only really becoming a mass financial market over the past 100 years or so.

Today insurance is a vast global business. Total 2008 global premiums are estimated by Swiss Re's Sigma Insurance Research as being $4,270 billion (*sigma No. (3/2009)*). Life premiums account for $2,490 billion, general insurance premiums the remaining $1,779 billion. Insurance premiums therefore account for approximately 7 per cent of world gross domestic product.

Insurance cover is certainly not evenly distributed. The developed world is heavily insured, the developing world is often all but uninsured. The 30 members of the Organisation for Economic Development and Co-operation (OECD) account for 86.5 per cent of all insurance premiums. The G7 nations alone (the USA, Canada, Japan, the UK, Germany, Italy and France, also all OECD members) constitute 68.5 per cent of the global insurance market. US policyholders pay 29 per cent of global premiums (ibid.).

This book will concentrate on the UK insurance market, the importance of which is disproportionate to the size of the overall UK economy. The UK insurance market collected total premiums of $450 billion (£243 billion) in 2008, giving the UK a 10.5 per cent share of the world market. The UK is by a wide margin the largest insurance market in Europe, holding a 25.6 per cent share of the total European insurance premiums and a 27.8 per cent share of the European Union insurance premiums (ibid.).

As of 2008, the UK insurance market comprised 1,017 companies; 209 of these offer long-term insurance (life assurance and pensions), 762 are general insurance companies and 46 are composite insurance companies, offering both long-term and general insurances.

The primary function of insurance is frequently stated to be to act as a risk transfer mechanism. The accuracy or otherwise of this view is considered in Chapter 1, however insurance does have secondary economic functions, as discussed below.

Secondary economic functions of insurance

(a) *Stimulation via security* – The security that an insurance policy provides means that funds that would have had to be retained to meet possible losses can be released. In the case of individuals, this means increased consumer spending providing a stimulus to the economy. Industry and commerce is free to undertake greater investment in the business hopefully increasing both profitability and employment. In addition, insurance facilitates such investment by increasing the likelihood that it will be successful as additional assets purchased can then be insured. Equally it reduces the risks faced by external investors (such as shareholders) thus promoting such investment. This is what is meant when people refer to an insurance policy as providing peace of mind.

(b) *Availability of finance* – Associated with the above point is the role of insurance in providing security for bank lending. Loans are frequently secured on physical assets (most commonly in the case of domestic mortgages). Such assets only represent good security if they continue to exist in an undamaged state. The insurance of the asset means that it is fairly certain that the asset will continue to secure the loan, leading to a greater willingness on the part of banks to lend.

(c) *Business promotion* – By covering some of the risks associated with business contracts, insurance makes businesses more likely to enter into such contracts, leading to a greater level of business activity. Examples would include marine insurance covering goods in transit between buyers and sellers, and liability insurance covering the consequence of errors.

(d) *Business continuity* – By providing finance in the event of catastrophe, the level of business failure is reduced, with obvious benefits in terms of increased tax revenues and reduced unemployment.

(e) *Reduced tax burden* – Insurance provides a source of financial compensation for private individuals who would otherwise turn to the state for assistance. This would include two scenarios, either where the individual directly insures their assets or earning potential or where liability insurance provides a guarantee of compensation in the event of injury that might otherwise not be forthcoming. Note that this has a cost, the insurance premium. A benefit to society only arises if the insurance industry is able to handle the loss more efficiently than government.

(f) *Source of investment* – As well as stimulating investment, the insurance industry controls vast funds which provide an additional source of finance for industrial development and government borrowing. According to the Association of British Insurers, UK insurers had £1.6 trillion invested as at December 2007. As well as large holdings of government and corporate securities, insurers owned 15 per cent of all UK shares.

(g) *Loss reduction* – The insurance industry has a vested interest in accident/fire prevention and is a major source of research funding in this area as well as providing a natural forum for discussion and dissemination.

(h) *Promoting savings* – Many 'insurance policies' are in fact savings schemes. For example, many people fund pensions via insurance companies. Some life assurance contracts also are partially or mainly savings based. Up to a point the accrual of savings could be viewed as being beneficial to the economy. This provides financial stability for individuals, reducing dependency on state benefits. Taken to extremes, however, excessive saving could lead to recession as firms struggle to sell their products as consumer spending and hence demand falls.

(i) *Invisible earnings* – The insurance industry in the UK is a major source of overseas earnings. This arises in two ways. First, UK-based insurers insure overseas risks, exporting insurance and bringing the premium income into the UK. Alternatively many UK companies maintain branch offices or insurance subsidiaries overseas. Insurance is written locally, but profits would be remitted back to the UK.

Two themes run through these secondary functions: the reduction of risk and investment. This is the service that the insurance industry offers to its policyholders and given that demand for insurance continues to grow, the policyholders presumably find this service valuable.

This book will examine the nature of insurance, the structure of the market and the role of the market participants. The relationship between the insurance market and its policyholders and the government will also be explored. Where possible, suitable illustrative cases will be discussed and current issues explored.

1 Insurance as a risk transfer mechanism

What is risk?

Derived from the Italian word 'rischio', meaning a source of peril, this everyday word is defined by the *Oxford English Dictionary* thus:

> **noun 1** *a situation involving exposure to danger.* **2** *the possibility that something unpleasant will happen.* **3** *a person or thing causing a risk or regarded in relation to risk: a fire risk.*
> **verb 1** *expose to danger or loss.* **2** *act in such a way as to incur the risk of.* **3** *incur risk by engaging in (an action).*

This definition presents no fewer than six distinct meanings, distinguishable by context. Far from offering clarity, the insurance industry jargon adds a seventh meaning by referring to 'the risk' which in this particular context means whatever is being insured by an insurance policy (in other words, the subject matter of the policy) rather than the event which might cause loss or damage.

In seeking to define what constitutes risk, two key elements emerge. There must be an element of uncertainty, and there must be the potential for loss. At the basic level, risk can be defined as simply 'the uncertainty of loss'. This adequately defines risk as ordinary individuals understand it.

This is, however, rather too simplistic for the purpose of the insurance industry. The classical theory proposed by the prominent economist, Frank Knight, argues that there is a third ingredient in risk. This third ingredient is measurement and it is measurement that allows risk to be distinguished from uncertainty. Therefore, if we do not know whether a particular event will happen, then the possible occurrence of the event is termed an uncertainty. If we do not know whether a particular event will happen, but we can at least estimate the probability that it will happen, then the possible occurrence of the event is termed a risk. As will be seen, the measurement of uncertainty is a critical element of the insurance concept.

Furthermore, an insurance policy is a financial contract and therefore the only losses an insurer is interested in are economic or financial losses. For a risk to be insurable, it must be possible not only to estimate the degree of uncertainty, but also the extent of loss in financial terms.

An adequate definition of what constitutes risk from the perspective of insurance must therefore include all four ingredients: uncertainty, measurement of uncertainty, loss, and financial quantification of loss.

For the narrow purposes of insurance, risk can be then be defined as: 'the probability of an uncertain event, causative of economic loss'.

The language of risk

Having defined risk, it is equally important that risk-related terminology, commonly used in the insurance industry is properly understood. To the layman, the terms 'hazard' and 'peril' appear to be synonymous with 'risk'. In fact, their meanings are distinct:

- *Hazard* – Although commonly used to mean 'danger', in fact the technical meaning is somewhat different. A hazard is something that affects the probability of a risk occurring. Something that the layman would regard as 'dangerous' is indeed almost certainly a hazard. For example, if a car has defective brakes, it is self-evident that the probability of a collision is increased. However, if a car is fitted with an ABS braking system, this will also affect the probability of a collision, in this case making it *less* likely. This is also a hazard. It is perhaps helpful to think in terms of negative hazards that make loss more likely and positive hazards, which make loss less likely. Insurers need to be able to identify whether a particular policyholder represents an above average or below average risk. In order to do this they must be equally interested in both the positive and the negative.
- *Peril* – Although seemingly used as a synonym for risk, a peril is subtly different. Insurers tend only to use the term in the areas of property and marine insurance, although it does have wider application. If risk is seen as the broad threat, a peril is the precise means by which the risk could come about. Therefore, if the risk is physical damage to a building, then fire, storm, flood and earthquake are all perils. Hence a common form of policy, the 'fire and perils' policy, whereby property is insured against fire and a number of specified perils.

The classification of risk

To complicate matters still further, risk can be subdivided into various classifications (Figure 1.1). First, not all risks cause measurable economic loss. Outcomes such as disappointment, trivial injury or inconvenience can arise from events commonly termed risks, but are not the concern of the financial services industry. Second, risks can be classified according to outcome, the effect and the nature of risk.

Pure vs speculative risks

The first and most important distinction between economic risks examines the potential outcome of such risks. A speculative risk is a risk with a potential for either loss or gain. A good example would be a share purchase, as the future value may increase or decrease. Any change in interest rates, either up or down, will simultaneously create both winners and losers among borrowers and lenders. Alternatively, there may be no change in price or rate, in which case the risk has not materialised and wealth is unaffected.

In the case of a pure risk, if the risk materialises, the only potential is for loss. Examples would be the risk of physical damage to property or death/injury of a person. If the risk materialises, the owner of the property (or indeed life) can only lose, while if the risk does not materialise, the owner gains nothing that they did not already possess.

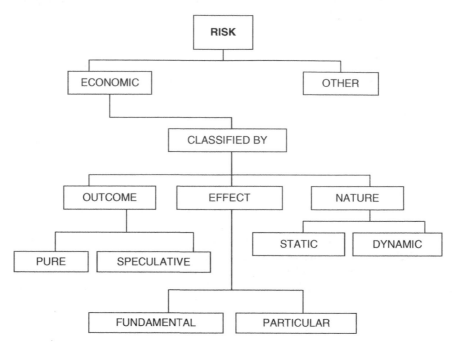

Figure 1.1 The classification of risk.

Particular vs fundamental risks

Alternatively, a risk can be considered according to its effect. A particular risk affects an individual or a small group of individuals. For example, there are around 30 million motorists in the UK. Even the most severe motor accidents can only affect a tiny handful of the total. If we are to consider that the occasional major conflagrations such as London in 1666, and Moscow in 1812 (where the true cause was war in any event) are unlikely to be repeated, the effect of fire is similarly limited.

Fundamental risks, on the other hand, affect a sizeable percentage of a given population or even the entire population. An interest rate change will have some effect on every borrower and lender, in other words, almost the entire adult population of a developed country. If a country is at war and the conflict extends to its territory, a significant number of its people will suffer violent injury and/or property damage. While it is generally easy to classify risks as pure or speculative, it is less easy to label risk as particular or fundamental. First, there is a large grey area, where the occurrence of a risk would affect a large number of people but not necessarily involve more than a small percentage of the population. Many natural disasters fall into this category, for example, floods or storms. In the case of flood, the risk is minimal for many home owners, only properties on low-lying land close to a body of water are likely to be affected. Is the population of all properties at risk or only properties in 'at risk' areas? In the first case, it could be argued the risk is particular, in the second case, fundamental.

Second, some broad risks can have exceptions. One individual's early death will generally have no bearing on the probability of other early deaths. Therefore, as a rule, early death can be considered a particular risk. If, on the other hand, the cause of death is infectious disease, it is possible that any single death will be one of many brought about by the same virus. Therefore, a risk may generally be particular but certain causes or perils may have a fundamental effect.

It is also worth considering that it is not necessarily the case that a risk is always either particular or fundamental. Consider, for example, the risks of unemployment or bad debts. Such events could be considered as particular on the grounds that they arise from the insolvency of a single company, perhaps due to poor management. If the economic outlook is benign, this may well be the case. On the other hand, if the economy is in recession, the difficult trading conditions causing the failure of one company will affect not only their competitors but other economic sectors as well. The result is likely to be a rise in the number of business failures and a commensurate rise in unemployment and bad debts. This could certainly be viewed as a fundamental effect.

Therefore, an alternative view is that particular risks tend to be independent. If the risk materialises, affecting one individual, does this increase the probability that other individuals facing the same risk will suffer? If a house in London catches fire, this will have no effect on the probability of a house in another part of the country catching fire. If, on the other hand, the house is damaged by storm, the likelihood is that the effect of the storm will be widespread, damaging many houses in different parts of the country.

Static vs dynamic risks

A third method of classifying risk is to consider the nature of the risk. The essential nature of some risks never significantly changes. The risk that property will be destroyed by fire is ancient. Major causes of fire in the twenty-first century include heat sources used for heating, cooking and lighting. Arson is also common, with riots and civil commotions forming a well-established sub-set. If fire losses occurring hundreds of years ago are considered, the same causes emerge. The Great Fire of London, for example, was caused by a failure to properly extinguish an oven in a bakery. Moscow was destroyed by arson in 1812, although perhaps it would be more accurate to consider the cause to be war. Such unchanging risks are termed static.

Other risks constantly change. The law, for example, does not stand still. Conduct that 100 years ago would not have resulted in any liability may be actionable in the modern legal environment. The development of technology has radically changed risks such as fraud. A bank account can be emptied and the contents transferred to another continent without the involvement of any bank employee. The internet has seen the rise of methods such as 'phishing', attempting to trick a bank customer into revealing their personal details, which has no pre-internet equivalent. Such risks are termed dynamic.

By classifying risk, the consequences and predictability of risk occurrence can be anticipated. As will be seen, this has significant implications for the insurance industry.

Human response to risk

There is a natural tendency to take the view that as risk involves danger to persons or property, representing the downside of life, it is consequently something to be avoided. Obviously some risks have to be incurred through the simple process of living, we need food, drink and shelter for basic survival and must take a degree of risk to obtain such basics. However, this does not explain why people take part in dangerous sports, gamble in casinos or engage in extra-marital affairs. These are extreme examples but everyone voluntarily incurs risk unnecessary for basic survival. Given that any rational person would want to avoid loss or detriment, there must be a reason why risks are intentionally incurred. The answer is that there is always a perceived upside or benefit to the assumption of risk, not necessarily capable of financial measurement and which might only be considered as a benefit by a tiny minority of individuals. It may not even exist in fact, being a product of false perception. However, it is this upside (the benefit) that is the reason why we accept the possible downside (the loss).

Economists, particularly those commenting on the financial markets, tend to divide people into three categories:

1   *The risk averse* – People who actively dislike uncertainty and therefore will be prepared to pay for certainty (or a close approximation) even if the cost of certainty exceeds the probable loss. They would also accept a lower certain return than a higher, uncertain expected value. They are the instinctive hedgers.
2   *The risk preferrers* (alternatively *risk lovers*) – The exact opposite, these people actively enjoy uncertainty and will tend to accept a degree of uncertainty even if offered the opportunity to pay for certainty (or a close approximation). Alternatively, rather than accept a lower certain return, they would tend to choose uncertainty if the potential return was higher, even if the expected return was equal to the certain return offered. They are the instinctive gamblers.
3   *The risk neutral* – Theoretically, some people exist who display no emotional reaction to risk. Their choices would be determined by cold calculation of probabilities and therefore expected outcomes. If we are to accept that such individuals do exist, they are the automatons.

However, this theory depends upon measurement of risk. If probable outcomes cannot be measured, the concept of risk neutrality becomes irrelevant as no judgement can be made as to the mathematically logical decision. Similarly, only extreme risk aversion/preference can be measured, in other words, those who will always hedge or always gamble, as it is impossible to say whether a particular choice is or is not risk averse.

More specifically, this theory depends upon the *financial* measurement of risk on the slightly dubious assumption that money offers a more or less equal reward to all. The motivation to run risk is reward. If an individual chooses not to run the risk, is this because they are risk averse or is it because they personally do not recognise that there is any potential reward? Presumably we would all consider money to be reward, but any other commodity is a matter of personal taste. A bag of peanuts has no value to a monkey with a nut allergy.

Therefore, risk decisions are not merely a factor of appetite for risk, they also depend upon individual perception and preference. Under- or over-estimating either risk or reward would distort the decision. Even if perception is accurate, different individuals would obtain variable utility from the potential reward, again affecting the decision. Equally, as economists tend to consider financial risks, the label 'risk averse' only means that a particular individual displays risk aversion when making financial decisions. This does not necessarily mean that they display risk aversion when confronted by other risks. An individual might adopt an extremely conservative investment strategy yet cheerfully partake in dangerous sports. Alternatively, the boldest entrepreneur may be extremely health conscious.

One alternative view is that we come fitted with a personal thermometer, which we use to measure subjectively the risks associated with everything we do. Proposed by Gerald Wilde, a Canadian psychologist, the hypothesis is that rather than possessing crude, inflexible attitudes, we are infinitely sensitive to risk.

The perceived rewards of taking risk incite us to assume risk. However, at the same time, the perceived losses make us equally aware of the dangers. We then balance possible reward against possible risk and make a subjective judgement as to the level of risk we are prepared to accept given the rewards. In some circumstances we may choose to avoid a risk completely, but it is more likely that we will seek to manage risk by adopting behaviour we perceive will reduce the possibility of loss even if this also reduces reward. Our aim is to achieve a comfortable risk temperature. This can be subject to wide variation between individuals, some like it hot, others prefer to play it cool.

The model suggests that everyone has the propensity to take risks, but this propensity varies from individual to individual. People are motivated to take risks by the perceived rewards of risk taking, but the perception of loss reduces willingness to take risks. The perceptions of the degree of risk are influenced by prior experience of loss, either one's own or others. Therefore, individual risk-taking decisions are a balance between perception of risk and propensity to take risks. Losses and rewards are the consequence of taking risks. The more risks are undertaken, the more loss and the more reward the individual is likely to incur.

As will be demonstrated, theoretically an insurance premium (or approximate certainty) must be greater than the expected cost of risk. Therefore, the act of purchasing insurance could be said to indicate risk aversion. However, it could not be inferred that the purchaser of an insurance policy is averse to financial risk. If, for example, the financial arrangements of all individuals whose investment portfolio demonstrated risk preference (i.e. higher than average risk) were to be studied, most if not all would hold insurance policies, voluntarily purchased. As to non-financial risks, any motor insurer will readily confirm that the voluntary purchase of motor insurance, over and above the legal requirement, in no way indicates that an individual will drive in a risk-averse manner.

What is in fact happening is that every individual is constantly faced with risks, whether physical, financial or social. We are all forced to make risk decisions on a daily basis. Consciously or not, we conduct cost/benefit analyses, possibly considering risk reduction measures, before deciding on a course of action. Of course a natural propensity to risk aversion or preference will be influential, but not conclusive. The potential loss may be so severe (e.g. loss of life or bankruptcy) that any sane person would be averse to it. Alternatively, the benefits may loom so large that even the naturally cautious may be blinded to the risks. We therefore continually revisit our prior risk decisions in the light of new information. While risk aversion is the most important driver of insurance purchase, in many cases, insurance covers losses of such magnitude that almost everyone would be averse. What is perhaps more important to insurers is that the claims experience is influenced by the risk decisions of their policyholders. Any change in circumstance that makes policyholders feel safer (for example, improved vehicle safety) is likely to worsen claims experience as the perception of risk diminishes, thus increasing the desire for benefit. Of course, the reverse is also true, fear is the insurer's friend. Articles in the press highlighting increased burglary rates are likely to lead not only to increased sales of insurance, but also for existing policyholders to act more cautiously, ensuring use of existing security measures and perhaps enhancing such measures.

The existence of risk is therefore the basic driver of the insurance industry. The occurrence of serious losses do of course cost the insurers money, however, they also reinforce risk aversion and therefore promote the purchase of insurance and improvements in risk control. Therefore, when an insurer looks gloomily at a satellite photograph of a hurricane developing in the Caribbean, they should look more closely at the edge of the cloud spiral. They may just detect a silver lining.

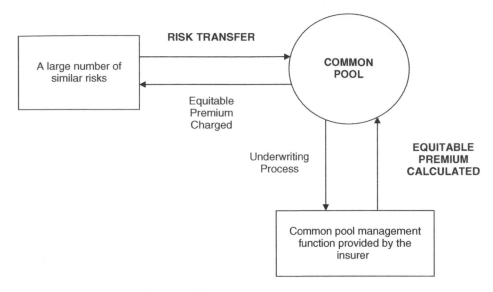

Figure 1.2 The insurance concept.

The insurance concept

There is a common misconception among insurance policyholders that they are entering into an individual arrangement with their insurance company. This is not surprising as this is how the law views the relationship. In fact, the insurance concept operates in a somewhat different manner (Figure 1.2). Insurance companies are financial intermediaries.

Risk transfer

The starting point is that a situation exists whereby a reasonably large number of individuals all face a similar economic risk with a reasonably low probability of occurrence. The risk is of a magnitude that it would at least seriously damage the wealth of the unfortunate few who suffer loss. Even if the probability of loss is low, the consequences are sufficiently severe to lead to risk aversion and therefore to a desire to avoid the risk. However, if the benefits gained are perceived to be so valuable that they cannot be foregone, for example, home ownership, then the risk has to be accepted. If you own a home, you have no alternative but to accept the risk that it may be damaged. If you drive a car, you must accept the risk that you may be injured in a motor accident. These are personal risks that cannot be transferred. However, the *financial consequences* of risk *can* be transferred. It is this transfer of financial consequences that forms the first stage of the insurance concept.

Common pool

The next point to consider is where the financial consequences of risks are transferred to. The superficial answer would be that they are transferred to an insurer. The problem with this argument is that recognisable insurance transactions were taking place thousands of years before the first insurance companies appeared. In fact, the risk is being transferred from a number of individuals to a collective pool. This pool contains the collective risk of its members, together with the collective resources these members have set aside to meet the occurrence of such risk. Each member surrenders a small sum to the pool with the intention that this be used to meet the collective loss, regardless of where the loss actually falls.

One reason for the false perception is the frequent claim made in insurance advertising that 'you will not be paying for the mistakes of others'. But this is *exactly* what a policyholder is agreeing to do. The reason that we are happy to do so is that we cannot know whether we will be the one who makes a mistake and need to draw on the pooled resource to meet the cost. Faced with the possibility of severe financial loss, it makes sense to elect to take a small, certain loss instead.

The term 'common pool' refers to the fact that the risks borne by the pool are all of a similar nature, even if they are not identical. It is this lack of total homogeneity that was influential in the establishment of insurance companies.

Equitable premium

Human nature being what it is, every risk holder would like to be a member of the pool and receive financial consequence in the event of loss. However, human nature also dictates that we would all like to contribute as small a sum as possible. If the decision regarding contributions is left to the members themselves, there is a danger that the understandable reluctance to pay means that collective contributions are insufficient to meet collective losses. In order to meet the potential losses, there are two approaches that can be taken: flat rate and equitable premiums.

The simplest method is to charge every pool member the average cost of loss for the average member (plus the cost of administering the pool). Deceptively straightforward, in fact, this methodology is fatally flawed. The risks in the pool may be similar, but they are not identical. If a flat rate premium based upon average costs is charged, those members who represent a better than average risk will be subsidising those members who are below average risks. This may arise either because the hazard factor is lower (i.e. it is less probable that the loss will occur) or because the greater wealth of certain policyholders means that their losses will be larger on average.

Premiums will look expensive to 'good' risks while seeming cheap to 'poor' risks. The likely result will be that below average risks are disproportionately represented in the pool as good risks are deterred and poor risks attracted, raising the average cost of loss per policyholder and leading to a shortfall in pool funding. This risk that only those more likely to claim will take out insurance is known as 'selection' by insurers and is feared due to its distorting effect on loss estimates.

Flat rate premiums are only workable where the size of the premium is so small that any differential will be so small that the distorting effect on the pool will be trivial. The cost of underwriting would also be out of all proportion to the benefits, raising the cost for all risks, good and bad. An example would be travel insurance where limited questions are asked and adverse hazards tend to be dealt with by exclusion of cover rather than premium adjustment.

The alternative is to charge each member of the pool a sum of money that represents the financial equivalent of the degree of risk that they have transferred into the pool, i.e. an equitable premium. This requires that a hazard analysis is undertaken to determine the probable frequency and severity of loss for each applicant. The expected cost of loss is its probable frequency multiplied by its probable severity. A sum equivalent to this expected cost can then be charged, known as the pure risk premium. This pure risk premium is the part of the premium that is going into the pool to cover the risk, as opposed to the part of the premium that is going to cover administrative expenses. Using this method, a fair premium will be paid by all based upon their risk, cross-subsidisation can be avoided (at least in theory) and therefore membership should be equally attractive to all, avoiding selection.

It is suggested that any pool that is not based upon equitable premium principles is unlikely to succeed. Only if there is a *very* high degree of homogeneity between risks can flat rating work, as in this case equitable premiums would be more or less equal and it could be argued that the saving in administrative costs would outweigh any benefit to be gained from the strict application of the equitable premium. This is rare indeed in the real world and when insurers do flat rate premiums, it is generally because the premiums are so low that differentiation is not cost effective rather than because they are truly highly homogeneous. Even this is becoming unusual as the use of computerised quotation systems and the internet allows insurers to distinguish between risks at minimal cost.

The role of insurers

Obviously the existence of insurance companies adds to the cost of the risk pooling arrangement we know as insurance. They must therefore provide a valuable service to justify this cost. This service is the management of the common pool, which can be broken down into seven key responsibilities.

Controlling membership of the pool

As will be seen, insurance presumes that the policyholder possesses a financial interest in the risk being insured. There is also a presumption that risk of loss is reasonably low. The first duty of an insurer is to limit membership of the pool to those who seek to cover against the possibility of financial loss. (See subsequent comments headed 'Insurable interest' and 'Reasonably low probability of loss' in the discussion of the insurability of risk.)

Calculation of the equitable premium

As stated, calculation of the equitable premium is a critical part of the insurance concept in all major insurance classes. The primary role of the insurer is to undertake such calculation in order that the common pool may be constructed. Known in the industry as underwriting, insurers carry out an 'arm's length' analysis of the relative hazards for each proposal for pool membership to determine the required premium. The greater the expected loss for a given proposal, the greater the premium. Conversely, risks possessing good features should attract a discount.

The use of an insurer as an independent arbiter allows vastly larger pools to be established, to the point where the members lose awareness of the collective principle underpinning insurance. The benefit, however, is that insurers are generally experienced risk assessors and can also apply economies of scale, thus greatly increasing efficiency.

Arrangement of reinsurance

Although insurers will calculate the mathematically expected cost of losses, the actual outcome will almost certainly differ. In order to ensure that the pool is not unduly exposed to catastrophe loss and to smooth out variance in the results from year to year, insurers arrange reinsurance. In the same way that the policyholders make a small certain loss to reduce larger unexpected losses, insurers achieve the same via a transfer of excess risk to a reinsurer (see Chapter 7).

Risk improvement

Although proper calculation of the odds is a fundamental part of the underwriter's art, insurance companies then seek to modify these odds in their favour by seeking to improve the risk insured. This can be general, by imposing minimum security requirements before offering theft cover, for example. Alternatively, it can be specific, physically inspecting the risk and requiring particular improvements based upon the survey.

Investment of the pool funds

As a general rule, premiums will be paid in advance; however, claims may arise at any time during the period of insurance, possibly close to the end of the period. The actual payment of claims will occur at a later date to permit investigation of the loss or due to the time necessary to carry out repairs. In the case of life assurance, the claim payment may be decades after the inception of the policy, although premiums would normally be paid in monthly instalments rather than in advance. In order to maximise the financial efficiency of the pool, insurers invest the premiums prior to claim settlements to provide further income to the pool.

Control of claim payments

Often referred to as the acid test of insurance, insurers must avoid gaining a reputation for slow or unfair claims payments, while at the same time managing the pool effectively. Premiums have been collected on the basis that the policy covers defined risks. If an insurer settles a claim for a risk not envisaged by the policy, no premium will have been collected in respect of this risk and, if repeated, may lead to a deficit in the pool. Even where the peril that has occurred is clearly covered, most insurance offers no more than an indemnity against incurred losses. If an insurer frequently pays more than a fair indemnity, insufficient premium will have been collected to cover surplus payments. While this may be to the benefit of individual claimants, if the pool becomes insolvent as a result, this is greatly to the detriment of subsequent claimants.

Guaranteeing the solvency of the pool

Finally, the insurer, having taken responsibility for managing the pool, has one further duty. They must stand as guarantors of the pool's solvency. If the pool is in deficit, that deficit must be funded by the insurer's own assets, even to the point of the insurer's insolvency.

In the past, risk pools operated by a relatively small number of participants on their own behalf were not uncommon, indeed, many modern insurers began life in this fashion. This is a very unusual arrangement today. The greater efficiency of insurance companies in managing the common pool combined with the additional financial security of the insurer's own assets, means that co-operative risk pools are unlikely to be encountered except in circumstances where insurance companies are unwilling to offer cover.

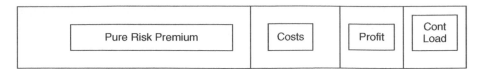

Figure 1.3a Traditional model of pure risk premium.

The components of an insurance premium

The role of the insurer as the manager of the common pool can be demonstrated by considering the component parts of an insurance premium.

Traditional insurance premium model

The traditional model is as shown in Figure 1.3a. The pure risk premium is the premium necessary to cover the mathematically expected loss. Note it is highly unlikely that this would be the actual loss, it may even be impossible that it would be the actual loss. However, over a large number of policies the total pure risk premiums collected should approximate to the total loss. Although variable according to the class of business and the efficiency of individual insurers, the pure risk premium for general insurance is likely to be around 65–75 per cent of the total premium paid.

The insurers incur costs in underwriting the risk (including commissions), issuing documentation and settling claims. These costs are added to the pure risk premium which means that an insurance premium will always be more expensive than the probability of loss truly demands.

Theoretically, an insurer will add a profit margin to the premium and possibly a contingency load, an additional sum to cover the possibility that the actual losses will exceed the estimated losses. In fact, it is far more likely that there will be no profit or contingency load.

Probable insurance premium model

Figure 1.3b Probable insurance premium model.

Although superficially this would seem to indicate that there is nothing in the transaction for the insurer, due to the unusual nature of insurance transactions, this is not case. As previously mentioned, insurance premiums are generally paid at the commencement of cover. The majority of the costs incurred by the insurer (the cost of administering and settling claims payments) are not incurred until some time after receipt of the premium. This can be contrasted with manufacturers who incur most of their costs before the point of sale.

The generation of investment income on the pool funds is then of critical importance in insurance. The insurers can take advantage of two delay periods in order to generate this investment income. First, the delay between the payment of the premium and the loss arising.

Second, the delay between the loss occurring and the claim being settled, this being the legitimate delay caused by the reasonable investigation and negotiation of the claim. The period of delay will vary according to the class of insurance. During the delay period, the funds will be in the possession of the insurer who will earn investment income on the application of these funds. Where a market is both predictable and competitive (e.g. motor insurance), contingency and profit loads may be foregone and the insurer's profits will be provided by the investment income.

This is demonstrated by Houston's formula, giving the true cost of insurance to the policyholder:

$$I = P(1 + r)^t$$

Where:

I   = The cost of insurance
P   = The premium
$1 + r$ = The return potentially gained by investing the premium
t   = The period the premium can be invested for

The true cost of insurance is then the premium, plus the investment income that could have been derived from the premium had it not been paid over to the insurer.

There is then an opportunity cost to the policyholder and converse benefit to the insurer based on the fact that it is the insurer who holds the premium and derives investment income from it.

The insurability of risk

Not every risk is a suitable case for insurance. The nature of the insurance concept means that risks covered by insurance companies tend to possess certain features:

1 *Financial measurement* – The loss insured against must be capable of financial measurement. If this were not the case, insurers would be unable to calculate likely losses and therefore estimate the equitable premium. They would also be uncertain as to how much to pay in the event of a claim. In the case of life and limb, such calculation of loss becomes difficult; however, given that such policies are generally not indemnity policies, a reasonable advance estimate or lump sum suffices.

2 *Insurable interest* – The financial interest the policyholder has in the subject matter of a policy. It can be viewed as the measure of financial value, but it also limits membership of the common pool to participants who face loss should the risk occur and may therefore be expected to manage the risk. After all, insurance cannot compensate for distress, inconvenience or in most cases the full financial cost, therefore despite the existence of insurance, the policyholder is better off if the risk does not occur. Insurance then relies on the common pool being comprised of (occasionally incompetent) risk managers trying to prevent the loss, as opposed to a pool of speculators hoping the risk will occur and possibly prepared to assist the loss process.

3 *Pure risk* – Insurance is in the business of loss. There is nothing in an insurance contract that permits the insurer to share in a gain. The natural territory of insurance is the field of accidental *loss*. When a speculative risk is insured, problems are likely to emerge arising out of the nature of such risks. We choose to specifically run these risks, they do not arise naturally.

Clearly we expect gain, but are aware of the possibility of loss. Pure risks, on the other hand, are a by-product of our choices. We buy a house in order that we have somewhere to live, not to run the risk of its destruction in a fire.

The existence of insurance does not determine to any significant extent which house we purchase. While it can be argued that it is possible that some policyholders are less careful because they know they are insured, it is equally arguable that the work that insurers do in promoting loss prevention plus the fear of higher premiums counteract this effect. Therefore, it is reasonable to assume that the existence of insurance does not affect the underlying risk insured to any great degree.

If speculative risks are insured, the insurance itself can distort the risk to the detriment of the insurer. Such insurance might, by indemnifying the downside of the risk, create a one-way bet and it would be irrational not to speculate when you cannot lose. The catalyst for risk management is the prospect of loss, so when this catalyst is removed, then risk management will also tend to be removed.

By minimising the perception of loss, the perceived reward is magnified. The result is that the existence of insurance encourages riskier speculations. The probability of loss is then increased and the existence of insurance has negatively affected the underlying risk. This is termed *moral hazard*, meaning a hazard introduced due to human reaction to the very existence of the insurance.

4 *Particular risk* – Insurance works best when it covers particular risks, indeed, it can be argued that insurance companies cannot safely cover fundamental risks. One of the basic insurance principles is that the many compensate the few. Clearly when the risk is particular, the individual or small group affected are easily compensated from the resources of the pool. When a fundamental risk occurs, a danger exists that the majority of the pool are affected, begging the question, can a minority compensate a majority? The answer generally is that the solvency of the pool is difficult to guarantee in such circumstances.

However, insurers do cover natural disasters such as earthquakes, floods and storms, events which could be considered fundamental. How can this be? The answer is twofold. First, such cover is not available in every country. In the UK, earthquake cover is cheap and freely available as earthquakes are infrequent and localised, i.e. earthquake is a particular risk. This is not the case in Japan or California where the availability of cover requires governmental support. Second, while risks may be fundamental in the eyes of local insurers, they are particular to global reinsurers. A hurricane that sweeps across Florida would cause serious, possibly fatal losses to a Florida property insurer. However, it would only affect a small percentage of the policies reinsured worldwide.

5 *Common risk* – The construction of an insurance pool requires that a reasonably large number of potential policyholders exist, all facing a similar type and level of risk. The smaller the variation in the risks, the easier and therefore cheaper it will be to underwrite as premiums are tightly grouped around the average risk. Risks which deviate greatly will require individual attention at greater cost. This might be acceptable in commercial insurance where premium levels are higher, but not in mass market personal lines cover where margins can be small. For all types of insurance, however, a point is reached where the risk is so unique that it could be argued that it can no longer be considered a part of the pool and becomes difficult to underwrite. It could also be argued even if the premium is commensurate with the risk, the higher administrative cost is unfairly subsidised by the other policyholders. The likely response is that insurers refuse cover.

By way of example, many mainstream motor insurers refuse cover to high risk motorists, not because they cannot price the risk but because it is too time-consuming to do so.

Other insurers have chosen to specialise in this risk sector and, in their case, the high risk motorist becomes the norm rather than significantly sub-standard.

6 *Reasonably low probability of loss* – The basic principle of the unfortunate few being compensated by the contributions of the fortunate many has already been mentioned. In the medium and certainly the long term, all insurance pools require that only a minority of policyholders claim. It goes without saying that the occurrence of loss must be less than certain within the policy period, otherwise it would not be a risk. But in fact an insurance pool becomes financially unworkable long before certainty approaches.

This is due to the way that premiums are calculated. As previously noted, only a percentage of the premium paid is the pure loss premium. Therefore, the point at which the cost of insurance purchase exceeds the potential indemnity is reached long before the probability of loss reaches 100 per cent.

It is also the case that the greater the potential for a catastrophic loss, the lower the probability of loss must be. A motor insurer might consider a 20 per cent probability of loss within a year to be reasonably low. An aviation insurer would expect the probability of loss to be a tiny fraction of this figure.

7 *Fortuitous loss* – As discussed, insurance covers possibilities not certainties. It is a feature of an insurable risk, that the occurrence of loss is fortuitous from the perspective of the policyholder. Indeed, if the policyholder were to deliberately bring about a loss and claim, that would constitute fraud.

The only exception to this would be circumstances where the best efforts of the policyholder could not guarantee not to bring about the loss. Such policies are rare, but insurers have insured golfers against scoring a hole in one or, to be more accurate, the cost of buying everyone in the bar a drink having performed the feat! Football teams have been insured against winning the league, specifically the cost of paying promised bonuses to the players. In both cases the insurer accepts that the policyholder will be trying to bring about a claim, but even their best efforts cannot guarantee success.

Although the deliberate actions of the policyholder would be excluded, most policies would cover honest mistakes. Indeed, most liability insurance is specifically designed to cover the negligence of the policyholder. Only when the policyholders conduct becomes reckless, defined as realising a serious risk existed and proceeding not caring whether it is averted, might the policy be invalidated. In such circumstances it could be considered that the existence of insurance might influence such behaviour and theoretically at least, insurance should not increase the probability of loss.

8 *Conforming to public policy* – Insurance receives considerable support from the law. Where common law principles are insufficient, legislation has been enacted to give effect to a functional insurance contract. The general view of government has been that insurance is a prudent practice which should be supported. So long as insurance is seen as beneficial to society in general and the economy in particular, this seems certain to remain the case. However, it is expected that insurance will not be misused for purposes that might be considered immoral or which might conflict with other areas of public policy. It goes without saying that attempting to directly insure an illegal act would be unlawful, for example, a marine insurance policy covering contraband would not be upheld by the courts. The principle goes beyond illegality, so a policy that offers to indemnify the policyholder against being fined by the courts would certainly be deemed contrary to public policy. The effect of insuring would be to spread the cost of the fine among the general public, thus defeating the deterrence and retribution arguments that justified the fine in the first place.

Table 1.1 Insurability of risks and perils

Naturally insurable	*Generally insurable*	*Difficult to insure*
Fire	Flood	Terrorism
Theft/malicious damage	Storm	War
Damage to motor vehicles	Legal liabilities	Nuclear accidents
Accidental death	Riot	
Death from cancer	Death from infectious disease	
Explosion	Bad debts Earthquake Pollution	

Put these factors together and the insurability or otherwise of risks or perils can be mapped, for the UK at least (Table 1.1). The perils in the naturally insurable category are freely insurable not only in the UK but around the world. In each case, the risks are particular, independent and a sufficiently large pool of such risks can be created. The generally insurable risks are all commonly insured in the UK, however they are in some way problematic for insurers. A number of these risks are arguably fundamental, flood and bad debts being examples. Others, while easily insured in the UK, are not necessarily easy to insure in other countries. Legal liability risks are not static, and where personal injury is involved, have a long 'tail' (claims appear many years after the period of insurance). Pollution is in many cases not fortuitous as the pollutant may be released deliberately as a part of an industrial process. In other countries this map would look very different. Earthquake risk in countries like Japan and Iran would be in the difficult-to-insure category. Flood risk would certainly be exceptionally difficult to cover in Bangladesh. Riot cover may not be available in some countries where the political situation raises the probability of such an event to an unacceptable degree.

The difficult-to-insure category includes risks that are generally uninsurable, although terrorism cover may be available via special schemes (see Chapter 13). The terrible destructive effect of war is of a scale that no insurer can offer cover. The Second World War caused heavy damage to countless cities. Some were almost completely destroyed, Hiroshima, Stalingrad and Berlin being prominent illustrations. Similarly, the loss of tens of millions of lives, a large percentage of which were young lives, could not be covered by a life assurer. War risks are excluded from the great majority of policies issued worldwide. The exception is marine and aviation where although cover is excluded from the standard policy, it may be offered as an extension if a conflict is localised. This is because the global nature of transportation risks means that only a small percentage of insured risks are likely to be in the war zone at any one time. Even so the probability of loss can rise to a point that insurers refuse cover.

Why buy insurance?

There are three primary reasons for purchasing insurance:

1   *Risk aversion* – Few people have a risk thermometer set so high that they would never become risk averse. Insurance is purchased in situations where the individual feels that the risk insured against is such that it does represent an unacceptable financial loss. The initial setting of the thermometer will control at what point the individual feels that a risk is unacceptable and this is highly variable.

2   *Legal compulsion* – In some cases the purchase of insurance is mandatory. In the UK, the main examples are third party motor insurance and employers' liability insurance.
3   *Contractual obligation* – Many individuals and companies enter into contracts under which they are obliged to purchase insurance. A prime example is a mortgage contract. The borrower would certainly have to agree to insure the property concerned as a condition of the mortgage and would also be required to insure their life. It is also common in commercial contracts for one or both parties to agree to arrange insurance.

The primary function of insurance

The function of insurance can be considered in three rather different ways. It can be considered as either a risk transfer mechanism, a risk-spreading mechanism or even as a risk transformation mechanism.

The traditional view is that insurance is a risk transfer mechanism. The policyholder transfers the risk of what to them might be catastrophic financial loss. If such loss occurs, the consequences are transferred from the policyholder to the insurer.

A second and usually more realistic view is that the policyholder is spreading the risk. This requires consideration of the long-term position. General insurance is mostly provided by means of annual policies. In any single policy period, the risk is transferred, in that a claim, if it arises, will likely be greater than the premium paid. However, this single period should not be looked at in isolation. The risk will be continuing and in most cases further cover will be purchased at the expiry of the policy.

In the case of motor insurance, the policyholder enters into a long-term relationship with the insurer. They must by law purchase insurance for as long as they drive a motor vehicle, a period that could be 60 years or more. It is self-evident that the majority of motorists will over this extended period contribute more in premiums than they collect in claims. Were this not the case, motor insurers would be forced into insolvency. If the claims payments received are more than accounted for by the premiums paid, no risk transfer has occurred. What has taken place is a risk-spreading mechanism whereby the policyholder's lifetime risk cost is spread over many years in manageable annual instalments (Figure 1.4).

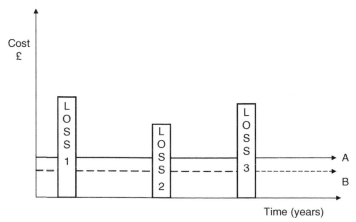

A = Average annual premium cost over the insurance buying lifetime
B = Average annual claims cost over the insurance buying lifetime

Figure 1.4 Insurance as a risk-spreading mechanism.

A minority of policyholders will incur a catastrophe loss. In the case of motor insurance, this would mean a large third party liability. A loss of several million pounds cannot be recouped from subsequent premiums over the policyholder's insurance-buying lifetime. Such policyholders can fairly to be said to have transferred risk. Of course, we cannot know in advance which category we as individuals will fall into, however the probability is that we will be risk spreaders rather than risk transferors. The surplus insurers generate from the large number of policyholders who suffer no catastrophe loss is required to compensate the small number who do suffer catastrophe loss, hence the probability that most policyholders will pay more in premium than they recover in claims over their lifetime.

As this view envisages the possibility of an unknown number of losses of an unknown cost spread over an extended period, it does not apply to life assurance. Life assurers would be surprised to say the least to receive multiple claims from the same policyholder! This form of insurance, it is fair to say, is a risk transfer mechanism.

A further view of the function of insurance is that it is a risk transformation mechanism. A range of pure risks can in financial terms be converted by the medium of an insurance policy to a credit risk founded on the solvency of the insurance company. It would be ludicrous to suggest that any private policyholder would consider insurance purchase in this way and due to the consumer protection available, it would be incorrect for them to do so. However, large corporations can and do view insurance in this fashion. The purchase of insurance does not eliminate the risk of financial loss as it can never be guaranteed that the insurer will have the financial resources to meet a claim. In the event of insurer default, large companies would have to consider the unsettled claim as a bad debt.

Finally, within risk management, insurance would be viewed as a risk financing mechanism. The risk management function can be divided into three areas: (1) risk analysis (the identification and measurement of risk); (2) risk control (the reduction of the frequency and severity of risk); and (3) risk financing (the sourcing and application of funds to meet the cost of risk occurrence). Insurance to a risk manager is just one of the risk financing options available, albeit an important one.

Why speculative risk should not be insured

It is suggested above that insurance should not cover speculative risk due to the existence of moral hazard. By offering insurance, the downside of a speculative risk is eliminated while the upside remains available. The result being that risks are taken that would not be acceptable if the downside remained a threat. Where insurers attempt to cover speculative risks, it tends to go horribly wrong.

This was illustrated by the Time Variable Contingency policies offered to the film industry in the 1990s by the London insurance market. These policies offered to cover a shortfall between the costs of making the film and the revenues generated within a specified time period. This is unquestionably a speculative risk. Nothing in the 'insurance' contracts allowed the insurer to share in the spectacular success of a film; however, the payment in respect of a box office disaster could be huge. This is an excellent example of moral hazard in operation. Normally a film producer would have to think long and hard about whether to make a film and the budget available, knowing that losses were possible. If the producer was unsure of recouping the investment, the film would be sent back to the drawing board or the project shelved. Once this loss could be covered by insurance, there was no reason not to speculate. If the film succeeded, a profit was made, if it turned out to be the mother of all flops, the losses were passed on to the insurers. The inevitable result was that films were made that would not have been made in the absence of insurance. The number of flops greatly exceeded expectations and insurers lost hundreds of millions of dollars.

This could be regarded as part and parcel of the rough and tumble of insurance life. The London market has reputation for innovation, here they over-innovated and strayed over the line, treating an investment opportunity as an insurance opportunity. Heads rolled, but no insurers collapsed as a result. The effective collapse of AIG was of an entirely different order of magnitude.

A complete analysis of the AIG crisis is beyond the scope of this book; however, this was another example of an insurer attempting to insure speculative risk. The products in question were credit default swaps (CDSs) written on collateralised debt obligations (CDOs). A CDO is a bond backed by the income produced by repayment of secured debt, often but not necessarily domestic mortgages. The purpose is to pass the credit or default risk from the original lender to the CDO. In the case of default of the underlying debts, the CDO will be unable meet its obligations. To reduce the risk to the investors in the CDO, CDSs were created.

Under a CDS, the buyer makes a series of payments to the seller. In return, the seller makes a payment to the buyer if the CDO defaults. Payment may also be triggered by other specified contingencies such as a downgrade in the credit rating of the CDO. On the face of it, this looks a lot like an insurance transaction, a premium is paid and if the contingency occurs, a claim flows in the opposite direction. Indeed, CDSs were often referred to as insurance. This is fundamentally wrong. CDSs are derivatives and therefore not bound by any principles of insurance law that might serve to protect the position of the seller or 'insurer'. The buyer of a CDS did not need to have any exposure to the underlying CDO, the CDS could be purchased purely for speculative purposes. It follows then that the payment was not necessarily based upon any financial loss sustained by the buyer. As a result, the payments made under a CDS could far exceed the actual loss on the underlying CDO. This would clearly not be acceptable under insurance law, in particular, the principles of insurable interest and indemnity (see Chapter 2).

However, all the evidence is that AIG treated CDSs as if they were insurance policies, in effect insuring a speculative risk. Insurance operates on the principle of the law of large numbers. The likely losses are estimated and reserves set aside to cover the possibility that actual losses will be higher than expected. This only works if the degree of volatility in the result is relatively limited (as one would expect from traditional insurance risks such as motor or life).

Risk management in the derivatives market works on a very different principle. Derivative risks are hedged. The potential losses are covered or at least reduced, by taking an opposite position. Most CDS sellers were therefore also buyers. The cost of their payments as sellers would then be offset by the recoveries from their buying positions. In the pure risk scenarios insurance ought to be covering, hedging is not possible as if the risk occurs, there are only losers. Losses cannot be recouped from the 'winners' if there are no winners.

AIG's fundamental mistake was to treat CDSs as insurance products and fail to hedge. They were exposed to a reported $441 billion of risk as sellers, but there is little evidence that this risk was hedged by counter-positions taken as a buyer.

The problem was exacerbated as the risk they were insuring was essentially fundamental. The rate of default on loans is intimately connected with economic conditions. A sharp downturn in the global economy will produce a sharp increase in the rate of default. The collapse of the US housing market in 2006/07 led to recession and an inevitable rise in loan defaults. The problem was not so much payments on CDS transactions to cover actual defaults, but the contractual terms of the CDS. The buyers of the CDSs invoked clauses requiring AIG to provide additional collateral in the event that the risk of default increased. By providing this collateral, AIG found that their credit rating had been lowered. This then required them to post additional collateral to back the CDS transactions as *their* risk of default had increased. Before long, AIG found that it did not have the capital to meet all the collateral demands. Many of the buyers were banks and in their already severely weakened condition, it was feared that the failure of AIG could precipitate systemic collapse of the banking system. The US government was forced to support AIG to the tune of $180 billion and at the time of writing (July 2009) it is still not clear what the ultimate cost will be. What is known is that AIG posted the largest ever recorded quarterly loss in US history in the last three months of 2008 of $61.7 billion and a loss of $99.3 billion for the year. To put these figures in some kind of perspective, the global premium income for general (non-life) insurance in 2008 was $1,779 billion according to Swiss Re (*sigma No. (3/2009)*). Taking into account the $180 billion of government support provided, a relatively small division of a single insurer (albeit the largest) has apparently managed to lose 10 per cent of the entire global non-life insurance premiums for the year, although it must be said that the ultimate losses may not be that severe.

The message seems clear. Either insurance companies should avoid speculative risks or alternatively they should at least refrain from attempting to manage them as if they are insurable.

Can fundamental risks be insured?

In part, the AIG crisis was caused by the insurance of a fundamental risk. There are other examples. It is usually clear whether a risk is pure or speculative. It is far harder to assess a risk as fundamental or particular as a significant grey area exists containing a number of commonly insured risks.

A fundamental risk is one where if the risk occurs a significant percentage of policyholders will be affected. This begs the question, what is significant? By way of example, the UK insurance industry has been concerned about flood losses for some years. Large losses were incurred in Autumn 2000 leading to concerns that UK insurers might not be able to continue to offer flood insurance to all homes and businesses. Heavy rainfall in the summer of 2007 resulted in large-scale flooding costing an estimated £3 billion. There were other smaller but still significant losses in the intervening period. The question is, is flood a fundamental risk? If so, can the UK insurance industry continue to afford to offer cover?

In March 2008, the ABI estimated the cost of the 2007 floods to be £3 billion arising from 160,000 property claims and 20,000 motor claims. It was implied that this was a gross figure before reinsurance recoveries which would reduce the net cost to an extent (see Chapter 4 for further details of the effect of reinsurance recoveries on an insurer's financial position). This seems a reasonable estimate given that total property claims (domestic and commercial) rose from £4.562 billion in 2006 to £6.675 billion in 2007. Remember reinsurance would reduce the cost to an extent and a proportion of the loss fell on the motor insurance market. A £0.517 billion underwriting profit on property insurance in 2006 plummeted to a £1.485 billion loss in 2007. Note that this would be offset by investment income which is not accounted for in calculating underwriting profit or loss (see Chapter 4).

This demonstrates why insurers are frightened of fundamental loss events. The foundation that the common pool is constructed upon is that the premiums collected from the majority who suffer no loss will be used to compensate the minority who do suffer loss. As the ratio between the two narrows, the risk that the pool funds will be exhausted increases. Furthermore, the larger the potential losses arising from the event, the wider the ratio between non-claimants and claimants must be. The 2007 floods appear to have cost around a third of the total property insurance premiums for that year.

This kind of disastrous result can be withstood once in a while. However, coming only seven years after the heavy losses of 2000, insurers are understandably worried that such losses are becoming more common. It is possible that climate change is affecting weather patterns. The argument is also raised that due to increasing demand for housing we are now building in unsuitable locations at greater risk of flooding. Regardless, the ability of insurers to meet loss is finite and from 2000 onwards they have been working with the government to establish an acceptable solution for the future.

The government is clearly keen that affordable flood insurance will be available. Insurance underpins the mortgage and therefore housing market. If private insurance is unavailable, then the problem will fall on government. They are equally concerned that commercial insurance remains available due to the economic impact of business failures brought about by uninsured loss.

The deal struck in 2000 saw the insurers promise not to raise flood premiums or refuse cover altogether. This of course means that policyholders not at risk from flooding are subsidising those who are, contrary to the principle of equitable premiums. The government in turn promised to improve flood defences in an attempt to reduce the risk to manageable proportions. Even before the 2007 floods, the ABI frequently criticised the government for failing to spend the promised amounts. Although initially increased after 2000, by 2002 spending on flood defence was frozen, reducing spending in real terms. This is despite an increase in the number of properties deemed to be at risk. In the aftermath of the 2007 floods, significant increases were promised, but given previous promises it is easy to be sceptical.

It is worth noting that in many European countries compensation for flood damage is the responsibility of the state. Spain, France and (unsurprisingly) the Netherlands are examples. The same is true in the USA. Although controversial, a government-sponsored pool may be the long-term outcome in the UK.

It all depends on whether the risk veers so far in the fundamental direction that the insurance industry cannot safely handle the risk. At present the risk of flood is arguably fundamental in the eyes of a UK property insurer in that 160,000 claims arising from a single event can certainly be termed a fundamental loss. It is not, however, necessarily fundamental when seen from the perspective of a global reinsurance company. So long as UK floods do not produce unacceptable losses to the reinsurers, UK insurers will be able to transfer a proportion of the surplus flood risk. One role of reinsurance is to convert risks that are fundamental on a national scale to risks that are particular on an international scale. If the reinsurance market refuses or restricts cover in the future, the insurers may be forced to refuse or restrict cover to individuals.

It is noticeable that the insurers' original undertaking not to increase terms for vulnerable properties is being eroded. In July 2008, the ABI revised their statement of principles. Standard cover will only be offered if the risk is not significant (annual probability of flood 1 in 75 or lower) or where the Environment Agency has announced plans to reduce the risk below significance within five years. Crucially, the ABI stated that although standard cover will be offered, this does not mean that it will be on standard terms. The principles do not apply to homes built after 2008.

It seems possible that government may have to take an increasing role in property insurance in future. For further discussion as to how this may develop, see Chapter 13 where governmental involvement in insurance schemes is discussed in further detail.

2 Fundamental legal principles of insurance

An insurance policy is a contract and is therefore governed by normal contractual legal principles, such as the requirement that there be offer and acceptance, consideration and capacity. Given that it is a commercial contract, an intention to create legal relations can be presumed. However, the nature of an insurance contract requires special legal treatment in order that the contract operates as intended. First, insurance policies are aleatory contracts. Although the premium (or the means of calculating the premium) is certain, the insurer's obligations depend upon whether the insured event occurs and if so, its magnitude. Clear rules are required to determine the extent of such obligation. It is also important that the common pool operates as intended, which in turn requires the calculation of an equitable premium. As will be seen, legal intervention has been deemed necessary to ensure that the insurance concept works. Indeed, although there is significant scope for argument concerning the precise nature of such legal rules, their absence renders the insurance contract unworkable. It is therefore impossible to distinguish a rule of law from a principle of insurance, as the fundamental principles of insurance are essential to the proper operation of the insurance system and as such have to be supported by law if the contract is to be properly enforceable.

Sources of insurance law

Our judges tell us that English common law was established in an inviolable form in 1189 and exists, ancient and unchanging. Occasionally, while applying this venerable system, they may find one of their distinguished predecessors may have strayed from the path of wisdom and incorrectly stated the law. In such circumstances this error will be corrected, but must not be considered as being a change in the common law. It has merely been revealed that for perhaps several centuries, we have been mistaken as to the law, which of course was permanently laid down in 1189, and has simply reverted to the purity of the original. Given that there was no recognisable insurance system operating in feudal England in 1189, it is therefore somewhat surprising to find that the common law is an important part of insurance law. The reality of course is that while adhering to core principles, judges have been inventing new law for new situations.

The roots of insurance law, however, lie outside the formal legal system. By the late medieval period, merchants increasingly found that the courts offered a far from satisfactory forum for the resolution of disputes. Not only were the costs often out of all proportion to the amount in dispute, but courts might not view the more complex commercial transactions that began to appear at this time in the same way that they were understood by the merchants themselves. The result was the development of 'pie powder' courts (a corruption of the French term pied poudre meaning dusty feet). This was an informal system whereby a respected merchant would be asked to arbitrate on a dispute, with the two parties agreeing to be bound by his decision. The principles established in the pie powder courts were to prove influential in the subsequent development of the law of contract of which insurance law is a branch.

Until the latter half of the seventeenth century, 'insurance' was no more than a number of collective risk pools established by merchants to share the risk of marine ventures. There were no insurance companies and the development of a mass insurance market covering the majority of the adult population to some degree or other lay hundreds of years in the future. This was, however, the era when the foundations of what was to become the British Empire were laid down, an empire based upon maritime trade. As this trade became vital to the English economy in general and in the days before income tax, government revenue in particular, Parliament began to take a close interest in protecting the source of such revenue.

Recognising that a trustworthy insurance system was one factor in the preservation of volumes of trade, Parliament and the courts started to play an active role in the development of insurance law during the eighteenth century. Particularly prominent was the distinguished judge, Lord Mansfield, Lord Chief Justice from 1754 to 1788. A Scotsman, practising at the English bar, Lord Mansfield could be viewed as the father of modern insurance law, introducing a number of concepts that continue to govern the law to this day.

In so doing, he was to a large extent influenced by the established practice of the insurance industry itself, following the decisions handed down in countless arbitrations over two hundred years. Unsurprisingly the common law principles that were laid down at this time were favourable to the insurers' position, to say the least. Indeed, it could be argued that insurance law was conceived not by the courts but by the insurance companies themselves. A quarter millennium later and English law is still struggling to deal with this legacy.

The purpose of insurance law

It is often impossible to distinguish a rule of law from a principle of insurance, as the fundamental principles of insurance are essential to the proper operation of the insurance system and as such have to be supported by law if the contract is to be properly enforceable.

All the main insurance law principles (Figure 2.1) exist to give effect to the concept of insurance discussed in Chapter 1 or to permit the insurer to fulfil their role as the managers of the common pool.

Legal principles: contract formation

Insurable interest

Chronologically, the first principle to consider is insurable interest which arises before the contract is concluded and is often a prerequisite for the formation of a valid insurance policy. The purpose of insurable interest is to govern membership of the common pool and thereby reduce moral hazard. Moral hazard comes about when the existence of insurance modifies

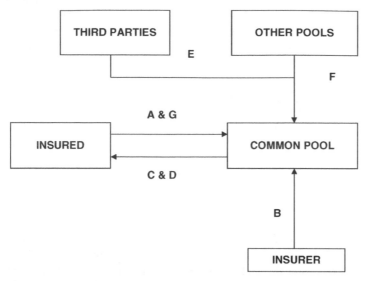

KEY
A = Insurable Interest – Governs pool membership
B = Uberrima Fides – Setting the equitable premium
C = Proximate Cause – The basic validity of a claim on pool funds
D = Indemnity – Quantifies the claim on the pool
E = Subrogation – The recovery of pool costs from third parties
F = Contribution – The sharing of claims costs with other insurance pools
G = Average – A partial pool membership according to partial risk transfer

Figure 2.1 Insurance law and the insurance concept.

the behaviour of the policyholder by causing them to be less careful than they would have been had they faced the financial consequence of loss.

The concept of the common pool requires that a reasonably large number of individuals facing a similar risk transfer the financial consequences of the risk to the pool. Such risks should be pure, therefore if they occur, loss will result. Theoretically, the pool should only contain members who do not wish the risk to occur and it is presumed will take reasonable measures to avoid the occurrence of the risk. Again theoretically, they do not gain financially from risk occurrence.

Some degree of moral hazard is inevitable as the frequently stated purpose of insurance is to provide peace of mind and therefore a more relaxed attitude to the prospect of loss might exist in a proportion of policyholders. However, because policies are unlikely to cover all financial consequences of loss, do not offer any certainty of recovery and do not compensate for the stress and inconvenience caused, there remains a motivation to avoid loss.

If, however, the pool contains members who do not face financial loss should the risk occur, their behaviour is likely to be significantly altered. In this instance they have taken out the policy not for the purpose of protection but for the purpose of speculation. Given that it is in their financial interest that the loss occurs, there is no motivation to avoid the risk, indeed there is a strong temptation to take active steps to ensure the risk does occur! The justification for the law of insurable interest is that it is designed to deny access to the insurance pool to these speculators who pose an extreme moral hazard.

The nature of insurable interest

It may appear that when you purchase buildings insurance, you insure a physical structure. However, as made clear in *Castellain v Preston (1883)*, 'What is it that is insured in a fire policy? Not the bricks and materials used in building the house, but the interest of the insured in the subject matter of the insurance.' Insurance is a financial contract and as such can only protect a financial interest.

Insurable interest can be defined as 'the legal right to insure arising out of a financial relationship, recognised at law, between the Insured and the subject matter of insurance'. Three essential ingredients must then be present for insurable interest to exist:

1   There must be an asset, liability or life capable of being insured and this asset, liability or life must be the subject matter of the policy.
2   The insured's relationship with the subject matter must be such that he benefits from the continued safety/existence of the asset/life or non-existence of liability and would be prejudiced by the loss/damage of the asset/life or materialisation of the liability.
3   Whatever the nature of the relationship, it must be recognised by law.

This final criterion is well illustrated by the case of *Macaura v Northern Assurance (1925)*. Macaura insured a quantity of timber in his own name. The timber was, however, owned by a company in which Macaura was the sole shareholder. As legally a shareholder cannot claim ownership of company property, it was held that Macaura's claim failed for a lack of insurable interest even though he was financially prejudiced when the property was destroyed. It is the company that possesses the insurable interest and decides whether or not to insure its property.

The principle of insurable interest enables the courts to distinguish between an insurance contract (which they will uphold) and a wager (which they will not uphold). Macaura may be viewed as unfortunate as a shareholder seeking to protect their investment could not be viewed as gambling. Nonetheless, a shareholder's interest in company property is almost certainly less than the value of the property.

Historical development

There is some authority that insurable interest was a common law requirement (*Sadler v Badcock (1743)*). However, insurable interest is predominantly a creation of statute. By the middle of the eighteenth century, it had become increasingly common practice to make wagers disguised as insurance policies, for example, taking out a life assurance policy on the life of a prominent public figure such as an army commander in time of war. Although betting that a General will lose an argument with a cannonball might be viewed as being in poor taste, it is not in itself damaging to society. By way of example, numerous policies were effected on the life of Admiral Byng when he faced court martial for the capital offence of dereliction of duty. The Admiral was executed in 1757 'pour encourager les autres' as Voltaire famously commented. Presumably the 'claims' were duly paid. The Government's concern was, however, that use of insurance as a means of wagering was an inducement to murder, the sabotage of shipping or arson. This threat was sufficiently serious to justify government action, manifest in a number of Acts of Parliament to direct the business of insurance. The practice was also problematic for life assurers as speculators would naturally seek to take out cover on lives known to be unhealthy or likely to come to an abrupt end. This distorted the pool, leading to higher premiums for legitimate policies.

Acts are as follows:

1   Marine Insurance Act 1745 – This rendered unenforceable any marine insurance policy, covering either hull or cargo, where:

(a) The policyholder did not have proof of interest; or
(b) The policy was taken out 'by way of gaming or wagering'; or
(c) Where the salvage benefit did not accrue to the insurer.

This essentially makes the same point three times over as a lack of interest would automatically mean that salvage rights could not pass to the insurer and the policy would in law even if not intent, constitute a wager.

2   Life Assurance Act 1774 – The Marine Insurance Act only covered ships and cargo and therefore it was still possible to gamble on lives. The Act prohibited making a policy 'on the life or lives of any person or persons, or on any other event or events whatsoever' where the beneficiary of the policy 'shall have no interest or by way of gaming or wagering'.

The main features of the Act were:

(a) Insurance contracts for life and other events are null and void if the beneficiary does not have an interest in the subject matter (Section 1).
(b) A policy for life or other events will not be lawful unless the beneficiary is identified in the policy (Section 2).
(c) The sum recoverable under a policy is limited to the Insured's interest in the subject matter (Section 3).

The Act was amended by the *Insurance Companies Amendment Act 1973* which allows unnamed persons to benefit, provided that they fall within certain classes or descriptions stated within the policy (i.e. they can be identified as being a part of the class in the event of a claim). This was to facilitate employer-sponsored group life or accident schemes for employees.

The current position

Marine hull and cargo insurance

The position is governed by the *Marine Insurance Act 1906* which repealed and consolidated previous Acts. Marine insurance contracts are void under Section 4 of the Act 'where the assured has not an insurable interest as defined by this Act, and the contract is entered into with no expectation of acquiring such an interest'. The *Marine Insurance (Gambling) Polices Act 1909* made it a criminal act to effect marine insurance if no interest or expectation of interest exists.

Due to the nature of international marine trade there can be no certainty when a ship will arrive in port and therefore when a cargo is loaded. This was even more the case in the age before electronic communications. For this reason, insurable interest is not required at the time the policy commences if there is at least an expectation that such interest will be acquired in the future. The insured must, however, possess an interest at the time of the loss for the policy to be valid.

Goods and merchandise (marine policies)

Where covered by marine insurance (and this is not limited to goods forming part of a ship's cargo), the position is governed by the *Marine Insurance Act 1906*. Section 6 states that insurable interest must exist at the time of the loss, but is not necessary at the time the policy is taken out.

It is even possible to recover when no interest existed if it was reasonably believed that such interest existed. This concerns 'lost or not lost' policies where goods are sold during transit and the possibility exists that unknown to either party, the goods have already been lost at the time of sale. In this case the 'purchaser' is entitled to recover even though the loss pre-dates the sale and no interest existed at the time of the loss.

Property and all other insurances

As regards all other forms of property (and this would include motor vehicles and livestock, for example, as well as goods and merchandise insured on a policy other than a marine policy), the position is far from clear.

For two centuries, it was assumed that buildings insurance at least was covered by the *Life Assurance Act 1774* in that the wording 'any other event or events whatsoever' referred to any risks other than life or marine. As the range of insurable risks in 1774 was to a large extent limited to marine, life and fire, this was a reasonable assumption.

This is not the modern position. In the recent cases *Mark Rowlands Ltd v Berni Inns Ltd (1986)* and *Siu Yin Kwan v Eastern Insurance Co (1994)*, it was held that the Life Assurance Act 1774 does not apply to property insurance.

There are grounds to question this position. As mentioned, *Sadler v Badcock (1743)* indicates that there may be a common law requirement of insurable interest. The *Marine Insurance Act 1788* closed a loophole left by the 1745 Act by requiring insurable interest on policies covering 'any goods, merchandises, effects or other property whatsoever' rather than merely ships' cargo. Those parts of the Act relating to marine insurance were repealed by the *Marine Insurance Act 1906*; however, the 1788 Act remains in force, arguably requiring interest for all non-marine property insurance. It should though be noted that the 1788 Act could be viewed as archaic and its implied provision that policies be in writing has not been supported as verbal contracts have undoubtedly been upheld.

It is unlikely that liability insurance was in existence in 1774, but this could reasonably be considered to fall within the category of 'any other event or events whatsoever' and if insurable interest is required for property insurance, then this should also be the case with liability insurance.

Although academically interesting, in practice, this argument becomes semantic as far as indemnity policies are concerned. The policyholder will need to demonstrate financial loss before recovering under the policy; if no insurable interest exists, then they will be unable to demonstrate such loss and the policy will be ineffective even if valid (see the section on Indemnity below).

Insurance of the person (life and personal accident)

The Life Assurance Act 1774 makes it absolutely clear that insurable interest is required at the commencement of the policy. Section 3 makes it equally clear that the amount recoverable under any policy is limited to the insured's interest. This then raises questions as to the extent of interest.

Due to the evidential difficulties in valuing one's own life, it is presumed that any individual has an unlimited interest in their own life, *Wainwright v Bland (1835)*. It is equally presumed that an unlimited interest exists in the life of a spouse, *Griffiths v Fleming (1909)*. No such presumption extends in law to co-habitees (note there is no such thing in English law as a 'common law marriage'!). The Financial Ombudsman Service would unquestionably find policies on the lives of co-habitees to be valid. Same sex partners have an interest under the provisions of the *Civil Partnerships Act 2004*.

Parents do not have an interest in the lives of their children even if they intend to rely upon their support in old age. While the law is prepared to recognise an obligation of support within a marriage, no such legal obligation exists to require a child to support a parent, *Halford v Kymer (1830)*. Similarly, children do not have a general interest in the life of a parent. Although a child might have an expectation that they will be maintained until reaching majority, during this time the question arises as to how they would be able to afford the premiums, even if the problem of contractual incapacity as a minor were to be overcome. In reality of course, the expectation of the courts is that it is for the parents to insure their own lives for the benefit of their children.

The exception to this rule concerns limited value policies effected by children to pay for funeral expenses on the death of a parent. *Harse v Pearl Life Assurance Co (1904)* held that no insurable interest existed in such circumstances as there was no legal obligation imposed upon the child to meet funeral costs. The *Assurance Companies Act 1909* authorised funeral expense policies taken out on the lives of close relatives, a statutory insurable interest that exists today as a part of the Financial Services and Markets Act 2000.

In other cases, in law if not in practice, insurable interest must be demonstrated at the commencement of the policy. Usually, the interest is based upon a debt owed by the life assured to the beneficiary; however, there is a mutual insurable interest between employers and employees and between business partners. Insuring the life of a creditor for the amount of the debt is uncontroversial, but any cover beyond the value of the debt is irrecoverable. The employee/employer relationship is not so straightforward. There is no doubt that there exists a financial relationship between the two parties and that one party may be prejudiced by the death of another. The difficulty lies in quantifying the financial interest. If a fixed term contract exists, then the interest of the employee is limited by the value of future payments at the commencement of the policy, as confirmed in *Hebdon v West (1863)*. If a contract of employment is determinable by notice, the interest is no more than the contracted payments during the notice period.

In fact, most policies are taken out by the employer on the life of employees, what are termed 'key man' policies. Again, s3 of the Life Assurance Act 1774 prohibits the recovery of any sum greater than the policyholder's interest. This would be the value of the services lost in the event of the employee's death (*Simcock v Scottish Imperial Insurance Co (1902)*). It is suggested that it is extremely difficult to put a monetary value on this loss. Not only will the value vary from employee to employee, but the value of the employee's service will vary over their working lifetime. The argument can also be raised that as the employee can give notice at any time, the sum should be limited to the value of services performed during the notice period.

There appears an unwillingness to challenge the validity of key man insurance on the quantification of insurable interest. The insurers do not wish to lose a valuable source of premiums and the courts appear reluctant to apply s3 strictly with all the evidential difficulties this entails, given that some interest at least exists. As it does not appear that any significant moral hazard arises, it can be argued that the apparent redundancy of s3 causes no problems. It should also be noted that key man policies should be distinguished from group life policies where the benefit is paid to the dependants of the deceased.

The next issue to consider is when the interest must exist. Life policies can be distinguished from other forms of insurance not only due to the long-term nature of the contract, but also because a whole life policy (see Chapter 10 for more information on life policies) is as much an investment contract as an insurance contract. It would then be unfair if after many years of premium payment, a life contract taken out on the life of a spouse was void because the policyholder got divorced, thus losing any insurable interest. Initially, however, the courts interpreted s3 as meaning that life policies were policies of indemnity, limiting recovery to the value of the interest at the time of loss. In the case of *Godsall v Boldero (1807)*, it was held that a creditor's insurable interest in the life of a debtor was extinguished by repayment of the debt, preventing recovery of any sum assured after this time.

The question was reconsidered in the key case, *Dalby v India and London Life Assurance Co (1854)*. In this case, a policy on the life of the Duke of Cambridge was reinsured by the claimant. The original policy was cancelled, however, the reinsurance policy was continued. When the Duke died, the reinsurers refused to pay the claim on the grounds that at the time of the loss, the Claimant had no insurable interest. It was held that s1 of the Life Assurance Act required only that insurable interest existed at the time the policy was 'made'. The courts therefore interpreted s3 as limiting the sum insured to the interest the policyholder could demonstrate existed at the commencement of the policy. As insurable interest is only required at the outset, there is no legal impediment to claiming the full sum insured even if the insurable interest has long since evaporated. Divorce does not invalidate life policies between spouses and a creditor can recover on the death of a debtor even if the debt has already been repaid.

The same principle applies to policies covering accidental death, issued by general insurers. However, as these policies are normally renewed on an annual basis, after the insurable interest is lost, the policy will only remain valid up to the next renewal date. If the policyholder then attempts to renew without an interest in the life insured, the policy will be void.

Although this might appear to create precisely the kind of speculation the Life Assurance Act 1774 sought to prohibit, in practice, this is not the case. Even after divorce, former spouses often retain a legitimate financial interest in each other's lives, particularly when there are children to consider. The great majority of policies protecting creditors are in fact effected by the debtor for the creditors' benefit as part of a mortgage agreement. It is the norm for such policies to remain in force only for the period of the loan and for any surplus over and above the outstanding loan at the time of death to be passed to the deceased's estate or beneficiaries.

Unenforceable policies

Clearly no claim need be paid by the insurer if a court refuses to enforce a contract for lack of insurable interest. If the claim has already been paid and the argument is between the beneficiaries, the courts will, however, ignore the defect and proceed as if the policy was enforceable. There is, however, a fundamental difference between void and illegal policies. Normally when a contract is void, the parties are put back in their pre-contractual position, meaning that goods or money that has passed under the contract would be returned. As taking out insurance without interest is rendered illegal by the *Life Assurance Act 1774* and the *Marine Insurance (Gambling Policies) Act 1909*, in law, insurers are under no obligation to return the premium. In practice, insurers will return premiums on void policies in the absence of any fraudulent intent on the part of the policyholder.

Creation of insurable interest

Insurable interest can be created in three ways:

1   *Common law* – Through ownership of property (legal or equitable) or legal obligations in tort.
2   *By contract* – The terms of a contract may impose responsibility for property on someone who does not own the property, e.g. a tenant may be responsible for repairing a house. Debts give rise to an interest in the life of a creditor.
3   *By statute* – Legislation may create an interest in another's property or a right to insure, for example, the provision in the *Civil Partnerships Act 2004* giving same sex partners an insurable interest in each other lives.

Uberrima fides or utmost good faith

While the concept of the common pool is that similar risks are transferred, they are not of course identical. The tertiary concept, the charging of an equitable premium is crucial if the insurance pool is to run successfully.

A basic principle of English contract law is one of *caveat emptor* or buyer beware (slightly misleading as the principle applies to both parties). Therefore a seller is not obliged to draw the buyer's attention to a defect or drawback so long as he does not make any false or misleading statements, a duty of good faith. It is for the buyer to elicit the information, not for the seller to offer it.

In the case of an insurance contract, a policyholder is transferring a risk to an insurer. The policyholder is presumed to know everything about his risk, the insurer's knowledge of the risk will be limited to what the policyholder tells them. Clearly the policyholder may be in an advantageous position. The insurer has, however, got to decide upon an equitable premium, taking into account the risk that is being brought to the pool. It is crucial therefore that the insurers can distinguish between good and poor risks and to do this they are to an extent dependent upon the information provided by the prospective policyholder (the proposer). By failing to reveal negative information about the risk, the proposer can obtain a lower premium than the risk justifies to the detriment of other pool members who must subsidise the proposer's insufficient contribution and the insurer who must guarantee the solvency of the pool.

This problem was considered by Lord Mansfield in the case of *Carter v Boehm (1766)* where an insurer had refused to pay a claim for damage to a Sumatran fort as the policyholder took out the policy without disclosing that the French were likely to attack. Dismissing the principle of caveat emptor, Lord Mansfield ruled that

> the special facts, upon which the contingent chance is to be computed lie most commonly in the knowledge of the insured only, the underwriter trusts to his representations and proceeds upon the confidence that he does not keep back any circumstance in his

knowledge, to mislead the underwriter into a belief that the circumstance does not exist and to induce him to estimate the risque [*sic*] as if it did not exist.

Lord Mansfield intended that this principle should apply to all contracts; however, it is insurance uniquely that has been influenced by this judgment. What is often overlooked when considering this judgment is that Lord Mansfield clearly stated that the duty is reciprocal and found for the policyholder as he ruled the underwriter was aware that the policyholder anticipated an attack and suspected that he 'signed the policy with a secret reserve in his own mind to make it void'.

Nonetheless much of the development of the principle has solely been concerned with the duty owed by the policyholder to the insurer, a duty reinforced by the later case of *Rozanes v Bowen (1928)* where it was stated that:

> As the underwriter knows nothing and the man who comes to him to ask him to insure knows everything, it is the duty of the assured ... to make a full disclosure to the underwriter without being asked of all the material circumstances. This is expressed by saying it is a contract of the utmost good faith.

From this case is drawn the commonly cited definition that utmost good faith is 'a positive duty to voluntarily disclose, accurately and fully, all facts material to the risk being proposed, whether asked for them or not'. Therefore, full and accurate completion of a proposal form cannot be considered to discharge the duty of utmost good faith. Even if no question is asked, the information must be provided voluntarily.

Materiality is defined by s18(2) Marine Insurance Act 1906 (since considered applicable to insurance generally) as 'every circumstance which would influence the judgment of a prudent insurer in fixing the premium or determining whether they would accept the risk'.

Underlying this duty of disclosure is the law of misrepresentation which applies to contracts generally. Therefore, the policyholder owes:

1   The basic contractual duty to tell the truth. Misrepresentation is prohibited.
2   An additional contractual duty unique to insurance to disclose material facts. Non-disclosure is prohibited.

A breach of either duty will render the contract voidable. Just to confuse matters, a misrepresentation will often constitute non-disclosure as well. A false statement that a policyholder has not been convicted of any driving offences is clearly misrepresentation. It is also non-disclosure as the convictions have not been notified. Insurers generally plead both misrepresentation and non-disclosure where possible.

If a representation of fact (as opposed to opinion) is made, it must be accurate. Representations of opinion require honest belief (see *Economides v Commercial Union (1997)* below). Misrepresentations can be fraudulent, a representation made without belief in its truth or recklessly, not caring whether it is true or not. They can be made negligently, where the representor believes their statement to be true but fails to verify its truth where it would be reasonable to do so. They can be innocent, where the representor honestly and reasonably believes the statement to be true. The effect is the same in all cases, the contract is voidable at the option of the representee. If the representation is fraudulent, then damages may be awarded under the tort of deceit.

Non-disclosure can equally be fraudulent. If the proposer knows full well that the insurer will charge a higher premium or refuse cover if the fact is disclosed and then deliberately fails to disclose, this constitutes fraudulent non-disclosure.

If the proposer honestly believes that the fact is not material when a hypothetical reasonable proposer would realise that it *was* material, this would be negligent non-disclosure.

Negligent non-disclosure also occurs if the proposer intends to disclose but either they or more likely their brokers forget to do so. A broker acts as the agent of the proposer when advising on the completion of a proposal and the proposer is therefore responsible for their acts or, in this case, omissions (see Chapter 8).

The possibility exists that this hypothetical reasonable proposer would also fail to realise the materiality of the fact and this can be termed an innocent non-disclosure. An alternative view would be that all are presumed to know the law and that any failure to disclose a known fact is at least negligent if the fact proves to be material.

A clearly innocent non-disclosure would seem to occur where the fact is not known to the proposer. This, however, is not actually non-disclosure as the proposer is not required to disclose what they do not know.

This duty was examined in *Economides v Commercial Union (1997)*. In this case, the policyholder's father came to live with him bringing a quantity of silver. The father reckoned the silver to be worth £3,000 and the policyholder increased the sum insured on his home insurance by £4,000 to allow a margin for error. In fact, the silver proved to be worth £30,000 and the insurers refused a burglary claim on the grounds that the presence of such a quantity of valuables at the property was material, the policyholder had misrepresented the value and had failed to disclose the true value. Neither the policyholder nor his father had the expertise to properly value the silver, but could of course have sought expert opinion. As it was accepted that the policyholder acted honestly, the case turned on whether he acted reasonably in not making further enquiries. The court felt that given honest belief, the policyholder was not required to demonstrate reasonable grounds for such belief. In other words, the court did not impose a duty on policyholders to make further enquiries so long as they do not close their eyes to the obvious.

This conflicts with the general law of contract, where representations of opinion must be made honestly *and* with reasonable grounds. The *Economides* decision could be said to cloud already murky waters.

Materiality

The requirement is to disclose *material* facts, defined as 'influencing the judgment of the prudent underwriter'. Materiality is then determined by what the underwriter would consider to be material, not what the reasonable proposer believes that the underwriter might consider to be material. It is not a defence for the proposer to claim that they could not reasonably have known that the underwriter would have wished to know the fact.

The next point to consider is the meaning of 'influence the judgment'. This could mean that the fact is merely something that the underwriter might wish to know about when forming an opinion, but would not necessarily affect the decision. Alternatively it could mean something that would cause the underwriter to reach a different decision, a concept known as decisive influence.

This has been considered in two relatively recent cases. First, in *Container Transport International Inc v Oceanus Mutual Underwriting Association (Bermuda) Ltd 1984*, the policyholder failed to disclose the fact that the previous insurers had refused to renew the policy and submitted inaccurate information concerning previous claims, but argued that had the new insurer known, the terms would have been the same. The Court of Appeal decided that 'influence the judgment' means the fact must be one the insurer would like to know. It need not be one that would cause them to act differently and therefore it was no defence to claim that the terms would have been unaltered. As a previous refusal to insure was something that the underwriter would at least have wished to know, the fact was material and the insurers were entitled to avoid the policy.

The point was reconsidered by the House of Lords in *Pan Atlantic Ins v Pine Top Ins (1994)*. By a narrow margin (3 to 2), *Container Transport* was upheld. A material fact did not have to have decisive influence, merely influence. Incorporating a concept from the law of misrepresentation, the House of Lords went on to rule that the material fact must 'induce' the contract; however, it would appear that such inducement is presumed. Nonetheless there is evidence from subsequent cases that 'inducement' is interpreted as requiring the insurer to demonstrate that they would not have entered into the same contract had they known the fact, in other words, decisive influence. For evidence of this, consider *Drake Ins v Provident Ins (2003)* where a speeding conviction was not disclosed. This would certainly have led to an increase in the premium. However, the court held that if this had been the case, the policyholder would have protested and it would have been revealed that a previous accident, initially held to have been their fault, had been determined as being the other driver's fault. This would have negated the premium increase, therefore the non-disclosure could not have induced the contract and the insurer could not avoid. It appears that despite *Pan Atlantic*, there remains some doubt as to the application of the law.

Which facts are material?

Unfortunately there is no clear answer to this question, it depends on the particular circumstances. Although it is impossible to construct a definitive list, there are certain categories of facts that are generally material.

Previous insurance and loss history is certainly of interest to insurers. Previous losses are material, even if uninsured at the time. A refusal by an insurer to offer cover will be material (although not in the case of marine insurance). It is possible that this is the case even when the refusal involves a separate class of insurance from that proposed for, if the refusal implies dishonesty or supra normal claims experience.

Facts that would either make a loss more probable or more expensive than would ordinarily be the case are material. This could be anything from the construction of a building to pre-existing medical problems to modifications made to a motor vehicle.

In the case of non-indemnity policies (accident or life), the existence of other similar policies is material in order that the insurer can assess the overall level of insurance purchased by the policyholder.

Then there is the issue of moral hazard. Insurance policies are personal contracts between the insurer and the policyholder. The honesty of the individual or company insured is of general materiality. Previous convictions should be disclosed even if the conviction was many years ago, subject of course to the conviction not being spent under the provisions of the *Rehabilitation of Offenders Act 1974* which permits offenders not to mention certain offences after a specified period of time.

The law, however, is not altogether clear on this point. In *Woolcott v Sun Alliance (1978)*, a fire policy was voidable due to an undisclosed conviction for armed robbery 14 years prior to inception even though no specific questions were asked regarding prior convictions.

However, in *Reynolds and Anderson v Phoenix Assurance Co Ltd (1978)* a prior conviction for handling stolen goods 11 years prior to inception was not deemed material to a fire policy. It could be argued that the seriousness of the offence is the crucial factor, as in *Woolcott* the policyholder was sentenced to 12 years imprisonment, while in *Reynolds* the policyholder was only fined (and the conviction would not have had to be disclosed had the Rehabilitation of Offenders Act 1974 been in force at the relevant time). So whether a conviction will be deemed material seems to depend on the severity of the offence and the time that has since elapsed.

It was found in *March Cabaret Club v London Assurance (1975)* that despite the principle that a person is innocent until proven guilty, an allegation of dishonesty is material. In this case the policyholder was convicted of the offence, but only after the policy had been renewed. However, in *Reynolds and Anderson v Phoenix Assurance Co Ltd (1978)* it was decided that was not the case if the proposer knows that they are innocent, but they must disclose if they know they are guilty, on the basis that it is not the allegation that is material but the policyholder's knowledge that they committed the offence. In this case the policyholder was acquitted, again after the policy had commenced.

These cases were followed by *Inversiones Manria SA v Sphere Drake Insurance (The Dora) (1989)*, where a pending criminal charge was stated to be material even though the proposer knew that they were innocent and were subsequently acquitted. In *Strive Shipping Corporation and Royal Bank of Scotland plc v Hellenic Mutual War Risks Association (The Grecia Express) (2002)* the decision in *The Dora* was followed, however, with the qualification that any insurer who sought to avoid a policy knowing the policyholder to be innocent was in breach of *their* duty of utmost good faith! This utmost good faith argument was overturned in *Brotherton v Aseguradora Colseguros (2003)* as subsequent developments do not affect the duty to disclose at the time the policy is made. This conflicts with the decision in *Reynolds* that it is the commission of the offence that is material; *Brotherton* makes it clear that it is the allegation that is material.

It appears that allegations of criminality must be disclosed regardless of whether the policyholder believes that they are innocent or guilty. This can be considered unfair if the policyholder is denied insurance due to a possibly spurious allegation that they know to be totally unfounded.

If the policyholder has actually been convicted prior to the inception of the policy, the insurers are entitled to assume that the conviction was fair and the conviction must be disclosed even if the policyholder knows that they were innocent and therefore wrongly convicted.

It is though worth noting that despite the law, unless clear questions are asked, the Financial Ombudsman Service (see Chapter 12) would not permit an insurer to avoid a personal policy and possibly would not allow avoidance of a small commercial policy, due to a failure to disclose either convictions or allegations.

Which facts are not deemed material?

There are a number of facts that would unquestionably influence the judgment of a prudent underwriter and yet need not be disclosed.

1   *Facts not known to the proposer* obviously cannot be disclosed. *Economides* makes it clear that there is no duty to undertake a thorough investigation to reveal the truth so long as the obvious is not wilfully ignored or the proposer does not carry out very basic checks. In the unusual case of *Joel v Law Union (1908)* a proposer was not required

to disclose that she had suffered from acute depression as she had not been told of her condition even though she received treatment for it.

2   *Where the insurer has been put on reasonable enquiry*, if they fail to make such enquiry, they are deemed to have waived their right to disclosure. It would, for example, be common for a proposer to refer an insurer to their previous insurers for verification of prior claims experience and this is sufficient to discharge their duty.

3   *Where the insurer impliedly waives their rights*, the proposer need not disclose. For example, where a proposal asks for disclosure of losses within the last five years, older losses need not be mentioned.

4   *Where the fact is one of law*, this need not be mentioned as both proposer and insurer are deemed to know the law.

5   *Where the fact would reduce the risk*, the proposer is entitled to remain silent. As disclosure would be likely to result in improved terms, the non-disclosure operates to the insurer's advantage and it would be inequitable to allow them to avoid the policy.

6   *Facts of common knowledge* are considered to be known by both parties. Once the information is in the public domain, it no longer needs to be disclosed. Policyholders are not required to inform their home insurers of an increase in the burglary rate in their area. The source of the information would be police statistics, available to both parties equally.

7   *Facts covered by the policy terms* may be left unmentioned. If the risk is excluded by the policy anyway, there is no requirement to disclose exposure to that risk. The same principle applies if the policy wording provides that terms are amended if a certain circumstance exists. The insurer cannot argue in either case that the non-disclosure influenced their judgment as it can be presumed that they would have ignored the fact if disclosed.

When must you disclose?

In common law, disclosure is required from the start of negotiations until the inception of the policy. As renewed policies are in fact fresh contracts, the duty re-emerges during renewal negotiations and any material changes since the inception of the previous policy must be disclosed. Therefore a motorist is not required to immediately inform their insurers of a conviction that takes place after cover commences, but must disclose this fact before accepting an offer of renewal.

However, if the change is so fundamental that the original subject matter insured and the subject matter that now exists can be considered to be different, the insurer must be informed. This is not just because of a duty of utmost good faith, but on the practical grounds that the insurer has not agreed to insure the new subject matter and is therefore entitled to decline a claim relating to something they have not insured. The obvious example here would be the case of a motorist replacing their car halfway through a policy.

In practice, additional duties are written into the contract itself. Some merely confirm that the policyholder is required to tell the insurer of a significant change to the subject matter of the contract and are not controversial. Indeed, such clauses often serve to warn the policyholder of the need to protect their position by keeping the insurer informed.

More problematic are increase of risk clauses. Generally only seen on commercial property policies, these require the policyholder to disclose any material facts which might increase the risk during the period of insurance. A failure to disclose will render the policy voidable. Disclosure of such facts may lead to amended terms or even a refusal of further cover.

The result is that a policy purchased to provide peace of mind becomes an additional source of worry. The policyholder can never be entirely sure of the availability of cover and have no certainty as to terms. The courts have sought to limit the impact of such clauses by requiring that the change increasing the risk is a permanent state of affairs unless the contract expressly provides otherwise. It is to be hoped that an insurer would only seek to rely on such clauses in the most extreme cases, where it could be said that the risk bears little resemblance to that that they agreed to cover.

Remedies: the insurer

A breach of the insured's duty of utmost good faith renders a policy voidable at the option of the insurer. In legal terms they are repudiating the contract due the policyholder's breach of contract. They may elect to ignore the breach, but having done so waive any future right to avoid the policy due to that breach. However, if a further and separate instance of non-disclosure subsequently emerges, the insurer will not be considered to have waived their right to avoid in respect of this newly discovered breach.

If an insurer decides to declare the policy void, they are relieved of all obligations under the contract *ab initio* (from the beginning). The policy did, however, come into existence and remained so until actually avoided.

Policies can be avoided irrespective of whether the policyholder's non-disclosure is fraudulent, negligent or innocent. The nature of the policyholder's breach is, however, relevant as regards further action by the insurer:

(a) If the breach is fraudulent, the insurer may retain premiums paid and sue for damages based upon the tort of deceit.
(b) If the breach is negligent, the insurer may retain premiums paid. It is suggested that it would be good practice for an insurer to return premiums voluntarily.
(c) If the breach is innocent, premiums should be refunded.

A voidable policy should not be confused with a void policy. The likely reason for a policy to be void is if there is no insurable interest as required by the Life Assurance Act 1774 or the Marine Insurance Act 1906 (see above). A policy may also be void for illegality if it is taken out to protect an illegal enterprise. In this case the policy is deemed never to have come into existence.

Remedies: the policyholder

As Lord Mansfield clearly stated in *Carter v Boehm*, the duty of utmost good faith applies to both parties. An insurer that fails to voluntarily disclose material facts to the policyholder is in breach of contract.

The remedy for the policyholder in the event of non-disclosure by the insurer is avoidance and the recovery of any premium paid. The problem is that if a claim has arisen on the policy, the very last thing the policyholder wishes to do is declare the policy void as this would relieve the insurer of any responsibility to pay the claim!

It is settled that if an insurer is in breach of their duty of utmost good faith, there is no right to damages for breach of contract. This was considered in *Banque Financière de la Cité v Westgate (1991)* where an insurer's failure to disclose fraud by a broker was insufficient to support a claim for contractual damages.

Only if the insurer's non-disclosure was fraudulent would damages be available. This would not be contractual but under the tort of deceit. In practice, fraud is extremely difficult to establish. Evidentially it would be hard to conclude an insurer concealed information deliberately rather than negligently.

This is patently unfair on the policyholder. If, for example, a policyholder clearly states that they wish to buy insurance to cover a particular risk, but the policy sold does not insure that risk. In the event of a claim, the only legal remedy open to the policyholder is almost certainly the return of the premium rather than the payment of the claim. The Financial Ombudsman Service, however, not being bound by the law, would certainly award compensation for negligent non-disclosure by an insurer where appropriate. This would be the case for personal policies and perhaps for small companies as well.

Legal principles: the payment of claims

Proximate cause

Before considering how much the policyholder is entitled to receive, the question of whether they are entitled to receive anything must be considered.

Any insurance policy must state the events (or 'perils') that are being insured against (fires, storms, accidents, etc.). The principle of proximate cause controls access to the insurance pool. A participant may only call upon the pool in respect of loss or damage attributable to a particular peril if they have transferred the risk of that peril occurring to the pool. In setting the equitable premium, the insurer has not taken into account other perils and if the policyholder were able to recover in respect of such losses the premium could no longer be considered equitable. Therefore the principle is used to determine whether or not a particular loss falls within the range of perils, the risk of which has been transferred to the pool and for which an equitable premium has been charged.

Usually it is easy to establish whether or not the insured peril has occurred. However, on occasions it is not obvious when a particular peril has started to occur and when its effects have ended.

The problem is that losses are not necessarily attributable to one single peril; it is quite possible that two or more perils may operate consecutively or concurrently, all contributing to some extent to the damage or injury that is suffered. Proximate cause is concerned with establishing the order in which multiple perils occur and/or the duration for which they occur and/or the damage that is attributable to that peril. The aim is to identify the peril that will be recorded as actually causing the loss. It can be defined as:

> the active, efficient cause that sets in motion a train of events which brings about a result, without the intervention of any force started and working actively from a new and independent source
>
> (*Pawsey v Scottish Union & National (1907)*)

Proximate cause is not necessarily the first cause to occur or the last cause. It is the 'dominant cause' *Leyland Shipping v Norwich Union (1918)* or the 'operative cause' *Samual & Co v Duras (1924)*:

1   *Operative cause* – There is a direct link between the cause and the result, such that each event in the train of events is the natural and probable consequence of the

original cause until the result is brought about. This envisages two or more consecutive causes.

2   *Dominant cause* – If multiple causes are operating concurrently, the proximate cause will be the most significant in bringing about the result.

It is important to realise that a cause not deemed proximate will still have some bearing on the loss that has occurred. The principle recognises two types of causation, *proximate causation* and *remote causation*. A remote cause will have contributed to the loss but is not 'blamed' for insurance purposes. It is the proximate cause that determines liability under the policy.

This is well illustrated by *Leyland Shipping Co v Norwich Union (1918)*. A merchant ship was torpedoed by a German submarine in the English Channel during the First World War and badly damaged. The ship was towed into port and moored safely. However, as a storm was forecast, the harbourmaster ordered the ship to leave port due to the risk that it would sink and block the harbour. The ship was anchored outside the shipping channel and abandoned. The ship then sank during the storm. Although the storm appears to be the cause of the ship sinking, it is a remote cause. The proximate cause of the sinking was war as there is an unbroken chain of causation (or train of events) between the torpedoing of the ship and its eventual loss. The danger that the ship would sink due to the torpedo damage had never been eliminated, therefore even though but for the storm the ship would almost certainly not have been lost, the effect of the torpedo was the most significant or dominant. Note that although this is an excellent example of operative causation, the case was decided on the principle that the torpedo damage was the dominant cause. The ship was insured against the risk of storm, but war risks were excluded. As the proximate cause was war, the insurers were not liable.

This case can be contrasted with *Marsden v City & County Insurance (1865)*. In this case a crowd gathered to watch a fire, a riot subsequently broke out and the policyholder's windows were broken in this riot. The policyholder's policy covered fire, but not riot. The court rejected the policyholder's claim that the proximate cause was fire on the grounds that a riot is not a natural and probable consequence of a fire (although fire (arson) is a logical consequence of a riot). Some other factor other than the fire must have caused the crowd to riot, thus breaking the chain of causation.

Operative causation can be established by starting at the cause of the first event and considering what might logically occur next. If the second event is a natural and probable consequence, then the process is repeated. If the first event can be linked in this way to the final loss, then the cause of the first event is the proximate cause. If some new and intervening cause breaks the chain (it is not a natural and probable consequence), the process begins again from the break until an unbroken chain can be constructed from the peril to the loss.

The application of the two doctrines depends upon the occurrence. Operative causation relies upon tracing the effect of two or more consecutive (but possibly overlapping) causes. If two or more causes occur concurrently, there is no chain of events to consider and the dominant causation doctrine is more suitable.

It must be said that all too often real life throws up more complex problems. Perils do not occur in a neat and tidy sequence, with the effect of one peril concluding before the intervention of the next. In practice then, elements of both principles are deployed in reaching a decision, seasoned, it is to be hoped, with pinch of common sense. As Lord Wright put it: 'Causation is to be understood as the man in the street and not as the scientist or metaphysician would understand it.' An example would be the case of *Lawrence v Accidental Insurance Co Ltd (1881)* where a man suffered an epileptic fit and fell from a station platform in front of a train. The man in the street would, it is suggested, attribute his death to a freak accident rather than to natural causes and that indeed was the decision of the court. The case predates both the operative and dominant causation theories, however, applying these principles the same result emerges. Is falling in front of a train a natural and probable result of an epileptic fit? The answer is plainly no, therefore the fall from the platform is a new and intervening cause. Alternatively was the fit or the impact of the train the most important factor in the death of the policyholder? It is very rare for a fit to be the direct cause of death, on the other hand you would be considered very fortunate to survive being struck by a train.

The effect on claim payment

When considering the effect of the principle of proximate causation on claim settlements, it is not possible to provide a definitive guide within the scope of this book. The outcome will depend upon the precise wording of the policy and this can differ significantly between apparently similar policies, let alone between different classes of insurance. A full analysis of the interpretation of phrases such as 'attributable to', 'directly or indirectly', 'howsoever caused' and 'arising in consequence of' is beyond the scope of this book. Nonetheless certain broad guidelines can be set out.

There are three kinds of perils:

1   *Insured perils* – The policy provides cover against losses occasioned by the peril.
2   *Excluded or excepted perils* – The policy specifically states losses brought about by the peril will not be covered.
3   *Uninsured perils* – The peril is not mentioned by the policy. Clearly such perils are not covered, but neither is there an express refusal of cover.

Proximate cause insured

If the proximate cause is insured, a valid claim exists in respect of damage stemming from the operation of that cause. This is the case even if the remote cause was excluded. Therefore if in *Leyland Shipping* the proximate cause had been considered to be the storm, the shipowners could have recovered despite the operation of an excluded peril. Depending on the wording of the policy, insurers may be permitted to deduct the damage caused by the operation of an excluded or uninsured peril from the settlement if an excluded or uninsured peril occurred first and it is possible to estimate the extent of damage attributable to such peril. This relies upon the indemnity being calculated according to the value of the property immediately prior to the loss which is not always the case (and was not the case in *Leyland Shipping*, for example). This is not possible in the case of life assurance as the loss is not valued (see section on Indemnity, p. 42).

Proximate cause excluded

If the proximate cause is excluded, the insurer is not liable for the loss, even if a subsequent remote cause is insured. Again it is arguable that if the remote, insured peril occurs first and the effect can be isolated, a recovery is possible. In practice, it would be unusual for such separation to be calculated and in life assurance it is an impossibility.

Proximate cause uninsured

If the proximate cause is uninsured, the policyholder has no right of recovery. Again recovery may be possible in respect of a remote, insured cause occurring prior to the proximate, uninsured cause. There is an additional possibility that a remote, insured cause occurring after the proximate, uninsured peril may give rise to a recovery if the effects can be isolated. The difference arises because by excluding a peril, the insurer is indicating that they are not willing to pay losses stemming from the operation of that peril. If the peril is uninsured, no such indication is given, although obviously there is no intention to pay for losses directly caused by the uninsured peril.

It must be stressed that these are broad rules only and the precise policy wording must always be studied carefully when determining liability as exceptions to these very broad indicative guidelines certainly exist.

Indemnity

On the assumption that the claim is valid, the next consideration is the amount that the policyholder is entitled to receive from the pool. The principle governing this calculation is indemnity. Indemnity has been described as a 'controlling principle in insurance law' (*Castellain v Preston (1883)*). This is slightly inaccurate as although most insurance policies are indemnity policies, not all insurance polices involve the principle of indemnity at all.

Insurances of the person, life, personal accident and health, are not indemnity insurances. In many cases this is due to the practical difficulty involved in valuing life and limb, hence the presumed unlimited interest in one's own life and life of one's spouse. Most policies offer a pre-established benefit, payable on the occurrence of a specified event. The insurer would then be liable to pay the benefit without proof of financial loss. In any event *Dalby v India and London Life Assurance Co (1854)* relieves the policyholder of any obligation to demonstrate an insurable interest at the time of loss (effectively to prove that financial loss has occurred) so long as such interest existed at the inception of the policy.

Insurances on other lives ought to follow the provision of s3 Life Assurance Act 1774 which states 'no greater sum shall be recovered or received from the insurer or insurers than the amount of value of the interest of the insured in such life or lives'. Prominent in this category would be life policies effected by a creditor on the life of a debtor. In fact, subsequent decided cases have not followed a strict interpretation of the Act and there is no legal reason why a sum greater than the debt should not be recovered so long as the benefit under the policy did not exceed the outstanding debt at the commencement of cover.

The principle of indemnity can be defined as the financial compensation necessary to ensure that the policyholder's financial position after the loss is the same as their financial position immediately before the loss.

This principle is modified in the case of a policy covering the loss of future profits to the financial compensation necessary to place the policyholder in the financial position they would have enjoyed had the loss not occurred.

In absence of any contractual agreement to the contrary, the courts will assume that indemnity applies. As Lord Justice Brett put it in *Castellain v Preston (1883)* 'If ever a proposition is bought forward ... which will either prevent the assured from obtaining a full indemnity or which gives the assured more than a full indemnity, that proposition must certainly be wrong.'

The purpose of indemnity is to give effect to the common pool concept. Having transferred a risk of loss to the insurance pool, the policyholder can only require the pool to provide sufficient to cover that loss, but is entitled to receive full compensation for that loss. The policyholder has chosen to incur a small certain loss (the premium) and after that their financial position should remain unchanged irrespective of whether the insured risk occurs or not.

Provision of indemnity

There are four ways in which an insurer can provide an indemnity and normally they will provide in the policy that they have discretion as to which method they wish to use, although a fair insurer would certainly consider representations from the policyholder. It will, however, be for the insurer to demonstrate that the chosen method does indeed constitute a fair indemnity.

1   *Cash* – The simplest method of indemnity is to pay monetary compensation for the loss.
2   *Repair* – The insurer can elect to repair damaged property on behalf of the claimant. Clearly the property must be substantially returned to its pre-loss condition for this to constitute adequate indemnity.
3   *Replacement* – The insurer replaces the damaged item with a new item of at least similar quality and specification.
4   *Reinstatement* – Only applicable to property insurance (and in practice only to buildings insurance), the insurer elects to re-instate the building to its pre-loss condition. This is option is rarely exercised in practice as once exercised the insurer must carry out the work even if the cost exceeds the sum insured. Any failure to reinstate to substantially the same standard will entitle the claimant to claim damages. The insurer may validly elect to repair or possibly replace the building, therefore reinstatement need not be selected as the method of indemnity.

A brief summary of the practice in some major categories of indemnity insurance is provided below:

1 *Property* – All four options could be used depending upon the circumstances. As a general rule, if the property is partially damaged, an insurer would elect to repair or make a cash payment on receipt of evidence that the policyholder had carried out repairs, often direct to the repairer. If the property is totally destroyed or irretrievably lost, replacement or again cash payment on production of evidence of replacement would be normal. Insurers rarely offer straight cash indemnity to deter fraud. An honest policyholder should have no objection to replacement of property, as a fraudster's motivation is financial advantage which is maximised by a cash payment. Similarly, if fraud is suspected in a buildings insurance claim, insurers may elect to reinstate or repair to defeat the purpose of the fraud.

2 *Motor* – Partial damage to the policyholder's vehicle would usually be settled by repair. Insurers enter into agreements with repairers and benefit from favourable rates. Damaged third party vehicles would be dealt with in a similar fashion. If the vehicle is a constructive total loss (a write-off) in that the cost of repair exceeds the value of the vehicle, a cash payment would be made. The relevant indemnity would be the second-hand value of the vehicle at the time of loss.

3 *Liability* – These claims (including third party injury claims on motor policies) are usually settled by cash payments. Such payment would be made directly to the third party, their contractors or solicitors or paid into court. It would be highly unusual for the money to be paid to the policyholder.

4 *Marine* – Marine policies, whether covering hull or cargo, are unusual in that they are usually 'valued' policies. Insurer and policyholder agree an amount of indemnity in advance which is payable in the event of total loss. Under such policies 'the value fixed by the

policy is ... conclusive of the insurable value of the subject intended to be insured, whether the loss be total or partial' – s27(3) Marine Insurance Act.

This can produce results which could be viewed as being in conflict with the principle of indemnity. In *Glafki Shipping Co v Pinos Shipping Co 'The Maira' (1986)*, the construction of the ship was funded by a marine mortgage the terms of which were that the vessel be insured for 130 per cent of the mortgage debt. The ship was insured for $10 million when the actual value at the time of loss was $5 million. The agreed value was paid, however, 130 per cent of the debt was $12 million. The managers of the ship were liable to the owners for the $2 million shortfall. Clearly the court had no problem with a gross over-valuation in the absence of fraud and indeed would have been happy with an even higher valuation.

If there is a total loss on an unvalued policy, the indemnity is based on the value of the insured property immediately prior to leaving port. Where a partial loss occurs, the whole sum will obviously not be paid. The insurers will repair or make a cash settlement equivalent to the cost of repair. Partial losses on unvalued policies would be dealt with in the same fashion.

The right of a policyholder to insist on a particular method of indemnity

As insurers invariably reserve the right to determine indemnification in the policy, such rights are necessarily limited. Having reserved this right, the insurer must, however, be able to demonstrate that a particular settlement constitutes a fair indemnity.

This was examined in *Reynolds v Phoenix Assurance (1969)*. The claimant purchased an old commercial building for £18,000. They insured it for £628,000, being the cost of totally rebuilding the property. A fire caused significant damage to the property. The insurers declined to elect to reinstate, the parties could not reach agreement and the question of what would constitute a fair indemnity was put to the court. The court held that three possibilities existed.

One measure of indemnity would be the market value of the property. This would be considerably less than the cost of reinstatement. Alternatively, indemnity could constitute an amount sufficient to replace the building with a building of modern construction, again at a cost considerably less than reinstatement. Finally, the court could award the cost of reinstatement of somewhat over £200,000.

As this was an ordinary indemnity policy, the claimant had no automatic right to insist on reinstatement. However, the claimant did have a right to a fair indemnity. Given that the court found that there was a genuine and reasonable desire on the part of the claimant to reinstate the property, they were entitled to the reinstatement cost. It is worth noting that the policy as per standard practice required that the property be insured for its full rebuilding cost. It would seem harsh to expect the policyholder to pay the premium on a sum insured they could not hope to recover in the event of loss.

Contrast this with *Leppard v Excess Insurance (1979)*. Leppard purchased a property intending to resell it. He never occupied the property and never intended to in the future. The property was insured for the full rebuilding cost of £14,000 although the market value was £4,500. A fire caused £8,000 worth of damage. Given that a premium had been paid on the full rebuilding cost, Leppard felt entitled to £8,000 as a settlement. The court held that his intention had been to sell the property, that intention was frustrated by the fire and his true loss was the market value of £4,500.

The crucial distinguishing feature between *Reynolds* and *Leppard* was the intention of the claimant. In *Reynolds*, the claimant was occupying the building prior to the loss and intended to continue to do so. The high cost of reinstatement could not be viewed as unnecessary expenditure as it permitted the occupiers of the building to enjoy the benefit of the property in the future. In *Leppard*, the claimant was asking the insurer to spend £8,000 on a property that would immediately be sold for £4,500.

The position can be complicated by the Fire Prevention (Metropolis) Act 1774. This rarely used Act (applicable only in England and Wales) provides under s83 that where any person interested in or entitled to occupation of buildings so requests or where the insurer suspects fraud, the insurance company must ensure that insurance payments arising from a fire loss are expended as far as they will go in rebuilding, reinstating or repairing the building. A cash payment would clearly not satisfy this requirement, restricting the insurer's indemnity options. The most likely scenario whereby this Act is invoked is on behalf of a mortgage lender; however, tenants clearly have rights under the Act as well. Note that it was confirmed in *Reynolds* that the policyholder is not deemed to be an interested person within the meaning of the Act. In practice, the insurer can discharge their duty by obtaining the policyholder's undertaking to reinstate or repair. If an insurance company is in breach of this obligation, it appears the only remedy is an injunction and the interested party cannot demand resettlement of the claim. As the Act refers only to insurance companies it does not apply to Lloyd's syndicates.

Agreed value or valued policies

The normal operation of indemnity can be overridden by the agreement of the parties. As has been seen, valued policies are the norm in marine insurance. A similar practice is also followed in certain types of property insurance. If there is a risk of total loss of the subject matter (due to theft, for example) and it would be then be difficult to establish the pre-loss value, insurer and policyholder will agree the indemnity at the commencement of the policy, agreeing that this figure will be the indemnity in the event of a total loss, with the insurer reserving the right to repair or offer a lesser cash settlement in the event of a partial loss. The insurance of fine art and high value jewellery is usually on an agreed value basis, with a professional valuation forming the agreed indemnity. Bloodstock and classic car insurance are further examples. As in marine insurance, the insurer is contractually bound to pay the agreed value in the event of a total loss, with both parties accepting the risk that the value at the time of loss may have risen or fallen.

If the property suffers partial damage, the insurer may elect to repair. Alternatively, if this is not possible (say, in the case of damage to a work of art) the insurer should pay a percentage of the agreed value equal to the percentage of the reduction in the item's value as a result of the damage, *Elcock v Thomson (1949)*. It is possible that a combination of repair and compensation for reduction in value would be a fair indemnity if repairs could minimise the reduction in value but not eliminate it altogether.

Reinstatement basis or 'new for old'

Just to confuse matters, the term 'reinstatement' is not only used to describe a means of indemnity settlement in property, it also describes an agreement to vary the strict application of indemnity from the outset of the policy, again limited to property insurance.

The strict application of indemnity may leave the insured in a more advantageous position than they enjoyed prior to the loss. For example, if an insurer elects to replace, the policyholder would benefit by the replacement of used property by new property, a concept known as betterment. In such circumstances the insurer would be entitled to require the policyholder to contribute towards the cost of the replacement property, the amount determined by the age and condition of the original property. The aim being that the policyholder is left in approximately the same financial position they enjoyed before the loss.

This in practice is fraught with difficulty. Policyholders tend to object to being asked to pay a part of their own insurance claim. In some circumstances the principle could leave the policy near worthless. For example, the theft of a venerable, but still serviceable hi fi system could lead to a situation where the insurer assessed the value of the stolen property at only a small percentage of the cost of a modern replacement, essentially asking the policyholder to meet the loss. In the case of a major loss, deductions would need to be assessed on many separate items at considerable administrative cost, doubtless resulting in extensive negotiation with the claimant. This would also raise the question of whether a claimant could afford to meet their contribution. If not, they would be unable to replace all the damaged property and might fairly question whether they had received a full indemnity.

For this reason insurers introduced cover on a reinstatement basis as opposed to the traditional indemnity basis. While this terminology prevails in commercial insurance, in personal lines insurance, reinstatement cover is known by the plain English 'new for old'. By this agreement, the insurer offers to replace lost or destroyed property with new property of a similar quality and specification without deduction for wear and tear or depreciation. The policyholder is required to insure the property for the full cost of replacement as new and pay the enhanced premium that would result. The cost of settlement under this wording is clearly higher, however, this ought to be covered by increased premiums. The insurer would also benefit from less argument over the claim settlement, reducing the administrative cost and probably leaving the policyholder in a more benevolent frame of mind at the next renewal. The use of the reinstatement basis in now so widespread that a pure indemnity wording in property insurance should be considered archaic.

The concept of betterment still exists, but in modern insurance usually refers to the replacement of property with property of a higher specification. In such cases insurers would require the policyholder to meet the difference between the cost of direct replacement and the enhanced specification option.

Partial indemnity

There are circumstances where an insurer may quite legitimately offer less than a full indemnity:

1 *Sum insured or limit of indemnity* – With the exception of the third party cover in motor insurance, insurers always limit their liability under a policy. Property policies are limited by a maximum sum insured. Even where the insurer elects to reinstate and is ordinarily required to fulfil this obligation without regard to the sum, a clause is usually inserted in the policy limiting liability to the sum insured in the event of reinstatement. Similarly, marine policies whether valued or unvalued, have a sum insured inserted. Liability and loss of profit policies have limits of indemnity as the potential loss cannot be valued in advance. If the loss exceeds the sum insured or limit of indemnity, the policyholder must meet the shortfall themselves. In the jargon of the market, they are deemed to be their own insurer for the balance.

2 *Sub or inner limits* – Even if the sum insured is adequate to pay the entire loss, policies often impose inner limits in respect of particular kinds of loss. This again would permit a partial indemnity to be paid. An example is a clause common in home contents insurance limiting the insurer's liability in respect of valuables to no more than one-third of the total sum insured.

3 *Excess* – Also known as a deductible, this clause requires that the policyholder meets the first £X of the loss. The same principle applies to a co-insurance clause where instead of a fixed amount, the policyholder undertakes to pay a stated percentage of any loss. In either case the insurer will pay less than a full indemnity. A final variation is a franchise, where the policyholder is responsible for losses up to a specified level; however, if the total loss exceeds this level the insurer meets the whole of the loss. In the case of a franchise, the insurer either offers no indemnity or a full indemnity.

4 *Average* – This should not to be confused with marine insurance, where the term is used as a synonym for loss. Applied to property insurance, average refers to a policy condition designed to deal with underinsurance. In most cases property policies require that the policyholder insures for the full replacement cost of the insured property (the full rebuilding cost in the case of buildings). The premium is a percentage of this figure. It follows that a policyholder who understates the value of the property will be charged a commensurately lower premium. However, given that the vast majority of losses are partial rather than total, the risk borne by the insurer is not reduced proportionately. An average clause provides that where the sum insured is less than actual value at risk, the insurers' liability is reduced by the same percentage as the percentage of underinsurance. Therefore, if the sum insured is only 75 per cent of the true value, the insurer is only liable for 75 per cent of any loss that arises. The insurer may legitimately offer less than a full indemnity on the basis that the policyholder is their own insurer for any percentage of underinsurance. This is the case even where the sum insured exceeds the loss. It should be noted that average is not a general principle of insurance law. In the absence of an average clause, average will not be implied in the contract.

5 *Salvage* – This is not strictly partial indemnity as salvage rights only arise when an insurer pays a full indemnity. Nonetheless the result is that the cost to the insurer is less than the full indemnity. Salvage was initially a marine insurance practice but is now common in all property insurance (including motor vehicles). Where an insurer indemnifies a constructive total loss they have the right to take possession of the damaged property and recover what they can from the sale of such property. A constructive total loss arises when the property is not totally destroyed or irretrievably lost, but the cost of repair exceeds the repaired value of the property or the sum insured. By indemnifying the policyholder for the loss or paying the full sum insured, the policyholder has received all they are entitled to. If the value of the salvage accrued to the policyholder, they would receive more than a full indemnity. The insurer receives the benefit which is offset against the indemnity they have provided.

Subrogation

Developed out of indemnity principles, subrogation has two aims. First, it ensures that the policyholder does not obtain more than a fair indemnity. Second, it is designed to pass the cost of loss to the responsible party (or more probably their insurers). As such, it protects the common pool by, first, ensuring the pool members receive no more than a fair indemnity and, second, by ensuring that the pool only meets those losses that are properly the responsibility of the pool as opposed to another insurance pool.

Subrogation for the purposes of insurance may be defined as the right of an insurer having indemnified the policyholder due to a legal obligation, to take advantage of any legal rights or remedies available to the policyholder in relation to the loss indemnified. If such rights have already been enforced by the policyholder, the insurer can require the policyholder to reimburse them up to the amount of indemnification and may claim an equitable lien (giving them a preferential position in the event of the policyholder's insolvency or bankruptcy).

The case of *Castellain v Preston (1883)* is famous for its comments on the law of indemnity. It is properly a subrogation case, however. Preston contracted to sell his house to Rayner for £3,100. Before the sale was concluded, insured damage of £330 was caused to the property and Preston recovered this sum from his insurers. Repairs were not carried out and Preston did not account for this sum to Rayner or discount the purchase price. Rayner was, however, contractually bound to pay the full price, effectively negating any loss suffered by Preston. The insurers sued for recovery of their indemnity payment. As Preston had enforced his rights against Rayner by recovering the full purchase price, he was required to account to his insurers for this award, although only up to the amount of the indemnity. Preston was accordingly required to return the £330.

The most common application of subrogation is in motor insurance. Where the policyholder's vehicle is damaged by a third party, it would be normal practice, if the policy offers comprehensive cover, for the insurer to repair their policyholder's vehicle and then seek recovery of the costs from the third party under the policyholder's name. As the third party is legally obliged to insure, in practice this is a squabble between insurance companies. Money is reallocated between insurance pools based upon responsibility for the loss.

Subrogation and non-indemnity policies

It is important to note that subrogation is an extension of indemnity principles. An insurer who does not indemnify cannot inherit subrogation rights. Payments under non-indemnity insurances, such as life and personal accident, do not then give rise to subrogation rights. Although a negligent motorist who causes the death of a life assured is responsible for causing a loss to the life assurer, the life assurer cannot recover the cost of the claim. Similarly, a policyholder (or their estate) who recovers a benefit under a life or accident policy is not required to account to their insurer for any further recoveries in respect of death or injury from any person responsible for the loss.

Creation of subrogation rights

Such rights can be created by:

1   *Tort* – Most commonly the tort of negligence, although certainly not limited to negligence.
2   *Contract* – Insurers can benefit from the policyholder's contractual rights, particularly indemnity clauses where another party promises to indemnify the policyholder in respect of a particular loss. In practice, such clauses are usually backed by insurance clauses and the loss would be passed directly to the other party's insurers.
3   *Statute* – Any statutory rights possessed by the policyholder may also be subrogated. An oft cited example is the *Riot (Damages) Act 1886* under which a person who suffers damage due to riot may recover compensation from the police. Therefore, in 2002, the insurers of the private security firm Group 4 who ran the Yarlswood immigration

detention centre recovered £38,000,000 under the Act from Bedfordshire Police (in reality their insurers) following a riot at the detention centre, a riot that one would think that Group 4 were supposed to prevent. No conceivable claim would have succeeded against the police in the absence of the statutory provision.

4   *Salvage* – Some commentators feel that salvage rights properly fall within the ambit of subrogation. This is questionable as it is difficult to see how a pre-existing right to property can constitute a right or remedy of the policyholder within the meaning of subrogation which implies recovery from another source. Nonetheless this would have the same practical effect of mitigating the loss suffered by the insurer.

Prohibited subrogation

There are, however, some circumstances where insurers will not be permitted to exercise subrogation rights. If both parties are named in the policy, a legal action submitted by one at the instigation of the insurer against the default of the other would be ludicrous. If an insurer were to pay one insured only to recover from the other, there would seem little purpose to the policy. However, insurance policies often indemnify unnamed categories as insured persons, either specifically or by implication. An example would be a building subcontractor negligently causing damage to contract works. As a subcontractor has an insurable interest in the building work, they might reasonably be deemed to be within the definition of 'the insured'. If the insurer of the works attempts to recover the cost of a claim against them, they are essentially paying one co-insured only to recover the cost from another co-insured. This, the courts will not allow (*Petrofina Ltd v Magnaload Ltd (1984)*). There is some doubt as to whether this is due to the principle of circuity of action (courts will not hear a case if all parties are likely to end up back in their original positions) or whether the insurer's obligations to the defendant co-insured imply a term in the policy preventing the action. It is submitted that the latter interpretation is to be preferred as, strictly speaking, given the separate legal identity of the two parties, circuity does not occur. The result, however, is the same. Insurers may not sue one co-insured in the name of another co-insured even if the defendant is not named in the policy.

An analogous position is the right of an employer's liability insurer, who pays a claim due to the policyholder's vicarious liability for the negligent act of an employee, to pursue that negligent employee. This was examined in *Lister v Romford Ice and Cold Storage Ltd (1957)* where an employee negligently injured another employee (in fact, his father). The insurers having paid the claim sued the employee in the policyholder's name. It was reluctantly held that they were entitled to recover, but such was the criticism of the insurer's action, that the insurance industry undertook not to pursue such claims in the future. This undertaking would not apply if an employee caused intentional harm or collusion existed between the employees involved.

It is arguable that the law now prevents such actions. *Morris v Ford Motor Co (1973)* concerned a contractor of Ford suing an employee of Ford after his negligence required the contractor to indemnify Ford. The scenario is essentially the same as in *Lister*, however the Court of Appeal ruled that subrogation would not be allowed.

Such actions will always be contentious as they conflict with the unwritten subrogation principle that insurers are in reality pursuing defendants who are insured or who have decided not to purchase readily available insurance. Where the defendant cannot reasonably protect themselves via insurance purchase, it is harder to justify an insurer, who has charged a premium for assuming a risk, seeking to avoid the financial consequences of that risk once it occurs.

Waiver of subrogation rights

In many cases, insurers voluntarily agree not to pursue subrogation against certain parties. It is common practice for insurers to insert a clause into the policy agreeing not to subrogate against the policyholder's subsidiary or associated companies. Other grounds for a waiver would include situations where the policyholder is engaged in a common enterprise with other parties and undertakes to insure the enterprise for the benefit of all. Construction contracts often fall into this category, but it may also include other situations. Presumed benefit is another basis for a waiver. This occurs where a potential subrogation target benefits from the policy even though they are not insured by it. An obvious example would be a landlord and tenant relationship. The landlord may arrange the insurance, but the tenant clearly benefits.

Even where the insurer does not waive subrogation rights, the policyholder may have waived their right to sue. As the insurer can only inherit rights possessed by the policyholder, if the policyholder surrenders the right, the insurer cannot subsequently subrogate.

There is a practical benefit to such agreements as in their absence multiple policies would need to be effected covering the same risk.

Knock-for-knock agreements

As the exercise of subrogation rights frequently means that one insurer is in reality, if not in law, taking action against another insurer, as a matter of commercial common sense the two insurers may agree not to pursue subrogation against each other's policyholders. This was most commonly seen in motor insurance and was termed a 'knock-for-knock' agreement. Each motor insurer would agree not to recover the cost of repairing their own policyholder's vehicle from a negligent driver insured by the other company (although this would not affect the rights of the policyholder). The reason being that in the long run, the amounts claimed by each insurer would be likely to be similar and the administrative cost of collection would be saved. Both parties would expect to be financially better off under such agreement. The emergence of direct writers (i.e. selling cover direct to the policyholder rather than via a broker) in the 1980s has all but ended such agreements. Many of the direct writers chose not to enter into knock-for-knock agreements and pursued their subrogation rights. The existing market was forced to adopt the same practice against the direct writers and once they were forced to incur the cost of establishing departments to recover such costs, much of the rationale for knock-for-knock agreements disappeared. By the mid-1990s knock-for-knock agreements had almost disappeared.

Part of the premium paid by the motorist now includes a provision for insurers to engage in arguably pointless squabbles and therefore this development is not in the interest of consumers generally. On the other hand, under the agreements, comprehensive policyholders were effectively subsidising policyholders who chose to insure on a third party or third party, fire and theft basis. This is because if a comprehensive policyholder was at fault, a non-comprehensive policyholder would recover from the comprehensive policyholder's insurer. If the non-comprehensive policyholder was at fault, a knock-for-knock agreement would prevent recovery.

Responsibilities of insurer and policyholder to one another

Both parties have a general duty not to prejudice the position of the other. A right or remedy can be exercised only once, therefore it would be unfair for one party to sue, agree a settlement that only considers their interests and thereby prevent the other party from recovering further sums. Such conduct is inconsistent with the general duty of good faith imposed by the contract. Therefore, a motor policyholder who has been fully indemnified by their insurer, while perfectly entitled to sue for the recovery of uninsured losses (including any policy excess), must sue for the whole amount of the damage, including losses already indemnified. If they fail to do so, the insurer's right to subrogate will be lost and they will have to account to the insurer for any damages the insurer would have been likely to recover. This would effectively mean repaying any insurance claim. Note that this only applies if legal proceedings are commenced; if an uninsured loss claim is settled by the third party's insurer without recourse to the courts, this does not prevent a subsequent action by the policyholder's insurer. The duty operates in reverse, as an insurer may not recover solely the indemnity paid, extinguishing the policyholder's right to recover uninsured losses.

Contribution

This principle is designed to operate in conjunction with indemnity and prevent a policyholder from collecting more than a fair indemnity. It also acts so as to ensure a fair distribution of loss between insurers. It arises out of the equitable principle that an unjust enrichment will be remedied, whether accruing to the policyholder receiving more than a fair indemnity or an insurer evading their share of a claim.

Contribution can be defined as the right of an insurer to call upon other insurers similarly, but not necessarily equally, liable to the same insured in respect of the same loss or series of losses, to share the cost of an indemnity payment. It can arise in a number of circumstances:

1 *Mistake* – The policyholder purchases more than one policy. This is rare but within a firm or indeed a marriage, the left hand does not always know what the right hand is doing. Where it is clear that one policy was effected in error, normal market practice is to allow cancellation of the erroneous policy and a return of premium. Strictly speaking, though, this is a contribution situation.

2 *Policy overlap* – Although insurers do try to minimise the overlap between different covers, it is not always possible to eliminate them. This is particularly the case where the cover in question is not the primary cover. An example would be pet insurers offering legal liability cover for amounts owners may be liable to pay due to the misbehaviour of the pet as an extension to the policy. This liability would also be covered by the more general liability cover under home contents insurance, again as an extension to the primary cover. Should such a loss arise, both insurers would be liable.

3 *Multiple interest* – It is frequently the case that more than one party may have an insurable interest in property or a liability. Although usually the two parties would agree who will take responsibility and therefore arrange insurance, it is possible that both will take out cover.

In order for contribution to arise the following criteria have to be satisfied, known as the five commonalities:

1 Two or more policies of indemnity must exist.
2 The policies must cover a common interest – the same insured must be covered by both policies although either may cover additional interests as well. This is the case even if the common interest is not named in both policies, just so long as they are entitled to recover from both policies.

3   The policies must both cover the event which gives rise to the loss – the same peril.
4   The policies must cover the same subject matter – the same asset or liability.
5   Both policies must be liable for the loss – i.e. the loss is not excluded by one of the policies.

Note: It is not necessary that the two policies cover the *exactly* the same interests, events or subject matter so long as there is an overlap.

It follows then that there can be no contribution between non-indemnity policies. The full benefit can be recovered from life or personal accident policies irrespective of how many policies are held.

The definition of interest has a strict legal meaning, rather than merely an insurable interest. In *North British & Mercantile Ins Co v London, Liverpool & Globe Ins Co (1877)* (generally known as the King & Queen case), a fire at a warehouse destroyed a quantity of grain. The grain was insured by the legal owners. The operators of the warehouse also held a policy covering their liability as bailees (a person entrusted with property and responsible for its safe return). The bailee's insurers paid the whole loss and sought contribution from the fire insurers of the owners of the grain. It was held that they could not succeed as the proprietary interest of the owner was not the same as the legal duty of a bailee. Had the loss been paid by the fire insurer, they would have had the right to *subrogate* against the bailee, whose insurers would have ended up paying the whole loss.

In practice, as a result of this case, fire insurers agreed irrespective of the law, that they would consider losses involving buildings to be contribution cases even where the interests were not the same. Although outside the agreement, there is evidence that this principle is often applied to the insurance of building contents as well.

The position in equity

If a policyholder has more than one policy covering the same loss, they can elect to recover an indemnity from just one insurer. The insurer would be fully liable and would then have to seek contribution from other liable insurers. The expense of so doing together with the risk that contribution might not be forthcoming would rest with the insurer.

The position in contract

To avoid these problems, insurers include a condition in their policies stating that they will only be responsible for their 'rateable proportion' of each loss. This is supported by a standard question in claim forms requiring the claimant to disclose the existence of any other policy that might cover the loss that has occurred. This prevents the policyholder recovering more than the insurers' share of the claim and requires them to make claims against all other liable insurers if they want a full indemnity. By forcing the policyholder to recover from both, contribution between insurers rarely arises.

Where it does arise, problems can ensue due to the operation of rateable proportion clauses. In *Legal & General v Drake Ins (1991)*, Legal & General paid the full loss, unaware of the existence of another policy that would also have indemnified the claimant. When they discovered the existence of the other policy, they sought a contribution from Drake. Although the court supported the right to contribution in principle, the operation of the rateable proportion clause rendered each insurer legally liable for only half the loss. Contribution can only be claimed where an insurer has indemnified under a legal obligation to do so.

Any payment over 50 per cent of the loss was deemed voluntary and therefore could not be recovered as a contribution. This decision appears harsh because although in law the excess payment was voluntary, the insurers when making it honestly believed that they were fully liable and were not consciously making a voluntary payment.

This case was complicated by the failure of the claimant to inform Drake of the loss, breaching a policy condition and allowing avoidance of the claim. However, the court dealt with this problem easily by ruling that the right to contribution arose at the time of the loss. As the breach of condition occurred later, Drake were liable at the time of the loss. Therefore contribution could not be ruled out on these grounds. In the event of non-disclosure, the position would be different as this occurs prior to the loss and the insurer would not be liable when the loss occurs, even if they are unaware of this at the time.

This definition of voluntary has already been challenged to an extent in *Drake Ins v Provident Ins (2003)*. Provident refused to pay on the grounds of non-disclosure. Drake, who also insured the claimant, then settled in full and sought a contribution, challenging Provident's avoidance of the policy. This challenge was successful, the non-disclosure was not deemed to be material and it was established that Provident were equally liable at the time the claims were made. As Drake had clearly contested Provident's avoidance from the outset and they paid the full sum under protest, no part of the payment made was considered voluntary and they could recover a contribution.

Non-contribution clauses

Rateable proportion clauses are clearly recognised by the courts as they do not restrict the right of a policyholder to ultimately recover a full indemnity. Far more controversial are clauses that refuse any indemnity at all if another policy is in force covering the loss that has occurred, i.e., non-contribution clauses.

If such a clause only appears in one policy, the policyholder can recover from the other. However, if both policies contain such clauses, on the face of it the policyholder having paid the premium for two policies, in fact receives nothing at all. The courts have held that if the policy contains a rateable proportion clause as well (and usually they do), given the inconsistency of the two clauses, the rateable proportion clause will be applied and the non-contribution clause ignored. The position as regards policies that do not contain rateable proportion clauses has not been specifically addressed by the courts. However, there is clear indication in other judgments that if this situation arises, each clause will cancel out the other due to the fact that contribution is an equitable provision and the equitable maxim that equity imputes an intent to fulfil an obligation applies.

Property more specifically insured

A further contractual restriction on contribution can be imposed by insurers covering a general category of property, the contents of a home, for example, refusing any cover if a particular item is more specifically insured, say, in the case of a separate policy covering the policyholder's bicycle. Given that such a clause does not seek to deny the policyholder an indemnity, merely qualify which insurer should pay, these are not so controversial from the policyholder's perspective. Although the superior courts do not appear to have considered these clauses to any extent, it is suggested that there is no reason why they should not be upheld. One proviso might be that the definition of 'insured' might be narrowly interpreted to mean that the policyholder can actually recover under the more specific policy.

The liability of each insurer

The cost is not necessarily equally distributed between the insurers involved. Instead it is determined by applying one of two methods to determine what the rateable proportion of each will be.

The first method is the maximum liability approach based upon the sums insured of the insurers involved. Suppose that two home contents insurance policies are in existence, policy A with a sum insured of £23,000 and policy B with a sum insured of £18,000. The loss that has occurred is £1,500. The liability of each is calculated according to the following formula:

$$\frac{\text{Sum insured of policy A}}{\text{Total sum insured of both policies}} \times \text{Loss} = \frac{£23,000 \times £1,500 = £840}{£41,000}$$

$$\frac{\text{Sum insured of policy B}}{\text{Total sum insured of both policies}} \times \text{Loss} = \frac{£18,000 \times £1,500 = £660}{£41,000}$$

The problem with this method is that it assumes that each insurer would be fully liable for the loss and therefore ignores the possibility of average or inner limits. If both policies offered legal liability cover to an unlimited level as would be the case in motor insurance, the outcome would be incalculable.

In practice, the market will use the independent liability method, whereby liability is determined by the insurer's actual liability for the loss. In the example previously given, assume that both insurers would be independently liable to pay £1,500 in the absence of a rateable proportion clause. The apportionment would be determined as follows:

$$\frac{\text{Liability of policy A}}{\text{Total liability of both policies}} \times \text{Loss} = \frac{£1,500 \times £1,500 = £750}{£3,000}$$

$$\frac{\text{Sum insured of policy B}}{\text{Total sum insured of both policies}} \times \text{Loss} = \frac{£1,500 \times £1,500 = £750}{£3,000}$$

It follows that where the loss is less than both the sums insured the loss will be shared equally. When the loss exceeds the lesser of the sums insured, the insurer offering the greater sum insured will pay a larger proportion. Therefore if the loss was £21,000, the independent liabilities would be £21,000 and £18,000 respectively and the result would be:

$$\frac{\text{Liability of policy A}}{\text{Total liability of both polices}} \times \text{Loss} = \frac{£21,000 \times £21,000 = £11,308}{£39,000}$$

$$\frac{\text{Sum insured of policy B}}{\text{Total sum insured of both polices}} \times \text{Loss} = \frac{£18,000 \times £21,000 = £\ 9,692}{£39,000}$$

The proportionate liability of the insurer covering the greater sum insured will then increase as the size of the loss increases. Once the loss equals or exceeds the liability of both policies, the proportionate shares will be the same as under the maximum liability method.

This method is used in property insurance as a matter of practice. It is used in liability insurance as a matter of law, settled in *Commercial Union v Hayden (1977)*. While in property insurance the premium received is a percentage of the sum insured, in liability insurance the premium is not based upon a percentage of the limit of liability. The justification for the use of a maximum liability method is that the insurer with the larger sum insured will have received a proportionately greater premium. This assumption cannot be made in the case of liability insurance.

Utmost good faith – the case for reform

The English law of utmost good faith has been strongly criticised for being too favourable to the insurer's position. Indeed, so extreme is the English position that the insurers themselves recognise that their position is unfairly advantageous, particularly when applied to consumers as they are often termed. Consumers in this context would refer to private individuals as opposed to commercial buyers. A more cynical view would be that voluntary reform was the price the insurance industry paid for insurance being excluded from the ambit of the *Unfair Contract Terms Act 1977*. Whether due to altruism or self-interest, the Statements of Insurance Practice were introduced in 1977, subsequently modified in 1986 and for general insurance superseded by the Insurance Conduct of Business Sourcebook introduced by the Financial Services Authority in 2005 (ICOBS).

However, before consideration of industry or regulatory measures, the essence of the problem must be analysed. The current law can be criticised on two main grounds:

1 The average policyholder cannot reasonably be expected to discharge their duty of disclosure. It is not unreasonable for a policyholder to assume that providing honest answers to questions put to them is sufficient. This is not of course the case as they would then have to consider whether there was any other information that the insurer might wish to know that is not covered by the responses provided.

This in itself creates a problem for the non-expert policyholder. The problem is then exacerbated by the test of materiality. Rather than require the policyholder to reveal what they might reasonably be expected to realise was material, they are forced to put themselves in the position of a professional underwriter and consider what an experienced market professional would deem material.

This already difficult task is made harder by the decision of the court in both *Container Transport International* and *Pan Atlantic* that a material fact need not decisively influence the judgment, but merely be something that the insurer might want to know. Most policyholders would be very surprised to learn that they need to disclose a fact that would not actually lead to any change in the insurer's terms. The requirement of inducement may somewhat alleviate the situation, but it is quite unreasonable to expect most policyholders to recognise the nuances of this ruling. The result is that an honest and careful policyholder may inadvertently fail to discharge their duty of disclosure and this cannot be acceptable.

2 The remedy offered to the insurer is disproportionate to the prejudice suffered while the remedy offered to the policyholder is usually worthless. Irrespective of the quality of the policyholder's non-disclosure, be it fraudulent, negligent or innocent and without regard to the prejudice suffered by the insurer, significant, trivial or possibly non-existent, the remedy is the same. The insurer may avoid the policy in its entirety. The operation of utmost good faith cannot be considered compensatory, it is a penalty. If a motorist deliberately conceals a drink driving conviction with the intent to obtain a cheaper premium or any cover at all, it is difficult to have any sympathy for them if they are penalised. It is equally difficult to justify why a policyholder should lose the entire benefit of the policy for failing to reveal a

fact that would have led to a small increase in premium, when they did not realise that this increased premium might be required. It is unconscionable that an insurer can avoid a policy where had the fact been fully disclosed, cover would have been offered on the same terms anyway.

Lord Mansfield made it absolutely clear that the duty is imposed equally upon the insurer, a view that has been consistently supported by the judiciary ever since. Yet, the insurer faces no effective penalty if they are in breach of this duty as the policyholder's only recourse is to avoid the policy. Therefore, if a policyholder clearly expresses that they wish to cover a particular risk and the insurer fails to disclose that such a risk would not be covered by the policy, the law is of no real assistance. If no loss has occurred, the policyholder may of course avoid the policy and demand the return of the premium. If a loss has occurred, avoiding the policy will not provide any worthwhile remedy. In this instance, the policyholder requires that the insurer meet the claim, not as a contractual right as the policy does not cover the loss, but as damages for the insurer's breach of duty. This they cannot recover as a matter of settled law, confirmed by the House of Lords in *Banque Financière de la Cité v Westgate Insurance (1991)*.

Voluntary and regulatory measures

To be fair, some attempt has been made to reform the practice of insurance if not the actual law. The right to avoid does not have to be exercised and reputable insurers have always been prepared to overlook minor breaches and settled claims that in law they were entitled to refuse. Indeed, where an insurer invokes utmost good faith in circumstances where the breach is trivial, it is often an indication that they suspect but cannot prove fraud.

As already stated, the price of exemption from the Unfair Contract Terms Act 1977 for the insurance industry was voluntary reform. This took two forms: the Association of British Insurers' (ABI) statements of insurance practice (the intent); and the Insurance Ombudsman Service (the enforcement of this intent).

The statements of insurance practice

There were two statements: a Statement of General Insurance Practice and a Long-Term Statement. The statements only applied to consumers and did not offer to modify the position of commercial policyholders.

1   Statement of General Insurance Practice:

> An insurer will not repudiate liability to indemnify a policyholder:
>
> (a) on the grounds of non-disclosure of a material fact which the policyholder could not reasonably be expected to have disclosed;
> (b) on the grounds of misrepresentation unless it is a deliberate or negligent misrepresentation of a material fact.

2   Long-Term Statement:

> An insurer will not unreasonably reject a claim. In particular an insurer will not reject a claim or invalidate a policy on grounds of non-disclosure or misrepresentation of a fact unless:

(i) it is a material fact; and

(ii) it is a fact within the knowledge of the proposer; and

(iii) it is a fact which the proposer could reasonably be expected to disclose.

(It should be noted that fraud or deception will, and reckless or negligent non-disclosure or misrepresentation of a material fact may, constitute grounds for rejection of a claim.)

The General Insurance statement clearly and the Long-Term statement by implication prevent avoidance on the grounds of innocent misrepresentation. On the issue of non-disclosure, the position is more ambiguous. By whose standard will reasonable disclosure be judged?

Did this mean material facts that an insurer would reasonably expect them to disclose or material facts that another reasonable policyholder would expect them to disclose? The two are not one and the same, given the insurers' greater knowledge of the underwriting process. If it is the reasonable policyholder standard, then this was a genuine reform, the reasonable underwriter standard was no reform at all. Although subsequently taken to mean the standard of the reasonable policyholder, this was by no means clear at the time.

The statements also required insurers to publish warnings on proposal forms and renewal notices. They were also required to ask clear questions regarding facts that they have generally found to be material.

Being a voluntary code, the statements could not modify the law. While the courts were aware of them, they could not apply them to the exclusion of the law. Therefore, as of 1977, insurers were volunteering not to rely upon the full rigour of the law; however, it was at the insurers' discretion whether they chose to do so and the only appeal if the policyholder felt that they had not applied the statements correctly was to the courts. The courts would be bound by the law and could not order the insurer to follow the statements. There was therefore no way to ensure that the statements had the desired effect. For these reasons, the statements could not be considered to be the full answer to the problem.

Note that the statement of General Insurance Practice has ceased to be applicable since 14 January 2005 when it was superseded by new conduct of business rules drawn up by the FSA (see below). The Long-Term statement continues in force.

The Insurance Ombudsman Service

Much more is said regarding the Insurance Ombudsman Bureau (IOB) and its successor the Financial Ombudsman Service in Chapter 12. For the present, it is sufficient to say that this was an independent body established and funded by the insurance industry in part to enforce the statements. Surprisingly perhaps, the payer of the piper did not call the tune and the IOB proved more than willing to hold insurers to account where appropriate.

The ABI needed to ensure that the statements of insurance practice were applied as anticipated. The courts could not perform this function in the absence of legislation and in any event this would be an expensive means of resolving disputes.

The result was the establishment of the IOB in 1981. Funded by ABI member companies, Lloyd's and indeed any non-ABI company that chose to join, the IOB was a self-regulatory body. However, it proved (as intended) to be independent of insurance industry control. Crucially, it was also independent of the constraints imposed by English law. This meant that they were able to enforce the statements irrespective of any conflict with the law and indeed in such cases preferred the statements to the law and in so doing gave a voluntary code the necessary teeth to be effective. Initially giving effect to the statements (considered to be 'good insurance practice'), the IOB then decided to arbitrate on the basis of what they deemed 'fair and reasonable' allowing them to go far beyond the statements. It is fair to say that as regards consumer contracts the IOB created a parallel body of informal 'law' that in practice governs the great majority of insurance policies issued in the UK.

Initially, the IOB applied the statements as definitively 'good insurance practice', interpreting the standard as requiring disclosure only of facts that a reasonable policyholder could be expected to realise were material.

Increasingly, however, the IOB began to look beyond the issue of materiality and consider the remedies available when even by the more liberal standards of the Statements there had been negligent non-disclosure.

In the IOB Annual Report 1989, the Ombudsman declared an intention to impose the concept of proportionality. Avoidance would no longer be available as an automatic remedy, but the insurer would be required to settle a claim in proportion to the ratio the actual premium paid bore to the premium that would have been charged. If only 90 per cent of the correct premium had been paid, the policyholder would be entitled to 90 per cent of any claim. The idea originated in France and has since been incorporated into Australian law.

In the IOB Annual Report 1990, an intention to prevent avoidance of the policy for some cases was announced. Although the insurer would be entitled to avoid some or all of a claim, the policy would continue in force. The argument raised was that in most cases the problem was not non-disclosure but misrepresentation, in other words, incorrect answers on a proposal form. S(2) of the *Misrepresentation Act 1967* gives the courts the discretion to award damages in lieu of rescission and this is analogous.

As a result of the Financial Services Act 1986, responsibility for most life assurance policies was transferred to the Personal Investment Authority Ombudsman. As of November 2001, the IOB ceased to exist, subsumed within the new Financial Ombudsman Service (the FOS) which brought all ombudsman services in the financial sector together in a single body.

This has led to a slightly different statement as regards general insurance (the long term statement remains in force). Clause 8.1.2 of the Insurance Conduct of Business Sourcebook (ICOBS) states:

> A rejection of a consumer policyholder's claim is unreasonable, except where there is evidence of fraud, if it is for:
>
> (1) non-disclosure of a fact material to the risk which the policyholder could not reasonably be expected to have disclosed; or
> (2) non-negligent misrepresentation of a fact material to the risk.

Although the wording is slightly different, this essentially restates the old Statement of General Insurance Practice, making it clear it does not apply to commercial policies.

Further guidance is provided in Clause 5.1.4, applying to all policies and requiring that:

> A firm should bear in mind the restriction on rejecting claims for non-disclosure. Ways of ensuring a customer knows what he must disclose include:
>
> (1) explaining the duty to disclose all circumstances material to a policy, what needs to be disclosed, and the consequences of any failure to make such a disclosure; or

(2) ensuring that the customer is asked clear questions about any matter material to the insurance undertaking

Again, this is similar to the requirement in the statements, but is not as specific. Indeed, it could be said to be a backward step as there is no duty to ask questions about facts generally found to be material as was previously the case. In addition, there is no clear requirement to provide warnings on all proposal forms and renewal notices, although most insurers would do this as a matter of course. It is of course arguable that as this standard applies to all policyholders not merely consumers, this clause has to cover commercial contracts, which limits the duty that can reasonably be placed on insurers.

The effect of ICOBS is to modify the practical application of the law (it does *not* modify the law itself) as regards consumers in the area of materiality. The test of whether a fact is material is not the test of *CTI v Oceanus Mutual (1984)*, what a reasonable insurer would wish to know. Rather it is what a reasonable policyholder would realise an insurer would wish to know. This *implies* even if it is not definitively stated that such a fact would have to have a decisive influence on the underwriting decision.

It is also clearly the case that insurers are ordered to overlook innocent misrepresentations. This would require honest and reasonable belief in the truth of the representation.

Possibly the most important change, however, is that ICOBS is not a voluntary code, it is enforceable by the FSA and non-compliance can lead to fines or even to authorisation being revoked.

Despite the fact that it is not referred to in ICOBS, the approach taken by the IOB in relation to proportionality and the avoidance of claims rather than the entire contract continues to be followed.

As regards consumer contracts, it is fair to say that the Courts are now somewhat of an irrelevance and the FOS, due largely to the work of its predecessor, has deviated significantly from the law in the way that it demands insurers practice their trade. Calls for a definitive change to the law remain, however.

Law Reform Recommendations

The Law Reform Committee recommended change as far back as 1957, arguing in its 5th Report that the law of non-disclosure led to an unacceptable degree of prejudice in its treatment of honest policyholders. None of the recommendations made were acted upon. In 1980, the English Law Commission (which replaced the LRC in 1965) returned to the topic, considering the Statements of Insurance Practice as well as the law. The conclusion was that the law was 'undoubtedly in need of reform' and that such reform had been 'too long delayed'. Again nothing came of the recommendations, largely because the insurance industry successfully argued that voluntary self-regulation was an acceptable solution, particularly as the Insurance Ombudsman scheme was established in 1981.

In 2007, the ELC in conjunction with the Scottish Law Commission, tried once more. While recognising that the FSA's Insurance Conduct of Business Sourcebook (ICOBS) and the Financial Ombudsman Service had ameliorated some of the injustice, the report concluded that this was no substitute for law reform.

A number of specific criticisms were raised:

1 *The duty of disclosure may operate as a trap* – Many policyholders may not realise the extent of the duty of disclosure or even that the duty exists at all. The quoted example

was that a consumer taking out household contents insurance may not realise that the insurer wants to know about outstanding county court judgments.

2 *Policyholders may be denied claims even when they have acted honestly and reasonably* – An inaccurate but honest response allows the insurer to avoid the contract, even if the question was ambiguous and the response was reasonable.

3 *The remedy for misrepresentation and non-disclosure may be overly harsh* – Where a policy is 'avoided', the insurer can refuse all claims, even claims which the insurer would have paid had it been given full information. The provided example was of a failure to disclose a hearing problem permitting a critical illness insurer to refuse a claim for leukaemia. The penalty was felt to be reasonable where the policyholder acted dishonestly, but inappropriate if they were merely negligent and certainly inappropriate if they were honest and reasonable.

4 *The policyholder often bears the consequences of mistakes or wrongdoing by intermediaries* – Intermediaries are usually considered to be the policyholder's agent rather than the insurer's agent, despite a close relationship with the insurer. This means that any misrepresentation or failure to disclose by the intermediary entitles the insurer to avoid the policy, even though the policyholder has done all that can be required of them and will not know that the breach has occurred. Indeed many policyholders may not appreciate the finer points of agency law and believe that in telling the intermediary they have told the insurer.

The impact of ICOBS and the FOS was considered. The point was made that the law says one thing, ICOBS says another and the FOS may seek a third interpretation. This leaves both policyholder and insurer in an uncertain position. Of course ICOBS is not the law and although the courts may consider this, if in direct conflict with the law, the law must prevail. ICOBS 8.1.2 only applies to private individuals, while the law as regards businesses is officially applied in all its rigour, irrespective of the size of the business. FOS practice can and does differ, but this leads to further uncertainty.

Specifically, although it was recognised that the FOS offers a number of advantages to the consumer in comparison to court action, the following criticisms were levelled:

1   The FOS very rarely holds oral hearings and where the facts are in dispute, witnesses cannot be cross-examined.
2   The awards are not binding above £100,000.
3   Decisions are private and discretionary. Clear precedents are not set for the industry to follow in the future.
4   Although complaints from small businesses can be heard, if the turnover of the policyholder exceeded £1 million at the time the policy was incepted, no complaint will be accepted.

In addition, the report felt that the FOS process was stressful. With respect this is not a valid criticism as the FOS process is considerably less stressful than the alternatives (arbitration or the formal court system) and any dispute resolution must involve a degree of anxiety by its very nature.

The following recommendations were made, based upon two laws of utmost good faith, one for consumers and one for businesses.

Consumer law

1   The duty of disclosure should be abolished. If the insurer fails to ask a question they cannot complain if facts relevant to that question are not disclosed.

2   Although general questions will be permitted, they may not avoid the policy unless the reasonable policyholder would have realised that the information that the insurer complains about should have been provided.
3   A duty to answer question honestly and reasonably would remain. The insurer would have no remedy unless they could demonstrate:

   (a) The consumer made a misrepresentation, defined as either untrue or misleading.
   (b) This decisively induced the contract in that the insurer would, knowing the true facts, not have entered into the contract on the same terms or at all.
   (c) The reasonable person in the circumstances would not have made the misrepresentation.

4   The remedy of avoidance would only be available for deliberate or reckless misrepresentation (i.e. fraudulent misrepresentation).
5   In the event of negligent misrepresentation, the remedy would be that the insurers would be placed in the same position they would have been had the misrepresentation not occurred. This would operate as follows:

   (a) If an increased premium would have been required, a reduction in the claim, proportionate to the reduced premium paid, would be made.
   (b) If the claim would have been excluded, the claim would not be paid at all but the policy would continue.
   (c) If a excess or warranty would have applied, the claim would be treated as if the policy had been so amended.
   (d) If the policy would not have been issued at all, the insurer is entitled to avoid the policy.

6   There was a recommendation that there be discretion to refuse avoidance where the degree of fault was minor and an adequate remedy is available in the form of a reduction in claim value.
7   It was recommended that after five years, a life assurer could not refuse a claim for negligent misrepresentation. Rejection for fraudulent misrepresentation would, however, remain available.

Business law

Despite the suggestion in the 1980 report that there be separate laws for marine, aviation, transportation and reinsurance, this is now considered unworkable. A new regime was suggested for all commercial contracts on the following basis:

   1 The duty to disclose would remain due to the existence of unusual risks.
   2 The test of materiality should be changed. The reasonable insurer test would be jettisoned in favour of a test based upon the reasonable policyholder. If the policyholder actually realised that the fact was one the insurer would want to know about or a reasonable policyholder would have known, then the fact is material and is to be disclosed. The standard of the 'reasonable policyholder' would be flexible according to the size of the business, their own expertise and the degree to which they were professionally represented. The standard is envisaged as varying from almost no change to the current law to a standard not much different from the proposed consumer law, with the onus on the insurer to ask questions.

3 Innocent misrepresentations would no longer give any remedy to the insurer. The test of what constitutes a misrepresentation differs, however, from the consumer law recommendations.

The insurer would need to show that:

(a) The business made a misrepresentation,
(b) Which induced the insurer to enter the contract, and
(c) Which a reasonable person in the circumstances would not have made.

In this case, inducing the contract is not defined and it remains open to question whether this means decisively influence or the broader *CTI/Pan Atlantic* test. It is suggested that this must mean decisively influence. After all the justification for utmost good faith is that the insurer would not have entered into the same contract had they known the true facts.

4 On the much more difficult issue of whether the right of avoidance should be available to insurers in the case of negligent non-disclosure or misrepresentation, no recommendation was made.

It was recognised that this would operate as a penalty when an insurer can avoid a large claim even though the non-disclosure would have resulted in a minor difference in the premium received or maybe even no change to terms at all. The point was made that normally a penalty requires culpability beyond mere carelessness.

The counter-argument was that proving fraud is difficult as far as corporations are concerned, which might remove avoidance as a remedy except in rare and clear-cut cases. It was also pointed out that proportionality would be difficult to enforce as, unlike consumer insurance, it is often unclear what difference the correct facts would have made to the premium charged. In addition, there should be an incentive to businesses to act with due care. The conclusion was that 'we welcome views on this issue'!

5 However, the recommendation was that the parties would be free to contract out of what are described as the default provisions. It is easy to envisage abuse of this right as far as small businesses are concerned, so where standard policy wordings were concerned the policyholder's reasonable expectations of cover would be protected. It is worth noting that most firms in this category would fall within the FOS scheme and it could be effectively policed. What is not clear is why this is recommended in the first place. One purpose of reform is to clarify, but this can only create confusion. The Joint Law Commission should have the courage of its convictions and prohibit the contracting out of the new provisions.

The role of intermediaries

The current position that genuinely independent brokers, clearly acting for the policyholder, are deemed the agents of the policyholder for the purpose of disclosure is not challenged.

However, tied or multi-tied agent intermediaries (see Chapter 8 for an analysis of the various categories of intermediary) are considered to be so closely linked to the insurer that the policyholder, consumer or business, might reasonably identify them with the insurer or even as the insurer. In this case it is recommended that they should be deemed the agent of the insurer for the purpose of determining whether a material fact was disclosed. This is reasonable as far as tied agents go, but the multi-tied agents have such a degree of independence that it may be difficult in practice to separate them. Given that they are now regulated, there seems no great harm in continuing to consider all intermediaries agents of the policyholder, except for tied agents. This argument is revisited in Chapter 8.

Conclusion

Most of the recommendations have been implemented in other territories without causing insurers undue problems and cannot therefore be considered revolutionary. Reform has long been held up due to the insurance industries' claims, entirely supportable, that consumer insurance and commercial insurance are different markets. Since the introduction of the IOB in 1981, few consumer insurance disputes have reached the superior courts and the law is being developed in cases involving large companies, particularly in the areas of marine insurance and reinsurance. The resulting decisions, however, apply to all insurance as the law at present does not recognise a difference between consumer and commercial insurance. This is unsatisfactory and it seems sensible to introduce different laws for each market.

As far as consumer (or personal lines) policies go, it is difficult to envisage that insurers will suffer any noteworthy detriment if the standard of disclosure is limited to the provision of full and honest answers to questions posed. A two- or three-page proposal will cover all commonly material facts. The number of occasions where a genuinely material fact is not covered by a standard proposal question is likely to be extremely small, so small in fact that no real prejudice to either the insurer or other policyholders would be caused. The benefits in terms of the reduced cost of disputes and improved public relations would in any event be likely to outweigh what little prejudice might exist. So, one solution would be one law for private individuals and another for commercial enterprises or a consumer law and a business law as the Joint Law Commission puts it.

The problem is that although large corporations can be presumed to have the expertise to deal with insurers on an equal footing, the same is not true of small companies. There is therefore a persuasive case for treating companies differently according to their size and resource. What is difficult to establish is the point at which a company no longer deserves the protection offered to consumers. This point is too complex to settle via legislation and would lead to the situation whereby both insurer and policyholder (and indeed their brokers) would be uncertain which category a firm fell into. It is suggested that as far as the law is concerned the law regarding commercial contracts should apply to all companies and that the FOS can modify its application to small businesses where 'fair and reasonable'. Larger companies would be left to fend for themselves.

Some 52 years after the first serious call for reform, the attempt is being made once more. The Law Commission envisages drafting a bill on consumer insurance in the summer of 2009. Despite the lack of government response to the two previous recommendatory reports, it appears that the Law Commission is confident this time. Only time will tell.

3   The insurance contract

As discussed in the previous chapter, an insurance policy is a legal contract. This chapter discusses the construction of such contracts and considers common insurance contact clauses and their interpretation as well as the proposal forms which, if used, form the basis of the contract.

Proposal forms and the formation of the contract

Although completion of a proposal form (either written or online) is not a legal requirement, they are almost invariably used in all forms of personal lines insurance (including life assurance) and are common in small commercial insurance. Larger commercial arrangements (often termed corporate insurance) tend to use individual risk presentations, an often lengthy written description of the company and the risks it wishes to insure.

The purpose of a proposal is to provide the insurer's underwriters with the necessary information to calculate the equitable premium and thereby provide a quotation to the proposer. This is critical to the formation of the contract. Although insurance contracts have their own unique legal rules, the basic principles of contract law generally apply, including a requirement that there be an agreement between the parties evidenced by offer and acceptance of the contract.

In legal terms, completion of a proposal would constitute an invitation to treat, designed to provoke an offer (the quotation) from the insurance company which the proposer can choose to accept or refuse.

In some circumstances, completion of a proposal form may constitute acceptance. However, this requires the proposer to already be in receipt of an offer containing the fundamental terms of the proposed contract such as the premium, the nature of the risk to be insured, the subject matter and the duration of the policy. It may be that sufficient information has already been provided by the proposer over the telephone to enable a quotation to be provided containing these fundamental terms, in which case completion of a proposal form may be deemed acceptance of the offer contained in the quotation.

This is occasionally problematic if additional information is given in the proposal form that was not provided over the telephone. In this case the proposal form would constitute a counter-offer, extinguishing the insurer's original offer (the quotation). If this was not the case, the insurer would be bound by their original offer, even though this new information would have led to an increase in premium or even a refusal to offer cover. Where an insurer is made aware of additional information in this manner, they can elect to issue cover on the original basis accepting the counter-offer. Alternatively, they can issue an amended quotation (a further counter-offer) for the proposer to accept or decline. In reality a prudent insurer will always qualify a quotation with the term 'subject to completion of a satisfactory proposal form' or similar phraseology, making it clear to the proposer that the quotation is not necessarily binding.

Note that it is not necessary for the proposer to be aware of all the proposed terms in the proposed contract, only those terms that are so fundamental that if were they unaware of them they could not be said to have agreed to the contract (see above).

The leading case of *General Accident v Cronk (1901)* states that the courts will assume that both parties have contracted to deal on the basis of the insurer's standard policy wording for the particular class of insurance in the absence of specific agreement to the contrary. It is not therefore necessary for an insurer to provide a copy of the full wording in advance. It would, of course, be good practice to make a specimen wording available for inspection, should the proposer desire.

Generally, it will be necessary for acceptance by either party to be communicated, often by the completion of a proposal or the issue of policy documents or certificates, but verbal confirmation is equally binding if the offeror does not specify written acceptance. It would be usual for insurers to impose a time limit for acceptance of a quotation, anything from 7 to 30 days depending upon the class of business. The offer lapses at the expiry of this period and is no longer capable of acceptance.

Exceptionally, a contract may be formed without actual communication of acceptance. The most likely scenario is where after receipt of a written quotation, a proposal form is completed and posted by the proposer, accepting a quotation. If the proposal form should be lost in the post, the postal rule will apply. First expounded in the case of *Adams v Lindsall (1818)*, the rule holds that where written acceptance is posted to the offeror, acceptance is deemed to have been communicated as soon as the letter is posted, irrespective of whether it is actually delivered. It should be noted that the proposer must actually be accepting an offer rather than making a counter-offer (see above). The principle works equally when it is the insurer's acceptance that goes astray. Note that this principle does not apply to instantaneous methods of communication such as faxes or e-mails, where the sender ought to be aware that the message has not been communicated.

Even more exceptionally a contract can be formed where communication of acceptance has not even been attempted. Although silence can never constitute acceptance, it is possible to accept an offer by conduct. This involves behaving in such a fashion that the offeror reasonably concludes that the offer has been accepted. Very few cases exist concerning acceptance by conduct; however, one leading case did involve a life assurance policy, *Rust v Abbey Life (1979)*. A life policy was issued to Mrs Rust following submission of a proposal form. The court rejected her argument that the proposal form was an invitation to treat and found that the proposal was an acceptance of an offer. However, the court went on to state that even if Mrs Rust was correct, the issue of the policy would have constituted an offer. As she retained the policy for seven months without dispute (although without payment of premium either), her conduct was such that Abbey Life reasonably concluded that the policy was in force and would unquestionably have settled a claim had she died within this period. She was therefore liable for the outstanding premiums.

Today, a significant amount of insurance is being transacted online. Although the postal rule does not apply, all other principles remain the same as if the process was conducted by post, albeit that the entire process may be completed in a few minutes. Filling in an online proposal is an invitation to treat. The insurer's instant quotation is an offer that can be accepted by the proposer by a single mouse click unless it is stated to the contrary. The insurer will be bound even though the entire process is automated from their perspective.

The contract or policy

While insurers are free to draft their policies as they see fit, certain components are likely to be present in most cases. This is not to say that all policies are similarly structured and on occasions the structure might be far from clear to the uninitiated.

The contract as a whole will generally be formed by three or four separate documents: the proposal (or risk presentation), the policy wording, the schedule and if a compulsory class such as motor or employer's liability, the certificate.

Recital clause

Also commonly referred to as the preamble, the clause identifies the insurer and declares a basic intent to insure in consideration of receipt of the premium, possibly identifying the broad class of insurance. In the case of long-term policies such as life assurance, the provisions for the future payment of premium will probably be stated. It would not be uncommon for the clause to state that any proposal is incorporated in the policy and forms the basis of the contract. It may also incorporate the schedule into the contract as a whole, in conjunction with the policy wording and the proposal, making it clear that the contract is based upon all three (or four) documents. Part or all of the recital clause may well be contained within the operative clause.

Operative clause

Also known as the insuring agreement, this defines the risks that the policy is intended to insure against. Put another way this sets out how the policy will operate, hence the reason it is termed the operative clause. Dependent on the complexity of cover the length of the clause varies and if there are multiple sections within a policy there may be multiple operative clauses identifying the purpose of each section. The promise to indemnify against the stated risks will be qualified by reference to policy exclusions and conditions. These clauses will usually be standardised for each class of business and form the starting point for subsequent tailoring of the policy to the individual requirements of both insurer and policyholder.

The schedule

The operative clause will be standardised, the schedule is personalised. The schedule will often take the form of a separate document to be attached to the policy wording and read in conjunction with it.

The schedule will first identify the policyholder. This is straightforward enough for personal policies, but care must be taken if the policy covers a business and cover is required for subsidiary or associated companies as their interest must be noted if they are to benefit from the policy. It would not be uncommon, once the primary policyholder is identified, for additional interests to be noted by category rather than name. For example, 'Acme Ltd &/or subsidiary &/or associated companies', 'insured & spouse' or 'the insured and family members normally resident at the insured address'. General categories of insured parties present no problem as long as the insurer and if necessary the courts can identify with sufficient precision whether an individual or company falls within the category.

The schedule may also mention other parties who may have an interest in the risk insured. The most common example would be lenders holding a mortgage on property insured.

Once the lender's interest is noted, the insurer is required to inform them of major claims and seek their approval of proposed claims settlements. Failure to do so may leave the insurer open to a further claim from the lender if their position has been prejudiced.

The schedule will then proceed to identify what parts of the standard policy wording apply and to what extent. This is generally achieved by noting a sum insured, benefit or limit of indemnity on the schedule for each part of the policy that applies. Any excesses or inner limits may be noted on the schedule but are just as likely to be contained in the policy document.

Exclusions or exceptions

Such clauses are generally referred to as exclusions, but may be described as exceptions. The effect is the same in either case. These clauses must be read in conjunction with the operative clause and set out circumstances in which, notwithstanding the offer contained in the operative clause, the insurer will not be liable. These clauses then serve to qualify the cover offered in the operative clause and have a number of purposes:

1 The clause may exclude fundamental or uninsurable risk. Losses caused by war are excluded from property policies as a matter of course, although in the case of marine insurance it may be possible to arrange separate cover. Losses caused by nuclear risks are also habitually excluded. Non-fortuitous losses are regarded as uninsurable, therefore normal wear and tear would be excluded from property coverage or medical costs arising from pre-existing conditions excluded from travel insurance. While standard shop insurance would cover burglary, shoplifting would be excluded as such losses can be viewed as inevitable.

2 The exclusion may clarify that a particular circumstance will not fall within the definition of the peril insured. For example, a buildings policy covering subsidence usually excludes losses caused by coastal erosion which might otherwise be considered a form of subsidence.

Alternatively, the exclusion might modify the cover offered only in particular circumstances. For example a life policy would exclude death caused by suicide occurring within the first one or two years of the policy. A policy covering product liability will generally contain a standard exclusion of liability for products exported to North America (although this may be removed if additional premium is paid).

3 The exclusion may exclude cover for particular types of subject matter otherwise falling within the broad description of the subject matter. This can be total or only in particular circumstances. A travel policy may cover valuables but exclude cover if the property is left unattended.

4 Most exclusions are standard and applied to all policies of that type. However, additional exclusions tailored to the individual risk insured may be included. Where a health insurance proposal discloses a serious pre-existing condition, that particular condition may be named as uninsured by the policy.

5 The exclusion may exist for no reason other than to avoid policy overlap and therefore wasted premium and contribution. A commercial public liability policy will exclude personal injury claims brought by the policyholder's employees as this risk is properly insured by an employer's liability policy. The exclusion of property more specifically insured is a subset of this class.

6 Many policies contain limitation clauses. These can be viewed as exclusions but the provision may well be contained in the operative clause removing the need for a subsequent exclusion. An example would be geographical limits imposed by travel and marine insurance. The geographical limit (or cruising range as it is known) on a private marine insurance may

be defined as UK coastal waters. If the vessel is taken beyond this limit, cover does not apply. Liability policies may similarly provide that the policy only covers events occurring within the UK.

Many policies cover more than one category of risk. Such policies would have a general exclusion clause which would apply to all sections of the policy. Each section would then have its own exclusions applicable to that section only.

A common criticism made by, frankly, lazy and ill-informed journalists is that insurers rely on 'small print' to exclude losses. It would in fact be astonishing to find a consumer policy in the modern UK insurance market that is not printed in the same font throughout and is not written in plain English. Indeed, most small commercial policies also now benefit from plain English wordings.

Extensions

It is not all negative. As well as excluding risks, insurers frequently offer to extend cover beyond that offered by the operative clause. Such extensions can be standard or tailored to the particular requirements of the policyholder. Standard clauses would be pre-printed in the policy document, perhaps with an indication in the schedule as to whether they are operative or not.

Tailored extensions could be invoked in the same manner, but in the London market particularly, it is more likely that the insurer will adopt a 'cut and paste' approach, only inserting those extensions that apply.

Conditions and warranties

Although conditions and warranties are different, they must be considered simultaneously as they can be difficult to distinguish. What is stated to be a condition may in reality be a warranty and vice versa. Both impose obligations on the policyholder, the difference lying in the effect on the contract if the policyholder is in breach of such obligations.

Normally, in contract law, a condition goes to the very heart of the agreement and a breach permits repudiation of the contract and/or damages. A warranty is not so fundamental and a breach only permits an action for damages. In insurance law, the relative importance of the two clauses is somewhat reversed. Breach of warranty extinguishes the contract and discharges the insurer of any liability under it, while a breach of condition leaves the contract intact, but may give the insurer the right to elect to avoid the contract or to avoid a specific claim. A breach of warranty extinguishes the contract irrespective of any effect or otherwise on the insurer, while a breach of condition must cause some prejudice to the insurer.

Warranties

In the insurer's arsenal of weaponry, warranties can be considered the heavy artillery. If a warranty is breached, the policy will be obliterated. They must be strictly complied with and there is no need for the insurer to demonstrate that they have suffered any detriment. The mere fact of breach is sufficient to invoke a warranty.

As with utmost good faith, the modern law derives from the judgments Lord Mansfield handed down in the mid-eighteenth century. The harshness of law relating to warranties can be demonstrated by the case of *De Hahn v Hartley (1786)*. It was warranted that a ship would leave Liverpool on a voyage to the West Indies via Africa with at least 50 hands on board. In fact, there were only 46 hands on board when the ship sailed, but a further 6 were picked up in Anglesey. It was held that a warranty had to be strictly complied with and therefore the moment the ship left Liverpool, the insurers were relieved of all obligations. The fact that the warranty was complied with at the time of loss was not relevant. Note though that given the voyage, the ship was unquestionably a slave ship, so perhaps there is no reason to feel much sympathy for the policyholder. The principle established is, though, problematic.

Lord Mansfield commented: 'A warranty in a policy of insurance is a condition or a contingency, and unless that be performed, there is no contract. It is perfectly immaterial for what purpose a warranty is introduced.' This comment can be criticised as being contrary to the proper function of warranties. They do have a legitimate risk management function. They ensure that risk controls are put in place and where necessary remain in place, with the intention that losses are reduced for the benefit of both the pool as a whole and the insurers. If the warranty has no bearing on the loss that has occurred, its existence or otherwise is immaterial as regards that particular loss and it assumes the character of a penalty clause rather than a risk control clause.

It is perhaps unfair to criticise Lord Mansfield for failing to recognise a risk management function long before the concept was developed. However, while his ruling has been somewhat eroded, the lack of any requirement for a true warranty to be causative of the loss to be enforceable, stands unchallenged in an era when risk management is well understood.

Warranties must be a term of the policy. An express warranty written into the contract would naturally be upheld in principle. They may also be contained in other documents, principally the proposal form, but this document must be incorporated into the policy (one function of a recital clause). Strict compliance is required with the letter of the term.

It is possible that warranties may be implied even where not mentioned in the policy wording or incorporated document. Even though not mentioned, the fact/circumstance would have to be so obviously fundamental, that a warranty (as opposed to a condition) would be implied as the only reasonable interpretation of the intent of both parties. In marine insurance, this is unquestionably the case. The *Marine Insurance Act 1906* specifically states that there are implied warranties that the ship is seaworthy (s39), fit to carry the goods (s40) and the purpose of the voyage is legal (s41). However, none of these implied warranties can be inferred in other types of cover. It is suggested that in other cases conditions rather than warranties should be implied (see below).

Given that strict compliance is required and the consequences of a breach are so serious, the courts are strict in their interpretation of warranties. Where, if the clause is interpreted as a warranty, it will produce an unjust result, judges have often been quick to use any ambiguity to strike out the putative warranty or downgrade the clause to a condition. In the case of *Provincial Ins v Morgan (1933)* a statement that a lorry would be used to carry coal was deemed to mean that it would usually be used for that purpose. The insurer could not claim that a warranty was breached because on one occasion (prior to the loss) the lorry carried timber. The court commenting that 'a warranty ... though it must be strictly complied with, must be strictly though reasonably construed'. If the insurer wished to impose a warranty that the vehicle would only be used to carry coal, it was for them to introduce a clear, express warranty to that effect.

Warranties may be distinguished according to their nature.

1   *Warranties as to present or past facts* – Any breach would discharge the insurer from liability ab initio or from before the very beginning of the contract. Any subsequent

change to the fact would not constitute a breach. In *Kennedy v Smith (1976)* a statement that 'I am a total abstainer from alcohol' was deemed a present not a promissory warranty. When the policyholder fell off the wagon subsequently, this was not a breach of warranty.

2   *Warranties as to the future* – Generally known as promissory or continuing warranties, these promise that a particular circumstance will continue. An insurer would be liable under the policy up until the date of breach.

3   *Warranties of opinion* – These are less onerous as they need only to be true to the honest belief of the policyholder. An insurer seeking to rely upon a warranty of opinion would have to demonstrate that the policyholder was dishonest or reckless or failed to exercise reasonable care. The fact that the opinion was clearly wrong is insufficient in itself.

Basis of contract clauses

A variation on warranties of past and present fact, basis of contract clauses are created by terms found at the bottom of a proposal form stating that the proposal form forms the basis of the contract. This has the effect of making all statements warranties and possibly even promissory warranties. This would automatically relieve the insurer of all liability if any inaccuracy existed. This goes beyond the law of utmost good faith, where the insurer can only avoid the contract for non-disclosure if it was a *material* fact. As we have seen, materiality is irrelevant to warranties. The impact of the already harsh law of utmost faith is then worsened by the inclusion of basis of contract clauses.

For example, in *Dawsons v Bonnin (1922)* a statement that a lorry was garaged in central Glasgow when it was actually garaged in the suburbs was not material as if, anything, it improved the risk. The insurer could still avoid for breach of warranty even when they would not have been able to avoid for non-disclosure.

It is important that warranties of fact created by basis of contract clauses are distinguished from warranties of opinion. A warranty of fact is breached by any substantial inaccuracy. If it is a warranty of opinion, inaccuracy alone is insufficient to create a breach.

The effect of breach of warranty

There is a noticeable contradiction in the law as it is impossible to reconcile an insurer's discharge of liability and an apparent discretion to waive such rights. For many years, the view was that breach of warranty gave the insurer a right to repudiate, a right that they of course did not have to exercise. This construction has, however, been rendered incorrect.

In *Bank of Nova Scotia v Hellenic Mutual (The Good Luck) (1991)*, the insurer had agreed to inform the bank promptly if the insured ship became uninsured. The insurer discovered a breach of warranty after the loss of the ship but failed for some weeks to inform the bank. Between the discovery of loss and notification to the bank, the bank made further loans secured against the value of the ship. The insurer tried to avoid both the claim and liability to the bank, arguing the ship only became uninsured when the insurer decided to refuse the claim.

It was held that the cover automatically ceased when the warranty was breached. The insurers were therefore under a duty to inform the bank as soon as they became aware of the breach. Their failure to inform the bank could only be justified if the insurer chose to waive their rights as the ship would not then be uninsured. The insurer could deny liability either to the bank or to the policyholder, they could not deny liability to both.

This view that the contract automatically comes to an end at the time of the breach creates an inconsistency. If the contract is no longer in existence, how can the insurer elect to waive their rights and allow the contract to continue?

If an insurer elects to ignore the breach and pay the claim, the matter is highly unlikely to come before the courts. Both sides would be satisfied and no dispute would exist. However, a question then arises as to the validity of future cover. If the insurers' liability was extinguished by the breach, is it then the case that any claims paid after that date are paid ex gratia and cannot be enforced? Alternatively, have the parties entered into a new contract analogous to a renewal, commencing immediately after the breach? If so, does this mean that there is a requirement to disclose material facts on the same basis as at renewal? The right to repudiate an argument does avoid these inconsistencies, even if it would have produced a patently unfair result in the *Good Luck*.

A further complication is introduced when subrogation or contribution exists. If a warranty has been breached but the insurer pays the claim anyway, this payment is surely voluntary. A voluntary payment is not made under any obligation to indemnify and therefore prevents subrogation and contribution. If the payment was or would be ordered by the Financial Ombudsman Service notwithstanding the law, then it seems clear it will not be deemed voluntary. In other cases there could be problems.

Note that this is clearly different from an insurer electing not to enforce their right to declare a policy void for non-disclosure. Once such election is made, the insurer is obliged to settle a claim.

Conditions precedent to contract

These may also be referred to as conditions precedent to liability which can be misleading as 'liability' could mean liability to pay a single claim. These are conditions that must be met if the contract is to come into existence in the first place. The duty of disclosure is a general example, but other conditions specific to the risk proposed can be specified as well.

Conditions subsequent to contract

These are conditions that must be complied with during the period of the policy, alternatively known as clauses descriptive of risk. A breach would suspend policy cover but if subsequently complied with, cover would operate once more. In *De Maurier (Jewels) Ltd v Bastion Ins (1967)* a jeweller failed to fit a vehicle with the locks required by the insurers. A theft took place after which the correct locks were fitted. A second theft then occurred. The failure to meet what was deemed to be a clause descriptive of risk, suspended cover and the insurer was not liable for the first loss. Once the condition was complied with, and cover reattached, the insurer was liable for the second loss. Alternatively, motor policies commonly stipulate that the policyholder holds a valid driving licence. If the policyholder receives a one-month driving ban in the middle of the period of the policy, third party cover at least is suspended for the duration of the ban. Once the ban has expired, cover commences once more. These clauses are very easy to confuse with warranties, particularly as the term 'warranty' may appear in what is actually a clause descriptive of risk. The effect is very different. Not only would a descriptive clause only suspend cover, there would also need to be a causal connection with the loss for the insurer to avoid a claim. It is also entirely possible that other cover offered by the policy would continue while a part of the cover was suspended. In the driving licence example, there seems no reason why, unless the policy states the contrary, if the vehicle is laid up in a garage during the period of the ban, that fire and theft cover should not continue to operate.

Conditions precedent to claim

Such conditions set out the obligations of the policyholder if they wish the insurer to meet a particular claim. Although a breach may entitle the insurer to avoid that claim they may not avoid the policy. If the condition is complied with on a subsequent claim the insurer is liable. Examples are conditions requiring notification of the loss within a specified time or the recording of information in an accident book. Late notification of one claim will not automatically allow an insurer to avoid a subsequent claim properly notified.

Implied conditions

These conditions are not mentioned in the policy but are so fundamentally important to the contract, that both parties are deemed to have unconsciously agreed to them. Put another way, in the absence of the implied condition would the parties have entered into the agreement? If not, then the condition will be implied. A breach of implied conditions may be fatal to the entire contract or to an individual claim depending on the nature of the condition.

A major category of implied conditions is that the law of insurance applies to the contract. Therefore, even if the policy does not mention insurable interest, utmost good faith, indemnity, *et al.*, these legal principles are implied in the contract. This does not directly give the insurer any rights as any rights would arise out of the application of the principle. It merely prevents a policyholder from arguing that where non-disclosure or insurable interest, for example, are not mentioned in the policy they do not apply.

Although often referred to as implied warranties this is questionable other than in the case of marine insurance. If it were the case that these were implied warranties, then if the policyholder were to insure a number of specified items of property and failed to possess an insurable interest in any one, the insurer would be relieved of all liability under the policy. In the absence of fraudulent intent, this would not be the case.

There are a number of generally implied conditions that will be inferred across all categories of insurance. An example being that the policyholder will not intentionally cause a loss (although such a term would usually be expressed in any event). The fact that a loss must be fortuitous is so fundamental to an insurance contract that the policy would be nonsensical if the term was neither expressed nor implied. Another example would be an implied condition that the subject matter of the contract is actually in existence.

Alternatively, conditions may be implied in specific contracts due to the nature of the agreement between the two parties. In such circumstances a condition implied in a contract in one class of insurance would not necessarily be implied in a different class of insurance and often could not be. One example would be that a motorist hold a valid driving licence.

Warranties, conditions and combined policies

Many forms of insurance are in fact composite policies, combining a number of different classes of cover. Sometime this is made clear in the title (commercial combined policies), sometimes it is not (travel or comprehensive motor cover). There is judicial support for the idea that combined policies are not necessarily to be treated as a single contract but as a conglomeration of a number of individual contracts bound together and governed by a central contract that does not itself provide cover.

This can be important as a breach of warranty on one section of the policy may permit the remainder of the sections to survive intact. This was the decision in *Printpak v AGF Ins (1999)* where a warranty was attached to the end of section B of a commercial combined policy. Section B covered theft and the warranty required that a burglar alarm be maintained in working condition. The warranty was clearly breached. When a fire, covered under section A, damaged stock, the insurers relied on the breach of the burglar alarm warranty to deny liability. In a novel judgment the court held that the policy 'should not be treated as a seamless contractual instrument'. Accordingly, although the insurers were relieved of liability under section B, all other sections of the policy remained in force and therefore the insurers were liable for a loss arising under section A. This is no more that common sense and does bring the courts very close to requiring that the breach of warranty be connected to the loss. It should be noted that there is no suggestion that there will not be warranties that by their nature apply to all sections of a policy.

Endorsements

Where there is a change to the subject matter or to the cover available during the policy period, such change will have to be recorded in the contract. To avoid the expense of reissuing the entire contract, this is achieved by the issue of an endorsement varying the original agreement. The endorsement is attached to and incorporated in the original contract. Its provisions will override any prior agreement.

Cancellation clauses

Policyholders might reasonably suppose that a contract is binding and that if they fulfil all their obligations that cover will continue until the agreed expiry of the policy. In fact, policies commonly contain a clause permitting the insurer to cancel cover at any time, normally it must be said with notice.

The courts clearly uphold such clauses. In *Sun Fire Office v Hart (1889)* the cancellation of a fire policy after several losses and receipt by the policyholder of an anonymous threat to start another, was upheld.

There is no general duty to provide reasons. Neither is the insurer required to return any part of the premium unless provided for in the policy. As a matter of practice, pro rata return of premium is usually required by such clauses. Any notice period specified must be complied with and losses occurring during the notice period will be covered.

Cancellation clauses may potentially be abused by the insurer to avoid single losses the policyholder might reasonably expect to be covered. To be fair to UK insurers, there seems little evidence that any such practice has been widespread. The convention appears to be that the clause is invoked only in extreme cases after the insurer has met a number of claims. *Birds' Modern Insurance Law*, p. 96, cites an Indian case, *General Assurance Society v Chandermull Jain (1966)*, that illustrates the problem. Here flooding upstream threatened inevitable flooding of the insured's riverside premises some days later. The insurers promptly cancelled cover. The Supreme Court of India upheld the unrestricted cancellation clause and rejected the policyholder's argument that the loss occurred prior to cancellation as the flood was already inevitable. They correctly ruled that the flood occurs when the water enters the premises, as this was after the policy was cancelled no cover was in force.

There are, of course, circumstances where such a clause is perfectly reasonable. If, for example, a policyholder contracts to pay the premium in instalments and then defaults, the insurer is quite entitled to cancel. The clause should not be viewed as giving an insurer a right inconsistent with fair conduct.

Such clauses will commonly set out the policyholder's right to cancel. Usually if the cancellation is involuntary in that the policyholder no longer has an interest in the subject matter of the policy (they have sold their car, for example), a return of premium will be made. This is unlikely to be on a pro rata basis to take account of the insurer's expenses.

This clause is not used in life assurance policies as the justifiable intent of such clauses is for an insurer to say enough is enough after a number of claims. This is not a scenario that could arise in life assurance. It would be unconscionable for an insurer to collect premiums for years and then seek to cancel cover if the policyholder was diagnosed with a critical illness. A life assurer is then committed to the contract for its full term, save in the case of a breach of obligation by the policyholder such as a failure to pay the premium.

Conduct of business regulation permits cancellation by the policyholder in the early stages of the contract, generally known as the 'cooling off' period. The Insurance Conduct of Business Sourcebook (ICOBS) provides in section 7 that the policyholder may cancel a life, accident or payment protection contract within 30 days of inception and other contracts within 14 days of inception without giving reasons. A full refund must be offered.

This does not apply to travel policies of less than one month duration. Neither does it apply to life and accident contracts of less than six months, unless they are 'distance' contracts (sold by phone or internet with no face-to-face contact). The right may also not be exercised where the policy has been arranged via an unauthorised intermediary. No such cancellation rights are available for business insurance, only to private consumers.

The ICOBS rules will be applied by the Financial Ombudsman Services irrespective of the contractual position. Reputable firms will no doubt incorporate the rules into contracts and sales literature. If within the contract, such rights would be upheld by the courts.

Interpretation

The full law on the interpretation of contracts is outside the scope of this book. The important principles should be noted, however.

The basic approach of the courts to the interpretation of a contract is to give effect to the agreement between the parties. In general, if the intent is clear it will be enforced. This is the case even if the clause conflicts with established principles of insurance law. It has already been seen in Chapter 2 that rateable proportion clauses override the common law of contribution. However, the more a clause appears to favour one party (and in an insurance contract that is always going to be the insurer), the greater the presumption that the other party could not have agreed to it and therefore an alternative meaning should be considered:

1   *Ordinary meaning* – The first consideration is the ordinary meaning of the wording used. If from this only one reasonable interpretation emerges, that is the interpretation that will be applied.
2   *Technical meaning* – The ordinary meaning approach will not apply if the word in question has a technical meaning. This is often a technical legal meaning, but can apply to other kinds of technical meanings. 'Theft', for example, is a word that has ordinary meaning, but as it is legally defined in the *Theft Act 1968* it is the legal meaning that will be ascribed to the word.

3   *Context* – The ordinary meaning of words can also be modified when they are used in conjunction with other words, such that the use of the other words implies that such a modification is intended. Therefore, in *Young v Sun Alliance (1977)*, flood was defined as meaning some kind of abnormal event rather than mere entry of water into the premises. The decisive factor was the use of the phrase 'storm, tempest or flood' implying that the intent was that the policy cover some kind of extreme event.

4   *Contra proferentum* – Despite the application of the principles outlined above there will always be cases where a word or phrase might reasonably have two (or more) meanings. This might present problems in contract law generally, but in insurance the position is relatively clear. The decisive factor is that it is the insurer who has written the contract. They have had the opportunity to plainly express their intent. If they fail to do so, they must pay the price. This is termed the contra proferentum rule (literally against the one who brings (into existence)). Under this rule, if one party wrote the contract and a genuine ambiguity exists, the meaning preferred will be that favourable to the other party. Therefore, as it is the insurer who writes the policy, the courts will favour the policyholder if the insurer fails to make the meaning of the policy clear.

The basic law is modified by the *Unfair Terms in Consumer Contract Regulations 1999* which states:

> A contractual term which has not been individually negotiated shall be regarded as unfair if, contrary to the requirement of good faith, it causes a significant imbalance in the parties' rights and obligations arising under the contract, to the detriment of the consumer.

This might appear to threaten many long-cherished insurance clauses, but for the qualification 'in so far as it is in plain intelligible language, the assessment of fairness of a term shall not relate ... to the definition of the main subject matter of the contract'. This would prevent the Regulations from affecting clauses setting out cover and exclusions. Just how much more of the policy would be removed from scrutiny is open to question, but for the present at least these questions are not being asked. Insurance contracts are specifically excluded from the jurisdiction of the Unfair Contract Terms Act 1977.

The reason why UTCCR 1999 is not influencing the law to the extent that it might, is because it only affects consumer contracts. Almost all disputes concerning consumer contracts will be adjudicated by the Financial Ombudsman Service, not the courts. If the matter is not brought before the courts, they are denied the opportunity to comment.

The stated aim of the FOS is to produce a result that is 'fair and reasonable'. The strict rules of construction adopted by the courts will be overlooked if they conflict with this basic aim. As the decisions of the FOS are not public and would not create precedent even if they were, it is difficult to assess the effect of the system on the practice of insurance. Suffice to say that the FOS and its predecessor the Insurance Ombudsman Bureau have in the past cheerfully ruled entirely contrary to the law and in the case of the FOS with statutory blessing.

Renewal

It is very easy to view policies as potentially long-term contractual arrangements and indeed in life assurance this is the case. As long as the policyholder meets their obligations, the contract exists for as long as they wish or until the contract is determined by death or the expiry of the term if it is not a whole life contract.

In general insurance, the pattern is one of a series of independent contracts each individually negotiated. Therefore, the duty of disclosure re-emerges at each renewal, although if a material fact has already been disclosed and remains unchanged, it need not be re-disclosed.

Each renewal is freely negotiated and although policyholders have in the past tried to argue to the contrary, insurers are under no legal obligation to offer renewal terms or even to advise that renewal terms would not be offered. Any such obligation would contradict the insurer's right not to enter into a new policy. It would of course be considered good practice to do so and insurers generally would consider a moral if not legal obligation exists to warn policyholders that a policy is soon to expire and to either offer terms or confirm that terms will not be offered.

ICOBS now requires insurers to issue such warning in good time. A minimum period of 21 days is specified for consumer policies, though no such period is specified for business policies.

The case for reform of the law of warranties

Statements of General Insurance Practice/ICOBS

From 1977, the voluntary agreement of the ABI (enforced by the IOB from 1981) was that 'an insurer will not repudiate liability to indemnify a policyholder ... on grounds of a breach of warranty or condition where the circumstances of the loss are unconnected with the breach unless fraud is involved'.

In addition, basis of contract clauses were prohibited by the statement that 'neither the proposal form nor the policy shall contain any provision converting the statements as to past or present fact in the proposal form into warranties'. Since January 2005, this area has been regulated by the FSA, in particular, Clause 8.1.2 of ICOBS states:

> A rejection of a consumer policyholder's claim is unreasonable, except where there is evidence of fraud, if it is for:
>
> (3) breach of warranty or condition unless the circumstances of the claim are connected to the breach and unless (for a pure protection contract):
>
>   (a) under a 'life of another' contract, the warranty relates to a statement of fact concerning the life to be assured and, if the statement had been made by the life to be assured under an 'own life' contract, the insurer could have rejected the claim under this rule or
>
>   (b) the warranty is material to the risk and was drawn to the customer's attention before the conclusion of the contract.

This is somewhat ambiguous. Does 'connected' mean a causal connection between breach and loss or merely that the warranty that was breached was of a type intended to minimise the risk of the type of loss that occurred?

Basis of contract clauses are not prohibited, although the requirement that breach and loss are 'connected' does reduce their impact. This is surprising given that the Statements so clearly prohibited their use. It is hoped that insurers would not use such clauses in consumer contracts anyway, but why not make it clear that their use is unacceptable?

FOS interpretation

Despite the lack of clarity in ICOBS, it is unlikely that the FOS would permit an insurer to rely on a basis of contract clause in a consumer contract. The position with businesses is less clear, given the FOS approach of applying a sliding scale of protection dependent upon the size of the business.

As regards warranties in consumer contracts, the position on causality is clear. The breach must be causally connected to the loss. It appears that this principle is extended into commercial insurance as well, at least regarding very small firms. In Issue 74 *Ombudsman News* (January 2009) a case was reported concerning what might be considered a warranty. A policy contained a 'condition precedent', stating that theft claims would only be paid if specific security devices were installed and in use, and all the doors of the insured premises were made of solid wood. The devices were in place as required but the door was not of solid wood and thieves gained entry through the door. In law, this was a clear breach of warranty entitling repudiation. There is also no question that the warranty was intended to reduce the risk of theft. The FOS was clear, however, that the breach would have to be connected to the loss. An extremely narrow view was taken and it was concluded that as the thieves gained entry by lifting the door off the hinges, that the construction of the door was unconnected with the loss.

Joint Law Commission proposals

Unsurprisingly, the joint Law Commissions have turned their fire on warranties as well as utmost good faith. In their 2007 report, a number of proposals were made, as shown below.

Basis of contract clauses prohibited

These would be prohibited in all consumer contracts. All statements would be treated as representations, requiring materiality and with remedy dependent upon the culpability of the policyholder (see Chapter 2). In commercial contracts, each statement warranted must be set out in the policy. This prohibits blanket clauses but does allow important statements of fact to become specific warranties. This is a sensible proposal as basis of contract clauses are difficult to justify. Why should insurers seek greater protection than they already enjoy from a law (non-disclosure) that is already regarded as unduly harsh?

Statements of past or present fact

Again, all statements would be considered representations as regards consumer contracts; however,with the prohibition of basis of contract clauses most of the problems are removed. In reality, no warranty would arise unless specifically written into the policy which it is implied would not be permitted.

Two proposals were submitted as regards commercial contracts. First, that they would also be prohibited in these contracts in the same way as in consumer contracts. Second, that insurers could use warranties of specific facts but could only rely upon them if the claim was causally connected. Either proposal would represent a significant improvement. It is suggested that the greater diversity of risks in the commercial arena should permit such warranties, but only when they are clearly set out in the policy.

Promissory warranties

First, it is proposed that a warranty would only come into existence if it is in writing, either in the main contract or referred to in the main contract and in the case of consumer contracts if it has been sufficiently brought to the attention of the policyholder.

Consumers would be entitled to be paid a claim if *they* could prove the breach did not contribute to the loss. If the breach only caused a part of the loss, the balance should be paid. Views were invited as to whether this principle should be extended to commercial contracts. Further doubt was expressed as to whether reform should extend to marine and reinsurance contracts.

A requirement of causal connection between breach and loss would certainly bring warranties back to their intended risk management function. They exist to promote good risk control practice, thus minimising loss for the benefit of all. They should not operate as penalty clauses.

The counter-argument is that culpable failure to adhere to the terms of a warranty indicates poor moral hazard. A lax attitude to risk control in one area, implies a poor attitude to risk control in other areas. Failure to comply with specific instructions could be viewed as evidence of a failure to comply with the policyholder's general duty to act as if uninsured. Insurers may argue that they want nothing to do with policyholders of this type and that withdrawing from the contract in its entirety is justified. However, it is questionable whether the penal nature of the existing law is a proportionate remedy for this problem, given that the insurer can refuse to offer terms at next renewal and can avoid claims caused by a failure to comply with a warranty during the policy period.

Effect of breach

Views were invited (presumably for commercial contracts only, although it is not made clear) as to whether, given a breach has occurred:

1   Insurers should retain the right to repudiate the entire contract.
2   Insurers could elect to repudiate a claim but continue the contract.
3   Policyholders should remain liable for future premiums following repudiation.
4   Insurers should be liable to make a pro rata return of premium following repudiation.
5   Insurers should be required to give reasonable notice that the contract is to be terminated.

In other words, very few firm proposals were made with regard to commercial contracts!

Given the possible effect on employees and third parties, not to mention other insured interests such as mortgagors, sudden withdrawal of cover is difficult to support in the absence of fraud. Even if insurers are to be allowed to repudiate the contract, do they suffer unacceptable prejudice if they are required to provide reasonable notice of this intent, say, 14 days? It is suggested not. Indeed, this can be brought about by refusing any right of repudiation for breach of warranty save in the case of fraud. The insurers can then consider whether the policyholder's conduct is sufficient to justify invoking the cancellation clause. As there is a commendable reluctance among insurers to rely on these clauses, this might change insurers' attitude from an automatic assumption that the policy should be instantly avoided, to proper consideration of the justification for avoidance.

There seems no reason why the basic principle should not be that the policyholder pays for the cover they have enjoyed. This means that there may be liability for future premiums as a number of categories of cover in a commercial policy are subject to subsequent adjustment based on exposure.

Whether such liability should extend beyond this period is less clear. Fraud should clearly entitle the insurer to refuse any return of premium as the compensation accruing to the wronged party. If it is the insurers' decision that they will withdraw from the contract, knowing that this will leave the policyholder having to find replacement cover hurriedly with a significant increase in premium in all probability, it seems fair that the policyholders' financial prejudice is eased by a return of the unused premium.

Conclusion

Again this is an example of a body of law that has for many years been recognised as unduly harsh and yet has gone unreformed. Again, self-regulation and the Ombudsman have alleviated some of the problems as regards consumer contracts and very recently for some small businesses. However, once more the problem arises that the law says one thing, the FSA (through ICOBS) another and the FOS practises a third and far from transparent system. As the FOS system is now by far the most influential due to the larger number of consumer policies, is there any reason why it should not be put on a proper legal footing?

Deal now, detail later

The issue of policy documentation became a major issue in the insurance market in the aftermath of World Trade Center attack in September 2001. Astonishingly, given that the policy was covering $3.5 billion of risk, no documentation had been issued in respect of the coverage on the World Trade Center at the time of the attack. The policyholder argued that there were two attacks and that they could claim for two losses. The insurers contended that it was a single attack. Two different courts were presented with two different wordings by two different groups of insurers. Unsurprisingly they delivered two different verdicts, one in favour of the insurers and one in favour of the policyholder. The lack of documentation led to nearly six years of litigation over the issue of whether the attack was defined as one loss or two by the policy, before a compromise settlement was negotiated via the mediation of the New York state regulator. Vast legal costs, reported as several hundred million dollars, were incurred. The WTC case was not, however, an isolated incident.

This highlighted what became known as the 'deal now, detail later' culture. Although dealing in contracts for premiums of many millions and much larger potential claims, all too often once the deal was struck, the issue of documentation clearly recording the contract was delayed for months. Far too frequently cover would commence with some details of the cover to be provided yet to be finalised. Insurers above all should be familiar with the first corollary to sod's law (usually known as Finagle's law to those of the American persuasion) which states, 'Whatever can go wrong will go wrong, and at the worst possible time, in the worst possible way.' Therefore, according to this law, a major loss will occur the day before cover is finalised and not the day after.

In the days of computerisation and instant electronic communication, this was seriously embarrassing to the insurance industry. A fair accusation was that a sales-orientated industry soon lost interest in the more mundane aspects of providing an efficient after-sales service.

It should be noted that the focus here was on the London market and large corporate policies. In personal lines insurance, standard policy wordings are the norm and if doubt exists, this is the contract that will be applied.

As a result, in 2004, the FSA set the London market a target. Contract certainty would be defined as full agreement being reached on all terms between the policyholder and all insurers before the inception of cover. Appropriate evidence of cover should then be provided within 30 days, either by a traditional policy or by some other bespoke document.

If the market did not make satisfactory progress, regulatory intervention was threatened. In 2007, the FSA congratulated the market on 'achieving contract certainty' as 90 per cent of contracts met the standard outlined above. Put it another way, the market deserved a pat on the back as only 10 per cent of policyholders having handed over large sums of money to the market, were left unsure of what they had bought for more than a month.

To be fair, this is a significant improvement. The initial target set in 2004 was for the market to achieve contract certainty on just 30 per cent of contracts by the end of 2005, indicating that in 2004 a much smaller percentage of contracts were being finalised with due expediency.

Surely, though, the market is being unduly complacent. The deal now, detail later culture will not be eradicated until it is exceptional for any contract not to be finalised on time. One in ten would not appear to meet any reasonable definition of exceptional.

4   Financial and accounting principles

Actuarial science is a predominantly financial discipline that uses mathematical and statistical techniques to predict future outcomes. In insurance, this is the means by which the equitable premium is calculated, as given an estimate of future losses, insurers are in a position to calculate the necessary premiums to charge. It is equally important in estimating future losses on policies already written, particularly critical in the practice of life and liability insurances. The mathematics of actuarial science is beyond the scope of this book, however, the principles are important.

Actuarial science was developed in stages from the seventeenth century by a series of mathematicians (although the efforts of the third-century Roman mathematician Ulpian should be recognised), with a view to predicting life expectancy. Early pioneers such as Edmund Halley and James Dodson constructed mortality tables, predicting the probability of death within 12 months for an average individual of a known age. This could then be used to estimate remaining life expectancy by adding the annual probabilities until the age at which the probability equalled 0.5 or 50 per cent. The point at which half of a large group of people will have died can be said to be the age that any individual within the group can expect to live to. In 1762, the Equitable Life Assurance Society was founded to provide a commercial application for Dodson's work.

The importance of mortality tables for the development of life assurance is discussed further in Chapter 10; however, these actuarial principles underpin insurance generally. Insurance is an unusual business in that not only are the majority of operating costs incurred after the income is received, as these costs are primarily the costs of claims, the amount cannot be known with certainty when the premium is set. Compare this with the position of manufacturers and retailers where costs will be incurred and largely quantified prior to the point of sale.

Insurers must be in a position to estimate future losses and ensure that sufficient premium is collected to meet these losses as they arise. It is not simply a matter of estimating whether the loss will occur, insurers must also consider when the loss will occur and when the claim will be settled. This creates different problems for different classes of insurance as losses can be divided according to three criteria:

1 *Certainty/Uncertainty* – Most policies cover fortuitous risks, that is to say the event insured against may or may not happen. Examples would be fires, accidents or legal actions. Life assurers, however, when issuing whole life or annuity contracts, offer to cover a certain event, the death of the policyholder or annuitant. The risk insured is not the occurrence of death but the timing of death.

2 *Immediate loss/deferred loss* – Assuming that the risk occurs, is it likely to be known by the policyholder and reported to the insurer within 12 to 15 months of the inception of the policy? Alternatively, will there be a significant delay between the commencement of cover and the occurrence or notification of a claim?

Most property damage covers fall in the former category. Policyholders tend to notice immediately if their house burns down or their car is damaged in an accident and will usually inform their insurer promptly. Not only will insurers know the loss has arisen, but they will be able to estimate the cost of loss.

Other types of cover can be trickier. Life assurers expect the majority of claims to occur years after the inception of cover, often decades later. Permanent health insurance follows a similar pattern. Legal liability covers encounter further problems. Although most liability policies only cover incidents occurring during the 12-month period of cover, the third party does not always realise at the time that they have been injured or that their property has been damaged. Obviously if they are involved in an accident it is usually immediately apparent that they have suffered harm, similarly property damage is often noticeable soon after the incident. However, if they are exposed to chemicals that may give rise to an industrial disease, this disease may not manifest itself for years. Other types of harm, deafness, for instance, develop slowly over a period of time. Consequently, there can be an extended period between the incident and discovery of the harm. Even once this harm becomes apparent, under UK law they have three years from the date they discover the harm to commence a legal action for personal injury, rising to six years in the case of property damage. As a result, valid claims may be received by the insurer 20 or 30 years after the incident took place. Claims for asbestos-related disease are particularly notorious for this lengthy deferral of notification (see Chapter 6 for further discussion of asbestos losses). Drawn-out claims of this nature are known as 'long tail' claims.

3 *Early settlement/delayed settlement* – Once the claim has been notified, in many cases, settlement by the insurer ought to follow promptly. Although the occurrence of loss may be long deferred in the example of life assurance, in most cases investigation of the loss will not be a lengthy process. Similarly, payment of straightforward property damage should not take more than a few weeks, with the caveat that serious damage to buildings, for instance, might involve a long rebuilding period (Figure 4.1).

A legal liability claim, on the other hand, may be significantly delayed. If liability is disputed, it may be necessary to determine the case in court, a process which might take more than a year and longer if either party appeals. Even if liability is not disputed, in the case of personal injury, the long-term effects of the injury may not be immediately apparent, resulting in a delay to establish whether the third party's condition improves or deteriorates. It would not be unusual for a personal injury case to take several years to settle from first notification.

In all cases, there is a clear distinction between the legitimate delay caused by the reasonable investigation and negotiation of a claim and the illegitimate delay caused by an unreasonable tardiness in dealing with the claim.

The equitable premium

Relative frequency

The basic tool of the insurance industry is a form of probability known as relative frequency. Casino operators know that given a pack of well-shuffled cards, the probability of drawing

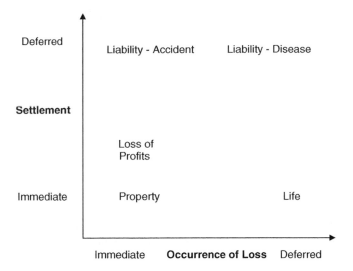

Figure 4.1 Pattern of payments.

a spade is one in four or 0.25. They know that there are 52 cards in the pack and that 13 of them are spades. All possible outcomes are known, all possible outcomes are equally likely and it is simply a matter of dividing the outcome sought by the total possible outcomes. This is known as *a priori* probability as the future result can be predicted by examining the problem.

When considering an insurance proposal, insurers can never know what the probability that there will be a loss in the next year will be. What they do, however, know is the outcome of insuring similar risks in the past. By analysing these outcomes and assuming that the hazards that caused these outcomes remain more or less the same, they can estimate the probability of loss in the future, essentially assuming that the future will resemble the past. This method is known as relative frequency. It forms the foundation of actuarial calculations from the construction of mortality tables in life assurance to setting premium rates for motor insurance.

The process can be as crude or sophisticated as the insurer wishes. A UK motor insurer will certainly calculate the base probability of a vehicle being in an accident within the course of a year (around 1 in 6, rather worryingly). However, they will, for example, want to know the age of the driver, the type of car and the usual location of the vehicle, as these vary the base probability. Although a life assurer will obviously need to know the base probability of a 35-year-old proposer dying in, say, the next 25 years, they again will adjust their estimate to take account of smoking, obesity or known health problems, for example. The estimate produced will then be adjusted to take account of known trends. If, for example, the number of motor accidents has been increasing by 3 per cent per annum for the last five years, it is reasonable to assume that next year will see a further 3 per cent increase. Life assurers need to take account of the fact that life expectancy has been steadily increasing throughout the last century.

As the probability of risk occurrence varies according to hazard, an analysis of the relevant hazards is critical to a sound estimation of risk. Insurers then need to consider whether there are any factors that lead them to suppose that the future will not resemble the past. In other words, have the hazards that produced the frequency of loss in the past changed? If so, is the change likely to lead to an increase or a decrease in losses? A good example of this would be where a change in legislation or a key legal decision increases legal liability. Incidents that would not have resulted in a claim in the past will now lead to losses and legal liability insurers must provide for this increase in their premiums.

The total cost of claims must take into account not only the expected number of claims, the average cost of claims must also be considered. For life assurers offering fixed benefits, this is not an issue, but must be carefully studied in the case of indemnity insurance where the settlement is not usually fixed. The obvious element to be factored into the premium calculation is a provision for inflation. This is not necessarily the consumer price index or other such broad indices. Inflation in legal awards has for many years been running above background inflation. Currency fluctuation can influence the cost of repair or replacement if parts or products are imported, a particular issue for motor insurers.

It is of course too much to expect that even the most experienced actuaries and underwriters will accurately predict loss every year. It is, however, important that in the medium term, say, any three- to five-year period, total estimates are reasonably close to total claims.

The law of large numbers

Insurers accept the risks that their policyholders find unacceptable. They do, however, have a natural mathematical advantage. For the policyholder, it is an all-or-nothing gamble, they get lucky or they face possible financial ruin. The insurer, on the other hand, is indifferent as to the outcome of any single policy, just as long as the overall outcome of all policies is close to expectations. That the insurers can survive and (usually) prosper is down to the law of large numbers.

The law of large numbers states that the greater the number of trials, the greater the probability that the actual loss will equal the expected loss. Therefore if an insurer seeks to predict the average loss on an individual policy to within, say, a 5 per cent margin of error, as the amount of policies written by the insurer increases, the probability that the result will be outside the 5 per cent margin of error decreases. Note this margin of error extends above and below the expected figure. Large insurance companies are not only less likely to experience nasty shocks, they are also less likely to be pleasantly surprised. Technically this is the weak law of large numbers, as no matter how large the number of trials, the probability that the insurer's estimate will be out by more than 5 per cent will never fall to zero. Alternatively, it could be argued that this is the empirical law of averages as it cannot be mathematically proven that this is a 'law', although in innumerable trials it has been found to work.

This can be demonstrated by considering the expected standard deviation on the basis that the outcomes of multiple underwriting years will be normally distributed. If insurance is reduced to a binomial distribution (i.e. the problem is broken down to a simple loss or no loss scenario), the distribution of loss should approximate to a normal distribution.

The formula to calculate the standard deviation is $\sqrt{npq}$ where n is the number of trials, p is the probability of loss and q is the reciprocal probability of no loss. Therefore, if we assume that the probability of a random vehicle being involved in a motor accident during the course of a year is 1 in 6 (or 0.167), the expected volatility in the results of motor insurers of varying sizes can be estimated.

Motor insurer A has 200,000 policyholders.

$$\sqrt{npq} = \sqrt{200{,}000 \times 0.167 \times 0.833} = \sqrt{27{,}822} = 167$$

Motor insurer B has 1,000,000 policyholders

$$\sqrt{npq} = \sqrt{1,,000,000 \times 0.167 \times 0.833} = \sqrt{139,111} = 373$$

In the case of insurer A, 200,000 policies might be expected to produce 33,400 accidents. The standard deviation is 167, therefore one standard deviation is equal to 0.5 per cent of the expected number of claims.

In the case of insurer B, 1,000,000 policies might be expected to produce 167,000 accidents. The standard deviation is 373, therefore one standard deviation is equal to 0.22 per cent of the expected number of claims.

As according to normal distribution theory, 68 per cent of outcomes will lie between one standard deviation of the mean, 95 per cent of outcomes will lie between two standard deviations of the mean and 99 per cent of outcomes will be within three standard deviations, in our example (Figure 4.2).

Therefore, theoretically insurer A has a 68 per cent probability that their estimate will be within 0.5 per cent of the actual result. Insurer B has a 68 per cent probability that the estimate will be within 0.22 per cent. As the number of policies sold increases, so in theory will the margin of error reduce.

This must be qualified by the comment that the problem is not strictly binomial as a motorists may of course have more than one accident in the course of year, meaning that the question can be defined not as whether there will be an accident or not, but rather how many accidents will occur. That being said, if a life policyholder submits more than one claim, the claims manager's eyebrow may be raised. It can also be noted that the total cost of claims is the frequency of claims multiplied by the severity. Therefore the outcome does not wholly depend upon the number of accidents. Nonetheless there is a demonstrable theoretical advantage to the large company and Voltaire's theory that God is not on the side of the big battalions must be doubted.

This concept does though rely upon the trials being independent, in other words, the outcome of one trial should not affect the outcome of any other trial. The real world is never

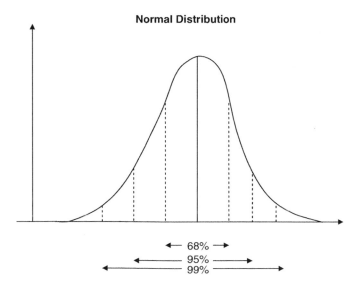

Figure 4.2 Normal distribution.

this neat and tidy. Therefore, where the risk is particular, the law of large numbers works well in practice, if the risk is fundamental, the trials are not independent as many losses will be caused by the same risk occurrence.

It is equally important that the expected loss is estimated with reasonable precision. If an underwriter fails to consider developing trends or changes in the underlying hazards, the estimate they produce will not be the real expected loss. Even when the law of large numbers operates, the outcome will tend to approximate to the real expected loss and not the underwriter's erroneous figure.

The operation of the law of large numbers can be observed by comparing the results of Lloyd's motor syndicates with their aviation and energy brethren. Obviously the number of motor policies issued is vastly greater than the number of aviation policies. One would expect the outcome of the motor syndicates to be more predictable as they obtain greater benefit from the law of large numbers. Similarly, while the motor and aviation risks are geographically well spread, the energy risks are clustered around major oil and gas fields and are in contrast geographically concentrated and not fully independent. As the energy risks are so concentrated, some of benefits of the law of large numbers are lost and a more volatile outcome is to be expected. By analysing the combined ratio (the ratio of claims and expenses to premium, see below for further explanation) from 2003 to 2008, the predictability of the various market sectors can be estimated (Figure 4.3).

Exactly as the law of large numbers would have it, the motor sector is the most predictable with a range of outcomes from 91.2 per cent to 99.6 per cent over the six-year period. The smaller aviation pool exhibits a much wider range from 65.1 per cent to 93.0 per cent. The energy sector is by far the most volatile with outcomes ranging from 73.4 per cent to 146.9 per cent. The full protection of the law of large numbers is not extended to all classes if the number of risks is not truly large or the risks are not independent.

There remains an element of doubt and unforeseen circumstances can lead to poor results in individual years. However, a further mathematical theorem then operates to stabilise longer-term outcomes. This is the central limit theorem, which states that the distribution of averages tends to be normal. What this means in practice is that given a number of trials (and a year's

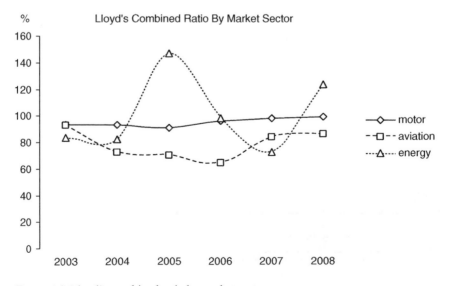

Figure 4.3 Lloyd's combined ratio by market sector.

underwriting result may be considered a trial), the outcomes will follow a familiar bell curve with the majority of outcomes grouped tightly around the average outcome. Therefore, an insurer might expect that in the long run in most years the result will be close to expected, with the occasional bad year balanced by the occasional good year. Again this depends upon accurate estimation of the expected result in the first place.

The effect of the central limit theorem is to iron out the wrinkles brought about by fundamental type losses. A certain number of such losses are to be expected in a normal year, as some years will be benign, others catastrophic. A well-capitalised insurer can, by reserving funds in the benign years, release them to meet the costs of the occasional disaster. A less well-capitalised insurer will use the services of a reinsurer to achieve the same result. By way of example, the average combined ratio for Lloyd's energy syndicates in the six years studied is 101.5 per cent, an acceptable result in the long term.

Stochastic modelling

There is an alternative means of considering the problem. A stochastic process does not assume that the future will resemble the past. Instead the future is viewed as a number of different pathways producing different outcomes with the probability of a particular pathway being taken being variable.

The stochastic process can be modelled by considering a number of random variables. These might include the number of claims, the number of catastrophes, the severity of losses, the timing of loss and settlement as well as non-claim-related factors such as investment performance or other economic variables. A particular set of variables would be chosen and the model would be run. The outcome would then be noted and the process repeated with one or more of the variables altered. After a very large number of such runs (this method does require significant computational power!), the distribution of the outcomes will produce a distribution curve. This will show not only the most likely range of outcomes, but enable an estimate to be made of the probability of extreme outcomes and the factors that would bring about such a result.

The usual practice in relative frequency of projecting a past trend into the future as a means of forecasting is arguably a very limited stochastic process. The distinction is that rather than deciding what the established trend is based upon prior observation, stochastic processes examine multiple possible trends moving forward from the present. The stochastic process is not limited by what has happened in the past. This overcomes the difficulty encountered in relative frequency in that if the event has not happened in the recent past, it will not be recorded in the data and therefore it is easy to make the false assumption that it cannot happen in the future.

Life assurers may use such a methodology due to the long-range forecasting that they have to undertake, perhaps requiring them to consider investment returns, inflation and interest rates over a period of 20 years or more, while also factoring in possible changes in mortality. Liability insurers may wish to examine how the 'long tail' will develop, using similar economic factors to the life assurers, but replacing mortality with consideration of the number, size and timing of future claims that may come crawling out of the woodwork. Another application is in estimating the cost of natural catastrophes. The effect of storms, for example, can be modelled, varying the intensity, size and path of the storm in each case to assess the probable damage. This is obviously a complex and expensive methodology; however, where the stakes are sufficiently high, the expense may be considered worthwhile.

The effect of investment income

Calculating the equitable premium is not simply a matter of calculating the likely losses and ensuring that pure risk premiums equal this amount. Insurers also have to consider when losses are likely to arise. This is central to life underwriting, but is also important in certain general insurance categories when loss is deferred and/or settlement delayed, particularly liability insurance. Insurers must match cash inflows (the premiums) to uncertain future cash outflows (the claims). Even when the number and cost of claims are accurately predicted, the greater the period between the two flows, the greater the uncertainty that remains.

If the nature of the loss is such that it will be immediate and settled early, for example, minor motor accidents, the timing of loss will have a limited effect on the two cash flows (except in a high inflation economy). Any adjustment to the premium to take account of the time value of the premium will be minimal.

If, however, either the loss is deferred or settlement is delayed, insurers will seek to collect the net present value of a future claim as the pure risk premium.

The present value (PV) of a loss is:

$$PV = \frac{FV}{(1+r)^n}$$

Where FV is the future value (the actual sum paid), $1 + r$ is the anticipated rate of investment return and n is the number of periods for which this return can be earned.

If an insurer offering public liability insurance anticipates that incidents during the course of an underwriting year will produce £10,000,000 in claims settlements, how much pure risk premium will they need to collect to meet this future liability?

This depends on two main factors. First, the rate of return they expect to receive from the investment of premiums prior to settlement. Second, when these settlements are likely to be made indicating the period that premiums can be invested. This is demonstrated in the following (highly simplified) example. Assume that 30 per cent of claims are settled in year 1 (the period of cover), 40 per cent are settled in year 2 and the final 30 per cent settled in year 3. Assume also that claims are settled bi-annually six months into the year and at the year end. Finally, assume that the £10,000,000 premium is received on day one of the first year.

If the premiums are invested and produce a return of 10 per cent, the cash flow will be as shown in Table 4.1, bearing in mind that there are 6 periods and a return of 5 per cent in each period.

Therefore, assuming that all assumptions prove correct, a pure risk premium of £8,456,650 will be sufficient to meet future claims totalling £10,000,000. This is a contrived example as in reality premiums will be collected over the course of a year and claims will not be neatly settled in 6-month instalments; however, this is the broad principle applied and is equally applicable to other deferred losses such as life assurance.

The longer the period, the greater the risk that assumptions will be inaccurate. Predicting investment returns even over two to three years is not an exact science, as over 20 years significant economic changes can occur that might render the original assumptions wildly inaccurate (see the discussion in Chapter 11 of the failure of Equitable Life). Similarly, the risk of loss may change over time as changes in the underlying hazards affect the probability of loss. For example, improvements in medical treatment may increase life expectancy or changes in legislation may increase the number of successful liability claims.

Table 4.1 Premium investment returns

	Settlements (£)	Discount factor	Present value @ 5% (£)
Period 1	1,500,000	0.9524	1,428,600
Period 2	1,500,000	0.9070	1,360,500
Period 3	2,000,000	0.8638	1,727,600
Period 4	2,000,000	0.8227	1,645,400
Period 5	1,500,000	0.7835	1,175,250
Period 6	1,500,000	0.7462	1,119,300
Total			8,456,650

Actuaries must therefore not only consider the likely number, severity and timing of losses, but must also consider trends, both established and anticipated, that might influence not only losses, but investment performance and future income. Insurers then have to deal with the accounting complications caused by acceptance of premiums today for policies that may produce claims many years into an uncertain future.

Accounting for insurance

Accounting can be considered in very simple terms, even if the practice can be rather involved. It is primarily concerned with three factors:

1 *Solvency*: Assets − Liabilities = Solvency. This is set out in the balance sheet.
2 *Profitability*: Revenue − Costs = Profit. This is set out in the profit and loss account (also commonly referred to as the income statement).
3 *Liquidity*: Liquid assets − Short-term liabilities = Liquidity. This can be derived from the balance sheet, although cash flow statements are invariably provided as well.

Although seemingly straightforward, the complications are introduced when these terms have to be defined. This is particularly the case in insurance where claims can occur long after the policy has been sold and the income generated. This affects both liabilities (and therefore solvency) and costs (and therefore profit). There are also differences in approach between general insurers and life assurers due to the different nature of the risks they are covering.

Insurance accounting terminology

Although the basic principles of accounting apply to the accounts of insurers in just the same way as they apply to the accounts of any other company, there are some distinct terms used in insurance accounting.

• *Technical accounts* – The term 'technical' when used in connection with insurance accounting denotes that the accounts refer to the insurance activities of the company, rather than the general business activities common to all companies. The term 'technical reserve' indicates therefore that the reserve is created to meet insurance liabilities as opposed to general liabilities.

- *Gross written premium/net written premium* – The gross written premium is the amount of premium policyholders are required to pay during the year of account. The net written premium is the gross amount less any reinsurance premiums paid by the insurer.
- *Earned premium/unearned premium* – The insurer will be writing policies throughout the year of account. In the case of general insurers, these policies will usually be offered for a period of one year. Therefore, unless the policy commences at the same time as the year of account, the policy will continue to operate after the year of account has ended. The earned premium is the proportionate part of the premium that is payable for cover actually offered during the year of account. Therefore if an annual policy commences three months into the year of account, 75 per cent of the premium is deemed to have been earned during that year of account and 25 per cent will be carried over to the next year of account as unearned premium. Unearned premiums are deducted from the gross written premium, however unearned premiums from the previous year will be added to the figure. Unearned premium should not be confused with unpaid premium. Unearned premiums have been received by the insurer, unpaid premiums have not and may indeed be accounted for as a bad debt.
- *Loss ratio* – The loss ratio is calculated by dividing the total claims paid during the year of account (usually including the claims handling costs as well as the actual payment) by the earned premium during the year. Therefore, if the earned premiums are £312 million and the cost of claims amounts to £243 million, the loss ratio is 243/312 which equals 77.88 per cent. Two slightly different ratios can be produced, depending on whether the insurer includes claims payable or claims actually paid. The former includes provisions for claims notified to the insurer but not actually paid.
- *Expense ratio* – The expense ratio is calculated by dividing the total operating costs for the year of account (usually less claims handling costs accounted for in the loss ratio) by the earned premium during the year of account. Therefore if the earned premiums are £312 million and the operating costs are £64 million, the expense ratio is 64/312 which equals 20.5 per cent.
- *Combined ratio* – The combined ratio is total claims paid and the operating costs during the year of account divided by the earned premium during the year of account. Using the above examples, the total claims paid amount to £243 million, the operating costs are £64 million and the earned premiums are £312 million. The combined ratio is therefore 307/312 which equals 98.39 per cent. If the ratio is less than 100 per cent, the insurer has made an underwriting profit, if the ratio exceeds 100 per cent, they have made an underwriting loss. Note that this does not mean that an overall profit or loss has been made as this does not take into account investment income. An insurer can therefore produce a combined ratio of 102 per cent yet still make an overall profit. Similarly, an underwriting profit can be eliminated if the investment returns are negative. This is the most commonly used ratio, providing as it does a snapshot of the insurer's underwriting profitability. It should be noted that these ratios are a feature of general insurance only.
- *Technical reserves* – These are reserves an insurer must create to meet future claims costs arising from policies already written. The need to create such reserves arises from three main sources. There are also voluntary reserves an insurer may choose to set aside in certain circumstances.
- *Unearned premiums* – The proportion of the policies already written that has still to run at the end of the financial year can be anticipated to produce claims in the next financial year. Unearned premiums are transferred to the next financial year as a reserve to meet these claims.

- *Claims provisions* – At the financial year end there will be a number of claims still being investigated and/or negotiated. Insurers estimate the cost of these reported claims and create a reserve to pay them in the future. Because they have arisen in the year of account the cost must be assigned to that year of account even if the final settlement of the claim occurs in subsequent accounting periods.
- *Incurred but not reported claims (IBNRs)* – In the case of long tail claims, in particular legal liability insurances, insurers must also consider that only a relatively small percentage of claims will be promptly reported to them. As most liability policies cover incidents arising during the period of cover irrespective of when the claim is actually notified (occurrence wordings as they are known) a reserve has to be created to meet these claims in future. Insurers study past underwriting years in order to estimate the number of IBNRs they expect to emerge in the ensuing years and seek to transfer reserves from year to year to meet the costs as the IBNRs appear. As discussed above, the longer the period, the more uncertain the process and it can be argued the greater the need for the insurer to reserve conservatively to allow for a margin of error.
- *Unexpired risk reserve* – While the creation of technical reserves is mandatory for insurers, they may also create a voluntary unexpired risk reserve. This is where they identify that the unearned premiums may be insufficient to meet the cost of claims arising from the unexpired period of cover. If claims arising from the expired period of cover exceed expectations and produce an underwriting loss, it is reasonable to suppose that this trend will continue. The unearned premium reserve can be augmented to meet these anticipated losses. This will form a part of the overall technical reserve.
- *Claims equalisation reserve* – As has been noted above, the claims paid by insurers can be subject to extreme volatility from year to year. In order to avoid lurching from triumph to disaster one year to the next, insurers can create equalisation reserves designed to smooth the results in the medium term. In years when loss ratios are well below expectations, the surplus underwriting profit is added to the claims equalisation reserve. This is then released in the years when loss ratios exceed expectations. The aim is to seek to provide a steady, relatively predictable return to investors. This reserve is voluntary, but forms a part of the technical reserve if it is created.
- *Accounting for reinsurance* – As has been noted, premium income is adjusted to take account of the fact that a proportion of the premium is ceded to the reinsurers. Reinsurance recoveries will be offset against claims payments, with the net cost to the insurer ultimately recorded. The reinsurance policy can be viewed as an asset, if it might be expected to produce 'revenue' in the future by way of reinsurance claim payments. Reinsurance assets are then stated in the balance sheet, based upon estimated future reinsurance recoveries with an allowance made for the possibility that not all such amounts will in fact be recovered.

Insurance company accounts: the profit and loss account

Accounting practices are governed by the *EU Directive (91/674)/EEC* on the annual accounts and consolidated accounts of insurance undertakings (generally known as the Insurance Accounts Directive or IAD). Once the EU assumed responsibility for the regulation of insurance companies (see Chapter 5), it was desirable to impose common accounting standards to allow easy comparison of the financial position of insurers across Europe.

The IAD was then intended to harmonise rules on the presentation and publication of annual and consolidated accounts by EU insurers. The IAD specifies how the balance sheet is to be structured and sets out the contents of the various balance sheet items. Similarly, the structure of the profit and loss account and the items it must contain are stipulated. The directive goes on to set out rules for valuation of investments and technical reserves and specifies the information that must be provided regarding the calculation of premiums and claims. Consolidated accounts are required from insurance groups. The IAD must be considered in conjunction with other directives aimed at the harmonisation of accounting standards in general as it deals with issues specific to insurers. It should also be noted that the IAD is more concerned with what information will be reported and the disclosure of methodology rather than the manner in which the figures will be calculated which is influenced by other principles, notably the IFRS, EEV and MCEV, all of which are discussed later in this chapter.

By way of example, Article 28 states:

> The provision for claims outstanding shall be the total estimated ultimate cost to an insurance undertaking of settling all claims arising from events which have occurred up to the end of the financial year, whether reported or not, less amounts already paid in respect of such claims.

Article 30 states: 'The equalization provision shall comprise any amounts set aside in compliance with legal or administrative requirements to equalize fluctuations in loss ratios in future years or to provide for special risks.'

Articles 34 and 35 stipulate how profit and loss accounts will be laid out for general and life companies respectively. The two requirements are broadly similar, however greater detail is required from life assurers in the reporting of investment income. Life assurers are also required to disclose investment management charges, together with value adjustments and both realised and unrealised losses on investments.

The requirement for the technical account for general insurers is as follows:

1 Earned premiums, net of reinsurance:

   (a) gross premiums written
   (b) outward reinsurance premiums
   (c) change in the gross provision for unearned premiums and, if permitted, the provision for unexpired risks
   (d) change in the provision for unearned premiums, reinsurers' share

2 Allocated investment return transferred from the non-technical account
3 Other technical income, net of reinsurance
4 Claims incurred, net of reinsurance:

   (a) claims paid
       (i) gross amount
       (ii) reinsurers' share
   (b) change in the provision for claims
       (i) gross amount
       (ii) reinsurers' share

5 Changes in other technical provisions, net of reinsurance, not shown under other headings
6 Bonuses and rebates, net of reinsurance

7 Net operating expenses:

  (a) acquisition costs
  (b) change in deferred acquisition costs
  (c) administrative expenses
  (d) reinsurance commissions and profit participation

8 Other technical charges, net of reinsurance
9 Change in the equalization provision
10 Sub-total (balance on the technical account for non-life-insurance business).

In reality, published accounts are simplified. There may be nothing to report under certain categories, and other categories will probably be published as a single figure rather than subdivided. A real world profit and loss account might be similar to the example in Table 4.2.

Some insurers may choose to produce two accounts. A technical account stating the operating profit or loss and a non-technical account considering finance costs, taxation and other income or expenditure unrelated to insurance activities.

Accounting for profit and loss: life assurers

The position for life assurers is somewhat different due to the long-term nature of the policies and the fact that their products are often investment rather than insurance-based.

Table 4.2 Profit and loss account for Xanadu General plc

Income	2008(£m)
Gross written premiums	865
Less: reinsurance premiums	(78)
Net written premiums	787
Change in the gross provision for unearned premiums	(37)
Less: change in provision for unearned premiums, reinsurers' share	3
Change in provision for unearned premiums	(34)
Net earned premiums	753
Net investment return	59
Other operating income	12
Total income	824
Expenses	
Gross claims incurred	(678)
Less: claims recoveries from reinsurers	46
Net claims and benefits	(632)
Underwriting and policy acquisition costs	(98)
Other operating expenses	(41)
Total expenses	(771)
Results of operating activities (Income–Expenses)	53
Finance costs (interest on long-term loans, for example)	(6)
Profit/(loss) on the sale of subsidiary companies	14
Profit before tax on continuing operations	61
Income tax expense	(13)
Profit for the year from continuing operations	48

A profit and loss account will be produced in a similar fashion to those produced by general insurers. The main difference is that life assurers will be accounting more for benefits than claims, recording the anticipated maturity of policies. As explained above, investment management charges must be separately identified as an expense due to the greater importance of this item in comparison with general insurance.

The problem faced by life assurers is that while profit or loss is calculated annually, the policies that give rise to profit or loss are much longer term. A property insurer will know within a year or so of the end of the financial year whether the year's underwriting has been profitable as the policies have expired and the great majority of claims will be reported within a few months of expiry at the latest. As only a very small number of claims would be expected in the first year of a life assurance contract, if premiums are insufficient, the life assurer will not discover this for many years. Indeed, they have no way of knowing whether the life policy will be continued for the full term. The declaration of profit or loss depends to an extent on assumptions made by the life assurer as to life expectancy, the number of lapsed policies and investment returns. These assumptions may or may not prove accurate in the future and can vary from company to company.

In recent years, life assurers have attempted to introduce a degree of transparency to the process by producing an additional profit and loss report on the European Embedded Value (EEV) basis. This is a voluntary measure agreed by the Chief Financial Officers of a number of major European life assurers. The aim is to allow reasonable comparison of the value of life assurers in terms of anticipated future profit.

An embedded value is the present value of anticipated future profits plus the market adjusted net asset value (which represents past profits). This embedded value is the sum of the existing surplus funds allocated to the policies currently in force, the regulatory capital held by the life assurer to support the policies in force (less the cost of such capital) and the value of future cash flows attributable to shareholders arising from such funds. The EEV measure seeks to introduce consistency and transparency in the manner in which these two figures are calculated.

The EEV permits two approaches. First, the calculation can be real world. Also known as the 'top down' approach, a risk discount rate is calculated based on the risk-free rate (the anticipated return from government securities) plus a margin based upon the weighted average cost of capital which is based in turn upon the capital asset pricing model. Alternatively, a market-consistent or 'bottom up' approach can be adopted. Assets are valued at current market values. Again a risk discount rate is assumed which will be the risk-free rate, plus a margin for operational and market risk. It appears that the market-consistent approach is becoming standard practice.

Note that the EEV calculation is produced in addition to the profit and loss account prepared in accordance with the International Financial Reporting Standards requirements (IFRS 4). The EEV will tend to produce a more conservative figure as it does not allow some intangible assets (such as goodwill) to be included. As from the end of 2009 a new standard is due to be adopted, the Market Consistent Embedded Value (MCEV). Derived from the EEV, this will require greater consistency in the calculation of the risk discount rate and will standardise the market-consistent or bottom-up approach.

Insurance company accounts: the balance sheet

While the shareholders might be particularly interested in the profit and loss account, the regulatory bodies might be rather more concerned with the balance sheet, reporting as it does the amount of capital held by the insurer and therefore the solvency margin. The regulatory requirements are discussed at greater length in Chapter 5; briefly, however, all insurers are required to demonstrate that they meet minimum capital requirements as a condition of continued authorisation. The aim is to ensure that the insurer has the financial strength to meet a reasonably foreseeable deterioration in either claims or investment returns. In particular, the balance sheet will identify future liability for claims, which can then be compared to assets held by the insurer to meet such future liabilities. The structure of a real-world balance sheet might be similar to the following example (Table 4.3).

As can be seen, assets are divided into two categories, long-term assets held by the insurer and assets owed to the insurer (such as expected reinsurance recoveries, outstanding premiums and tax rebates) or held in cash. Equity is calculated by subtracting the total liabilities from the total assets. Whatever is left over can be said to 'belong' to the shareholders, although they have no right to such equity until the company is wound up and all liabilities have been met.

Two items can produce particular difficulties. The insurance contract liabilities and the reinsurer's share of such liabilities (booked as an asset) are dependent upon the development

Table 4.3 Balance sheet for Xanadu General plc

Assets	£m
Goodwill and other intangible assets	71
Property and equipment	29
Investment property	36
Investments in associated companies	12
Financial assets	1,256
Total investments	1,404
Reinsurers' share of insurance contract liabilities	172
Insurance and reinsurance debtors	291
Deferred acquisition costs	63
Current tax assets	5
Deferred tax assets	11
Other debtors and other assets	148
Cash and cash equivalents	158
Total assets	2,252
Equity and reserves	
Share capital	46
Retained earnings	287
Other reserves	63
Total equity and reserves	396
Liabilities	
Loan capital	128
Insurance contract liabilities	1,489
Insurance and reinsurance liabilities	52
Borrowings	28
Current tax liabilities	22
Deferred tax liabilities	19
Provisions	24
Other short-term liabilities	94
Total liabilities	1,856
Total equity, reserves and liabilities	2,252

of known claims and the emergence or otherwise of IBNRs. These figures are then assumption based and are hard to verify. (See the section on p. 97 concerning the demise of Independent Insurance for further discussion of this point.)

Again, life assurers' balance sheets will be broadly similar. Increasing numbers will produce an alternative balance sheet compiled under EEV principles. The main difference will be the exclusion of intangible assets such as goodwill or brand value. This should report an embedded value based upon shareholders' funds and the present value to the shareholders of existing policies.

Current developments

Annual basis v funded basis

In the UK, Generally Accepted Accounting Principles (GAAP) have since 2005 required that the accounts of UK general insurance companies be prepared on what is known as the annual basis. Under the annual basis, the profits and losses of premium written during the year of account are calculated at the end of the financial year. This is achieved by establishing provisions for outstanding claims, unearned premiums and unexpired risk provisions. A portion of the underwriting costs will also be deferred.

Prior to 2005, an alternative method was available. Known as the funded basis, this deferred declaration of profit for up to three years from the end of the financial year during which the policies had been written. After three years, the position will be that much more certain and the need to make assumptions about future claims is reduced (but not eliminated). This was the standard practice at Lloyd's up until 2005, however the Lloyd's market has now moved to the annual basis.

Accident year or underwriting year?

An accident year considers the events taking place during the course of the financial year. The premium earned during the year is compared with the claims paid or reserved against during the year for the purpose of establishing underwriting performance. Under this system, it does not matter whether the policy giving rise to the claim incepted during the financial year or not. Alternatively, the underwriting year method only considers profit or loss arising out of policies incepted during the course of the financial year, even though the claims and expenses attributable to the underwriting year may be incurred after the end of the financial year. In other words, unlike the accident year basis, unearned premiums are not deducted, but neither is the loss arising from the unearned premium.

If the financial year runs from 1 January 2008 and a policy incepts on 1 July, under the accident year basis 50 per cent of the premium is deemed earned in the 2008 year. Losses arising between 1 July and 31 December are also attributable to the 2008 year. The remaining half of the premium would be deemed to have been earned in the 2009 year and losses arising from 1st January 2009 would likewise be accounted for in the 2009 year. Under the underwriting year basis, all of the premiums and claims paid under the policy would be accounted for in the 2008 year of account.

Whether the underwriting year method will be much used in the future is open to some doubt. It is certainly a practical proposition when accounting on a funded basis as this allows time for the outcome of the policies written during the year to be estimated. If accounting on an annual basis, the insurer will have some tricky estimates to make at the end of the financial period as some of the policies incepted during the underwriting year will only just have commenced, in some cases only the day before the end of the financial year. Again this was once normal practice in the Lloyd's market, due to the special nature of Lloyd's syndicates (see Chapter 6 for more information about the operation of the Lloyd's market). Now that Lloyd's is operating on an annual basis, it would be surprising if any syndicate did not also operate on an accident year basis as well.

Insurance premium tax

For many years, insurance was zero rated for VAT purposes in the UK. In 1994, a specific insurance premium tax was introduced, initially at a rate of 2.5 per cent, rising to 4 per cent in 1997 and the current level of 5 per cent in 1999. This affects all UK located insurance risks with certain stated exceptions. Long-term policies such as life and permanent health are exempt, as are commercial marine and aviation insurances and all reinsurance.

A higher rate of 17.5 per cent is levied on fees for insurance-related services as opposed to actual insurance cover. Due to government concerns that tax was being avoided by travel agents inflating the cost of travel insurance and then discounting the cost of the holiday, this rate is also levied on travel insurance. The same rate applies to insurance arranged by suppliers of cars and domestic appliances and for the same reason. This does not affect ordinary motor or property insurers.

The collapse of Independent Insurance

Independent Insurance appeared to be one of the success stories of the UK insurance market. Originally a small and unregarded subsidiary of the US insurer Allstate, the company was taken over by the recently formed Independent Insurance in 1986. The new company grew rapidly throughout the 1990s and in 1999 was declared the British Insurance Awards General Insurer of the Year, with their Chairman Michael Bright receiving the achievement award for 'outstanding contribution to the success of the insurance industry'. This followed their 1998 win in the Underwriter of the Year category.

By December 2000, Independent was the ninth largest general insurer in the UK. In March 2001, the company announced a profit of £22 million and declared that net assets were in excess of £300 million. However, by June 2001, trading in Independent Insurance shares had been suspended and the company went into liquidation a few days later. Quite apart from the 1,000 employees who lost their jobs, the Financial Services Compensation Scheme (see Chapter 12) paid out a reported £366 million in compensation to private policyholders. Commercial policyholders (a major part of Independent's customer base) went largely uncompensated and Cotesworth & Co, a Lloyd's syndicate with a history dating back for almost 150 years went into run off when their reinsurance cover with Independent proved worthless. The question then arises as to how an insurer could collapse so swiftly, particularly given that they operated in a regulated industry and their accounts were subject to scrutiny both by independent auditors and the regulatory body.

The problem lay in the manner in which Independent reported their liabilities. It will be recalled that Article 28 of the IAD requires that an insurer calculate 'the total estimated ultimate cost to an insurance undertaking of settling all claims arising from events which have occurred up to the end of the financial year, whether reported or not'. However, because these are future liabilities and particularly because a proportion of the losses have not yet been notified, this figure is subject to considerable uncertainty when legal liability insurance is written.

When a personal injury claim is notified to an insurer, they face two major uncertainties. First, they must consider whether the policyholder is legally liable for the loss. If it is believed that liability exists, they must next judge the amount of compensation payable (the quantum of loss). These estimates are constantly subject to review as new information emerges regarding the incident and the medical prognosis. The insurer must be prepared to reconsider the provision and if necessary increase reserves in the light of new information. This is very difficult for an auditor to review as the exercise is largely subjective and requires careful analysis of the claim file if the provision in respect of an individual claim is to be questioned.

Originally concentrating on relatively stable personal lines business, Independent found that in order to continue to grow rapidly new lines of business needed to be developed. From the early 1990s, they became increasingly involved in commercial insurance and in particular commercial liability covers. They expanded rapidly by undercutting the premiums charged by existing players and apparently managed to do so profitably. Independent claimed that this was due to superior underwriting and a concentration on improving risks to reduce future claims. However, there was increasing disbelief in the commercial insurance market that they could improve risks to the extent necessary to justify the low reserves for future claims posted in their accounts. Indeed there was frequent comment that their rates were so low that they were below the long-term average claims costs other insurers had experienced underwriting the same business, making heavy underwriting losses almost certain. As commercial liability business involves both deferred loss and delayed settlement, there was no immediate proof that this was indeed the position.

The collapse of the company demonstrated that the reserves established were clearly inadequate. The question then arose as to whether this was due to incompetence or fraud. The Serious Fraud Office (SFO) clearly felt that the degree of under-reserving was such that it could only have been deliberate and charged the Chairman, Michael Bright and two fellow directors, Philip Condon, the managing director, and Denis Lomas, the financial director, with conspiracy to defraud. The specific allegations fell under two headings.

The first allegation was that from 1998 (and probably in fact much earlier), the defendants had deliberately withheld claims data from their independent actuaries Watson Wyatt. This led Watson Wyatt to approve a claims reserve considerably lower than should have been the case. The effect was twofold. The lower figure resulted in profits being overstated in the profit and loss account, indeed in the final years it disguised trading losses. The insurance contract liabilities were also understated in the balance sheet, overstating the solvency of the company, and again towards the end concealing the fact that the company was actually insolvent. This was achieved in three ways:

1 Serious claims when first notified were marked up on a whiteboard in the claims department. The idea was that they would be inputted into the computerised claims system once sufficient information about liability and quantum was available to enable the company to estimate a reserve. The SFO case was that claims were left on the whiteboard long after they had been quantified and that they were deliberately being left off the computer system. As the actuaries were working from the computer system they would not take these claims into account.

2 When new information emerged that led claims handlers to increase a reserve, the increase in reserves had to be approved by senior management before the reserve could be altered on the computer system. Such approval was often not forthcoming, with the result that lists of cases all requiring increased reserves were known to exist by the management but were not provided to the actuaries.

3 In many cases, investigation was delegated either to loss adjusters or solicitors. They would recommend reserves on written bordereaux which should have been entered into the computer system. Again these reserves were not entered and the actuaries were not provided with the paper records.

The second allegation was that the defendants misled the auditors and actuaries as to the value of reinsurance contracts with the effect that the reinsurer's estimate share of claims was inflated in the profit and loss account. This also affected the balance sheet as the reinsurer's share of insurance contract liabilities was booked as an asset, an asset that was deliberately overstated.

Of course, what could not be disguised were the actual claims payments. Once these started to mount, what reserves existed were eroded to the point that the actuaries began to have concerns about the reserve levels for the claims they did know about. As the under-reserving problem could not be concealed any longer, the SFO alleged that the directors they had charged sought to disguise the situation by purchasing reinsurance cover and misleading the actuaries and the auditors about the nature of the cover provided. A premium of £77 million was paid which, according to the prosecution, had the effect of converting a £105 million loss for the year 2000 to a £22 million profit. These reinsurance contracts were not written on future policies, but instead covered a deterioration in the claims position on polices that had already been written. Effectively the contracts purported to cover Independent against the possibility that the claims reserve was inadequate, but it was already known that the reserve was inadequate. The contracts appeared to be financial suicide on the part of the reinsurer, but when Michael Bright was asked by the auditors whether any subsidiary agreements existed, he denied that this was the case. In fact there were concealed agreements which amounted in effect to a promise by Independent to compensate the reinsurer for any loss that they might suffer. The 'reinsurance' contracts were then nothing of the kind and had the full terms of the agreement been disclosed, the auditors would not have agreed the accounts as they were ultimately presented.

All three defendants were found guilty of deliberately withholding claims data. Bright and Lomas were also found guilty of non-disclosure of the full details of the reinsurance contracts. They received prison sentences of between three and seven years.

The case reveals the difficulties of establishing the true financial position of an insurer when so many of the liabilities lie in the future and these liabilities arise from many thousands of individual claims that cannot easily be audited. The result is that the accounts are based on the insurer's opinion of their financial position. Compare this to the case of a manufacturer where the majority of costs are incurred prior to the point of sale and can be verified relatively easily. Past incurred losses leave a paper trail of paid invoices that can be followed, future estimated losses do not.

Independent were in all probability doomed well before 2001. Had the accounts been honestly presented, the company would have failed sooner, perhaps as early as 1998. Had this been the case, a reasonable percentage of outstanding claims should have been met at least, lessening the damage to the policyholders. It is not suggested that Independent was operating fraudulently from the outset. It is probable that the concealment of claims data began on a small scale to illegally boost the profitability of the company rather than to conceal losses, in the erroneous belief that the problem would be eliminated by future profits. As the underlying pricing of insurance was insufficient, the problem could not be resolved, however, and the fraud then grew in scale as the degree of under-reserving had to grow to disguise the financial difficulties.

Nonetheless, it is surprising that Independent's figures were not questioned earlier. Although both actuaries and auditors were deliberately misled, they have a professional duty not to allow themselves to be misled. Had a benchmarking exercise been carried out, it would have emerged that Independent were charging lower rates than their competitors and were setting aside lower reserves for future claims than their competitors. It is not credible that they could also produce higher profits in terms of return on equity than their competitors at the same time. During the trial the prosecution alleged that the reserves were understated by between £110 million and £250 million. Given that the Financial Services Compensation Scheme paid out £366 million and provided only limited compensation to commercial policyholders, it is suggested that the true figure must have been towards the upper end of this range.

In the case of the reinsurance contracts, the auditors did note that the reinsurance contracts were almost certain to cause heavy losses. There were only two realistic explanations. Either, as was the case, there were undisclosed subsidiary agreements in place protecting the reinsurer's financial position. Alternatively, Independent had failed to provide full disclosure to the reinsurer. In this case the reinsurance contract would be voidable for breach of the duty of utmost good faith. In either event, the auditors were not entitled to accept the unverified word of Michael Bright that no other agreements were in force. Indeed, the auditors, KPMG and the partner responsible, were heavily fined by their professional body for failing to verify the statements, given that there should have been 'obvious suspicion'.

As will be seen in later chapters, the reserving of long tail liabilities has caused the insurance industry significant problems and indeed was a major contributory factor in the crisis that came close to causing the failure of Lloyd's of London. Despite initiatives such as the IAD and increasing regulation of the insurance markets, it is disturbing that investors and policyholders alike can be so easily duped by a small group of dishonest directors. It is equally disturbing that professional actuaries and auditors and the regulatory body were unable to detect the fraud until the financial position of the company had deteriorated to the point that it could be considered to be hopelessly insolvent.

5 The structure and regulation of the UK insurance market

A brief history of insurance company development

The development of insurance

The first record of insurance is considered to be contained in the code of Hammurabi, written in ancient Babylon around 1790 BC. This ancient legal code states in clause 23:

> If the brigand be not captured, the man who has been robbed shall in the presence of God make an itemised statement of his loss and the city and the governor in whose province and jurisdiction the robbery was committed shall compensate him for whatever was lost.

This is arguably a form of state insurance. Private insurance can be traced back to around 350 BC with the emergence of marine contracts in Ancient Greece through a process known as 'bottomry' (a loan on a ship and cargo with repayment waived in the event of loss). This is analogous to modern marine insurance, but these days would be considered a catastrophe bond rather than insurance. By the first century BC, the Romans had a rudimentary form of life cover with the development of burial societies. However, for practical purposes, insurance has developed gradually since the thirteenth century in tandem with the development of the modern industrial society.

It follows that the first insurance was introduced to alleviate the major worry of the late medieval merchant class, namely the loss of ships. The idea of merchants banding together to produce a simple risk pool is usually attributed to the Lombards (a dominant trading force during this period), although insurance records exist from Flanders and Lübeck around this period. This concept of risk sharing was copied by London shipowners, ultimately creating Lloyd's of London. The earliest record of marine insurance in London dates back to 1547.

Life Assurance in the UK can be traced back to 1553 with the issue of a term assurance policy with a period of 12 months on the life of one William Gibbons in the sum of £382. He duly expired before the policy, giving rise to possibly the earliest example of an insurer seeking to unfairly avoid a policy. They claimed that 12 months meant 12 lunar months (a period of 28 days) and that Gibbons had died after the policy had expired. The court had no problem finding that a month meant a calendar month and found against the insurer.

The Great Fire of London in 1666 unquestionably led to a boom in the issue of fire insurance, although policies were in existence before this date. This was followed by a gradual development of property insurance in the nineteenth century due to the Industrial Revolution bringing about larger-scale investment and hence a demand for such investment to be protected.

Developments in the law in the latter half of the nineteenth century saw a commensurate development in insurance of legal liabilities. The counter-argument could, however, be that the increasing sophistication of the insurance industry provided the financial environment for more adventurous legal decisions. The invention of the motor car and aeroplanes in turn created a demand for related insurance products. Further innovations have led to new forms of cover, nuclear risks, satellites and computers being examples.

The development of insurance companies

Until the mid-nineteenth century, cover was generally offered by individuals or partnerships trading with unlimited liability (most notably Lloyd's of London) or alternatively (and far more commonly) mutual insurers established and owned by their own policyholders. Proprietary insurance companies, owned by shareholders, were rare. During this period, corporate bodies could be established only by Royal Charter or by a private Act of Parliament, neither easily (or cheaply) arranged. Some insurers were, though, formed in this manner. In 1720, royal charters were granted to London Assurance (now part of Royal Sun Alliance) and Royal Exchange Assurance (now part of AXA insurance). The charters were procured by a small sweetener to the King at a price of £300,000 each, a vast sum in 1720. The result was to give the two companies a duopoly of the marine insurance company market, protected by an Act of Parliament which lasted until 1824 when the Act was repealed and the Alliance Marine Insurance company was founded. Lloyd's of London, not being an insurance company, were unaffected by the duopoly and there was no restriction on the formation of mutual insurers. London Assurance and Royal Exchange were permitted to offer fire and life cover in 1721 but not on a duopoly basis. A number of proprietary fire and life companies were established in the eighteenth and early nineteenth centuries, but the majority of new companies were mutuals.

The *Joint Stock Companies Act 1844* made it easier to incorporate, however shareholders still faced unlimited liability. *The Limited Liability Act 1855* permitted limited liability companies but excluded insurance companies. Not until the *Companies Act 1862* was the establishment of limited liability insurance companies permitted. Once the restrictions on incorporation were removed, an increase in the number of insurers became possible. This had the potential for increased competition leading to lower cost and wider cover for the policyholder. On the other hand, the policyholder was more vulnerable to loss brought about by insolvency or fraud.

The structure of the UK insurance market

The UK insurance market is made up of three groups: the buyers, the intermediaries and the insurers (Figure 5.1). A number of other groups exist, uninvolved in the initial insurance contract, but providing associated services in support of the insurance contract. Prominent among these associates are the reinsurers and claims specialists (particularly loss adjusters). Their role is discussed in detail in Chapters 7 and 9 respectively. In addition, there are law and accountancy firms who specialise in providing services to the insurance industry, but they should properly be considered a part of their respective professions.

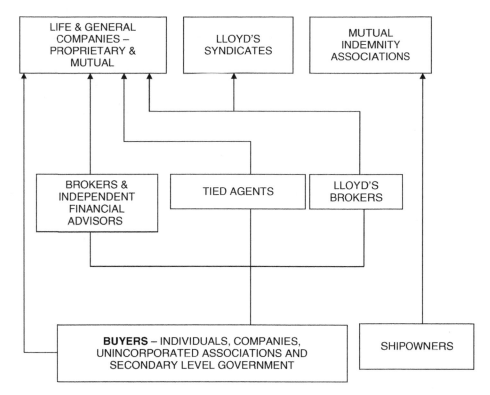

Figure 5.1 The structure of the UK insurance market.
Source: After S.R. Diacon and R.L. Carter.

The buyers

Three principal groups of purchasers exist:

1   *Private individuals* – They are by far the largest group in terms of number of policies. They form what is known as the personal lines market, but are often referred to by regulatory bodies as consumers. Motor, life, personal pensions, household and travel are the main covers offered, although a range of other policies are available, including private marine and aviation insurance.
2   *Industry and commerce* – Although fewer policies are issued, the cost and complexity of the cover are much greater than personal lines. Major covers include property, business interruption, liability, motor and employee benefits (group life, health and pensions). Again a range of covers is available, tailored to the needs of specific industries. Due to the added complexity, commercial buyers are more likely to use a broker.
3   *State-funded organisations* – Central government does not purchase insurance but local government, NHS trusts and other secondary or tertiary levels of government are major purchasers. The actual cover offered is similar to that available to industry and commerce.

The intermediaries

Various categories of intermediaries exist ranging from professional brokers and consultants to organisations which specialise in other areas but offer insurance subsidiary to the main business activities (e.g. travel agents selling travel insurance). UK purchasers have historically bought insurance mainly through intermediaries, although a move towards purchasing direct from the insurer has been prominent in recent years, particularly in personal lines.

Intermediaries can be categorised according to whether they offer cover with a range of insurers (brokers or independent financial advisors) or a single insurer (tied agents). Tied agents may well be part-time, selling insurance as a sideline to their main business. Lloyd's brokers, authorised to place business in the Lloyd's market, are a separate category. They will, however, also place business in the insurance company market.

The insurers

The insurers can be categorised according to whether they are proprietary insurance companies, mutual insurance companies or Lloyd's syndicates. A further stand-alone category exists, protection and indemnity clubs. These are mutual associations formed by ship owners to cover their legal liabilities. Both life and general insurance companies can be either proprietary or mutual, although, as discussed below, mutualisation is becoming increasingly rare in both cases. All Lloyd's syndicates today offer general insurance only.

Mutualisation

The risk pooling concept at the heart of insurance led to the development of many mutual insurance societies. Formed by deed of settlement or under the provisions of the Companies Acts, they differ in that they are owned by their policyholders. Usually they have grown from risk pools established by a particular group. In the case of general insurance, the group often comprised members of an industrial sector or type of government body, for example, Municipal Mutual formed by local authorities. In the case of life assurance, the name of the mutual often provided a clue as to their origins. It was the medical profession who were behind the formation of Clerical Medical. Other mutuals had geographical origins, Norwich Union and Scottish Widows being examples. Note that although all of the insurers mentioned or their descendants remain in business today, none remain as mutuals, having all been merged with or purchased by proprietary financial firms. Mutuals were an important part of the emerging insurance market, but are not of such significance now.

The main distinguishing feature of a mutual is that profits (or surplus as it will be known) belong to the policyholders and, given adequate reserves, may be used to fund lower premiums in the future or returned to the policyholders. It used to be the case that the policyholders were also liable for the debts of the mutual; however, this is now rare with the liability limited by guarantee to the premium or a nominal additional sum. After all the major creditors will be the policyholders themselves.

The mutual structure has a number of theoretical advantages:

1   Profits (or surplus) revert to the policyholders, potentially lowering insurance costs.
2   They were often narrowly focused, leading to specialised knowledge of the policyholder's risks. This was not always the case as a number had a broad scope of operation. This narrow focus could, however, inhibit the opportunity for growth, as once a sizeable percentage of the available pool has become policyholders, any future growth will be sluggish at best.

3   The close relationship between mutual and policyholder could engender greater loyalty and therefore stability. The broader the scope of operation, the less likely they would be to benefit from greater loyalty.

However, the proprietary company structure likewise had theoretical advantages:

1   Their generally wider scope of operation and broader potential customer base provide the opportunity for increased growth. Economies of scale could then provide the profits for shareholders.
2   Proprietary companies can raise share capital as well as loan capital, while a mutual is in modern times limited to loan capital alone, it being unlikely that a mutual today could successfully seek a subscription from its membership. This provides greater flexibility in the way the business is capitalised, increasingly important in a regulated market.
3   A broad spread of business reduces vulnerability to downturns in particular market sectors and promotes greater stability.
4   Although their customers do not have the same loyalty motivation, the insurer is, on the other hand, operating at arm's length from policyholders. It is far less likely that the policyholders' opinion would prevent the proper underwriting of the risk.

The problem of mutuals being too close to their policyholders was vividly demonstrated by the collapse of Municipal Mutual Insurance, the local government mutual, in 1992. Founded in 1903, Municipal Mutual became the dominant insurer of local authority risk. Although an attempt was made in the 1980s to broaden the scope of the company, local authorities still provided most of their business. In the late 1970s, the sector began to experience large increases in the number of legal liability claims. Premium levels were inadequate to meet this increased level of loss, however, under pressure from the membership Municipal Mutual did not increase premiums to the extent that they should have. Losses continued to rise sharply. As premiums had not been gradually increased over the preceding years as they should, Municipal Mutual had to impose steep premium increases and much higher deductibles in the late 1980s. This was not only to match premiums to current loss levels but also to recover deficits built up over the years. The premiums they were forced to charge were often higher than the market rates and they started to lose business, thus exacerbating the problem. In 1992, they were forced to close to new business and go into run off. The ongoing business was taken over by Zurich Insurance, however the debts were not. The old Municipal Mutual business is still being run off today.

Throughout the 1980s and 1990s, many of the established mutuals demutualised and most became a part of larger financial groups. Some remain as mutuals, such as Liverpool Victoria (or LV = as they insist on calling themselves), Royal London, National Farmers Union Mutual and Co-operative Insurance, all offering both life and general insurance.

Proprietary insurance companies

Insurance companies can be further defined as to whether they are:

1   *Composite insurers* – A composite insurance company in the UK is defined as an insurer authorised to offer both life and general insurance. In fact, there will be at least two separate companies within the overall corporate structure as the two businesses must be kept separate.

2   *Life or general insurers* – Alternatively, a company may only write either life or general business, but cover a range of different classes of insurance within the broad life or general insurance category. These companies are sometime erroneously referred to as composites.

3   *Specialist insurers* – A specialist insurance company only offers a single class of insurance. They are quite common in general insurance, for example, specialist motor insurers. It would be unusual for a life assurer to limit their activities to a single class, as if they are offering life and annuities, they would naturally offer pensions and other investment products as well.

Note that mutual insurance companies can be categorised in the same manner.

Ownership

Proprietary insurance companies can be public liability companies. As at June 2009, seven insurance companies appeared among the FTSE 100 (the 100 largest companies by value quoted on the London Stock Exchange), Admiral, Aviva, Friends Provident, Legal & General, Old Mutual, Prudential and Royal Sun Alliance. Other smaller insurance companies are also publicly quoted.

Alternatively a number of substantial insurance companies are wholly owned subsidiaries of conglomerates (companies which engage in a number of business activities), most commonly as a part of a financial conglomerate alongside banking and investment interests. Such conglomerates are almost invariably publicly quoted themselves. A good example would be Direct Line, which is a subsidiary of the Royal Bank of Scotland. A number of well-known life assurers are now banking subsidiaries, including Scottish Widows and Clerical Medical which are both owned by Lloyds Bank.

There remain a number of private limited liability insurers companies. These tend to be small specialist insurers, often servicing a distinct group of customers. Obviously the shares of such companies are marketable but they are not traded on the stock exchange.

The final category is the 80 Lloyd's syndicates currently operating in the Lloyd's market. They are owned by their investors (Names, as they are termed); however, their status is variable. Some are *de facto* subsidiaries of large insurance companies, others are private ventures capitalised by a group of private individuals (see Chapter 6).

The regulation of the insurance market

In the modern era, the regulation of the financial services industry is taken for granted. Surprisingly, perhaps much of the current regulatory structure is relatively new, even if the first tentative steps were taken some time ago. It is probably no coincidence that market regulation first appeared in the aftermath of the *Companies Act 1862* which, as noted above, permitted the establishment of limited liability insurance companies.

Approaches to regulation

There are in fact three distinct regulatory areas: systemic, prudential and conduct of business regulation:

1   *Systemic regulation* – This concerns the possibility that an event brings about mass, interconnected failures that cause the entire system to fail. In the insurance sphere, the

main systemic risk is the failure of a large reinsurer and therefore this area is discussed in Chapter 7.

2 *Prudential regulation* – This regulates the overall financial position of the market participants. It includes authorisation and licensing systems, the monitoring of accounts and other financial and statistical statements and if necessary intervention. This is regulation of the 'big picture' as regards the individual firm and provides only indirect benefit to policyholders. This form of regulation is the main focus of this section.

3 *Conduct of business regulation* – This involves direct intervention, whereby the regulator intervenes in the contract between the insurer and policyholder, either on an individual basis or en masse. This would include codes of conduct, the ombudsman scheme and policyholder compensation schemes. Obviously the intent is to directly benefit the policyholder where appropriate. This is discussed elsewhere in the book, in particular in Chapter 12.

Reasons for regulation

Government had considered the insurance industry before, of course. The first insurance legislation was the *Marine Insurance Act 1745* (now consolidated into the *Marine Insurance Act 1906)*. However, early legislation was concerned not with the regulation of insurers, but rather considered the question of insurable interest and was intended to give insurance policies legal effect by distinguishing them from wagers (which are, of course, unenforceable at law).

The primary purpose of government supervision ought to be the protection of the policyholder. This is not to say that other parties should not be protected as well, so long as by so doing this does not prejudice the policyholders. It can be argued that protection of the industry reputation is desirable, although insurance is not as sensitive to a loss of confidence as the banking sector. Certainly the honest and competent insurer deserves to be protected from unfair competition by the dishonest and/or incompetent. Finally, it is in the government's interest that financial market scandals be avoided where possible as the government is likely to face criticism and possibly a voter backlash if large numbers of people suffer financial loss.

There are a number of possible problems to consider.

Incompetence

As discussed in Chapter 1, insurers are responsible for managing the common pool on behalf of its participants. Their duties include calculating the equitable premium, arranging reinsurance, investing pool funds and controlling claim payments. An insurer who lacks the competence to fulfil these duties will endanger the solvency of the pool to the detriment initially of the insurer as guarantor of the pool. Ultimately, however, if their assets prove insufficient to cover the loss, members of the pool will suffer. Although not properly calculating adequate premiums is the obvious failure, a failure to invest pool funds properly and prudently can be equally disastrous, as indeed would be a failure to properly reserve for future claims. Clearly, there is direct detriment to the members of the pool if the insurer is unable to meet claims; however, if a company has been consistently under-pricing its policies, they will have damaged other insurers who will either have had to offer cover at uneconomic rates or lose market share. This will damage the sector as a whole.

Fraud

The nature of insurance makes fraud easy. The product only constitutes a promise and therefore the purchaser cannot then assess the worth of the purchase at the point of sale. Its value only becomes apparent after a loss has occurred (and of course a loss may never occur). The often lengthy delay between premium payment and loss allows a fraudster plenty of opportunity to defraud large numbers of people before the fraud is detected. While in practice it is not always easy to distinguish between incompetence and fraud, the effect on the policyholder and other insurers is much the same.

The theoretically unlimited supply of insurance

Most firms are constrained in the amount of product they can offer by availability of factors of production, land, labour and capital. Any large increase in production is difficult to achieve in the short term. By way of example, if a motor manufacturer seeks to increase production by 25 per cent, this will involve a long lead time and will only be achieved if they can secure the financial backing, extend (or build new) production facilities and find and train the workforce. However, there is no natural economic constraint on a motor insurer selling insurance over the internet, increasing their 'production' of insurance by almost any reasonably conceivable percentage. Even in the case of more complex insurances, while labour remains a possible constraint as the insurance will have to be marketed and explained to policyholders, availability of land is largely irrelevant (other than a limited demand for land in its usual sense, i.e. office space) and the nature of insurance is that most of the capital requirement occurs after the product has been sold.

The only tangible product that is offered is a piece of paper. It is the promise contained in this paper that constitutes the real product. It follows then that an insurer can massively increase the amount of promises made without a commensurate increase in the availability of factors of production. The consequences of this are twofold.

First, the individual insurer may be unable to fulfil its obligations in the absence of reserves of capital, adequate for the amount of cover offered. Although the law of large numbers ought to provide a measure of protection, the protection is not absolute. An insurer has to be able to withstand unexpectedly poor results within the boundaries of reasonable probability. The lower the capital in relation to premiums accepted, the lower the margin of error that can be tolerated before that capital is exhausted.

Second, an increase in supply which is not balanced by an increase in demand will lead to a reduction in price. This will endanger the industry as a whole as income may be insufficient to meet liabilities. This can be seen in practice. The insurance industry follows a cycle of 'boom and (hopefully not quite) bust'. When trading conditions are favourable, super-normal profits are achieved, attracting new entrants to the market and greater investment by existing firms to maximise business. This increase in supply will reduce prices and the favourable conditions will worsen, perhaps to the extent that severe losses are experienced. This will cause some insurers to withdraw from the market, offer less cover or even become insolvent. The reduction in the supply of insurance will then cause prices to rise and the whole scenario will be played out again. These cycles are known in the industry as 'hard' or 'soft' markets, referring to whether prices are increasing (hardening) or falling (softening).

Improper relationships

Insurance is largely marketed through networks of 'independent' agents and brokers. The policyholder therefore believes the advice offered by these intermediaries is impartial and is encouraged to enter into agreements that they might not have otherwise made. Surprisingly perhaps, there is no prohibition on an insurer owning a controlling stake in an 'independent' intermediary. For example, a major provider of motor insurance, Vehicle & General, collapsed in 1971. A large amount of Vehicle & General's business was introduced by a broker, Andrew & Booth Ltd, owned by Vehicle & General. Two questions arise. Would the policyholders have bought the policies had they known of this relationship? How likely is it that Andrew & Booth ceased to recommend Vehicle & General as an insurer once their financial position became apparent? The Lloyd's market has similarly encountered serious problems due to the cross-ownership of underwriting and broking interests, to the extent that this practice is now banned in the Lloyd's market (see Chapter 6).

Arguments against government regulation

However, the assumption that governments know best and that statutory regulation is the only solution cannot be left unchallenged. It is arguable that state regulation is both unnecessary and ineffective.

The nature of insurance

The great worry of regulators is systemic collapse. In particular, the concern is that a lack of liquidity or loss of confidence will lead to widespread failures in the banking system. In general, retail banks borrow short and lend long. They may be placed in the position that unusually high demand by their creditors cannot be met by increasing demands upon their debtors. The classic example is the position of mortgage lenders who borrow much of their capital in the form of deposits repayable on demand but lend on long-term mortgages over 20 or 25 years. The nature of banking is such that systemic collapse is an ever present risk. The US banking system came close to meltdown in the 1930s. The global banking system would certainly have collapsed in 2007/08 had it not been for government support on an unprecedented scale. The banks were not on the whole insolvent (although there were exceptions) but they lacked the liquidity to maintain day-to-day operations. The loss of consumer confidence is the likely effect of a failure of liquidity as customer demands cannot be met. Once customers start to queue to withdraw their money, a retail bank is doomed as only a small proportion of their assets are held in cash.

Maintaining confidence in the market is therefore of overriding importance in banking regulation. Not only does this protect the banks themselves but it is also in the interests of consumers as systemic collapse would be to the detriment of the majority of consumers. In the event of a run on a bank, the first customers to demand the return of their deposit might succeed, but once available liquidity was exhausted, subsequent demands could not be met.

Insurance does not face the same confidence risk. While a banking customer becomes a creditor as soon as they make a deposit, the customer of a general insurer only becomes a creditor when an insured, loss-causing event occurs. The risk for insurers is therefore that loss/losses of greater than expected magnitude occur(s). This is a solvency risk and can be reduced to acceptable levels by careful underwriting and proper reinsurance provision. As it can be generally assumed that an insurer would wish the business to prosper, it can be argued that they will take the necessary steps without government intervention. If a natural catastrophe occurs of unprecedented magnitude and that catastrophe is widely insured, the system will fail irrespective of any regulatory provision. As regulation cannot prevent such a catastrophe from occurring, it could be said that it provides no significant benefit.

(The counter-arguments to this position are explored in Chapter 7 as they are more related to the operation of the reinsurance market.)

Cost

Any regulatory systems will ultimately be paid for by the consumer. A regulated product will therefore be more expensive than an unregulated product. The question must then arise as to whether the regulator provides value for money. In the long term, does the cost of compensating the victims of insurance company failure exceed the cost of regulation? If the answer to this question is no, then why regulate? Is the regulator providing value for money?

Regulation can also add indirect costs. Market regulation distorts competition by acting as a barrier to new entrants. Theoretically this will reduce competition and increase prices. The counter-argument of course is that the firms that are barred from the market might damage the market to the detriment of providers and consumers alike. It can also be said that perfect competition is not a prerequisite for a genuine market price so long as there is sufficient competition. Therefore while there is a risk that regulation will distort prices to the detriment of the consumer, this is not an inevitable consequence.

One likely consequence of regulation is that it does distort the market in favour of larger firms for whom the cost of regulation as a percentage of income is lower. For evidence, consider the effect of regulation on insurance intermediaries, discussed in Chapter 8.

In practice, however, the risk is that the regulator will forget that it is supposed to provide value for money for the consumer by providing risk reduction at acceptable cost. This risk occurs when a regulator becomes overly concerned with its own reputation. Should a financial firm fail, the regulator is likely to face criticism. In such cases, individuals within the regulator could find that their jobs are threatened. The regulator may then become too risk averse and seek to increase the level of regulation more for the protection this increased level offers to the regulator than to gain cost-effective benefits for the consumer. In this case the market price will be distorted to the detriment of the consumer.

Stagnation

The risks we face are not static. Economic development and innovation constantly create new risks. Just over a century ago, motor and aviation insurers did not exist, as cars and aeroplanes had yet to be invented. A healthy insurance market must always be prepared to innovate in order to ensure that they are covering the risks of today not the risks of yesterday. Overly risk averse regulation can stifle this necessary innovation by making it harder to introduce new products to meet new risks. The result would be a stagnant market which no longer meets the needs of its consumers.

Alternative regulators

Although it is not always recognised, market participants play an important regulatory role:

1 *Intermediaries* – A high proportion of insurance in the UK is sold via intermediaries. They essentially offer advice for a fee and therefore will generally be liable to the consumer in the event that the advice they offer is negligent. Therefore when recommending an insurer, the intermediary must take reasonable steps to discover the financial position of the insurer

and advise the consumer accordingly. In the event that an insurer fails, the intermediary may find themselves liable if the weak financial position of the insurer were not brought to the attention of the consumer. For their own protection, many intermediaries will refuse to recommend insurers who are unable to demonstrate minimum levels of financial security (often based upon Standard & Poor or similar rating agencies). An insurer who permits their financial rating to fall too low may well be closed down by the market intermediaries removing support without the need for regulatory action. Of course, this effect is dependent upon intermediaries controlling a significant percentage of the market as most consumers are unlikely to be aware of the financial position of their insurers and indeed many would lack the knowledge to make such a judgement.

2 *Reinsurers* – Reinsurers play an important role in preventing inadequate pricing of insurance. In general, a proportion of the risk is passed to the reinsurer in return for a proportion of the premium. If an insurer's premiums are too low, they will tend to find reinsurance prohibitively expensive or unavailable, so in either case, they are forced to charge adequate rates. It is very difficult, perhaps impossible for a regulator to control pricing while maintaining a fair market price. The only realistic method is to set minimum premium levels (a tactic used by German regulators for many years). In a dynamic market, this level will almost certainly be, at times, greater than the equilibrium price to the detriment of the consumer. On the other hand, it should be noted that this system is not perfect. Reinsurers may at times offer cover below true cost, reinforcing inadequate pricing rather than preventing it.

3 *Self-regulation* – Theoretically, there is no reason why a market should not be left to police itself. After all, historically this has been the norm. It can be presumed that the market participants have a vested interest in maintaining consumer confidence for their future prosperity. It is then arguable that the market itself will do what is necessary to preserve consumer confidence. The counter-argument is twofold. First, even if there is a genuine desire to maintain high standards of discipline and integrity, the market may be unable to control rogue elements within their ranks. Second, there is the risk of a rogue market, deliberately seeking super-normal short-term gain to the detriment of consumers (price-fixing cartels being an example of such behaviour).

These arguments are, however, semantic. Insurance in the UK and indeed most of the world is subject to statutory regulation. This basic position cannot be viewed as subject to change.

Developments in government supervision

The development of government supervision has been a slow and incremental process. Basic measures have become progressively more complex, partly in response to lessons learned and partly in response to a more complex insurance market. Historically the main developments have been as follows.

Life Assurance Act 1870

This Act required that a deposit of £20,000 be lodged with the High Court before life assurance could be transacted. The idea being that this deposit could be used to compensate policyholders in the event of insurer insolvency. In addition, accounting and actuarial returns had to be made to the Board of Trade so that the assets could be compared to liabilities (solvency). Similar provisions were introduced by the *Employers Liability Insurance Companies Act 1907*. *The Assurance Companies Act 1909* extended supervision to fire, personal accident and bonds. The glaring defect, of course, was that the flat rate deposit requirement did not reflect the level of risk. £20,000 might not have been sufficient to cover the risk of insolvency involving one of the larger life assurance firms. Equally for a very small firm it may have been far more than what was required and acted as a barrier to market entry thus reducing competition.

Industrial Assurance Act 1923

Not only did this establish the class of Industrial Assurance separately from Life Assurance (this distinction has since been removed), it created an Industrial Assurance Commissioner to oversee the exercise of statutory powers on behalf of the Board of Trade. The idea of specific regulatory bodies was therefore introduced.

Assurance Companies Act 1946

This included motor, aviation and transit insurance within the regulatory framework. Its importance is chiefly that the deposit system was abolished and replaced with a solvency margin system, a margin between assets and liabilities which must be maintained. The precise requirement was a minimum paid up share capital of £50,000 and assets exceeding liabilities by £50,000 or 10 per cent of last year's premiums (whichever was greater).

The requirement was tightened by the *Companies Act 1967* to paid up share capital of £100,000 and a minimum solvency of £50,000 or 20 per cent of last year's premiums up to £2.5m, whichever was greater. The solvency margin was 10 per cent for premium in excess of £2.5m.

Clearly, the requirement in absolute terms would be dependent upon the size of the insurer. Although the margin is same in percentage terms, 20 per cent or 10 per cent of a large insurer's premium income would be a greater sum than that required of a smaller company. There is an element of differential regulation based on risk. However, this does not reflect the level of risk brought about by the nature of the insurers' activities (i.e. the class of insurance and the policy terms).

Despite the enhanced requirements, in the 1960s and 1970s there were calls for not only reform but extension of insurance regulation for a variety of reasons. A string of high profile insurance company failures prompted calls for a tightening of regulation. In 1966, Fire, Auto & Marine (FAM) failed, leaving 400,000 (mostly motor) policyholders uninsured. Run by the highly controversial Emil Savundra, the company expanded rapidly in just three years from its foundation in 1963. The company were pioneers of the use of computerisation in mass insurance. Despite Savundra's notably dubious past, the company was not necessarily an intentional fraud, although it could be said that the conduct of the business was reckless, to say the least. However, once FAM started to run into difficulties, Savundra did falsify financial records to disguise the under-capitalisation of the company, for which he was duly convicted in 1968.

In 1971, an even bigger failure involving 1.2 million policyholders occurred when Vehicle & General collapsed. Again, the majority of those affected were motor policyholders. Although the cause of the failure appears to have been inadequate pricing of policies and under-reserving for future losses rather than fraud, the Board of Trade (the regulator of the day) was criticised for not intervening at an earlier stage.

Although in a rapidly expanding motor insurance market, it could be said that there was a serious risk that some companies would be unable to make the necessary adjustments and that therefore casualties could be viewed as being not unexpected, this was not the case in life assurance. The failure of Nation Life in 1974 was then a serious embarrassment. The primary cause of the failure was the heavy exposure of the company to property investments, which were then badly compromised by the property crash of 1973.

Three highly publicised insurance company failures in such a short space of time would be sufficient for a call for reform of regulation. There was, however, a general movement towards greater protection for consumers in the 1970s with the passing of the *Unfair Contract Terms Act 1977* and the *Sale of Goods Act 1979*. It is arguable that even given stability in the insurance market, reform might well have occurred in any event.

The decisive factor was the UK's membership of the European Economic Community (as the EU was then known). This required the UK to enact the *1st Non Life Insurance Directive (73/239)* and the *1st Life Insurance Directive (79/267)*. The aim of the two directives was to pave the way for a single market in insurance by harmonising insurance regulation in all member states. These directives remain the basis for UK regulation today in law, if not quite in practice.

The Insurance Companies Act 1982

Applying to all parts of the insurance market with the exception of Lloyd's, the *ICA 1982* was intended to both strengthen regulation and harmonise UK regulation with the rest of the EU. Initially with the Department of Trade and Industry (the DTI), responsibility for insurance regulation was passed to the Treasury in January 1998. The Treasury delegated responsibility to the Financial Services Authority in January 1999, but remains the government ministry accountable.

The ICA 1982 was an important piece of legislation as far as the insurance industry as a whole was concerned. In 2001, the ICA 1982 was repealed by the *Financial Services and Markets Act 2000*; however, to a large extent this restated the ICA 1982.

The prudential regulatory function of the ICA 1982 was divided into five main categories: authorisation, solvency, monitoring, intervention and winding up.

1 *Authorisation* – No insurer can carry on any insurance business within the UK unless they have authorisation from the regulator or were already authorised under previous statutes prior to the ICA 1982 coming into force. The only exceptions were members of Lloyd's, Friendly Societies or Trade Unions or Employers Associations offering provident benefits or strike benefits. Since the Act came into effect, this position has been modified by EU legislation allowing insurers authorised in any EU state to operate in any other EU state, either by distance selling or by the establishment of a subsidiary in each state they wish to trade in.

The insurer has to obtain authorisation for each class of insurance business they wish to offer. General insurance is divided into 17 classes while there are seven life classes. The regulator is empowered to enquire as to the suitability and experience of the management and can refuse authorisation if they are not satisfied. Once granted, authorisation can be withdrawn if the insurer is in breach of the rules of a supervisory body. In addition, as the authorisation extends across the EU a breach of legislation in other member states could also lead to this sanction.

2 *Solvency* – The ICA 1982 continued the established 'rules-based' system. All authorised companies are required to maintain stated solvency margins at all times. Failure to do so can result in and has resulted in intervention by the regulator who has the power to withdraw authorisation and order the company to be wound up. For general insurance, the required solvency margin is based upon a two-stage test, both elements of which have to be passed.

In each case, an absolute figure is produced and the insurer then has to demonstrate that free reserves (i.e. not allocated to future liabilities) and shareholders' funds exceed this sum. These rules are set out in the 1st Non Life Insurance Directive (73/239).

The first test is the premium basis, which analyses the degree to which increases in premium income are supported by capital. A breach of this margin usually implies a company is expanding too fast. This may not in fact be a serious problem as additional capital would be likely to be readily available to a successful company. The aim is to ensure that the additional capital is put in place before expansion. This creates an artificial capital requirement imposing a factor of production constraint and preventing unrestrained growth. A return must be generated on the additional capital, forcing the insurer to consider whether the additional business from expansion will be profitable.

Alternatively, there is the claims basis. This considers the extent to which claims trends are covered by capital reserves. Problems in this area would be far more serious as a continuing downward trend would at some point lead to insolvency. In both cases, credit is given for reinsurance purchase which could reduce the requirement by up to 50 per cent. This encourages reinsurance on the basis that this brings greater stability to the reinsured. The premium basis is calculated as follows:

(a)   18 per cent of the first €10 million of premiums for previous year then 16 per cent of the balance.
(b)   Multiplied by 50 per cent or the ratio of net claims to gross claims in last year if higher than 50 per cent.

Therefore, if the premium income last year was €220 million and the gross claims paid totalled €200 million with €50 million recovered from reinsurers, leaving net claims of €150 million, the requirement would be:

$$
\begin{aligned}
10 \text{ million} \times 18 \text{ per cent} &= 1.80 \text{ million} \\
210 \text{ million} \times 16 \text{ per cent} &= 33.6 \text{ million} \\
&= 35.4 \text{ million} \\
\frac{150}{200} \times 35.4\text{m} &= 26.55 \text{ million}
\end{aligned}
$$

The claims basis is calculated as follows. Total *gross* claims over the past three years are calculated again in Euros in order that the figure is not distorted by the occasional bad year. This is adjusted by taking into account any change in reserves against future claims (technical reserves) established at the end of the last financial year in comparison to the previous year. The result is then divided by three.

Thus, 26 per cent of the 1st €7 million of the resultant figure and 23 per cent of the balance is then calculated. Again, this is multiplied by 50 per cent or the ratio of net claims to gross claims in the last three years if higher than 50 per cent. Therefore, if the relevant figures are:

2006	gross claims	€205 million		net claims	€155 million
2007	gross claims	€195 million		net claims	€145 million
2008	gross claims	€200 million		net claims	€150 million

the technical reserves at the end of 2007 were €30 million and at the end of 2008 €40 million. The average claims over the three-year period were €200 million, to which must be added the €10 million deterioration in the reserves. The relevant figure is therefore €210 million. The average net claims over the three-year period are €150 million.

7 million × 26 per cent   = €1.82 million

203 million × 23 per cent   = <u>€46.69 million</u>

                                €48.51 million

$\dfrac{150}{200}$ × €48.51 million   = €36.38 million

Therefore, in this example, the insurer would need to satisfy the regulator that it possessed €36.38 million in free reserves and shareholders' funds, the higher of the two figures. Minimum absolute levels of solvency were specified irrespective of the outcome produced by the application of the tests, dependent on the class of business. These are so low that they will only affect the smallest of insurers.

3 *Monitoring* – The ICA 1982 requires that revenue accounts, statements of profit and loss and a balance sheet be provided. Life assurers have to provide actuarial valuation of their funds annually.

4 *Intervention* – The regulator is given wide powers to demand further information and could call for accounts to be submitted more regularly as well as requiring further details or appointing its own actuary to review the figures provided. If there is a danger that the solvency margin or minimum capital requirement may in the future be breached, there are a number of steps that can be taken. Note the regulator does not have to wait for the minimum capital requirement to be breached and insurers are expected to maintain solvency levels well above the statutory minimum.

The amount of premium income accepted by the insurer can be restricted if insufficient capital is available to support rising levels of premium. This will not be likely to assist if a failure of the claims test is feared, as there will be a time lag before reduced premium levels bring about reduced claims levels. Alternatively, the insurer can seek to increase their capital. If the danger is that the premium test will not be met this may be feasible. A fast-growing company may be able to recapitalise via a rights issue, for example, although this is a lengthy process and cannot be used if the matter is urgent. Simply borrowing the required sum is likely to be ineffective. Unless the capital is in the form of subordinated debt (the lender ranks below ordinary creditors), the regulator will not accept this method as the increase in assets will be offset by an increase in liabilities and policyholders are no better protected. Interest on subordinated debt will be higher due to the increased risk to the investor, therefore this method is not attractive to the insurer in any event. An increase in reinsurance purchase will reduce the minimum capital requirement, always assuming that the ratio of net claims to gross claims is not already 50 per cent or less. This will not have any affect in the current year, however. If part of a larger group, the parent company may be prepared to inject more capital.

If there is a risk that the claims test will not be met, the problem is more serious. In this case it is probable that there is deterioration in the combined ratio, making the insurer a less than attractive investment proposition. Buying additional reinsurance may not stabilise the problem as although lower net claims will be paid, there will be less premium to pay them with, after taking account of the extra reinsurance cost.

If recapitalisation or additional reinsurance purchase is not an option, the next stage would be for the regulator to impose restrictions on the investment of premium or policyholders' funds. Normally this would mean that the insurer would be required to divert investment funds into safer areas such as government securities to minimise the risk that solvency might be eroded by investment losses. Of course, this would tend to reduce investment income. Such a step would usually indicate that the regulator fears that the insurer is likely to fail. Once this becomes public knowledge it may well be a self-fulfilling prophesy as intermediaries and well-informed policyholders lose confidence in the insurer. As a final step, the regulator could demand that no further policies be written, essentially winding up the insurer or in insurance jargon, putting it in run off.

5 *Winding up* – As a last resort, insurers can be wound up under the Act. Often a voluntary act by the insurer (with maybe a 'suggestion' from the regulator), the Act gives the regulator the power to make this compulsory. In practice, an insurance company cannot suddenly cease trading. Policies remain valid even in the event of insolvency and if cancelled would then require the insurer to return the unused premium (life policies of course contain no cancellation clause). Claims will already have arisen and must be met. Such claims can continue to appear for many years after the expiry of the policy in certain cases. Hence, the term 'run off' as it is by no means unusual for an insolvent insurance company to continue in existence for twenty years or more, before either funds run out or the company is finally wound up. Even winding up will usually require adequate reinsurance of any further claims that might yet come crawling out of the woodwork.

The intent of a solvency margin is that at the time an insurer's authorisation is removed, assets should exceed liabilities and the insurer should in theory be able to pay policyholder claims. In the real world, the damage to cash flow caused by the sudden cessation of premium income, the need to make redundancy payments to employees and the possible need to dispose of assets at 'fire sale' prices means that it is common for there to be a shortfall. Nonetheless, the creditors of an insolvent insurance company (mostly the policyholders) should in theory and in the absence of serious fraud, receive a reasonably high percentage of the debt that it owed.

Life assurance in the EU 1st Life Directive (79/278)

The EU 1st Life Directive (79/278) does not permit a single company to be authorised in respect of both life and general insurance, requiring separation of both funds and management. This does not prevent a company from offering both life and general insurance via separate subsidiaries; however, the assets of the life assurance subsidiary cannot be used to support the solvency margin of the general insurance subsidiary. If the general insurance subsidiary has surplus assets, they can be allocated to the life assurance side. The thinking behind this is that general insurers are more likely to fail than life assurers. The separation of funds ensures that policyholders' long-term savings and crucially pensions are not affected by the insolvency of the general insurance arm.

No set rules are established for calculating the solvency of a life assurer. Instead an actuarial calculation is required proving that the life assurer possesses the necessary reserves to meet future liabilities. Future liabilities include the benefits offered by any policies issued, together with any allotted bonuses and guaranteed bonuses, making due allowance for costs and commissions connected with the policies. The assurer then has to demonstrate how current assets, together with future premiums and investment income would be sufficient to meet these liabilities as they fall due. The calculation would be based upon a number of assumptions, the most important of which would be the life expectancy of the policyholder and the rate of return on investments. The regulator is empowered to intervene and demand a reassessment if the assumptions used seem optimistic. This solvency process is a complex mathematical procedure, a demonstration of which is beyond the scope of this book.

The Financial Services and Markets Act 2000

The ICA 1982 was repealed by the *FSMA 2000*. However, many of its provisions continue, carried over into the new Act, as the EU directives enacted by the original Act remain in force and must continue to be enacted. The Act confirmed the Financial Services Authority as the regulator, although responsibility for prudential regulation of insurance had already been delegated to the FSA in 1999.

The FSMA did, however, introduce changes of significance. Prior to the Act, Lloyd's syndicates had not been directly regulated. The Society of Lloyd's regulated the syndicates through the Council of Lloyd's and Lloyd's was supervised in this duty by the regulator. The FSMA gave the FSA direct regulatory powers over Lloyd's syndicates and, as from 2001, syndicates began to be regulated by the FSA in much the same way as an insurance company.

Although the EU Insurance Directives underpin all UK regulation and the FSA must enforce them as a minimum standard, the regulatory system has developed beyond this basic requirement. FSA prudential regulation of insurers follows some 'standards' which are published in the *FSA Handbook* and are intended to offer guidelines as to how the FSA will approach their task:

1   *High level standards* – These are overriding requirements imposed on all regulated firms, including insurers, reinsurers and insurance intermediaries. They tend to outline broad principles rather than impose specific rules. They are concerned with:

   (a)   *Principles* – A statement of 11 principles governing the overall standard of behaviour expected of financial firms, including integrity, diligence, prudence and avoidance of conflicts of interests.
   (b)   *Senior management arrangements* – These outline the broad corporate governance standards expected and highlight that it is the responsibility of senior management to ensure compliance with regulatory requirements.
   (c)   *Threshold conditions* – These confirm the basic requirements for FSA authorisation, including the legal form a regulated firm may take and that the firm is adequately resourced and managed by fit and proper persons.
   (d)   *Approved persons* – An approved person is anyone carrying out a controlled function. This would include directors or partners of the regulated firm as well as officers to whom regulatory responsibility has been delegated. The *Handbook* specifies the criteria by which approved persons will be judged, honesty, competence and financial soundness being key elements. Previous business background, criminal convictions and prior financial or regulatory judgments will all be taken into account. The section also prohibits taking out insurance against fines imposed by the FSA. It would after all be nonsensical for the FSA to fine an insurer for misconduct only for the fine to be paid by another, uninvolved insurer.

2   *Prudential standards* – There are two parts to this section, general prudential standards and INSPRU, the prudential sourcebook for insurers:

   (a)   *General prudential standards* – This confirms that the minimum capital requirement (MCR) is as stated in the *EU Consolidated Life Directive 2002/83* (which restated the

1st Life Directive), the *Reinsurance Directive 2005/68* or the *1st Non Life Directive 1973/239* as applicable. It is the insurer's duty to monitor their financial position and inform the FSA of any breach or expected breach of the Minimum Capital Requirement.

The section further provides that in the case of financial conglomerates, the capital resource requirement is the sum of the capital adequacy and solvency requirements for each financial sector the financial conglomerate is active in. Governed by the EU *Financial Groups Directive 2002/87*, the rules are complex. Broadly speaking, if an insurer is owned by a bank, the insurance subsidiary must be able to meet the minimum capital requirement as if it were an independent company. The Group is not permitted to 'double count' capital, i.e. use the same assets to support the requirements for more than one subsidiary.

The calculation of capital resources for insurers is also set out. This is a combination of tier one capital, share capital, free reserves and shareholders' funds, and tier two capital, preference shares and subordinated debt. The reason for the distinction is because preference shares and subordinated debt create liabilities which must be satisfied by the insurer.

(b)   *INSPRU* – More detailed rules are set out in INSPRU, specific to insurance. Briefly, these cover five categories of risk (Figure 5.2).

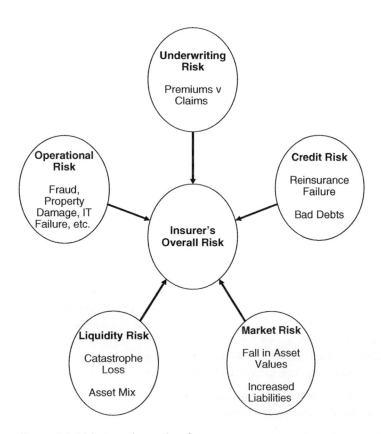

Figure 5.2 Risks to an insurer's solvency.

INSPRU categories of risk

1 *Capital resource requirement and technical provisions for insurance* – this covers the underwriting risk, being the risk that an insurer may fail to meet its liabilities to its policyholders as a result of occurrence, amount and timing of insurance losses. This therefore includes rules on technical provisions, reinsurance arrangements and for life assurers especially, matching of assets to liabilities (i.e. will the assets in future meet liabilities as they arise?).

The Non Life Directive requirements regarding the Premium and Claims tests are restated with the addition of a third test, the Brought Forward test. This is the capital requirement for the previous year multiplied if less than one by the ratio of the technical reserve (net of reinsurance) at the end of the previous year to the technical reserve at the beginning of the previous year. If there is no technical reserve at either the beginning or end of the previous year, the calculation must be repeated gross of reinsurance.

Therefore, if last year's capital requirement was €50 million, the technical reserve was €4 million at the end of that year and €5 million at the beginning, the brought forward amount would be:

$$€50 \text{ million} \times €4 \text{ million} = \frac{€40 \text{ million}}{€5 \text{ million}}$$

The Brought Forward amount will therefore be equal to the previous year's capital requirement unless technical reserves have fallen during the previous year. The aim is that where a company is shrinking in size, it must maintain its previous capital requirement until it can demonstrate that reserves for outstanding claims have reduced.

Another feature of the FSA regime is the Enhanced Capital Requirement. An insurer must calculate an enhanced figure for its capital requirement based upon the degree of risk inherent in the type of business it writes. This is achieved by adding a percentage to the capital requirement for each class of business written. The FSA will then take this into account in 'consideration of the appropriateness of the firm's own capital assessment'. In other words, this enhanced figure is not the legal minimum capital requirement, but any insurer that fails to meet the standard is likely to find that their relationship with the FSA becomes noticeably frosty. It should be remembered that the FSA do not have to wait until an insurer breaches the minimum capital requirement. They can (and probably are obliged) to intervene if a genuine risk exists that the insurer may breach the requirement at some time in the future. The broad approach is that personal lines insurance is deemed less risky than commercial insurance which is deemed less risky than marine and aviation. For example, the enhancement percentage for motor insurance is 10 per cent, for commercial liability it is 14 per cent, while for aviation it is 32 per cent. This is termed the capital charge factor.

For life assurers, the position remains broadly the requirement of the *Consolidated Life Directive 2002/83*. The life assurer must demonstrate that its financial reserves are sufficient to meet all future cash flows on every long-term policy offered. This must be achieved by using a prospective actuarial valuation based on prudent assumptions. In practice, policies will be aggregated and reasonable mathematical estimates of future cash flows made. Life assurers have a degree of discretion as to how they approach this task within the limits of accepted actuarial practice, subject to overriding principles. In particular, the approach taken must be consistent, allow a margin for error and must not conflict with the assurer's duty to treat customers fairly. The minimum capital requirement for life assurers has four components: the insurance death risk capital component; the insurance health risk and life protection reinsurance capital component; the insurance expense risk capital component; and the insurance market risk capital component.

2 *Credit risk* – Not to be confused with market risk, this refers to the risk that debts owed to the insurer will not be paid. There is a degree of credit risk brought about by non-payment of premiums; however, given the insurers' right to cancel the policy or deduct the outstanding amount from any claim payment, this risk is not significant. The main credit risk is a failure of a reinsurer to honour their obligations to the insurer. This would not include avoidance of the reinsurance contract for non-disclosure or other contractual breach, but rather the insolvency of the reinsurer. The existence of such risk is unavoidable, but can be minimised by using more than one reinsurer. The FSA recommendation is that no more than 20 per cent of gross premiums should be ceded to a single reinsurer. An insurer must also notify the FSA if their exposure to a single reinsurer exceeds their capital resources. Despite this, the failure of one of the principal reinsurers of an insurance company might well cause the insurer to fail as well. This is systemic risk as applied to the insurance market.

There is also a credit risk, albeit a lesser one, arising from the agency agreements with intermediaries. This will commonly permit the intermediary to collect the premiums and account for them to the insurer after a specified period (say, 60 to 90 days after inception of the policy). If the intermediary becomes insolvent, some or all of that premium will not be received, yet the insurer will usually be liable to meet claims arising on the policy (see Chapter 8). In most cases the insurer will only be exposed to a percentage of the annual premiums received from one broker among many that place business with the insurer. This credit risk should not therefore in itself threaten the solvency of an insurer. The normal operation of the market would tend to meet the FSA requirement that exposures are limited to prudent levels and adequately diversified. There may, however, be exceptions.

General insurers must calculate an asset-related capital requirement. The insurer's assets are divided into 30 categories. The value of the assets in each category is then multiplied by a capital charge factor. The lower the credit risk, the lower the charge factor. Therefore the capital charge factor for reinsurance debt is 2.5 per cent, for intermediary debt it is 3.5 per cent and for policyholder debt it is 4.5 per cent.

3 *Market risk* – The investment of premiums received is central to the operation of the whole concept of insurance. Market risk is the risk that market fluctuations will reduce the value of or expected return from investment assets. Market risk can also increase liabilities, for example, increases in interest rates will increase debt repayments and adverse movements in currency exchange can reduce the value of overseas premiums or increase the cost of claims if dealing in other currencies. Currency risk can also occur where investment assets are denominated in another currency.

Market risk can involve short-term fluctuations in the main investment markets, shares, securities and to a lesser extent property. This can result in the sudden reduction of the value of an insurer's invested assets. Such losses are often paper losses only, if the insurer continues to hold the asset and prices recover, the problem fixes itself. Only if the asset is sold will a loss be crystallised. However, even where a loss is not crystallised, there can be solvency problems where the investments concerned form a part of the insurer's minimum capital requirement, as a once sufficient portfolio of financial assets is re-valued at a lower figure. A sudden, sharp fall in the stock market or securities prices could result in an insurer's capital falling below required levels. Any technical reserves must be covered by a holding of assets sufficient to meet these liabilities. If the value of these assets falls, then the assets may be insufficient to meet estimated liabilities.

A more invidious problem is a long-term decline in investment returns as opposed to the cyclical peaks and troughs expected from the investment markets. There is a correlation between prevailing interest rates and investment returns, led by the returns on government securities or gilts, as they are known in the UK. Corporate securities as a class have to offer a higher return than gilts to reflect the higher risk. Equities have to offer the potential for still higher returns as the risk is still higher. If base rates fall, the interest paid on gilts will fall as well, as the government after all does not want to pay more interest than it has to. This will tend to have a cascade effect throughout the investment market. If good quality corporate bonds are priced at, say, 1 per cent above the prevailing return on gilts, they will follow the gilt returns down. This effect will then tend to be passed on throughout the investment market. Life assurers are particularly exposed in this regard. A general insurer charging annual premiums has the opportunity to adjust premiums to take account of lower investment returns. A life assurer entering into long-term contracts with fixed premiums and benefits cannot do this in the short term at least.

An additional market capital component is added to the Enhanced Capital Requirement for life assurers. A life assurer that does not maintain with profits funds or has with profits funds of less than £500 million is described as a regulatory basis life assurer and must meet the resilience capital requirement. A life assurer managing with profits funds of over £500 million is described as a realistic basis life assurer and must calculate the with profits capital component. The difference arises because with profits funds add annual bonuses to the fund based upon the profits of the assurer, thus creating liabilities in the future when the policy matures. The precise calculation of these requirements is complex and is beyond the scope of this book. Broadly speaking, however, life assurers are required to model falls in the equities and properties market by stated percentages and then demonstrate that they hold sufficient capital to withstand such falls.

General insurers are required to state their assumptions as to interest rates in their calculations of future claims payments. These assumptions must not be higher than the lowest of the insurers' own prudent estimate, the rate justified by earnings in the preceding five years and the rate justified by earnings in the previous year.

4 *Liquidity risk* – Insurers must be able to withstand sudden demands upon their cash reserves, in particular in the aftermath of a catastrophe loss. This concerns the short-term cash flow position rather than longer-term planning for future liabilities. By way of example, an event such as the World Trade Center attack in September 2001 resulted in a sudden and unexpected loss of around $35 billion, although not all of this amount was paid immediately (see Chapter 3 and the discussion concerning 'deal now, detail later' on p. 00). The effect of this is to force insurers to liquidate investments in a hurry, possibly at a loss. The knock-on effect of large-scale selling is to force the market price down and the major stock markets were indeed depressed for some time after the attack, although other factors were at work. Although the timing of some natural disasters is to an extent predictable (there is a well-recognised hurricane season between June and November, for example), the magnitude of the event is not predictable and anomalies do occur (for example, the widespread flooding in the UK during the summer of 2007).

Insurers are required to have in place a liquidity risk policy to manage such risks. For example, rather than selling an asset, it can be used to secure short-term borrowing, allowing the insurer to liquidate assets over a longer term and in a controlled manner. Assets can be

General Insurers Enhanced Capital Requirement Insurance-Related Capital Requirement Asset-Related Capital Requirement	Realistic Basis Life Assurers Enhanced Capital Requirement With Profits Capital	Regulatory Basis Life Assurers Enhanced Capital Requirement Resilience Capital
General Insurers **Minimum Capital Requirement** Highest of: Premium Test Claims Test Brought Forward Test	**Life Assurers** **Minimum Capital Requirement** Actuarial Valuation As required by the Consolidated Life Directive 2002/83 4 Components	
Base Capital Requirement Varies from €300,000 to €3.2 million according to the nature and activities of the company		

Figure 5.3 The capital requirements for insurers.

securitised, a type of borrowing that sells the future cash flows from the asset for cash up front. The debt is redeemed when the asset is sold in the future. The marketability of assets is also a factor. While financial instruments can be readily traded, property investments cannot be converted to cash in the short term. Insurers therefore need to have a sufficient proportion of assets held in a readily marketable form, in other words, the mix of assets must reflect the liquidity risk profile.

5 *Operational risk* – This concerns the risk of loss resulting from inadequate or ineffective internal processes, people and systems, or from external events. The four risks already discussed would fall into this heading but are obviously considered separately. To these risks can be added fraud (both internal and external), a failure to comply with the law (excluding regulatory law, of course), damage to premises with the consequential interruption to business, and the failure of information systems.

It is to be hoped that insurers will be adept at identifying and controlling such risks (Figure 5.3). After all, these are the types of risk that they offer insurance against. Nonetheless the risks that threaten their policyholders also threaten the insurers and as such, must be managed. If they are not adequately managed, the solvency of the insurer may be in doubt. The FSA requires that insurers demonstrate that they have systems in place to manage the identification, assessment, monitoring and control of such risks.

The future: Solvency II and risk-based regulation

The official approach to the prudential regulation of insurers has remained unchanged since its introduction in the 1980s and this implementation was based upon EU directives drawn up in the 1970s. In the meantime, the supervision of the banking sector has been reformed by the Basel Accords, leading to the Basel II standard intended to harmonise banking regulation around the world. In particular, Basel II was based upon a move away from a rules-based system towards a principles-based system. In a rules-based system the regulator draws up rules and the regulated firm then has to demonstrate that they comply with the rules. The solvency requirements of the 1st Non Life Directive (1973/239) is a good example of a rules-based system. A principles-based system puts a greater responsibility upon the regulated firm to consider the amount of capital they require given the particular activities of the firm. The role of the regulator is then to review the firm's own estimate of their requirements and to require amendment where necessary. The thinking behind this approach is that because all firms are different, it is impossible to draw up a set of rules that apply consistently and fairly to all firms. The result being that some firms will be required to over-capitalise increasing the cost of the product. Other firms will be under-capitalised, increasing the risk of insolvency.

By way of example, the Basel II principles concentrate on three pillars:

1 Minimum capital requirements in relation to risk assumed calculated by the bank.
2 Supervisory review by the regulator.
3 Market discipline must then be maintained in order that the risk assumed is not magnified.

Therefore, in broad terms, market firms will be judged by the degree of risk they represent to the health of the financial system. Alternatively it could be considered that they are judged according to the risk that they will prevent the Financial Services Authority from meeting its objectives. These objectives being:

1 Maintaining confidence in the UK financial system.
2 Appropriate levels of consumer protection.
3 Reducing financial crime.
4 Promotion of public understanding of the financial system.

Current thinking in the area of insurance is greatly influenced by these developments in banking regulation. This has led to the Basel II solvency approach, adopted by the banks, being identified by the European Union as the future for insurance regulation.

This has proved somewhat problematic as the Basel Accords were primarily designed to minimise the risk of systemic collapse, always the nightmare of a banking regulator. The basic banking operation brings about two major risks: credit and liquidity. The credit risk being that loans are not repaid. The liquidity risk being that either large numbers of small depositors will simultaneously demand repayment or the bank will have insufficient cash to repay large-scale, short-term inter-bank loans as they fall due. Risks in these areas tend to be fundamental, often brought about by the macroeconomic environment. Therefore, the system as a whole will be threatened, possibly resulting in multiple failures.

Indeed, from 2007, this is exactly what the world has seen. The property crash in the USA led to fears of large-scale credit defaults. This in turn led banks to be reluctant to lend to one another, partly due to their own liquidity requirements and partly due to the increased credit risk of short-term lending to another bank whose liquidity might be questionable. The result was the 'credit crunch' as banks were unable to borrow in the short term to meet their immediate liquidity requirements, initially in respect of large-scale inter-bank loans. Quite whether banks should have allowed themselves to get into the situation where repayment of a loan was dependent on their being able to take out another loan is another matter. Although the Bank of England and other central banks were ready to supply the necessary short-term liquidity, once it became known that a bank had been forced to approach the 'lender of last resort', confidence in the bank was lost. The result in August 2007 was a run on Northern Rock as long queues of depositors formed outside branches of the bank, desperate to withdraw their money. At that point Northern Rock was doomed. However, as the loss of confidence was general, rather than directed at a single poorly managed institution, this lack of confidence caused the system to fail rather than a single bank. Had it not been for government intervention on an unprecedented scale, the global banking system would have collapsed as the contagion spread.

The insurers are not as susceptible as banks to a loss of confidence. Of course if policyholders lose confidence in the market, the future for insurance companies will be grim; however, this will not bring about the collapse of the system in the short term. Unlike banks their customers are not automatically creditors. A policyholder only becomes a creditor on the occurrence of a loss-causing event covered by the policy. For the majority of policies this event will not occur during the period covered. There cannot be a 'run' on a general insurer.

If a particular insurer is in such difficulties that policyholders lose confidence in them, they often have no option but to insure the risk and will simply take out cover with another company. This will increase the business of the insurer's competitors and may cause a 'hardening' of premiums as the capacity of the affected insurer is not utilised, effectively reducing the supply of insurance. The effect of an insurer running into difficulties is generally to strengthen the rest of the market rather than to contaminate it. Such has been the experience of soft insurance markets in the past. Responding to classical Darwinian theory, the weakest fail, leaving the strongest to take advantage of the hard market that follows, enjoying increased market share at enhanced premium rates.

A run on a life assurer is possible as investment funds, in particular personal pensions, can be transferred to other providers. If large numbers of policyholders elect to do this in the short term, the life assurer will be unlikely to survive as they would struggle to find the necessary liquidity. For this reason, transfer penalties may be imposed as a deterrent. However, as pension funds cannot be withdrawn in cash and must be transferred to another pension provider, the rest of the market is once again strengthened by picking up the business of the failed competitor.

The spectre of short-term systemic collapse prompted by the failure of a single insurance company is highly improbable. The failure of a reinsurer is a horse of an entirely different colour and this scenario is explored in Chapter 7. There is therefore some question as to whether it is appropriate to apply regulatory approaches designed to prevent systemic collapse in the banking system to the insurance market.

Solvency II objectives

The problem with the current solvency requirement for general insurers (now known as Solvency I) is that it is a rather crude 'one size fits all' set of rules. Therefore the standard is the same irrespective of the business activities of an insurer. The degree of risk is, however, variable according to the mix of policies sold, as the volatility in the expected result is not the same for different classes of business. As previously mentioned, personal lines insurance is likely to be less volatile than commercial insurance. There are far more insured risks, therefore the operation of the law of large numbers indicates a more predictable outcome. The risks are also well spread and each individual exposure is small. There are fewer commercial risks and a greater value of risk is concentrated in each exposure. The specialised areas of commercial insurance, such as marine, energy and aviation can be more volatile still. The number of risks is relatively small and very large values are concentrated in a single location. While losses are very rare in comparison to motor insurance, for example, the cost is very high indeed. A new Boeing 787 airliner costs around $200 million, an Airbus 380 about $320 million. A single loss could cost the equivalent of about 10,000–15,000 motor insurance write-offs. A solvency standard that is adequate for a motor insurer can look dangerously low when applied to an aviation insurer. On the other hand, if the motor insurer is forced to adopt a level of capitalisation appropriate for an aviation insurer, the cost of motor insurance will be increased needlessly by requiring the motor insurer to hold more capital than the risk warrants.

It is, of course, possible to introduce revised rules applying different minimum capital requirements to different kinds of insurer. But even this approach is unsatisfactory, as there will be differences in the risk profiles of insurers covering the same class of business. For example, a motor insurer may specialise in insuring high value sports cars or rare collector's cars. If the overriding aim is that each insurer holds capital reserves appropriate to the risks they have assumed, a rules-based system would have to be of Byzantine complexity to cover all the possible risk permutations. There would then be the risk of endless arguments between insurer and regulator over precisely which rule should be applied.

Another criticism of the Solvency I approach is that it only considers underwriting risk. The rules are not designed to take into account credit, market or liquidity risk. The Solvency I system cannot be said to cover all risks to an insurer's financial position. Although as will be seen, underwriting risk is the main cause of insurer failure, it is not the sole cause.

The Solvency II exercise envisages a principles-based system, similar to the Basel II approach. Under the new system, the insurers themselves would need to assess their capital needs, which would reflect business activities, degree of volatility, availability of reinsurance and other risk-relevant factors such as credit, market and liquidity risk. This would be termed the *own risk and solvency assessment*. The role of the regulator would no longer be concentrated on the monitoring of rule compliance, but would become one of evaluation of insurers' risk profiles, solvency assessment, risk management and governance systems via the *Supervisory Review Process*. Finally, the system will be underpinned by *transparency, discipline and disclosure*. This requires full disclosure to the regulator together with the regulator adopting an inquisitorial stance where appropriate. The thinking here is that the standards of the first two pillars must be maintained.

Initially the EU announced back in 2001 that they would be moving towards implementation of Solvency II in 2004. This was rapidly put back as the complexity of the programme was realised. In July 2007, the European Commission announced that they were going to 'take a global lead in insurance regulation' … by 2012! So far it appears that this remains the deadline.

However, the FSA and some other EU regulators have already begun the move towards risk-based regulation. In addition to the basic requirement of the EU directives, general insurers are required to calculate an Enhanced Capital Requirement based upon the mix of insurance business that they undertake. Life assurers must consider either the With Profits Capital Component or the Resilience Capital Requirement. It is worth noting that the EU directive requirements for life assurers are arguably principles based anyway.

The requirements regarding credit, market, liquidity and operational risks are all measures taken to begin the implementation of Solvency II. The policy is clearly to introduce what will be a major change in regulatory policy in incremental steps.

A further example of the degree towards which the FSA is already partly applying Solvency II principles is their risk-based approach. Called ARROW which is almost an acronym for advanced risk responsive operating framework, this has been recently overhauled to produce ARROW II. Arrow follows a four-stage process:

1   *Risk identification* – An awareness of the risks faced by the firm.
2   *Risk measurement* – Consideration of the likely impact and probability of the risk occurrence.
3   *Risk mitigation* – Steps that can be taken to reduce either impact or probability.
4   *Risk monitoring and reporting* – The process is circular and requires that risk identification is re-visited to check whether new risks have emerged or the nature of existing risks has changed.

Risk in this context is the risk that the FSA objectives will not be met. The consumer protection objective will clearly not be met if a firm becomes insolvent; however, there are other aspects to this, in particular, the fair treatment of consumers. The ARROW system individually rates a variety of risks on a four-stage scale: low, medium low, medium high and high. Some key risks are given greater weighting and the 'score' is consequently more influential. The combined outcome gives an overall risk profile for the firm and indicates where attention is most needed. This also indicates to the FSA which firms are most in need of close supervision.

The standard expected of firms is variable according to need and resources. The complexity and demands made on the firms increase through the three versions of the system: Small Firms, Arrow Light and Arrow. There is a further category, close and continuous, that is applied to major firms (termed 'high impact' firms) and possibly to smaller firms identified as being in difficulties. In this context 'impact' refers to the impact that the firm might have on the FSA's regulatory objectives, and by implication this means the damage that might be done to the financial system. The failure of a small firm is highly unlikely to cause serious risk to the system, but this is not the case with the 'household name' companies. It is worth noting that the FSA regulates around 29,000 financial firms, of which almost 95 per cent are small firms and less than 0.5 per cent are 'high impact' firms such as major insurers and banks. Unsurprisingly, the high impact firms, although few in number, take up two-thirds of FSA resources.

The scope of the process is demonstrated in the FSA scoring chart in Figure 5.4, see opposite. As can be seen, the process goes far beyond an assessment of current solvency. Each box will be marked L (low), ML (medium low), MH (medium high) or H (high).

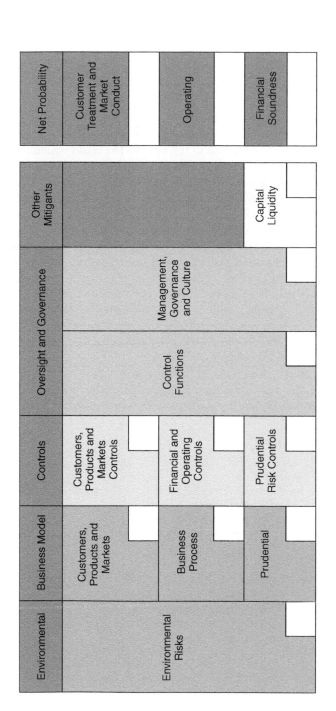

Figure 5.4 The ARROW process.

Where a firm fails to satisfy the FSA that their risks are appropriately managed, a risk mitigation programme will be required, setting out how the firm plans to bring the level of risk back within acceptable boundaries.

It is anticipated that this methodology will be form the basis of Solvency II implementation when it becomes mandatory in 2012.

Why do insurers fail?

The current regulatory thinking has moved away from a concentration on core underwriting risk and broadened out into a wide range of other issues. Although minimising the risk of insurer failure is certainly not the only FSA objective, it is the issue that will have the greatest impact on policyholders. In 1999, the ratings firm A.M. Best produced a report analysing 640 insurance company failures occurring in the USA between 1969 and 1998. The aim of the report was to identify, where possible, the cause of the failure. The result was illuminating (Table 5.1).

Most of these causes arise from underwriting risk. It can be argued that fraud is an operational risk (although the motivation for fraud may well be a desire to disguise underwriting losses) and that reinsurance failure is a credit risk (although if the failure was due to the avoidance of the policy by the reinsurer, this would be an operational risk). Insufficient reserves, rapid growth and catastrophe loss are generally underwriting risks. The significant change in business and impaired affiliate categories are likely to include failures brought about by underwriting risk, although other risks may have operated. Overstated assets may have been brought about by market risk, but fraud is another explanation. Therefore, between 62 per cent and 75 per cent of insurance failures can be attributed to underwriting risk. Certainly all the major insurance failures in the UK in recent years have their origins in the failure to underwrite the risk correctly. The Equitable Life, Municipal Mutual, Independent Insurance and KWELM failures are all examples.

This perhaps over-simplifies the issue. It is noteworthy that A.M. Best was unable to determine the primary cause of loss in more than a third of cases. Even where a primary cause was identified, it is probable that in many cases the failure was influenced by secondary causes as well.

Table 5.1 Reasons for company failure

Primary causes	*Number of companies*	*Total identified* (%)
Insufficient reserves	145	34
Rapid growth (under pricing)	86	20
Alleged fraud	44	10
Overstated assets	39	9
Catastrophe losses	36	8
Significant change in business	28	7
Impaired affiliate	26	6
Reinsurance failure	22	5
No primary cause identified	214	

The effectiveness of UK regulation

Having a sound regulatory structure is all well and good, but if it is not properly supervised, the system will fail to minimise the risk of financial failure. The failure of Independent Insurance was discussed in Chapter 4, where the insurer was able to conceal their true financial position from the regulators for an extended period, thus increasing the loss to policyholders when they finally collapsed. The other major insurer failure during this period was Equitable Life which failed in 2000.

The root cause of the Equitable Life failure was the offering of Guaranteed Annuity Rates (GARs) alongside their personal pension plans. The impact of this type of promise is explored in greater depth in Chapter 11, but the essence of the GAR is that the life assurer promises to pay a minimum percentage of the pension fund built up for the rest of the pensioner's life.

Equitable Life failed to build up any reserves to meet these future liabilities and once it became clear that the promises made were going to be very expensive to keep, they sought to renege on the agreement. They did this not by failing to pay the promised percentage but by seeking to restrict the size of the fund by offering lower bonuses to the holders of GARs.

The GAR policyholders sued, and won in the House of Lords (*Equitable Life v Hyman (2000)*). The effect of the decision was that Equitable Life was forced to pay the full bonus to the policyholders rather than the reduced sum. Prior to the House of Lords' decision, Equitable Life informed the FSA that their compensation bill in the event of defeat would be £200 million. More seriously, reinsurance cover worth over £1 billion was rendered invalid by the decision. It was a condition of cover that Equitable Life maintained differential bonuses for GAR policyholders. This Equitable Life were unable to do and a very large question mark hovered over the with profits fund, a question mark that is hard to quantify but is unlikely to have been less than £1.5 billion. At this point Equitable Life was clearly not able to demonstrate that their assets were sufficient to meet their future liabilities. Immediate action from the FSA was clearly called for.

The proposed solution was to put Equitable Life up for sale. Given the negative publicity generated by the trial and the unquantified GAR liabilities, a number of tentative enquiries failed to produce a firm offer. The issue was complicated by the fact that Equitable Life was a mutual and would have to be demutualised before sale. This process, however, stretched on for five months with little prospect of finding another life assurer prepared to take over a with profits fund with a multi-billion pound black hole in its finances. Eventually the FSA were forced to act.

Under the provisions of the Insurance Companies Act 1982, the FSA did the following:

1   Restricted the manner in which the company could invest policyholders' funds.
2   As of 8 December 2000, prevented new business from being written.

Effectively the company was in liquidation. The new management (the previous incumbents mostly having fallen on their swords) desperately sought to settle the 90,000 GAR liabilities while limiting the damage done to 360,000 policyholders holding other kinds of with profits policies. The with profits fund constituted about 75 per cent of Equitable Life's business. Although a compromise agreement was reached with the policyholders, the value of the policies suffered significantly.

Attempts have been made by policyholders to obtain government compensation, although no legal obligation exists requiring the regulator to pay compensation to policyholders irrespective of the circumstances of the loss; however, where it can be established that the regulator was at fault, it is possible that the government can be shamed into offering a settlement on a voluntary basis. The matter was complicated by the fact that although the GARs that brought Equitable Life down were written from 1957 to 1988, the problem started to materialise in the early 1990s. At that time the Department of Trade and Industry were responsible for the prudential supervision of insurers. This responsibility passed to the Treasury in 1998 and to the FSA in 1999.

Although consumer compensation was available in the event of an insurer failure in 2000 via the Policyholders Protection Board (now taken over by the Financial Services Compensation Scheme), it was inapplicable in this case as it only applies to sums the insurer is legally liable to pay. A fall in the value of investments is not covered (see Chapter 12).

An internal inquiry by the FSA (the Baird Report) concluded that Equitable Life was already doomed by the time the FSA took responsibility on 1 January 1999. The report states:

> The 'die was cast' and we have seen nothing which the FSA could have done thereafter which would have mitigated, in any material way, the impact of the court case as far as existing policyholders were concerned, or made any material beneficial difference to the final outcome as far as Equitable Life was concerned.

According to the FSA, it all happened on the Dept of Trade and Industry's watch and the FSA were helpless to prevent the collapse in the two years they were responsible. The DTI could claim that the collapse actually happened on the FSA's watch. In a fine example of teflon government, apparently no one was responsible. This is incorrect as the Government Actuaries Department had been responsible throughout, advising, first the DTI, then the Treasury and finally the FSA from start to finish of the Equitable Life saga.

An independent government enquiry was established under Lord Penrose in August 2001 to report on the circumstances surrounding the Equitable Life disaster. The Penrose Report was not delivered to the Treasury until 23 December 2003 and was not published until 8 March 2004, almost four years after Equitable Life failed.

The report concluded that, 'Principally, the society was author of its own misfortunes. Regulatory failures were secondary factors.' The report severely criticised Equitable Life's management commenting on a 'culture of manipulation and concealment' resulting in a failure to provide details of its financial position to either policyholder or the regulator. Particularly criticised was Roy Ranson who was both Chief Executive and Chief Actuary until 1997. It was pointed out that Equitable Life had over many years over-valued policies without the financial reserves to support the stated valuation. Non-executive directors were described as 'ill-equipped', 'ill-prepared' and 'incompetent' to supervise a major life assurer. The Penrose Report also commented that the light touch regulation applied by the DTI and the Treasury was 'inappropriate' and that the DTI in particular did not fully understand how to assess the solvency of a life assurer dealing in long-term future liabilities.

In the aftermath of this report the government refused compensation. Equitable Life policyholders took the matter to the Parliamentary Ombudsman claiming maladministration by the regulators of Equitable Life. Her report was published in 2008 and concluded as findings of fact that:

1   The regulator (the DTI at the time) failed to prevent the same individual holding dual office of Chief Executive and Chief Actuary from 1991 to 1997.

2   From 1990 to 1993, the Government Actuaries Department (GAD) failed to ensure that the submissions of Equitable Life's statements of assets and liabilities met regulatory standards. Consequently the GAD was unable to verify the solvency of Equitable Life. The imprudence of assumptions and unsustainability of bonuses were highlighted as being examples of areas that the GAD should have been raising questions about.

3   The GAD failed to draw the regulator's attention to the differential bonus payments planned by Equitable Life that came to their attention in 1994.

4   From 1994 to 1996, the GAD failed to ensure that the submissions of Equitable Life's statements of assets and liabilities met regulatory standards. Consequently the GAD was unable to verify the solvency of Equitable Life. Again the Ombudsman found that questions should have been raised concerning imprudent assumptions and unsustainable bonuses, but added questions should also have been asked about the lack of reserves for future GAR liabilities.

5   That the GAD failed to question why information concerning the resilience reserves was missing from the returns from 1996 onwards. This had the effect of making Equitable Life's financial position appear stronger than it actually was.

6   The FSA noted that there was no provision for GAR liabilities in 1998 and that an additional £1.6 billion of reserves needed to be demonstrated. They permitted Equitable Life to offset this amount via reinsurance even though the GAD had advised them that there were problems with the arrangement and that it was of little or no value in an assessment of Equitable Life's solvency.

7   The FSA knew that this reinsurance might be rendered invalid by the decision of the House of Lords and should have required Equitable Life to include details of their contingency plans in their 1998 and 1999 returns. These plans would have had to show how Equitable Life would be able to compensate policyholders and maintain solvency in the event that the reinsurance was in fact invalidated. They did remind Equitable Life but failed to act when the returns did not include such contingency plans.

8   Although the position of Equitable Life was perilous to say the least, in the aftermath of the House of Lords defeat in July 2000, the FSA decided not to order them to cease to accept new business. No record of that decision was made and it is not therefore known what factors the FSA took into consideration when reaching that decision.

9   In any event, the decision to allow Equitable Life to remain open was described as 'not grounded in a sound factual or legal basis'. This alluded to the fact that the FSA were under a duty to close a company once they were no longer in a position to demonstrate the required level of solvency.

10 After Equitable Life was closed to new business, existing policyholders were advised by the FSA that the company was solvent and was fulfilling and always had fulfilled its regulatory obligations. The solvency of Equitable Life was at the time in considerable doubt and the FSA knew that regulatory requirements had not been fulfilled.

In conclusion, the general complaint that the prudential regulators (the DTI, the Treasury and the FSA) and the GAD failed to properly exercise their regulatory functions prior to 8 December 2000 was upheld. The Parliamentary Ombudsman recommended that the bodies concerned should apologise and that the government should establish a fund to compensate those who suffered financial loss as a result of maladministration.

Not until January 2009 did the government respond. They fully rejected the 1st finding. The 2nd to 5th and 7th to 9th findings were in the main accepted in fact but it was rejected that any injustice to the policyholders resulted. Only the 6th and 10th findings were fully accepted. Although an apology was offered, no compensation scheme was established on the grounds of that Equitable Life was responsible to a large degree for the debacle, that the expense would be considerable and that it is not generally appropriate to pay compensation even when there has been regulatory failure. The government decided that the appropriate course of action would be to set up a further enquiry to consider whether ex gratia payments might be made to those who had suffered disproportionate impact, it being implied that they would be few in number.

This has resulted in a major political, some might argue constitutional, argument between the government and the Parliamentary Ombudsman. A second report has been laid before Parliament by the Ombudsman, only the fourth time this action has been taken in the 42-year history of the Ombudsman. Among many points made, not least some sharp criticism of the way the government has incorrectly cited both the Ombudsman's Report and the Penrose Report, the Ombudsman queries what the point of her enquiry was if no compensation was to be forthcoming. This matter remains unresolved at the time of writing.

Nine years after Equitable Life shut their doors, the arguments still rage. Many of those most badly affected were policyholders who were due to retire shortly after the failure of the company. Their retirement fund was seriously reduced, perhaps by as much as 50 per cent. They had no time to rebuild the fund and either had to delay retirement or accept a much lower standard of living than they were led to expect. Perhaps the worst affected were some of those who took out policies between July and December 2000. They joined an already doomed life assurer and while newly established policies could simply be cancelled and losses cut, others transferred large built up funds from other life assurance companies which promptly shrank alarmingly.

Equitable Life – effectively regulated?

The ten findings of maladministration made by the Parliamentary Ombudsman clearly indicate that in her opinion (after a four-year investigation), Equitable Life was anything but effectively regulated. It was known that Equitable Life was over exposed to GARs and that their terms were often more generous than other companies. When some life assurers started setting aside reserves against future GAR liabilities as early as 1994, the regulator should have expected to see the same from Equitable Life and ask questions when such reserves were not made. Once that failure had occurred, the policyholders were going to be hurt financially as at the very least the bonuses paid to the with profits fund would have to be cut at some stage to compensate. Nonetheless, even as late as 1999 when the FSA took over responsibility, the damage could still have been limited. Why did this not happen?

It is worth restating two of the FSA's objectives, consumer protection and preservation of market confidence, and to consider how these objectives informed FSA decisions.

The matter was never a simple case of the policyholders fighting a decision of their assurer. In keeping the GAR promise to the policyholders holding that kind of policy, Equitable Life would have had to cut bonuses to all with profits policyholders. This could have had the effect of transferring funds from the majority to benefit the minority. Equitable Life certainly portrayed their position as representing the non-GAR policyholders in a test case against the GAR policyholders. Their claim to the high moral ground is somewhat undermined by the fact that they had not met their regulatory obligations and that as a result did not have the reserves that they should have held. Nonetheless there was a case for allowing Equitable Life to follow a policy that led to a fair distribution of available funds for all policyholders.

On the other hand, the FSA were under a duty to protect the consumer and as such it is difficult to see how they could allow differential bonus rates when they ran so contrary to the policyholders' reasonable expectations. Equitable Life had made a promise and notwithstanding the fact that it was a promise that they should not have made, they should have been made to honour it. Differential bonuses were a back door method of reneging on the promise.

There is also the question of why the FSA did not intervene before the matter went to court. They were aware that the reinsurance cover would be invalidated by an adverse judgment and should have been aware that this would call into question the solvency of the company. Should the FSA have allowed Equitable Life to bet the company on the outcome of a single court case? It is difficult to see how this question can be answered in the affirmative. Had the FSA required Equitable Life to demonstrate that they had the required capital to meet the consequences of an adverse judgment before proceeding, it is probable that Equitable Life would have had to be put up for sale in 1999. At that point the reputation of the company had not been damaged by their court defeats and it is more likely that a buyer would have been prepared to take the risk presented by the Equitable Life with profits fund. The caveat here is that this could have presented the FSA with an even greater problem if Equitable Life's liabilities had contaminated the purchaser. This is precisely the problem that was encountered in 2008 with the Lloyds Bank takeover of HBOS, which led to Lloyds having to seek government support as the position of HBOS proved worse than anticipated. Given that the FSA did support attempts to seek a buyer for Equitable Life in July 2000, it is doubtful that this consideration would have been any kind of restraining factor.

This is the next difficulty for the FSA. Why, when they had cause to doubt the solvency of Equitable Life, did they permit them to continue trading for a further five months, during which time new policyholders were being enrolled? The Parliamentary Ombudsman rightly criticised the FSA for failing to keep any record of this critical decision. Any comment made in this regard must therefore be speculation; however, it is arguable that finding the objective to preserve market confidence in conflict with the objective to protect the consumer, the market confidence argument prevailed. The collapse of a major life assurer following closely on from the fall-out from the pension mis-selling scandal (see Chapter 11) would certainly have been unhelpful from the perspective of maintaining consumer confidence in pension providers. It is possible that this influenced FSA thinking and the desirability of a quiet takeover of the company was allowed to outweigh the need to protect policyholders. Alternatively it could be said that the successful purchase of the company was in the best interests of the policyholders and therefore met the consumer protection objective. This is unquestionably true, if it could be achieved. The risk, of course, was that if it could not be achieved, the policyholders' position would be worsened and the 'late joiners' (those taking out a policy after July 2000) would be needlessly entangled in the failure. Although a takeover was possibly feasible at an earlier date, this was highly optimistic by late 2000 as it would have required another life assurer to put their own policyholders' financial future at risk in order to rescue the policyholders of a competitor. The damage to the reputation of Equitable Life as well as the serious doubts that existed as to the extent of their liabilities meant that a serious takeover bid was never likely.

It is probably going too far to regard this episode as an example of financial crime. FSA bans have been handed out to some former directors, but none have faced criminal charges. They did not directly line their pockets, although they could be said to have collected bonuses they were not entitled to by concealing the true financial position of the company (according to both the Penrose Report and the Parliamentary Ombudsman's Report).

The FSA stated in their response to the Parliamentary Ombudsman that the regulatory regime has been reformed since the fall of Equitable Life. This is certainly true, however the failure of the company was not caused by any lack of regulatory powers but because they were not properly used. No amount of regulation will be effective unless it is accompanied by enforcement and sound judgement on the part of the regulatory body.

The system is set to be further tightened with the introduction of Solvency II. The proposals appear sensible and ought to lead to a reduced risk of insurer failure or at least an earlier warning if it cannot be avoided. However, the same could have been said of the Basel II Accords as applied to the banking system. Although apparently implemented, banks appeared wholly incapable of assessing the degree of risk inherent in their operations and indeed seem to have proceeded on the basis that property prices were a one-way bet despite a wealth of evidence to the contrary. Even more worrying, the FSA and their counterparts in other countries accepted the banks' risk assessments and evidently failed to identify huge risks that caused what would have been complete systemic collapse but for government intervention.

Conclusion

The challenge to a regulator is to protect two potentially conflicting consumer concerns. Obviously the consumer needs to be reasonably confident that insurers are properly managed and financed, without which there exists a danger that claims will not be met. The consumer is also seeking value for money, and the best way to achieve this is via a competitive market.

A draconian regulatory system, while offering security, will also deter new entrants and possibly limit participation in the market to a handful of large, wealthy firms. This creates a danger that the market will not be truly competitive. On the other hand, an overly competitive market may operate on thin profit margins which create a danger of frequent insolvencies. This is especially true of insurance as the profit cannot be calculated at the time the product is put into the market; only when the claims have been received and paid can profit (or loss!) be calculated.

Calls for tighter regulation should therefore be considered in the light of the effect on competition. A difficult balancing act is required. It is this balancing requirement which prevents government simply increasing solvency requirements to the point where insolvency is all but unimaginable. That being said, the existence of EU legislation in this area constrains a member state as far as minimum standards is concerned, although it is of course permissible to take action before a company falls below this minimum standard. The implementation of Solvency II will, it is envisaged, reduce the risk of insurer failures, but only if enforced correctly. This greater protection will come at a cost. The worst case scenario is that the additional costs of tighter regulation will be incurred, but due to defective enforcement, the expected benefits will not materialise. It is to be hoped that the lessons of Equitable Life and, even more pertinently, the lessons learned from the effective collapse of the banking system just a few years after the Basel II regime was rolled out, will ensure that Solvency II delivers the promised improvements.

6   Lloyd's of London

Lloyd's is one the most famous names in insurance; it is also an entirely unique organisation with no real comparators anywhere in the world. It is not and never has been an insurance company. It is a market place, some would say in the modern era a franchise, and although this would surprise many people, it has never itself offered insurance cover. What it does is provide the facilities, administration, regulatory structure and perhaps most importantly the brand that enables its member firms to offer insurance. Lloyd's can be considered the insurance market in microcosm, embracing as it does so many aspects of general insurance under one roof. Many of the issues affecting the market as a whole are thrown into sharp focus when they affect Lloyd's.

The development of Lloyd's

The history of Lloyd's can be traced back to 1688, the first record of a coffee house owned by Edward Lloyd in Tower Street, London (moving to Lombard Street in 1691). It was common practice for coffee houses to be used as meeting places by merchants in those days. Most merchants operated as sole traders or small partnerships and needed a recognised meeting point to transact business. No limited liability marine insurance companies existed. Merchants spread their risk by means of a system of risk pooling whereby merchants took reciprocal stakes in each other's risk, thus spreading losses among their number. However, the late seventeenth-century 'professional' risk takers had emerged. Although they had no risk of their own to exchange, they risked their wealth to cover the risk of marine ventures, in effect, taking a stake in the venture without the complication of actually owning or operating ships. In order to achieve this profitably, they needed to develop expertise in this area, expertise that the merchants began to rely on. Before long it became accepted practice for a professional risk taker to decide if a risk was acceptable and at what rate and the non-professionals would follow the professional lead, writing their names under the leader, the origin of the term 'underwriter'.

To take advantage of this, Edward Lloyd started to cater for the professional insurer. A room was set aside in the coffee house exclusively for the transaction of marine insurance, imaginatively entitled 'the room'. Box-like wooden desks were installed to provide insurers with a regular 'office'. To attract custom, Lloyd started to provide shipping intelligence publishing *Lloyd's News*, a shipping information newspaper, in 1696. Although this did not last, it was followed in 1734 by *Lloyd's List*, London's and possibly the world's oldest newspaper. In addition, a system of 'runners' was implemented to carry up-to-date news from the docks to the coffee house. This support led to Lloyd's rapidly becoming recognised as the place to arrange marine insurance.

By 1769, many of the Lloyd's regulars had become concerned that as well as the reputable marine contracts, there were many gambling contracts being arranged and a breakaway movement appeared. They persuaded a Lloyd's waiter to establish a new Lloyd's coffee house in Pope's Head Alley. In 1771, 79 underwriters and brokers subscribed £100 each and founded the Society of Lloyd's, moving to the Royal Exchange in 1774, ending the coffee house link.

Throughout this period Lloyd's did not exist as an entity, it was never anything more than a meeting place. But in 1771, the new Society of Lloyd's elected a nine-man committee to oversee the market. Lloyd's still did not exist as a legal persona, but this was the first step in that direction and resulted in the eclipse of the old Lloyd's left behind following the 1769 split. This was assisted considerably by the *Life Assurance Act 1774* which prohibited wagering contracts.

Despite the election of a committee, this body had no legal powers. They relied upon the consent of the market participants and, if defied, could not directly take action. Of course the nature of the market was such that if other market firms refused to do business with a rogue firm, they would rapidly be driven from the market as their income dried up. This, however, was unsatisfactory, particularly when the transgression was slight. The committee therefore sought to gain legal authority for their rulings, achieving this by the *Lloyd's Act 1871*. Under this Act, Lloyd's became an incorporated body with the power to make byelaws. Initially the market was incorporated purely as a marine market, but this was extended to embrace 'insurance of every description' in 1911.

More than 300 years later, this system is substantially the same. There is still a Lloyd's building, insurance is still transacted in the 'room' and the market continues to operate on a system of lead underwriters and following underwriters, all operating from a 'box'. As well as the transaction of insurance, Lloyd's remains a world centre for shipping intelligence.

How Lloyd's works

Transacting business

Lloyd's underwriters do not do business with just anyone; all risks must be introduced by a Lloyd's broker, a special category of insurance broker (the exception to this rule is motor insurance). The proposer must approach either a Lloyd's broker or another intermediary who approaches a Lloyd's broker on their behalf. The broker then prepares a slip, a document containing details of the risk.

The broker's job is then to enter the market and find a lead for the risk, an underwriter who will accept the risk and set the rate of premium and terms. Traditionally, this involved brokers queuing to see an underwriter to discuss the risk on a face-to-face basis. Although this still happens, modern communications are far more likely to be used for routine transactions. It is possible that the lead underwriter will take the risk in its entirety. If the proposer accepts the terms, the broker returns to the lead underwriter and the risk is placed.

If the risk is large, however, the lead underwriter will only take a percentage of the risk, possibly only 1 per cent. The broker will then approach other underwriters with the lead and try to convince them to follow the lead underwriter, i.e. take additional percentages at the same premium rate and terms, known as lines. This process continues until 100 per cent of the risk is placed. It is possible that Lloyd's will decline to take the whole risk and the broker will then need to seek additional cover outside Lloyd's, probably with other insurance companies operating in the London insurance market, but possibly in the international market. This may appear an expensive way to do business, but the costs should only be a small percentage of a large premium.

The job of the Lloyd's broker is to find the right lead, an underwriter whose expertise in the type of risk proposed is recognised. If the lead underwriter's judgement is trusted, the market will happily follow. If not, the broker will probably struggle to 'fill the slip' as other underwriters decline to take a share of the risk. A feature of Lloyd's has been that underwriters are able to develop special expertise, often in fairly narrow areas of insurance. They would then be a natural lead underwriter for that type of risk. They can then diversify their business by taking follow lines on different risks, based not so much on their knowledge of the risk, but on their knowledge of the expertise of the lead underwriter. This has enabled Lloyd's to handle successfully a wide range of business.

In some cases where acceptance of the risk is all but certain, a binding authority may be given. In this situation, an underwriter or group of underwriters gives a broker permission to accept risks on their behalf and will never see the individual risks placed under this scheme. Of course criteria for acceptance will be laid down, however the underwriter will be bound by the broker's acceptance even when the criteria are not met. The underwriter may, however, be able to recover losses from the broker should this situation arise. The aim of this system is the reduction of underwriting costs for small premium, high volume transactions.

The financing of Lloyd's syndicates

Naturally the financial promises contained in these insurance transactions must be backed by capital resources. Most insurance companies are capitalised by their shareholders' investment (by the membership in the case of mutuals). Lloyd's' approach is unique. Lloyd's is a market, not a trading entity in its own right, it merely provides the environment for other parties to trade. The Corporation of Lloyd's does not provide any insurance; this ultimately is provided by Lloyd's Names.

Right from the early days Lloyd's attracted investment from persons unconnected with either the risks or the underwriting of risks. Their role was simply to put up capital in return for a share of the proceeds and it was this capital which guaranteed the policies written. A Name was an investor in the market. To become a Name, the investor had to demonstrate that they possessed wealth up to a specified sum. They could then transact business, with the important proviso that they did so with unlimited liability for loss. In the words of Lloyd's, they had pay down to 'the last collar stud' (subsequently changed to 'the last shirt button' to reflect changing sartorial standards). Today the position has changed with the introduction of corporate capital, discussed later in this chapter. Nonetheless the system of financial backing being provided by Names continues even though the nature of the Names has changed.

These external Names are represented by members' agents, whose role is to advise the Names and assist the Names in complying with the rules of Lloyd's. In many cases, the members' agent will also have recruited the Name to the market. There are also internal or working Names, who are actively engaged in the Lloyd's market as brokers, underwriters or managing agents.

Names band together in a number of syndicates. Such syndicates vary in size and could in the past have involved hundreds, even thousands of individual Names. In the days of corporate capital, Names can be limited companies rather than individuals and the number of Names on a syndicate is accordingly lower. The number of Names and their wealth determine the amount of premium the syndicate can write or the capacity of the syndicate as it is known.

Note that the liability of Names is several but not joint. No Name can be called upon to meet the liabilities of another Name even if they are both members of the same syndicate. If the Name is responsible for 1 per cent of the syndicate's capital, they cannot be responsible for more than 1 per cent of losses.

Syndicates are controlled by managing agents. They appoint underwriters to accept risks on behalf of the syndicate. They are also responsible for ensuring that the syndicate complies with regulations and pays claims and arranges reinsurance.

It is standard practice for a Name to spread their capacity between a number of syndicates offering different types of insurance in order to spread the risk. Lloyd's was traditionally a marine insurance market, however, in 1887, the first non-marine policies were written. In the modern era, it was first split into four distinct operations, Marine, Aviation, Motor and Non-Marine (which covers all other types of insurance). More recently, the huge non-marine side has been divided into Property, Casualty (mostly liability insurance) and Energy (oil, gas, power stations and the like). Reinsurance is now separately noted irrespective of sector, meaning that there are now seven sectors of insurance in the current Lloyd's market (Figure 6.1). Lloyd's offers all types of short-term business and has in the past offered life assurance, although never on a large scale.

Although back in the seventeenth century, investors had little alternative to investing on an unlimited liability basis, by the mid-nineteenth century, limited liability investment opportunities had become commonplace. Nonetheless the unlimited liability system at Lloyd's persisted until 1994 and remains in existence today, albeit greatly diminished in scale. The reason why Lloyd's were able to attract unlimited liability capital was the nature of the investment. Although Names had to demonstrate a minimum level of wealth, they did not actually have to pay it over. Therefore the same capital used to support investment in Lloyd's could be invested elsewhere. For example, the prospective Name's share portfolio would be quite sufficient to secure their entry to Lloyd's, even though they continued to own those shares and benefit from the dividends. It can be viewed as a form of leverage, the original capital is being used to increase the total investment. The advantage offered by Lloyd's is that no money need be borrowed and therefore no interest paid. As in any leveraged investment, the potential return is magnified. Of course, the risk is also magnified.

Currently, in order to invest in Lloyd's, capacity has to be purchased in an annual auction, effectively buying a place in a syndicate from a current Name. Capacity is the ability to accept premiums, so if a Name buys £1 million of capacity, this means that syndicate can accept up to £1 million in premiums on the Name's behalf. The cost of capacity will vary according to market conditions and the reputation of the syndicate and will be quoted as a percentage of the capacity value. The capacity is an asset and can be sold if the investor decides to leave Lloyd's, very possibly at a profit. Of course, if the syndicate were to fail, the capacity would be worthless.

The Name must then deposit the required capital. On average, this is likely to be around 40 per cent of the capacity. Lloyd's applies risk-based capital requirements. Therefore this percentage will vary according to the nature of the risks underwritten by the syndicate. So a stable, low volatility risk such as motor might require a deposit of around 30 per cent of capacity, while a highly volatile risk such as aviation or energy might require 50 per cent or more. The deposit must be in the form of readily marketable instruments, so shares or securities will do nicely. These are held in trust by Lloyd's who have first call on the assets in the event of the syndicate making a loss. Crucially, however, any interest or dividends earned on the assets belongs to the Name.

FLOW OF CAPITAL

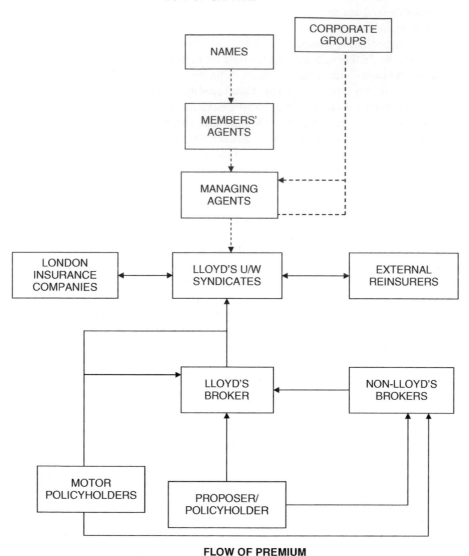

Figure 6.1 Capital and premium flows in the Lloyd's market.

Therefore, a Name possessing a capacity of £1 million might see an outcome as follows:

(a) Initial investment £400,000 (40 per cent of capacity) satisfied by the deposit of a portfolio of shares.
(b) £950,000 of premium is accepted in respect of the Names' capacity (note that it would be rare for the entire capacity to be filled).
(c) If the syndicate produces a return of 15 per cent, the Name would receive £142,500, a return of 35.6 per cent on the actual investment of £400,000. This is not unrealistic; in 2008, the return on capital was 13.7 per cent.

(d) If the share portfolio returns 8 per cent (£32,000), the Name will see an overall return of £174,500 or 43.6 per cent on their capital of £400,000.

Of course, if the syndicate makes a loss, these losses will be met from the deposit. If the Name is operating on limited liability the entire £400,000 is at risk. If they are operating on unlimited liability, they will have to meet their full share of the loss beyond the deposit they have paid, even if this means that they become bankrupt. The investor would also have to consider the cost of purchasing the capacity in the first place, which is over and above the capital deposit.

Prior to 1994, all Lloyd's capital was provided by individual unlimited liability Names. Since then, capital has increasingly been provided by a variety of corporate Names. These can be limited liability companies or limited liability partnerships (LLPs). Initially LLPs were established under Scottish law but since 2007, English LLPs established under the Limited Liability Partnership Act 2000 have been admitted. The term 'Name' has become confusing as a Name may well be a wholly owned subsidiary of a large insurance company, a limited liability investment company, a limited liability partnership or still a single individual.

Syndicate structure and accounting

A syndicate is traditionally the creation of a managing agent who attracts a group of Names who pool their collective capacity to provide the syndicate with sufficient capital to underwrite effectively. The managing agent appoints the underwriter and their team, who are responsible for the day-to-day insurance transactions. Most Names will be external, passive investors. In recent times, alternative structures have emerged. Where the Name is an insurance company subsidiary, the Name will control the syndicate which will be solely capitalised by that Name and they will obviously appoint their own underwriter.

A traditional Lloyd's syndicate is a single-year venture, beginning on the 1st January of each year. Technically the syndicate is dissolved at the end of the year and a new syndicate constituted the following day, even if the member Names remain unchanged. It is far more likely that some Names will have resigned and been replaced via the capacity auction. The calculation of profit or loss is, however, complex. At the end of the underwriting year, some of the policies will only just have commenced and will still have almost a year to run. For this reason, Lloyd's developed a unique accounting system whereby accounts were finalised after three years rather than at the year's end. This made it easier to arrive at a fair estimate of profit or loss and pay or issue demands to the Names as the case may have been. This system ended in 2005 and all syndicates now operate on an annual accounting basis, operating GAAP principles (see Chapter 4).

In order for a syndicate to distribute a profit, it must first be sure that a profit has indeed been made. As there can be no certainty that claims will not be made in the future on policies written in the syndicate year in question, such certainty is achieved by reinsurance. Called reinsurance to close, usually abbreviated as RITC, all future claims are covered by means of a single reinsurance premium. In many cases the next syndicate year would be the reinsurer, but cover could also be arranged elsewhere.

Security at Lloyd's

Policies at Lloyd's are secured by three layers of financial security (Figure 6.2). Initially losses are paid from syndicate assets, principally the premium funds, but reserves are maintained

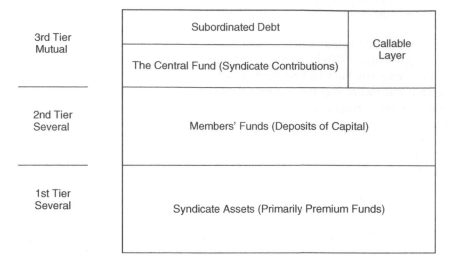

3rd Tier Mutual	Subordinated Debt	Callable Layer
	The Central Fund (Syndicate Contributions)	
2nd Tier Several	Members' Funds (Deposits of Capital)	
1st Tier Several	Syndicate Assets (Primarily Premium Funds)	

Figure 6.2 Lloyd's' capital base.

to meet shortfalls. Should this be insufficient, the Names must then contribute up to their capacity limit if operating on limited liability, or as far as is necessary, if they are operating on unlimited liability. If this proves insufficient, then the third tier of capital will be called into action. The first two tiers are several, the loss must first be met by the syndicate and its members according to their individual liability. The third tier is mutual and involves the Lloyd's community. This is based on the Central Fund.

The Central Fund was established in 1927 following the failure of the Harrison syndicate. The Names were unable to satisfy the liabilities and Lloyd's faced the prospect that claims might not be paid. Voluntary contributions were called for from the rest of the market and the claims were duly settled. Lloyd's then sought to prevent such ad hoc solutions in the future by raising an annual levy on the member firms, creating the Central Fund. Its express purpose is to settle policyholder claims in the event of syndicate failure. The fund is created by both syndicate contributions and subordinated debt issued by Lloyd's. In addition, Lloyd's can demand a further levy of up to 3 per cent of a member's premium limit to support the Central Fund, known as the callable layer.

The scope of Lloyd's operation

As stated above, Lloyd's is divided into seven sectors. Syndicates cannot be so divided as many will write business in more than one sector. Marine, aviation and motor remain distinct, while non-marine is divided into property, casualty and energy. Finally there is the reinsurance sector which includes risks from all of the other sectors. Together they produced annual premium income of almost £18 billion in 2008. Lloyd's is an important global market for marine and aviation risks, even if it is no longer the largest. The non-marine side has long specialised in handling difficult or unusual risks, again with a distinctly international flavour. The motor syndicates handle all aspects of motor risks but again with a bias towards the unusual as well as a strong involvement in commercial motor fleets. In addition, there is a significant amount of reinsurance transacted at Lloyd's,

35 per cent of all Lloyd's premiums which accounts for approximately 5 per cent of the global market.

In 2008, the remaining 65 per cent was divided between the six sectors thus:

Marine	8 per cent	Property	22 per cent
Aviation	3 per cent	Casualty	21 per cent
Motor	5 per cent	Energy	6 per cent

Lloyd's' operation is noticeably global. Currently approximately 78 per cent of its premium income comes from outside the UK. When you consider that almost all the motor insurance premium is derived from the UK, this becomes all the more striking, as roughly 82 per cent of non-motor premium comes from abroad.

The single most important market for Lloyd's, however, is North America, which accounts for 44 per cent of premiums. The USA has proved a source of significant income over the years. Unfortunately it has also proved the source of some heavy claims as well.

The strengths and weaknesses of Lloyd's

The original business model that led to the pre-eminent position of Lloyd's within the world of insurance has led to an insurance market that displays peculiarities, to say the least, in comparison with the structure that has more generally emerged. There have been advantages and disadvantages arising from the unique manner in which Lloyd's does business.

Strengths

1 *Security* – the promise by Lloyd's that Members will pay down to the last collar stud is borne out by the fact that valid claims on its policies have always been met in full over a period of over 300 years. Compare this to a limited liability company where shareholders can always choose to cut their losses, liquidate the company and lose only the value of their shareholding. Although the introduction of corporate regulation might be seen as diminishing this security, so far this has not affected the culture of Lloyd's that valid claims must be paid. Indeed, the reputation of Lloyd's was founded on a willingness to pay, best illustrated by a now famous telegram sent by its most famous son Cuthbert Heath to the Lloyd's agent in the immediate aftermath of the 1906 San Francisco earthquake. It simply stated 'Pay all our policyholders in full irrespective of the terms of their policy.'

2 *Globalisation* – Marine insurance is by its nature international. In servicing this business, Lloyd's developed a network of agents, correspondents and contacts throughout the world allowing them not only to attract business in other insurance areas, but to ensure that their exposure is well spread. It is indeed arguable that Lloyd's were the first global insurer.

3 *Specialisation* – the expertise of Lloyd's in marine insurance has long been acknowl-edged. This formula has been repeated, making Lloyd's a leading global market in a number of areas such as aviation and political risks. In modern parlance this is known as niche marketing.

4 *Boldness* – For many, Lloyd's conjures up an image of stuffy traditionalists operating a public school closed shop. In fact, Lloyd's has always been innovative in approach, leading the way in the development of many classes of insurance and thereby securing

a healthy market share of new markets. This is a result of the structure of Lloyd's. The lack of central management of underwriting allows syndicates to operate in a relatively unrestricted fashion, while their insurance company counterparts may be stifled by corporate attitudes and regulations.

Weaknesses

1   *Unlimited liability* – Although providing security for the policies offered, it also led to problems when Names suffered large losses. The understandable protests by Names were newsworthy, which only served to draw public attention to the fact that Lloyd's was losing money and implied that the Names might refuse to pay. This only served to unduly reduce confidence in Lloyd's despite the fact that the insurance companies were also losing money, many of whom were far more likely to fail than Lloyd's.
2   *Fascination with the USA* – It can be argued that Lloyd's is overly exposed to US risks in the non-marine area and has been for many years. Many of the storms that have battered Lloyd's have blown in from the other side of the Atlantic. Although the demand for non-marine insurance especially is high in the USA and has led to strong growth in premium income, it has all too often proved unprofitable.
3   *Boldness* – While boldness is one of the virtues of Lloyd's, it is also one of its vices. While some new ventures have been spectacularly successful, others have been just as spectacularly disastrous. This is an inevitable problem with new insurance products as the prior experience which is fundamental to cautious underwriting is simply not available.
4   *Market efficiency* – In the days before modern communications, the concept of grouping together a large number of underwriters in a single building served by teams of brokers, gathering daily to feed them business, was a business model that gave Lloyd's a competitive edge. This advantage was eroded by the development of an efficient postal service and the telephone. Once computers, fax machines and e-mail arrived, the idea of brokers queuing to speak to individual underwriters began to look outdated and excessively expensive.
5   *Market regulation* – Lloyd's has historically been relatively free and easy where the conduct of its members was concerned. There is the view that Lloyd's admitted them because they were gentlemen and they were then trusted to act like gentlemen. To be fair, many were and did. As will be seen, far too many rogues slipped through the net with distressing consequences.

Regulation of the Lloyd's market

The Lloyd's Act 1871, passed in the mid-Victorian age, continued to regulate the market until the latter half of the twentieth century. Regulatory power was vested in the Committee, the membership of which was drawn exclusively from the ranks of the internal names. By the 1970s, the committee comprised 16 members, mostly drawn from the underwriting side (one of whom would be the Chairman of Lloyd's) with limited representation from the brokers and members' agents. Of course this meant that the committee members were required to regulate their own firms, not to say themselves. It is, however, probably fair to say that despite the questions that this raises, Lloyd's did enjoy an excellent reputation for stability and probity. Unfortunately a string of very public scandals in the 1970s and 1980s indicated that the committee's supervisory regime was far from robust.

There was also the question of the capital structure of Lloyd's. In 1969, Lord Cromer, a former governor of the Bank of England, chaired an enquiry into this structure at Lloyd's, producing a report that made five major recommendations. This report was not published at the time. The first and second recommendations were that unlimited liability should remain, but that 'mini' Names should be permitted. In other words the demonstrable wealth required should be lowered allowing the not especially wealthy to become Names. These recommendations were adopted, but a recommendation that Lloyd's should consider corporate capital was rejected as impractical. Recommendations that managing agents' remuneration should be reduced to fairer levels and that brokers should not be permitted underwriting interests were also rejected. It is ironic that the recommendations adopted played a part in the near destruction of the Lloyd's market, while those rejected were all subsequently implemented after costly lessons had been learned.

The Sasse affair

The syndicate operated by Frederick 'Tim' Sasse was the first to cause major concern. This was a small syndicate with only 110 Names and therefore limited capacity to withstand major loss. In late 1975, Sasse sought to issue a binding authority to an American broker, allowing them to issue cover on his syndicate's behalf. The practice is known in the market as 'handing them your pen', an apt description as the syndicate would be bound without sight of the risks in advance. The use of non-Lloyd's brokers was permitted if they were sponsored by a Lloyd's broker and Lloyd's gave approval. In this instance, Lloyd's had reservations and refused such approval. This naturally should have been the end of the matter; however, Sasse simply changed the name on the binding authority to an associated company of the broker and allowed them to proceed. The amended binding authority was never submitted to Lloyd's for approval as it should have been. Had it been, there seems no question it too would have been rejected. Reinsurance cover on the business to be produced was obtained from IRB, the Brazilian state reinsurance company.

Rumours began to emerge of policies at Lloyd's being offered on properties in run-down inner city areas in the US at premium rates that might be regarded as not far short of suicidal. Reports were made to Lloyd's lawyers in New York in April 1976. Some business had been placed in March, but the bulk of the premium did not arrive until May. There was therefore the opportunity to act before serious loss was caused, but unfortunately no such action was taken. As Sasse had not registered the binding authority, there was no link to his syndicate and it appears to have been assumed that the policies were not in fact written at Lloyd's.

By June, it was clear that premium written on the binding authority was far in excess of what Sasse expected (much of which was never actually received by the syndicate). He should have withdrawn the binding authority immediately. It was not actually cancelled until 31st July and business was still permitted to be written up to 31 August.

By this time it was clear that large-scale losses were likely; however, a problem existed. As the binding authority had not been approved, any policies written under it were not approved Lloyd's policies. Nonetheless the syndicate had signed the binding authority. The proper course of action should have been to suspend the syndicate immediately and hold a full investigation. The Lloyd's committee instead sought to remedy this by ordering that the binding authority be retrospectively approved although they knew that market rules had been broken and that had the binding authority been submitted in advance, it would not have been approved. Neither did market rules permit retrospective approval. Sasse was allowed to continue underwriting and it was not until December 1977 that the syndicate was finally suspended. There is an implied suggestion that the Lloyd's committee appeared to think that the reinsurer would meet most of the loss and the whole affair could be quietly hushed up. IRB, however, quite reasonably voided the reinsurance policy on the grounds that Sasse had failed to disclose that the binding authority had not been approved.

The losses on the binding authority were appalling, indeed there is a strong suspicion of organised crime involvement in what might be considered a calculated insurance fraud. The overall loss to the 110 Names was in the order of £15 million in 1976 and £7 million in 1977. Lloyd's sent the bill to the Names on the Sasse syndicate and demanded payment. The Names refused on the grounds that while they had agreed to ordinary risks of insurance losses on properly written polices, they had not agreed to pay losses arising from the failure of Lloyd's to properly regulate its members. Lloyd's promptly sued them. After a bitter (and very public) dispute Lloyd's offered partial settlement and paid 60 per cent of the 1976 loss and the whole of the 1977 loss out of the Central Fund. This still left the Names with a loss of £6 million and posed serious questions about the conduct of the Lloyd's committee.

Howdens and PCW: the Gang of Four and the Dodgy Duo

To become embroiled in one scandal may be deemed a misfortune but to get entangled in a second seems like carelessness. Nonetheless the dust had barely settled on the Sasse affair before a second and far more damaging problem emerged in 1982.

At its heart was the failure of Lloyd's to implement the Cromer Report recommendation that brokers and managing agents should be kept separate as the cross-ownership of broking and underwriting created a conflict of interest. It is the broker's job to secure the lowest premium possible for the policyholder, while the underwriter seeks to maximise the premium for the benefit of the Names. While negotiations should not quite be adversarial, they should at least be at arm's length.

Many Lloyd's market firms at that time operated as both managing agents and brokers, allowing complete control over the insurance transaction to be vested in the hands of the senior directors of such firms. The result was that individual chairmen could, by utilising a combination of broking muscle and tame underwriters, seize control of the flow of premium. The firm's brokers could be directed to the firm's underwriters, who in turn could be influenced to accept a large line. Given such control over premium flow, a further more damaging possibility emerges. The director of a managing agent could seek to influence where the syndicate placed its reinsurance.

Two tame underwriter relationships became particularly notorious. Ken Grob, the Chairman of Howdens and his underwriter Ian Posgate, and Peter Dixon of Minets and the underwriter Peter Cameron-Webb. Following the sale of Howdens to the US broker Alexander & Alexander in 1982, auditors discovered that $55 million had been transferred from Howdens syndicates into offshore companies controlled by four directors or senior officers of Howdens. These transactions were described as reinsurance but were paid to companies not authorised to transact insurance and on such disadvantageous terms to the syndicate that they immediately appeared suspicious to the auditors. A & A went public, accusing Howdens' directors and officers of appropriating the money for their own purposes. Lloyd's subsequently expelled Ken Grob, Ronald Comery and Jack Carpenter of Howdens from the market for misappropriation of funds and false accounting. A fourth director, Allan Page was not charged due to ill health (these less than savoury characters became collectively known as the Gang of Four). Ian Posgate was expelled but received a six-month suspension on appeal. Grob and Posgate were subsequently acquitted of fraud in a criminal trial, the others being found to be unfit to stand trial due to their state of health. The purchase of Howdens caused Alexander & Alexander huge losses which led some years later to their acquisition (or merger as it was officially described) by Aon. Much of the loss, it must be said, arose on Howdens' interests outside Lloyd's, in particular the insurer Sphere Drake.

While auditing the Howdens' accounts, further suspicious transactions came to light involving Peter Cameron-Webb's PCW syndicates. Again, the cloak of reinsurance was used to disguise the transfer of funds to offshore companies in which Dixon and Cameron-Webb had an interest, under which large 'premiums' were paid with little chance of significant claims being made. This case also revealed a further fraud, the misuse of 'baby' syndicates with only a handful of Names. Dixon and Cameron-Webb set up two syndicates for the benefit of themselves and their immediate cronies (each syndicate had just seven Names). The very best business would be diverted to the 'babies' which were unsurprisingly far more profitable than the main syndicate. These were by no means the only baby syndicates at Lloyd's. Although it cannot be said that all were intentionally fraudulent, there can be no justification for insiders making private arrangements away from the syndicate proper. Dixon was fined and expelled by Lloyd's while Cameron-Webb resigned before proceedings could commence. The PCW syndicates faced unquantifiable losses. Lloyd's were forced to intervene and cover most but not all of the Names' losses. Such was the uncertainty that Lloyd's established a long-term run off company, Lioncover, to manage the run off of the PCW syndicates.

To complete Lloyd's' humiliation, the Chairman Sir Peter Green was found to have reinsured his syndicate with an offshore company in which he had a stake (albeit a minority interest). Although he had already resigned as Chairman, he was subsequently censured and fined by Lloyd's.

The Sasse affair was a major reason for the commissioning of the Fisher Report, published in 1982. The Howdens and PCW debacles led to the Neill Report, published in 1987. Both considered the regulatory structure of Lloyd's. The primary findings of the Fisher Report concluded that:

1   A new governing council should be established with representation for external Names and the public (i.e. policyholders).
2   The creation of an investigation and disciplinary panel.
3   Council control over the activities of underwriters and brokers.
4   Repeating Lord Cromer's finding, there should be divestment of broking and underwriting activities.

The Neill Report further suggested:

1   Greater information to be provided by syndicate accounts.
2   Reducing the influence of working Names on the Council.
3   A new complaints and arbitration system.
4   Revised agreements between managing agents and Names, standardising charges and introducing deficit clauses requiring managing agents to compensate Names for loss before paying themselves profit commission in the succeeding two years.
5   Clearer rules for syndicate access.
6   More onerous registration processes for managing agents, brokers and auditors.

Reform of Lloyd's

In the light of these embarrassingly public scandals, it was clear that a major reform of the structure and regulation at Lloyd's was required. In any event, this would have been required due to the *EU Non Life Directive (73/239)* which gave rise to the *Insurance Companies Act 1982* (which did not cover Lloyd's). The Fisher Report was available and influenced the new regulatory structure for Lloyd's. The reform was contained in the *Lloyd's Act 1982*, the main provisions of which are as follows:

The establishment of the Council of Lloyd's with the powers to make byelaws regulating the conduct of Names, brokers and underwriting agents. Essentially this added eight external Names and three appointees who could not be Lloyd's Names to the pre-existing 16-member Lloyd's committee. Lloyd's would select the appointees, but the Governor of the Bank of England would have to approve them. The Chairman and his two deputies would be internal Names. The byelaws did not have to be agreed at the annual general meeting as previously, thus allowing a more nimble response in a crisis.

A Disciplinary Committee and Appeals Tribunal were established to determine and enforce sanctions and penalties against transgressing Names, brokers and underwriting agents. The Act gave them power to fine or expel members of the Lloyd's community and award costs. The Act gave the Council the discretion to set up a separate arbitration panel to hear disputes relating to the business of insurance at Lloyd's.

Ownership or interest in both broking and underwriting interests at Lloyd's was prohibited (although a minority shareholding of less than 5 per cent was allowed). Market firms therefore had to decide whether to underwrite or broke, they could no longer do both. To avoid the provision being sidestepped, 'individual' was extended to mean an individual's spouse, children or trustees. Therefore transferring shares to a family member and exerting control through them would not be possible.

Section 14 granted the Society of Lloyd's immunity from suit in the manner that it exercised its powers unless the Society acted in bad faith (i.e. fraudulently). This only extended to the Lloyd's community and did not grant immunity from actions by policyholders. It is only fair to point out that the government enjoyed similar, indeed wider, immunity as regulator of the wider insurance industry and it would hardly be fair to expect Lloyd's to accept a liability that the government would not accept in similar circumstances.

This Act did indeed remedy some of the defects highlighted by the Sasse affair. A committee that was arguably slow or indeed perhaps reluctant to act against one of their own could now be held to account by the external Names and appointees on the new Council. The Council might be less concerned with protecting the reputation of Lloyd's than protecting the interests of Names or policyholders. The Council could through the arbitration and disciplinary processes determine disputes internally at far less cost to all concerned and could dispense punishment where deemed appropriate.

Further reform

In the immediate exercise of their new powers and in the wake of the Neill Report, further reforms were introduced by the Council via byelaws. In 1983, with remarkable prescience, they gave themselves the power to suspend one of their own members. The Chairman at the time was Sir Peter Green who resigned shortly afterwards, arguably in order not to become the first victim of the byelaw.

The constitution of the Council was changed several times, but with the overall aim of providing adequate representation for the three main constituencies, the market firms, external Names and policyholders. The principle would in future be that no one group could hold a majority. Today there are six internal Names, six external Names and six appointees.

New regulations governing submission estimates of proposed premium income for the forthcoming underwriting year were enacted. The intent was that the risk of 'overwriting' (accepting more premium than the capital base permits) be minimised. Further syndicate accounting regulations governed the required accounting standards. This included a requirement to provide details of reinsurance cover including policy wordings.

In January 1988, the first members' ombudsman took office to hear non-monetary complaints from Names against the Society of Lloyd's (excluding the Disciplinary Committee or the Appeals Tribunal). Later an arbitration system for compensation claims up to £100,000 was introduced to recommend compensation packages to the Council where losses arose other than in the course of normal underwriting.

Underwriting agents were required to disclose transactions with other parties in which the agents or individuals connected with the agent have an interest. This must be shown in the annual report to members of the syndicate. This would include multiple agencies, i.e. involvement in other Lloyd's syndicates and interests in external Reinsurers.

New registration processes were introduced giving Lloyd's greater control over entry to the market by managing agents and brokers.

A broker's code of conduct was produced. This quite properly stressed that the client's interests were paramount, but brokers must have 'proper regard for others'. Brokers were required to disclose to the client any additional remuneration (i.e. related reinsurance commissions). Brokers were instructed to advise clients regarding the principle of utmost good faith and could decline to act for a client if they felt this was not complied with and should then 'consider' obligations to insurers or regulators.

Lloyd's had existed for many years with minimal supervision, in effect, complete self-regulation. The losses and frauds of the 1970s and early 1980s meant that self-regulation looked perilously close to no regulation. The 'old boy network', while workable in principle, had been proved to be an unrealistic form of regulation in the modern financial markets. While still based on self-regulation, the new system was at least more robust. Unfortunately once again, as soon as a problem appeared to be solved, a new and even greater storm struck the market.

The Lloyd's crisis, 1988–1992

No sooner had Lloyd's taken steps to rectify the regulatory failures in order that the risk of future scandals would be reduced, than another far more serious crisis emerged. This crisis threatened to destroy the Lloyd's market. Although the activities of many Lloyd's professionals had badly damaged the reputation of Lloyd's for financial probity and although the members of individual syndicates had suffered as a result, the overall market had been profitable. Indeed, prior to 1988, Lloyd's had made an overall profit in every year except 1965 for as far back as anyone could remember. Even the 1965 loss was easily explained as heavy losses were caused when New Orleans was flooded due to Hurricane Betsy, regarded as the first ever $1 billion insurance loss.

However, in 1991, Lloyd's reported an overall market loss of £509 million for 1988 and it was clear that worse was to come (Figure 6.3). Over the next four years Lloyd's suffered overall losses amounting to a further £7.4 billion. This is the problem with a three-year accounting period. It makes it difficult for investors to get out at the first sniff of trouble. By the time losses are announced, they are already committed to a further three years of

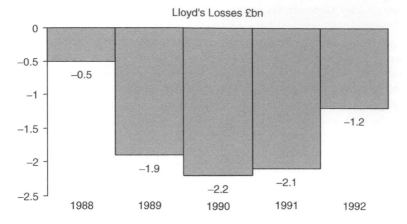

Figure 6.3 Lloyd's losses, 1988–1992 (£bn).

underwriting (indeed, more than two years of underwriting will already have taken place). Even if a Name then seeks to resign, they remain liable for their involvement in any 'Open Years', where the accounts cannot be closed for a particular year due to outstanding claims which cannot be reinsured to close. They must remain a member until the year is closed and their debt is paid. They are not though required to actively participate and will often be unable to if their losses are such that they can no longer provide the financial security required.

Lloyd's Names were then faced with losses totalling £7.9 billion in just five years, announced between 1991 and 1995. Put another way the 32,500 Lloyd's Names faced an average loss of over £50,000 per annum for five years. These losses were not, however, evenly spread. Half of Lloyd's 400 syndicates were profitable throughout most or all of this period. The motor syndicates were generally profitable and most of the marine and aviation syndicates produced respectable results with just the occasional disappointing year. The losses were largely concentrated in the non-marine sector and even then fell disproportionately on a small number of syndicates. Particularly affected were the Gooda Walker, Feltrim, Merretts and Outhwaite syndicates. It is noticeable that these syndicates had a large number of Names, many of whom had been newly recruited and did not have years of past profits to cushion the blow.

Between 1975 and 1987, the number of Names had expanded dramatically, from around 6,000 to 32,500. Lloyd's had, during this period accepted Names from outside the UK and Commonwealth for the first time. Although Names historically were seriously wealthy, many of the new recruits were not in this league and indeed some had total available assets of only £100,000. The unlimited liability of the Names meant that these losses threatened to bankrupt many of them. Tragically, a number committed suicide.

Causes of losses at Lloyd's

In the general blame game that followed a financial disaster of such magnitude, many were keen to attribute the results to single causes, specifically the single cause that most suited their position. The reality was that there were four major contributory factors.

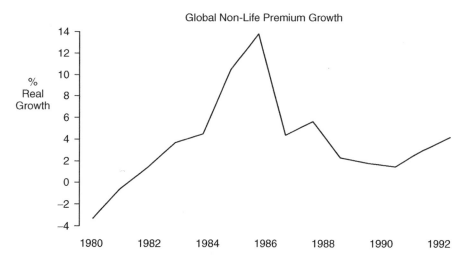

Figure 6.4 Global non-life premium growth, 1980–1992.
Source: Data obtained from Swiss Re Sigma Research.

Economic factors

There is no doubt that the losses at Lloyd's coincided with a period of over-capacity in the global insurance market. The insurance market has long struggled to maintain equilibrium between the demand for insurance and the market's capacity to supply that demand. The result was 'hard' and 'soft' markets (see Chapter 5). As can be seen in Figure 6.4, in the mid-1980s, premiums were growing strongly due to a lack of available insurance capital. Naturally insurance was perceived as a profitable investment bringing a commensurate increase in capital available. As this fresh capital was deployed, the supply of insurance increased and premium growth fell sharply after 1986 as the insurance 'commodity' became less rare. Effectively, the insurance market was writing the same risks for less money during the soft market that persisted from 1988 to late 1992. This problem was exacerbated by the 1990/1991 recession which led to further downward pressure on premiums due to reduced economic activity which meant that there was less business to be insured.

The Lloyd's market therefore saw a reduction in both insurance rates and available business during the 1988–1992 period, but without an equivalent reduction in the rate of loss. There is no correlation between recessions and hurricanes. There is, however, a known correlation between economic recession and *increased* rates of arson and theft. These economic factors meant that 1988–1992 were never going to be particularly profitable for Lloyd's, but they do not explain the level of loss experienced.

Catastrophes

Catastrophe losses refer to single events which cause either a single huge loss or more commonly an accumulation of very large numbers of small losses. They included weather-related losses such as storms and floods, natural disasters such as earthquakes and man-made disasters which would include industrial fires, terrorism and war. The period 1988 to 1992 saw an unusually high number of catastrophe losses. Indeed, the average rate of catastrophe

Table 6.1 Average annual losses, 1973–1992

Period	Average annual loss ($ bn)
1973–1977	6.6
1978–1982	7.7
1983–1987	10.3
1988–1992	27.2

Source: Swiss Re Sigma Research (*sigma No. (2/2009)*). All figures are rebased to 2008 price levels for comparison purposes *not* to values at the time which would have been considerably lower.

loss over this five-year period was very significantly higher than previous five-year periods (Table 6.1).

Given that the global insurance market was growing in real terms over this period, an increase in loss levels would be anticipated. After all, there is a strong correlation between the premiums received and claims made in the long term, as additional premium (after allowance for inflation) in the long term indicates new policies, extended cover or higher values insured (in the short term, this may only indicate fluctuations in pricing levels). The increase in catastrophe losses in 1988–1992 was, however, far greater than the increase in premiums during the period. Indeed, as can be seen, premium growth was sluggish over this five-year period.

Most losses involved non-marine business, however the Gulf War (1990/1991) saw a number of serious aviation and marine losses. In March 1989, the tanker *Exxon Valdez* was wrecked off Alaska, causing the biggest oil spill in US history.

Catastrophes affecting the non-marine market included those shown in Table 6.2 (note that the cost given is the total; Lloyd's were only liable for a percentage of these losses, albeit a high percentage in some cases).

Some catastrophe losses are only to be expected as, after all, that is what the insurance industry is there for. However, during the period 1988 to 1992, Lloyd's were undeniably unlucky.

Table 6.2 Global catastrophes, 1988–1992

Catastrophe	Year	Approx. cost ($ bn)
Piper Alpha oil rig	1988	2
Hurricane Gilbert	1989	1
Philli Petroleum Refinery fire (Texas)	1989	1
Hurricane Hugo (Eastern USA)	1989	4
UK subsidence losses	1989 to 1991	3
Oakland earthquake	1989	1
Northern Europe storms (4 in total)	1990	8
Forest fires (California)	1991	1
Typhoon Mirielle (Far East)	1991	7
Hurricane Andrew (Eastern USA)	1992	17
Los Angeles riot	1992	1
Baltic Exchange bomb, London	1992	1

Note: These are broad estimates of the cost at the time. Such events would be much more costly were they to occur today.

In particular, they had promised the Names that 1992 would see a return to profit and for most of the year it appeared that this promise would be fulfilled. Then, in August 1992, Hurricane Andrew struck. One of only three category 5 hurricanes to hit the US mainland in the twentieth century, Andrew was so powerful that the maximum wind speed is not known as the measuring devices were destroyed! Hurricane Andrew was at the time the most costly insurance loss in history and caused widespread destruction in Florida in particular.

Long tail liabilities

There was, however, a more invidious problem that had lain dormant at Lloyd's for decades. This was brought about by the manner in which liability policies were written. Although policies are issued for a period of one year, there are two conflicting views as to precisely what this period constitutes. The policy might cover all incidents occurring during the period irrespective of when the actual legal action is commenced (known as an occurrence wording). Alternatively, the policy may only cover legal actions commenced and claims actually made on the policy during the period of insurance, irrespective of when the incident giving rise to the claim took place (known as a claims made wording).

The big advantage of the claims made system is that this year's premium pays this year's claims. The insurer can therefore predict profit or loss at the end of the year with reasonable confidence. On the other hand, the policyholder cannot be sure that they have adequately insured their activities for that year as they must continue to purchase insurance. As soon as they cease paying premiums, they will be liable themselves for any future losses that may come crawling out of the woodwork.

An occurrence wording, on the other hand, provides reasonable peace of mind for the policyholder. Having insured a particular period, all incidents that occurred during that period would be insured even if the actual claim is not made until many years into the future. It follows therefore that the policyholder's peace of mind must be the insurer's uncertainty. At the end of the period the true profit or loss is difficult to calculate as the insurer cannot know how many claims will be faced in the future. In addition the effects of inflation may significantly increase the size of the claim rendering the premium charged hopelessly inadequate (and it must be said causing problems for the policyholder if the limit of indemnity is also inadequate).

Although most legal systems have limitation periods (rendering invalid legal actions not prosecuted within a certain number of years), claims can in practice be made decades after the incident took place. Under UK law, the claimant has three years to make a claim from the date they had knowledge of their potential right of action. In many cases knowledge will coincide with the incident; however, if the case involves industrial disease, this may not be the case. It may be 20 or 30 years after exposure that the disease materialises. The claimant will then have a further three years after diagnosis to make a claim. These types of claim are known in the insurance market as incurred but not reported claims or IBNRs. What is meant is that the incident giving rise to the claim has occurred, but the insurer and very possibly the third party as well do not yet know that the incident has occurred.

Back in the 1950s and 1960s, Lloyd's insured a number of firms involved in the manufacture and use of asbestos, both in the UK and elsewhere, with particular exposure in the USA. At this time the dangers of asbestos were not well recognised, however it unquestionably is the cause of a variety of serious lung conditions and cancers. Death all too frequently results from exposure to asbestos fibres. The problem, however, is that asbestos-related diseases can take 30 years or more to develop, so it was not until the 1970s and 1980s that the claims started to be made. The insurance was offered on occurrence wordings and as the risk often involved employee injury, the policies were often written on an unlimited liability basis (the standard practice in the UK until relatively recently). Syndicates found themselves potentially liable for an infinite amount for an infinite period. Also, by this time, not only were the awards made by the courts vastly higher than they would have been when the policies were written, but the claimant was much more likely to win. The result was that Lloyd's syndicates found themselves liable for losses on policies written decades in the past to the tune of billions of pounds. There are still INBRs being reported today on policies written 40 years ago or more.

In the 1970s and early 1980s, the asbestos claims were of manageable proportions, around 2,000 per year. In 1987, the number of claims increased sharply and by the 1990s was running at over 20,000 per year. Although this could not be known at the time, the annual rate of claim peaked around the year 2000 at 60,000.

As soon as these policies were written, a time bomb began ticking, even if this was not realised at the time. However, the purpose of insurance is to spread risk. This is not only achieved by primary insurance, but this risk is further spread by reinsurance. Effective reinsurance could have lessened the blow as far as Lloyd's was concerned. Unfortunately when put to the test, Lloyd's syndicates found that their reinsurance arrangements were seriously flawed.

Defective reinsurance

As discussed above, reinsurance to close (RITC) was a feature of syndicate management. It was common practice for many syndicates to buy RITC cover from the next syndicate year. Therefore the 1980 year would be reinsured by the 1981 year which would then in turn be reinsured by the 1982 year. The problem with this arrangement is that the 1982 year is not only reinsuring the 1981 year. As the 1981 year is liable for the 1980 IBNRs, the 1982 year is also covering the 1980 year as well. In some cases syndicates had been rolling up the liabilities for decades via RITC. When the asbestos crisis hit in the late 1980s, the current year could be liable for 30 years or more of accumulated liabilities. The syndicate years had been playing an extended game of pass the parcel with the asbestos time bomb. When the time bomb detonated, its full effect was often felt by a single syndicate year. The only way to avoid this problem was to reinsure outside the syndicate, assuming that such reinsurance would be available.

Certain syndicates specialised in offering RITC to other syndicates. Prominent among them were Gooda Walker, Feltrim, Merretts and Outhwaite. The result was that rather than spreading risk, the RITC system had the effect of concentrating it in a small number of syndicates which promptly collapsed under the weight of claims leading to appalling losses for their Names. This is exactly what happened in the Credit Default Swaps market in recent years, where the risk was overly concentrated at AIG and but for government intervention on a massive scale would have caused the collapse of the company. Again a device that was supposed to spread risk had only concentrated it. Sadly for the Names on the above named syndicates, no government intervention was forthcoming.

The problem was not limited to these four syndicates, however, as those syndicates who reinsured elsewhere found that they were not as well protected as they thought. This was due to the operation of London Market Excess of Loss reinsurance or LMX as it was known. This was a system whereby one syndicate reinsured losses above a certain level with another syndicate. This reinsuring syndicate then reinsured its excess loss with a third syndicate and so the process went on until everyone was reinsuring everyone else. The fatal flaw in the system was that when syndicate A claimed from syndicate B, it sparked off a series of

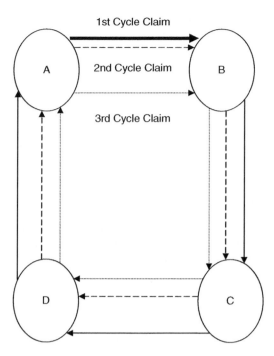

1st Cycle Claim

2nd Cycle Claim

3rd Cycle Claim

Figure 6.5 The LMX spiral.

claims across the market as syndicate B claimed from their reinsurers. All too often syndicate A would receive claims arising from the claim they themselves had originated. This could trigger a further claim from syndicate A and the whole merry-go-round began revolving again, a process now known as the LMX spiral (Figure 6.5). Because commission was paid on each transaction, a considerable percentage of the original premium had leaked away in the myriad LMX deals, thus reducing the ability of the overall market to meet the loss. The system also led to non-marine losses contaminating the entire market as syndicates outside the non-marine sector wrote LMX business. The essential problem was that reinsurance business was being reinsured (known as retrocession). Therefore each contract picked up risk not just from the syndicate reinsured but all the syndicates they had reinsured. This highly unpredictable mix was then passed on to another reinsurer. The problem has since been fixed by excluding all retrocessional cover on excess of loss reinsurance written in London (i.e. the policy only responds to claims on the insurance policies written by the reinsured, not on policies written by other insurers). However, the genie was out of the bottle well before this cork stopped it off.

By 1990, more than 16 per cent of all business at Lloyd's was no more than incestuous inter-syndicate reinsurance swaps. The large numbers of policies in existence could lead to absurdities in the way that the market reacted to major losses. By way of example, Lloyd's' actual exposure to the Piper Alpha disaster was approximately $1.5 billion. Due to the LMX spiral, the *apparent* claims (including all the reinsurance claims submitted between syndicates) were reported to be $15 billion!

Lloyd's did not seem to question whether or not the exposure was too great for the Lloyd's market to handle. If the surplus risk had been reinsured outside Lloyd's in the

London company market, then the damage to Lloyd's could have been reduced. Better still a proportion of the risk should have been ceded to the international reinsurance market, reducing the overall exposure in London.

The litigation

Clearly it could not be expected that Names would accept losses of this magnitude without protest. The protests were loud and *very* public and inevitably proceeded to the courts. Litigation fell into two categories. First, there were actions by the Names alleging negligence and/or fraud against their syndicates. Second, Lloyd's commenced actions for debt recovery against the Names. There were potentially enormous numbers of cases, raising the possibility that irrespective of the outcome, Lloyd's, its constituent firms and the Names would all be bankrupted by the legal costs, let alone the claims from policyholders.

Lloyd's did of course have the Central Fund, funded by levies on the syndicates. Its stated purpose was to guarantee the policies at Lloyd's by meeting the cost of claims only in the event of a syndicate's insolvency. Therefore it was initially intended that this fund would be used only after the Names had contributed to the full extent of their wealth. The Sasse and PCW scandals had forced Lloyd's to use the funds to assist Names, but both cases involved fraud. Now for the first time Lloyd's were forced to consider using these funds to assist un-bankrupted Names where fraud had not been proven (although alleged).

Although strenuously defended, Lloyd's were seeking an out-of-court settlement from an early stage. Essentially they were treating all the individual actions as one huge class action and attempting to reach agreement with as many Names as possible in one settlement. As early as 1993, a settlement offer of £900 million was made to 23,000 Names in respect of losses occurred up to 1990. Half of this was to come from Central Fund. Much of the rest came from the professional indemnity insurers of the underwriters and managing agents facing legal actions (ironically much of this business was placed in Lloyd's causing further losses for many Names!). Only around £50 million was to be contributed by managing agents directly. This settlement offer was rejected by the Names.

Realising that prospects for a successful defence of the legal actions by the syndicates were not good, Lloyd's made a further attempt to settle in May 1995. The overall offer was more than tripled to £2.8 billion, involving a considerably larger contribution from market firms, this time including brokers and members' agents. Again this was not accepted by the Names.

By now, however, the legal actions were reaching their conclusion. In a string of cases, Names successfully sued their syndicates for negligence (but not fraud). Examples include *Arbuthnot & Others v Feltrim (1993)* and *Deeny & Others v Gooda Walker (1994)*. Awards of hundreds of millions of pounds were won in some cases. In October 1995, the Names on the Merretts, Feltrim and Gooda Walker syndicates were successful in a conjoined action in the House of Lords which dismissed the syndicates' appeals against the earlier judgments (*Henderson & Others v Merrett Syndicates (1995)*). Unfortunately for the Names, almost before their celebratory hangovers had cleared, Lloyd's claimed the sums awarded in partial settlement of the Names' debts and added it to the Central Fund. Lloyd's argued that the payment of policyholders' claims was the overriding duty of all members of the market. No money could be released to Names until such time as the policyholders' claims had been settled.

It could be argued that these cases and the subsequent action by Lloyd's introduced a dose of much needed common sense to the warring parties. Clearly Lloyd's were going to have to come up with a realistic settlement offer. On the other hand individual Names were going to be unable to obtain a quick personal settlement and walk away from the market leaving the other Names to pay the bill.

In May 1996, an increased offer of £3,100 million was tabled, quickly increased to £3,200 million. This settlement would provide the Names with reinsurance against future liabilities, but would also end present and prevent future litigation. The matter was put to a vote and the offer was accepted by 94 per cent of Lloyd's Names. It involved contributions from the Central Fund, professional indemnity underwriters, managing agents and other Lloyd's firms. Note, however, that considerable losses were still sustained by the Names.

Lloyd's now had to deal with two issues, either of which had the potential to destroy the market if mishandled. First, having indemnified the Names, the outstanding liabilities had to be met if policyholder confidence in the market was to be maintained. Second, having caused so much financial damage to their Names, Lloyd's' capacity had been eroded as many Names were forced to resign, being unable to demonstrate the required wealth any more. Many Names who did possess the wealth left anyway, put off by the damage done to the reputation of Lloyd's as a sound investment proposition. Lloyd's desperately needed to attract fresh capital if they were to continue to write the large insurance risks they had become famous for. Bankrupting many of their previous investors could be considered as an impediment to this aim, particularly given the continuing problems of long tail liabilities and the LMX spiral. The process by which these twin problems were dealt with became known as Reconstruction and Renewal.

Equitas

Lloyd's themselves were well aware, however, that the long tail liabilities had not gone away and that a solution to the problem was needed. They were equally aware that replacing the departing Names' capacity would be impossible if new investors faced the possibility that they might be called upon to pay large losses from prior years.

The solution was to divide the operation into an 'old' Lloyd's and a 'new' Lloyd's and construct a firewall between the two. In order to achieve this, a reinsurance operation, Equitas, was established to reinsure all policies written prior to 1993. The settlement offer made to Names went to bankroll this operation, which promised to allowed them to finalise their open years and walk away, supposing of course that Equitas succeeded in meeting the liabilities.

Equitas is a single-purpose, run off reinsurance company. It received a single (rather substantial) premium at the outset and was then tasked with meeting all liabilities on all open years at Lloyd's prior to 1993, in effect, a vast RITC policy. The settlement offer, plus the total reserves of all syndicates relating to pre-1993 years, plus the reinsurance cover written on those years were pooled, together with the Names' outstanding contributions. As a condition of DTI approval, Equitas had to maintain a solvency margin of £500 million, Lloyd's had to stand as guarantor that contributions from Lloyd's market firms were received, and be prepared to inject further capital into Equitas should it prove necessary. As both assets and liabilities were likely to fall as claims were settled, the solvency requirement as a percentage of assets could be expected to rise steadily throughout the run off process.

Equitas commenced the run off in September 1996 to produce total assets of around £15.5 billion. This was set to be the largest insurance run off in history. Its scope was widened in 1998 when Lioncover, the reinsurer covering the run off of the PCW syndicates was transferred to the control of Equitas.

There was considerable uncertainty surrounding the operation. All Equitas projections were based on assumptions. Assumptions as to the number and timing of future claims. Assumptions as to the future reinsurance recoveries and collection of Names' contributions. Assumptions as to levels of future investment income. As Equitas was a reinsurer, in the event of failure, claims would revert to the syndicates reinsured and the Names providing the backing for such syndicates. Equitas did not offer the Names any guarantee. Furthermore, as time went by, the position was likely to become more uncertain due to the nature of the claims being made. At the outset in 1996, long tail liabilities, known as asbestos, pollution and health claims (APH) represented about 40 per cent of total claims. As the shorter tail claims were settled, so this highly uncertain class grew in importance, reaching 70 per cent of claims by 2001 and 80 per cent by 2003. Nonetheless, despite criticisms and predictions of swift financial disaster, Equitas managed to keep the run off process on a stable footing for the first ten years of operation. As can be seen in Table 6.3, liabilities were steadily reduced while the surplus was maintained at around the £500 million level.

By March 2006, Equitas had settled claims amounting to £17 billion and had recovered £7 billion in reinsurance recoveries. The liabilities stated above are the discounted liabilities and are calculated before taking into account reinsurance recoveries. When Equitas began, the liabilities were almost 26 times the surplus and even a small increase of 4 per cent in the liabilities would have wiped out this surplus. Ten years later, liabilities were nine times the surplus, a much healthier state of affairs.

In October 2006, a deal was announced which was intended to bring an end to the Equitas run off. The US insurers, National Indemnity (part of the Berkshire Hathaway Group) agreed to reinsure all Equitas liabilities (effectively taking over their responsibilities), provide a further $7 billion of reinsurance cover and take on the Equitas staff and operations. This involved handing over all of Equitas' reserves (less £172 million to cover costs) and an additional reinsurance premium of £72 million payable by Lloyd's. The deal was finalised in March 2007.

The second phase involved transferring the liability of the Names to Equitas Reinsurance Ltd. At this time Lloyd's contributed a further £18 million, and took up an additional $1.3 billion of reinsurance cover made available by National Indemnity for a premium of £40 million. Under this transfer the Names would no longer have any liability to the syndicate's policyholders as a matter of law. Policyholders' rights cannot be arbitrarily removed and this required the approval of the courts under s111 of the *Financial Services and*

Table 6.3 Equitas liabilities and assets in the run off

Date	Liabilities (£bn)	Surplus-assets in excess of liabilities (£m) (%)
Sept. 1996	14.9	580 (5.6)
March 1998	11.5	718 (8.5)
March 1999	10.3	772 (9.6)
March 2000	9.0	784 (11.2)
March 2001	8.9	700 (9.5)
March 2002	7.8	679 (10.3)
March 2003	7.0	527 (8.7)
March 2004	5.3	460 (9.8)
March 2005	4.4	476 (12.2)
March 2006	4.2	458 (12.0)

Markets Act 2000. The proposed transfer of liability was considered by the court and approval given in June 2009. The need to satisfy the court that policyholders' interests were properly considered was a major factor in the large amounts of additional reinsurance cover purchased. The relatively low premiums indicate that National Indemnity consider the possibility that Equitas Reinsurance Ltd may fail in the future to be very low. It is also worth considering just how valuable a right to recover from the Names actually was, given the length of time that had passed. According to Equitas, as of 2009, 6,806 pre-1993 Lloyd's Names had died and they were unable to trace a further 5,182. This transfer finally brings the crisis at Lloyd's to an end from the perspective of the Names. The run off though continues, possibly for many years to come. The risk, however, lies primarily with National Indemnity. Given the additional $8.3 billion of reinsurance, the Equitas liabilities would have to increase massively before the solvency of Equitas Reinsurance Ltd would be endangered and it is highly improbable that this could occur in the short or even medium term.

Continuing litigation

The Reconstruction and Renewal plan, the establishment of Equitas and the settlement offer made in 1995 to the Names were intended to end litigation. It was not entirely successful, although Reconstruction and Renewal did reduce the number of litigants from many thousands to a few hundred. Despite the fact that the overwhelming majority of Names accepted the settlement offer, 1,752 refused. Although a number subsequently came to an arrangement with Lloyd's, a hard core held out. They tended to be those Names who were unduly exposed to loss and/or were overseas Names.

There were frequent attempts to involve courts in other jurisdictions, particularly the USA. Although some rulings in favour of the Names were secured in State courts, the Federal court consistently overruled such decisions on the grounds that the matter lay within the jurisdiction of the English courts.

Pursuit of the syndicates was by now pointless. Most of the worst affected were insolvent and Lloyd's would unquestionably have laid claim to any award as before. The result was a string of cases against the Society of Lloyd's itself. The problem for the Names was that s14 *Lloyd's Act 1982* clearly gives Lloyd's immunity of suit unless they have acted in bad faith. The only recourse was to allege fraud on the part of Lloyd's.

An action was duly brought specifically alleging fraud, *Jaffray & Others v Lloyd's (2002)*. Neither the High Court nor the Court of Appeal was prepared to make any such finding. However, the argument raised by the *Jaffray* claimants was controversial and is not lightly dismissed. The core allegation was that in the 1970s and 1980s, Lloyd's, recognising that huge asbestos liabilities were likely to be incurred in the future, embarked on a massive recruiting drive with the aim of attracting new Names to meet the liabilities that their membership at the time could not have paid. What was termed the 'recruit to dilute' allegation. Furthermore it was alleged that market insiders dumped these liabilities on unsuspecting new Names, while ensuring that their own syndicates were free of such embarrassments.

Certainly the membership of Lloyd's did increase dramatically during this period (from 7000 in 1975 to 32,500 in 1988). It is equally the case that recently recruited Names were proportionately far more numerous on the syndicates facing the worst of the asbestos losses, many of which had assumed such liabilities due to RITC and LMX cover offered to other Lloyd's syndicates. In their evidence, the *Jaffray* claimants alleged that the average loss for internal Names was £120,000 and while external Names generally faced average losses of £263,000, the *Jaffray* claimants faced average losses of £469,000. Although embarrassing for Lloyd's, none of this is conclusive of fraud. Lloyd's could fairly argue that the purpose of recruiting additional Names was to expand the market and secure a fair share of a growing global insurance market. Newly recruited Names will tend to end up on either newly formed syndicates or expanding syndicates as the established syndicates were already adequately capitalised and had no need of the new recruits. Market insiders will always tend to be better informed than outsiders. One would expect those working in the stock market to enjoy better returns than external investors, for example, simply because they are closer to the action and benefit from better intelligence. Internal Names were far more likely than external Names to arrange personal stop loss reinsurance, thus limiting the extent of their loss.

But the most difficult hurdle for the *Jaffray* claimants to clear was the question of the identity of Lloyd's. Fraud is an offence of human commission. Where a corporate body is considered to have acted fraudulently, it is because individuals working for that corporation have acted fraudulently. Furthermore, these individuals have to be at a sufficiently senior level that their fraud can be imputed to corporation. For this to be conclusive, the individuals have to represent the controlling mind of the corporation. In the case of Lloyd's, the controlling mind was the Council. As the majority of the Council were either external Names themselves or appointees with no connection with Lloyd's, the court was unlikely to accept that the Council was implicated in such a fraud without incontrovertible evidence. The appointees stood to gain nothing and the external Names would have been acting contrary to their own interest. Even if it was established that individual internal Names did follow a 'recruit to dilute' policy (and the court made no such finding), this did not mean that the Society of Lloyd's had acted fraudulently.

Nonetheless, the judgment was certainly embarrassing for Lloyd's with the courts strongly critical of the way in which Lloyd's had regulated the market. Lord Justice Waller stating:

> So many syndicates were shown to be massively under-reserved … the system simply had not been producing reasonable estimates of outstanding liabilities over the years … It follows that the answer to the question … namely whether there was in existence a rigorous system of auditing which involved the making of a reasonable estimate of outstanding liabilities including unknown and unnoted losses, is no. Moreover the answer would be no even if the word 'rigorous' were removed.

Lord Waller did not though find that Lloyd's had acted in bad faith and the operation of section 14 denied the Names a remedy for the negligence that was found.

The matter did not rest there. An attempt was made in *Society of Lloyd's v Levy & Others (2004)* to hold Lloyd's liable for failing in their duty to regulate the market, exercising delegated powers from the Government under EU Directive (73/23). This failed as the Directive clearly gave no direct rights to investors and Lloyd's was not considered to be a public body. In *Society of Lloyd's v Henderson (2007)*, a claim for misfeasance in public office failed. Lloyd's had exercised powers delegated by the Dept of Trade and Industry, but this did not make them a public body. In *Harris v Society of Lloyd's (2008)* a further attempt was made to raise allegations of fraud which were duly struck out as the matter had been considered in *Jaffray* and were time barred anyway. In September 2008, a civil restraint order was granted preventing Names from bring any further actions against Lloyd's without the permission of the court. The matter may now be presumed to be laid to rest.

Corporate capital

Having dealt with the question of the outstanding liabilities via Equitas, Lloyd's then needed to address the issue of re-capitalisation. As might be expected, in the aftermath of the crisis years, large numbers of Names ceased to be participating members of Lloyd's (although they could not actually leave until any open years were finalised). If Lloyd's was to continue, new capital would be required to replace this lost capacity. There was little chance of attracting private investors to risk unlimited liability investment, therefore the only alternative would be to break with 300 years of tradition and allow investment on a limited liability basis. In 1994, Lloyd's permitted corporate Names to enter the market for the first time.

In just four years from 1994, corporate capital grew from zero to 60 per cent of Lloyd's' capacity. The number of corporate Names increased from 140 in 1995 to 435 in the same period. Throughout the period, Lloyd's' capacity remained static at around £10 billion; however, this then started to increase steadily. In 2008, Lloyd's' premium income was almost £18 billion. The number of active syndicates reached a peak of 400 in 1988. Today 80 are in business, but are on average considerably larger and therefore arguably more stable.

As can be seen in Figure 6.6, Lloyd's is primarily capitalised by the insurance industry. Just 15 per cent of total capital is provided by individuals and only 6 per cent by unlimited liability names. Just 703 unlimited liability Names remain in 2009 as active underwriting members as opposed to 1,238 corporate Names. It is, however, noticeable that the remaining unlimited liability Names do have significantly greater capacity than previously (in 2009, around £1.5 million each on average), suggesting that it is only the seriously wealthy that are continuing to underwrite. Given that Lloyd's are no longer accepting new unlimited liability Names, their numbers are set to dwindle still further, until eventually they are consigned to history as their membership is definitively terminated by death. Lloyd's has tried in the past to end unlimited liability investment, but has been defeated by the Names, who are after

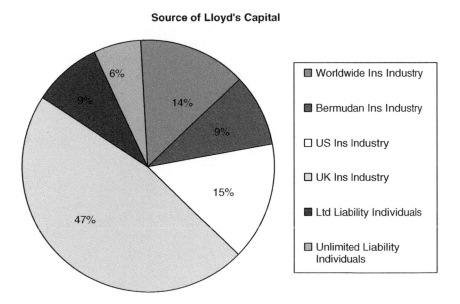

Figure 6.6 Source of Lloyd's capital.

all members of the Society and unprepared to vote for their own demise. This is what is commonly known as individual freedom.

Lloyd's has emerged from the crisis with their capacity not only intact, but enhanced. Most of the capital is now provided by the insurance industry and the remaining individual Names have demonstrated an ability to withstand loss-making periods and are certainly not wide-eyed innocents. It is therefore arguable that the quality of the capital has increased along with the quantity.

The future of Lloyd's

Since the crisis years Lloyd's may have recovered strongly, however not entirely smoothly. Benefiting from a hardening market, Lloyd's posted healthy results from 1993 to 1996. However, 1997 to 2001 saw a return to heavy losses. In fact, the losses totalled £8.72 billion, more than in the crisis years. It should be pointed out that the World Trade Center attack was a major cause of the record £3.11 billion loss in 2001. Since then the market has been highly profitable on the whole, posting record profits in 2008 of £3.84 billion. The only blemish was the 2005 year, when a small loss of £0.1 billion was posted due to the inundation of New Orleans by Hurricane Katrina.

Over the period 1988 to 2008, Lloyd's made an accumulated profit of £540 million, an average profit of £25.7 million per annum (Figure 6.7). This could be viewed as disappointing given the billions of pounds of capital deployed. Alternatively it could be said that Lloyd's made a loss of £12.84 billion from 1988 to 2001 and a profit of £13.38 billion from 2002 to 2008. The market could fairly be said to have been in need of modernisation in 1988, which led to an extended period of poor results as Reconstruction and Renewal took place. Perhaps the excellent figures of recent years indicate that this modernisation has been successfully concluded.

The transfer of the troublesome long tail liabilities into Equitas was certainly advantageous. However, the market has been more resilient in the face of catastrophe in recent years. 2004 was a bad year for catastrophe loss, with Hurricanes Ivan and Charley and the Asian tsunami. Lloyd's still managed to post reasonable profits. In 2005, Hurricane Katrina was

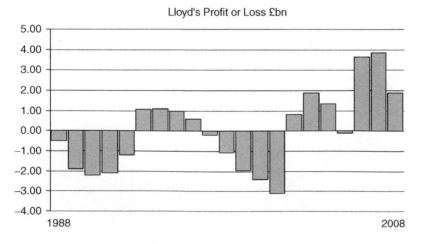

Figure 6.7 Lloyd's profit or loss, 1988–2008 (£bn).

even more damaging, yet Lloyd's posted a small loss. This compares favourably to 1992 when Lloyd's lost £1.2 billion due to Hurricane Andrew. Perhaps this is evidence of increasing professionalism among present Lloyd's Names and maybe the lessons of the LMX spiral have been heeded.

There can be no question that the reputation of Lloyd's suffered considerable damage as a result of the crisis years. In addition, the structure of Lloyd's has changed almost beyond recognition with the traditional names all but disappearing and corporate capital now dominating. The apparent success of Equitas leaves Lloyd's free to concentrate on the future rather than the past. The question is what is that future?

E commerce and the London market

The London financial markets have in recent years become almost entirely computerised. The stock market, for example, has switched to electronic trading. Some may lament the passing of traditional floor trading. There was no doubt considerable entertainment value to be gained from the sight of testosterone-fuelled men (and a few frankly equally testosterone-fuelled women) in garish blazers frantically barking at one other. The greater efficiency of the electronic trading platform is not to be denied, however. Shipping, foreign exchange and the commodities have followed suit. Banking transactions are equally computerised.

The insurance market is now the only major London financial market that is not automated. It must in fairness be said that insurance is far more difficult to automate due to the complex and varied nature of the products it offers. Several initiatives, involving major insurers and brokers have been piloted, but all have so far have failed to produce a single market system. Lloyd's are now trying once more with their Lloyd's Exchange system. If the admittedly significant problems can be overcome and the world's first computerised insurance trading platform can be established, London may regain some of the ground that it has lost to Bermuda and other offshore locations. The initial success of Lloyd's was due to the efficiency of the original coffee house model. That efficiency was eroded by modern technology and if it is to be regained, this technology must be harnessed.

7   Reinsurance

Reinsurance emerged at much the same time as the ancestors of modern insurers. Certainly reinsurance was a feature of the early medieval marine insurance markets as a means of further spreading what were the major insured risks of the day. However, coinsurance whereby insurers took a small proportion of the policy was a much more common method of spreading risk, with Lloyd's being an excellent example of this approach. Modern reinsurance practice, however, owes its origins more to the development of reinsurance of fire risks in the first half of the nineteenth century. Many of the early initiatives were taken by German insurers at a time before specialist reinsurers had appeared. This process was given impetus by a disastrous fire that destroyed a wide area of Hamburg in 1842, leading to the establishment of Cologne Reinsurance in 1846, the first specialist reinsurer.

In the UK, reinsurance was certainly practised in all major classes of business. Note that the seminal case *Dalby v India & London Life Assurance (1854)* concerned a reinsurance contract, not the original life policy which was no longer in existence. Again, it took a major disaster to prompt the development of a more formal market for reinsurance risk. In 1861, a huge fire engulfed a number of warehouses in Tooley Street, London. Insurance losses were appalling, leading to the introduction of the Fire Offices Committee and major reforms in the underwriting of fire insurance, including rules governing the arrangement of reinsurance. It cannot be entirely coincidental that in 1867 the Reinsurance Company Ltd was founded in London. Lloyd's rapidly followed, with the great Lloyd's innovator Cuthbert Heath writing the first reinsurance contracts in the 1880s.

As industrial development gathered pace in the twentieth century, so the demand for insurance grew. As the insurers' exposures grew, so did the demand for reinsurance, until the point was reached whereby the insurance market could not operate in its present form without the backing of the reinsurance market.

What is reinsurance?

Insurance is usually termed a risk transfer mechanism. As discussed in Chapter 1, this is questionable description as often the process is one of risk spreading rather than transfer. The law of large numbers dictates that the larger the common pool, the more predictable will be the result and therefore the risk associated with administering the pool is reduced. It is therefore in the insurers interests to create the largest common pool economically possible. There is, however, a limit to how quickly they can achieve organic growth within their own pool. In order to gain immediate benefit from the principle of the maximised pool, they must combine their pool with similar pools operated by other insurers.

The common pool concept is then taken to a higher level with the creation of a pool whose members are all insurance companies and the common risk transferred to the pool is the risk associated with administering the subsidiary insurance pools. This pool in turn needs an administrator, termed a reinsurer. Note that a reinsurance-based common pool is not formed simply by combining all the subsidiary pools into one 'super pool'. All that is being transferred is a proportion of the risk associated with administering the insurance pool and the insurer retains the responsibility for this subsidiary pool. Therefore, the predictable losses will be retained and the less predictable outcomes reinsured. This might be large single losses, an unexpected increase in the number of losses or even the deterioration in annual results brought about by a combination of factors. Just as the policyholder insures against the possibility of unexpected disaster, so does the insurance company. By way of example, a motor insurer would not be likely to seek reinsurance cover against ordinary claims arising from motor accidents. The bulk of the premiums charged would be retained to meet this liability. They may though reinsure against the possibility of very large third party claims, perhaps involving multiple deaths and/or injuries. While fortunately rare, the potential costs could be millions of pounds. Similarly, life assurers will not seek protection against predictable death claims. They may, however, reinsure the possibility that a number of policyholders are killed by the same event (a natural or man-made disaster) or against an unexpected rise in deaths due to an epidemic. Alternatively if a policyholder insures for an unusually large amount, they may seek to spread the risk of the early death of this one individual.

An alternative way of looking at the process is to consider the reinsurer as a wholesaler of insurance, 'selling' insurance to insurers who then offer insurance retail to the end consumer (or policyholder). This model relies upon looking at the generation of capital by the reinsurer as the 'production' of insurance. This model is conceptually harder to grasp as insurance is not a tangible product and it is not therefore possible to see a flow of insurance from reinsurer to insurer to policyholder (although the flow of premium in the opposite direction can be tracked). However, all insurers require the capacity to accept risk, but that capacity is limited by the capital they possess. By accessing the greater capital resources of the reinsurance market, they can significantly increase their own capacity. In some cases the insurance contract (retail) *predates* the reinsurance contract (wholesale). This is further complicated by the fact that many reinsurance contracts do not directly follow any underlying contract. However, the existence of the reinsurer makes it possible for the insurer to offer cover either because they can arrange cover in advance or they can use reinsurance to deal with subsequent difficulties.

The purpose of reinsurance

Capacity

One driver of demand for reinsurance is capacity. The ability of an insurer to accept risks into its pools is limited by the need to guarantee the solvency of the pool which in turn is limited by the financial reserves of the insurer. An insurer cannot prudently accept a risk if the possibility exists that acceptance of the risk will pose a serious threat to the reserves. Therefore no insurer would be prepared to risk losing more than a very small percentage of their reserves due to any single claim. Therefore if an insurer was unwilling to risk more than 0.25 per cent of reserves and the reserves totalled £500 million, their capacity for a single risk would be £1.25 million. If a potential policyholder wished to insure a factory worth £3 million, the insurer would not be able to handle the transaction. Reinsurance permits the insurer to accept the risk in its entirety, secure in the knowledge that the excess risk of £1.75 million can be passed to a reinsurer.

Catastrophe protection

The most basic function of insurance is to guard against financial catastrophe and insurers need protection in this area as well. Although they can ensure that the individual risks accepted are such that they are within the insurer's capacity, *accumulations* of loss can ruin these efforts. For example, an insurer without a wide geographical spread to its business may find that a significant proportion of its policyholders may be affected by a single storm, an arguably fundamental risk. A large number of claims on low value policies could accumulate to the point where the total cost of the insured event amounted to a catastrophic loss to the insurer. In addition to reinsuring individual risks, cover is available to insure events such as storms or floods that can cause this accumulation effect.

Loss spreading and stabilisation

Although avoiding losses that might compromise solvency is the priority, proprietary insurers do need to consider the demands of their shareholders. Investors are more likely to favour a company that produces good steady returns than one that lurches from triumph to disaster one year to the next. Although an insurer is in a better position than the policyholder to predict the distribution and likely cost of losses, there is still uncertainty in this area. Just as the policyholder seeks to reduce this uncertainty by means of accepting a small certain loss in exchange for an uncertain, possibly larger loss, so does the insurer. By purchasing reinsurance, a smoothing effect can be achieved whereby a share of the profits from a year when the claims environment is benign, can be exchanged for a share of the losses in the years when claims are heavier. The result ought to be a more predictable outcome, purchased at a known and presumably affordable cost.

Many insurers operate in one country or even in just one part of a country. As such, they vulnerable to natural disasters or downturns in insurance trading conditions affecting their domestic markets. Ideally a wider spread of risk should take place. The reinsurance market is international and allows risks to be spread into a global rather than domestic market, providing maximum smoothing of losses as premiums from one part of the world can be used to meet unexpected loss levels in another region. It is not unheard of, although less common than it was, for two insurers operating in different regions or markets to enter into a mutual reinsurance swap. These reciprocal deals allow the insurers to swap a proportion of their risks in order to diversify their portfolio of risks.

Confidence

A move into a new market is a dangerous time for an insurer. They rely on claims data often generated over many years in order to correctly price their policies. Clearly if the market is new to the insurer, they do not have the security of this experience and mistakes can prove expensive, damaging the insurer's capital base and possibly forcing an ignominious retreat. By heavily reinsuring in the early years, they can enter a new market confident that they are protected against unacceptable levels of loss. As they gain experienc, the amount of reinsurance can be scaled back to a level commensurate with the capacity of the insurer. In addition, the reinsurance rates may give them a good indication as to the adequacy of their own rates. If reinsurance seems expensive or is declined, it is probable that they are under-pricing the underlying insurance.

Regulatory compliance

As seen in Chapter 5, the minimum capital requirement an insurer is required to hold is affected by the degree to which they reinsure their business. The legal minimum requirement can be reduced by up to 50 per cent if suitably reinsured, allowing the insurer to accept twice the amount of premium income that their capital reserves would permit if not reinsured at all. This is of course subject to the insurer meeting the claims basis test and other provisions introduced in addition to the legal minimum requirement. This gives the insurer a much broader spread of risk and due to the operation of the law of large numbers, ought to produce a more predictable underwriting result. Additional reinsurance purchase can also be an alternative to increasing capital if growth in premium income outstrips existing capital. With the introduction of Solvency II, the simple test will be replaced with the own risk and solvency assessment. Nonetheless, insurers that retain most or all of their risk will be required to hold greater levels of capital than reinsured firms. On the other hand, reinsured firms now have to consider the credit risk. The impact of reinsurance on solvency requirements will not in future be as easy to see, but it will continue to be influential.

How insurance risks are spread

Reinsurance is not the only part of the risk spreading process. First, a number of insurers may combine to write a single large risk or a large number of small risks as part of an insurance scheme. This is known as coinsurance. This is best illustrated at Lloyd's, where as discussed in Chapter 6, the usual practice is for a risk to be underwritten by a number of syndicates, each taking a percentage. This is, however, also a well-established practice among insurers generally.

The insurer may then decide that although they only have a percentage of the risk, this is larger than they are prepared to retain. They will then choose to reinsure the excess risk, ceding a proportion of the risk to the reinsurer. The reinsurer may in turn feel that their capacity does not allow them to retain the whole of the ceded risk and may look to arrange a retrocessional cover whereby they retrocede a percentage of the risk to a retrocessionaire. A retrocessionaire is another reinsurer, and the term denotes that they have reinsured a reinsurer rather than an insurer. The resultant insurance structure is demonstrated in the (highly simplified) Figure 7.1.

By utilising coinsurance, reinsurance and retrocession, the insurance market spreads a large exposure into a number of smaller exposures with no single insurer or reinsurer liable for more than their safe capacity. In reality, the spread of risk on a very large single risk would involve many more participants. It would not be unusual to see 30 or more reinsurers and retrocessionaires taking a share of a single risk that might cause a claim of several billion.

It must be stressed that each contract is entirely separate. Therefore each coinsurer is independently liable for their coinsurance proportion. They are not liable for the failure of another coinsurer to meet their share of any loss. Similarly, the reinsurance contract is separate from the insurance contract. If the reinsurer fails to meet their liabilities, this does not relieve the insurer of any liability to the policyholder. The credit risk arising from the reinsurance contract lies with the insurer. Similarly, the reinsurer must accept the credit risk that comes with a retrocessional contract.

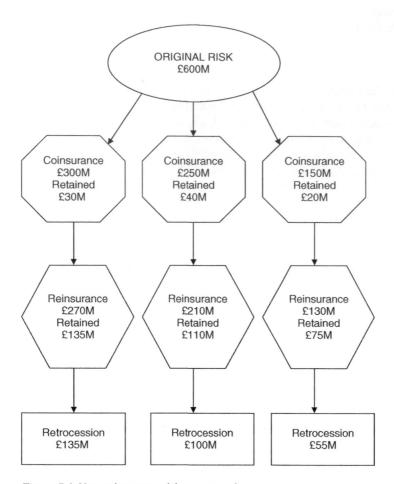

Figure 7.1 How reinsurance risks are spread.

Although a considerable proportion of the premium paid, possibly the great majority, is passed to the reinsurer, the policyholder generally inherits no rights under the reinsurance contract under English law. In the event that the insurer should fail, the receiver will invoke the insurer's rights under the reinsurance contract and recover any amounts owed. The amounts recovered will not, however, be passed to the policyholder but will be added to the general pool of assets. The policyholder will then be paid as an ordinary creditor usually receiving only a percentage of the value of their claim. The *Insurers (Reorganisation & Winding Up) Regulations 2004* at least prioritise insurance debts over other unsecured creditors; however, as the insurance debts are likely to account for the great majority of debts, this means that this will probably not make a big difference to the percentage recovered.

One possible problem is caused by the 'pay as paid' clause common in reinsurance contracts. Under this clause a reinsurer is only liable once the insurer has actually settled the claim to the policyholder. If an insurer is insolvent, they are obviously unable to settle and it has been argued in the past by (frankly less than honest) reinsurers that they were relieved of any obligation to pay under this clause. This is no longer the case; in the event of insurer insolvency, reinsurers are obliged to settle to the receiver once the liability of the insurer is established, not withstanding the 'pay as paid' clause. Reinsurers are generally entitled to offset any outstanding premium that the insurer may owe them.

Some policies may contain a 'cut through' clause allowing the policyholder to claim directly from the reinsurer, bypassing the insurer. The effect of such clauses would be to place the policyholder in an advantageous position in comparison to other creditors as they could recover the whole amount of their claim even where the insolvent insurer is only able to pay, say, 50 per cent of claims. This is in conflict with the basic principle adopted by the courts that all creditors should take a proportionate share of any loss, the *pari passu* principle as it is known. For this reason such clauses may well be considered invalid. In many countries relevant insolvency law will prevent their enforcement. It is, however, arguable that in some cases they may be upheld depending upon the wording of the clause and the situation. If the insolvent insurer is a 'fronting' insurer, the argument becomes more persuasive. In a fronting arrangement, the policyholder and reinsurer agree that an insurer will issue a policy and then cede 100 per cent of the risk to the reinsurer. The insurer charges a fee for the service but does not assume any risk, meaning that the reinsurer is the true risk bearer. This can occur for example where the class of insurance is compulsory and the reinsurer is not authorised to write such business in the particular territory. This situation is particularly likely to occur when the insurer is a captive insurance company (see Chapter 14 for an explanation of the structure and operation of captives). Although the *Contract (Rights of Third Parties) Act 1999* allows the policyholder to be specifically named in the policy as a beneficiary, this would clearly conflict with the provisions of the *Insolvency Act 1986* which confirms the *pari passu* principle. The effectiveness of cut through clauses is uncertain.

Methods of reinsurance

Although reinsurance in practice can appear fiendishly complicated, the basic theory is surprisingly simple. There are only two major methods of reinsurance: treaty and commission.

Treaty

Most treaties are agreed in advance of the year's underwriting by the two parties. The insurer agrees to cede and the reinsurer agrees to accept any insurance written by the insurer that falls within the scope of the treaty. The treaty will obviously set clear criteria in order that it can be established what must be ceded and also what the reinsurer is obliged to accept. Naturally the treaty will specify the class of business to be covered. Limits may be imposed on the nature of the risk, the sums insured or the domicile of the policyholder. Any policy falling within the scope of the treaty is automatically reinsured, any policy falling outside the scope will not be covered.

Under a treaty, the reinsurer will never see individual risks in advance, but will receive notification after cover has commenced. Statements are sent from the insurer on a monthly or perhaps quarterly basis detailing the new policies reinsured. It may even be, if the policies are low value, that broad statements of premium income are provided rather than individual risk details. The statement will also detail the claims paid and the reinsurer's share thereof. A reconciliation of premiums and claims will be provided and the insurer or reinsurer will pay the balance as the case may be.

The primary advantage of this method is that it is cheap to administer. The underwriting cost for the reinsurer is low, leaving more resources available for claims payments. Where there is a need to reinsure large numbers of low value policies, it is the only viable method.

From the perspective of the reinsurer, a treaty provides a spread of business with no 'selection'. Selection occurs when the insurer chooses only to reinsure the poorest risks while keeping the best for their own account. The compulsory nature of treaties eliminates this possibility. On the other hand the reinsurer is reliant upon the underwriting skill of the insurer, as once the treaty is in force, they will be bound without having had prior sight of the risks to be reinsured. Considerable attention will be paid by the reinsurer to the underwriting policy, underwriting team and prior performance of the insurer before entering into the agreement. The terms of the treaty can control the underwriting activities of an insurer. If a small premium policy is offered to the insurer, falling outside the terms of the treaty, they will probably decline to offer cover. The policy would not be reinsured and the costs of arranging such cover would be prohibitive in comparison to the likely premium. It is worth noting that even a private motor policy is capable of producing claims running into many millions of pounds.

Facultative reinsurance

As discussed above, treaties will impose limitations on the size of risk that can be transferred and often exclude certain kinds of risk. These can still be covered on an individual basis by means of facultative reinsurance. In facultative reinsurance, the insurer is free to decide which risks will be ceded and the amount of risk to be ceded. The reinsurer is then free to decide whether or not they wish to accept and at what terms. Obviously the transaction cost will be much higher, therefore such cover is unusual outside the field of commercial and transportation insurance, although very high value life assurance policies may well be covered on a facultative basis. Equally important is the time factor. The insurer will not want to issue cover until they are certain that reinsurance arrangements are in place, so the insurer cannot therefore make instant decisions on acceptance of business.

Facultative treaties are also undertaken between insurers as an alternative to coinsurance. Coinsurance is preferable as each insurer would then be independently liable for their share of any claim but coinsurance would require the policyholder or their broker to approach all insurers involved.

The big disadvantage of facultative cover is the cost. The risk has to be underwritten twice and that cost must be reflected in the premium charged to the policyholder. As a result, its use is limited to high premium business where the high underwriting cost will only be a small percentage of the premium. Such policies are usually high risk and there is then an advantage to the reinsurer in individually considering the risk before acceptance. In particular, they can ensure that the risks they reinsure are geographically well spread or independent risks as they are known. With treaty cover they can find themselves exposed to a cluster of risks all in the same location and therefore all exposed to an event such as fire that would normally be considered to be a particular risk.

Policy commission

The reinsurer will pay a commission to the insurer normally expressed as a percentage of the original gross premium paid by the policyholder. The reason for this is to acknowledge that the insurer faces significantly higher costs than the reinsurer. They must carry out the initial underwriting, pay broker commissions, issue the policy documents and do most of the claims handling. In the case of treaty reinsurance, the reinsurer's costs are much lower and a significant commission will be offered, say, around 30 per cent. In facultative reinsurance the reinsurer incurs much higher underwriting costs and for this reason the commission paid will be much lower.

In addition, it is common for the reinsurer to offer a profit commission on treaty reinsurance, whereby a percentage of the reinsurer's profits are paid to the insurer. The purpose of this agreement is to encourage prudent underwriting by the insurer to the benefit of both parties. Such agreements are less common in facultative reinsurance as the reinsurer will have underwritten the reinsurance policy rather than accept automatically and can therefore satisfy themselves as to the adequacy of the risk.

On occasions the two types of commission may be combined, with the commission varying according to the loss ratio. As the loss ratio increases, the commission paid decreases. The more profitable the treaty, the more commission the insurer will receive. The decrease will halt at a specified loss ratio around the point that the reinsurer will lose money on the policy. The percentage of commission remaining at this point will be intended to reflect the insurer's costs only and will not include any profit element.

Facultative obligatory/obligatory facultative

An unusual class of reinsurance cover is the facultative obligatory cover. Here the insurer is not obliged to cede all business within a certain area, but can choose which risks are ceded. The reinsurer is, however, bound to accept. Needless to say reinsurers are not keen on this type of cover due to the obvious potential for selection against them. Unless there is a long relationship between the insurer and reinsurer and the insurer is already placing treaty business with the reinsurer, it is improbable that such cover would be offered and such arrangements are few in number. The reverse contract, obligatory facultative is even rarer. This requires the insurer to cede all business within the scope of the agreement, however the reinsurer is free to decline the risk. As the insurer would be accepting business with no guarantee that reinsurance would be made available, they are most unlikely to enter into such agreement.

Reinsurance pools

Insurers do sometimes look to arrange reinsurance solutions without resorting to use of reinsurers, in effect, to establish a reinsurance mutual. This will usually arise where the reinsurers are either unwilling to offer cover or will only do so at prohibitively expensive rates, but the insurers are unable to refuse cover to the policyholder due to political or commercial pressure. Government clearly does not want to see major areas of cover excluded as they will very probably be under pressure to provide a solution themselves and may even legislate to force insurers to continue to offer cover. The use of legislation has not been used in the UK but certainly government has sought 'agreements' from the insurance industry with the veiled threat of legislation if no agreement is forthcoming. The moratoriums on flood cover are an example of this. In the USA, individual states have prohibited the exclusion of certain risks on occasions. Similarly, mortgage lenders exert very considerable influence over insurers due to the large amounts of home insurance business they control. In some countries, reinsuring risk abroad may be prohibited or heavily taxed, preventing domestic insurers from accessing the international reinsurance markets, even though the domestic reinsurance availability may be limited. Such pools may also be created by the reinsurers themselves, although these are more properly termed retrocessional pools (Figure 7.2).

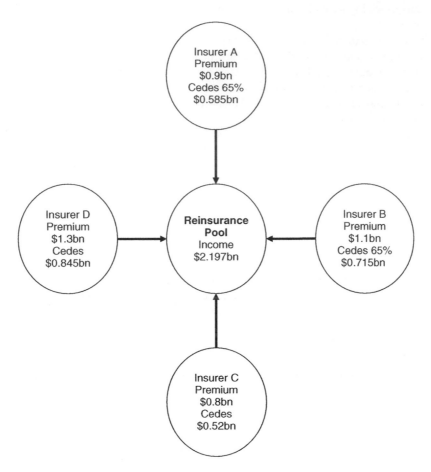

Figure 7.2 A reinsurance pool.

Whatever the motivation, pooling the risks via a mutual structure can achieve the risk-spreading outcome that conventional reinsurance is designed to provide. Such pools operate is a similar fashion to coinsurance, with the crucial difference that the participating insurers retain a proportion of the risk for which they are solely responsible. In Figure 7.2, a very simplified reinsurance pool structure is demonstrated. In this case the participating insurers have agreed to cede 65 per cent of premium along with 65 per cent of liabilities to the reinsurance pool (this type of arrangement is termed a quota share and is discussed more fully below). Each insurer retains a significant percentage of the risk themselves, which means that if their underwriting performance is worse than the performance of the pool, they will produce a worse overall result than the other participants. After all, good underwriting must have its reward. By mixing the majority of business in the pool, the participants gain a broader spread of business, they increase their individual capacity and the overall result of the much larger reinsurance pool is likely to be more predictable than the individual results of the participants (the law of large numbers again), leading to a more stable result. As this is a mutual reinsurer, any profit made belongs to the participants.

The danger with reinsurance pools is that they are normally narrow focus, usually covering one risk or one geographical region. They can then have the effect of concentrating risk rather than spreading it. If, for example, the pool is regionally based and an insured natural disaster occurs, all participants will be making heavy claims on the pool which may cause it to fail, taking its participants with it in all probability. However, the reinsurance pool may be able to purchase retrocessional cover in circumstances where the insurers could not purchase reinsurance. An example of a reinsurance pool is Pool Re, a UK company founded to provide reinsurance cover for terrorism. Pool Re is discussed in greater length in Chapter 13.

Reinsurance policies

Although there are many variations on the theme, there are in essence only four kinds of reinsurance policies: quota share, surplus, excess of loss or excess of loss ratio (often known as stop loss) (Figure 7.3). With the exception of excess of loss ratio, which can only be a form of treaty reinsurance, policies can be written on either a facultative or treaty basis.

Reinsurance policies can also be categorised according to whether they are proportional or non-proportional. In the case of a proportional policy, the proportionate share of any loss between the two parties is fixed at the commencement of the policy. In the case of non-proportional reinsurance, the proportionate share can only be determined after the amount of loss is known.

Proportional policies

Quota share

This is the simplest type of policy. A set percentage of all policies written by the insurer falling within the scope of the treaty are ceded (or a set percentage of the risk if facultative). The reinsurer receives that percentage of premiums (less commission) and in turn is responsible for that percentage of losses. If arranged via a treaty, the policy would impose a limit on the size of risk that would be transferred and restrict the type of risk covered by the treaty.

When arranged as a treaty, the great advantage of quota share is that it is very easy and cheap to administer. It can almost be viewed as a partnership between the two parties rather than a risk transfer mechanism. Under this policy the fortunes of the insurer and reinsurer will be the same for the risks covered by the policy. The reinsurer can be secure in the

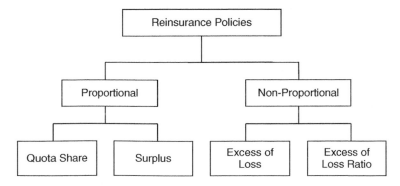

Figure 7.3 Types of reinsurance policy.

knowledge that there will be no selection against them and that the insurer will be motivated to ensure that they underwrite profitably as they will meet a proportionate share of any loss. The problem for the insurer, however, is that they would have to cede the set percentage of *all* insured risks, including smaller risks which they could safely retain. This is wasteful as they are purchasing reinsurance cover that they do not need. On the other hand, if a large risk is insured, the set percentage retained could be unacceptably large.

Quota share can be applied to almost any kind of insurance policy, but is perhaps best used for policies based upon a stated sum insured, where the sums insured are all of similar value. It is also especially suitable for dealing with the regulatory problems caused by accepting more premium than the insurer's reserves can support. The insurer can accept the risk, pass 50 per cent via quota share and then only need to demonstrate sufficient capital to support the 50 per cent retention. If their reserves increase in the future, they can then scale back reinsurance purchase.

Surplus

Where an insurer accepts risks with widely varying sums insured, quota share may not be suitable for the reasons discussed above. Therefore, in such situations a variation on quota share may be used, the surplus policy.

This method involves the insurer first deciding on its maximum acceptable retention for the class of business or policy concerned. This retention is termed a line and the first line is always the insurer's retention. The insurer then purchases additional lines of reinsurance, each line being equal to the first line or retention. Therefore if the retention level is £250,000, then each subsequent line will be for £250,000 as well. The insurer is free to purchase as many lines as they require.

In each case the percentage share between insurer and reinsurer(s) is determined in advance with reference to the sum insured. Premiums are ceded according to the proportionate share, after deduction of commission. This is straightforward enough if facultative reinsurance is used, but a surplus treaty requires more administration than a quota share treaty where the percentage share of premium is the same for all risks.

The example in Figure 7.4 shows how a surplus treaty operates. On the basis that the insurer has purchased four lines of surplus reinsurance cover above their retention of £200,000, this provides the insurer with the capacity to accept risks up to £1 million. In this example all lines have been purchased from one reinsurer, but in practice there may be multiple reinsurers all taking a few lines each. Of course, more lines of cover can be purchased to cover risks above £1 million if required. Let us assume that the commission is 30 per cent. Each risk written by the insurer will then be shared with the reinsurer in varying proportions dependent upon the sum insured.

In this example, as the insurer's retention is £200,000, any policy with a sum insured less than this will not be reinsured at all. Two policies have been written, one with a sum insured of £800,000 at a premium rate of 0.25 per cent and one with a sum insured of £400,000 at a premium rate of 0.3 per cent (Table 7.1). The premiums will be shared as follows:

Policy A £800,000 × 0.25 per cent = £2,000

Policy B £400,000 × 0.3 per cent = £1,200

The 5th line is not required and no premium is allocated to that line. In the case of policy A, the insurer is now responsible for 25 per cent of any loss while the reinsurer's proportion

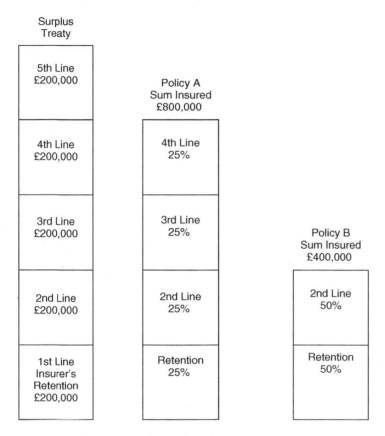

Figure 7.4 The structure of a surplus reinsurance policy.

Table 7.1 Surplus treaty example

Less commission	£2,000 – 30% = £1,400	£1,200 – 30% = £840
Retention	£1,400 × 25% = £350	£840 × 50% = £420
2nd Line	£1,400 × 25% = £350	£840 × 50% = £420
3rd Line	£1,400 × 25% = £350	
4th Line	£1,400 × 25% = £350	
Retained premium	£950	£780
Reinsurance premium	£1,050	£420

is 75 per cent. In the case of policy B, the insurer and reinsurer are each responsible for 50 per cent of any loss. Should a loss of £2,800 occur on policy A, the insurer will pay £700 and the reinsurer £2,100.

The effect of surplus reinsurance is that the larger the risk, the higher the proportion of the risk that is reinsured. Small risks where the sum insured falls within the first line would not be reinsured at all; as the size of the risk increases so the insurer's percentage share of the loss will decrease. The maximum the insurer could be called upon to pay in the event of a single loss would be £200,000 irrespective of the size of the risk. This would be acceptable as the retention is set according to the insurer's capacity.

This type of policy can be offered on either a treaty or facultative basis. If used in facultative reinsurance on a single policy, it would in effect operate as a quota share.

The advantage to the insurer is that under this arrangement they only cede that part of the risk that exceeds their capacity. Small value policies well within their capacity are fully retained, while they obtain an increasing measure of protection as sums insured increase. It is, however, much more complicated to administer as premiums have to be allocated on a policy-by-policy basis with a different apportionment for each different sum insured. That being said, in the modern, computerised world, the process can be automated. Even so, if the risks written by the insurer are all of a similar sum insured (for example, home insurance), a quota share would be preferable as the share of loss would be roughly equal in all cases on a surplus treaty, producing much the same result as if it had been written on a quota share basis. The administrative costs of quota share would, however, be lower. It should also be noted that unlike quota share, the insurer has a maximum liability for any one loss in surplus reinsurance contracts. Under quota share this liability is determined by the insurer's percentage share and on a large risk this could be commensurately sizeable.

Surplus is not suitable for all types of risk, however, as it requires the policy to contain a sum insured in order for the respective proportions to be calculated. Most insurance covering physical property does indeed have a stated sum insured; this would include marine and aviation as well as commercial buildings and contents.

Non-proportional policies

Unlike proportional reinsurance, non-proportional contracts do not involve a sharing of the underlying premium between insurer and reinsurer. The reinsurer charges a premium based on the degree of risk that the non-proportional contract exposes them to. While proportional reinsurance (especially quota share) operates as a partnership, non-proportional cover sees a relationship much closer to the supplier/customer model. It is also to be noted that non-proportional covers are not designed to share ordinary loss levels. Such contracts exist to protect the insurer against unusually high losses, peak exposures in the market jargon.

Excess of loss

Surplus reinsurance relies upon a sum insured to calculate the premium. An alternative means of reinsuring policies that do not have a sum insured is required, with liability insurances being prominent in this category. Again insurers will want to retain acceptable levels of risk for their own account while passing amounts over this level to reinsurers. The likely method will be excess of loss reinsurance.

Care must be taken not to confuse excess of loss with surplus as the structure of the policy is deceptively similar. It, in fact, operates on an entirely different basis. Excess of loss policies are non-proportional, therefore the policy does not allocate responsibility for loss in advance. Only after the loss occurs and has been quantified, can this be established.

Suppose a liability insurer offers policies covering a limit of indemnity of £5 million. If the policyholder is legally liable to the third party, the policy will pay up to that limit in respect of the compensation awarded and the third parties' legal costs. If the compensation and costs exceed £5 million, the policyholder will have to meet the additional amounts themselves. The insurer is prepared to pay up to £250,000 for any one claim, but wishes to

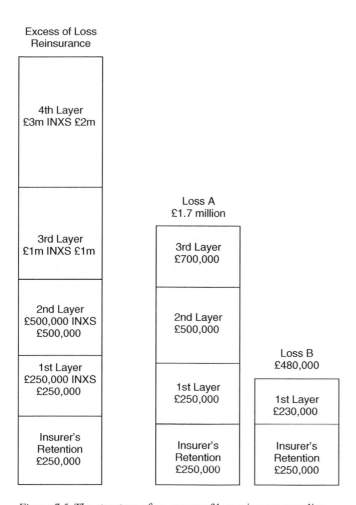

Figure 7.5 The structure of an excess of loss reinsurance policy.

reinsure above this level. An excess of loss reinsurance structure may be selected as shown in Figure 7.5.

The insurer purchases four layers of reinsurance as above. A reinsurer may accept more than one layer, however it is more probable that each layer will be with a different reinsurer. Unlike the lines used in surplus, the layers used in excess of loss are not equal. In almost every case, the layers will progressively increase in size. In the example, the four layers are for £250,000, £500,000, £1 million and £3 million, which together with the insurer's retention add up to the required £5 million. Although this may look to be similar to a surplus structure, it is not a proportional policy. The layers operate independently and each layer must become exhausted before the next layer can be called upon. Therefore all losses below £250,000 will not be reinsured. If the loss exceeds £250,000, the 1st layer is activated and continues to meet amounts up to £500,000. At this point the 1st layer is exhausted and the 2nd layer is triggered. In the example given, loss A at £1.7 million exhausts the retention and the first two layers. The 3rd layer is for £1 million in excess of £1 million and this is partially used, paying £700,000 on top of the £1 million already contributed by the underlying layer and the retention. In loss B, a claim for £480,000 only requires the involvement of the retention and the 1st layer. It follows that claims on the lower layers are far more frequent than on the higher layers. This is why the layers invariably start small and increase in size further up the structure as the probability of a claim reduces. The example provided shows reinsurance protection up to a £5 million limit; however, further additional layers of cover can be added.

Excess of loss reinsurance can be used to provide protection to the insurer in a number of different ways.

(a) *Per risk* – This is also known as working excess of loss. As in the example above, it is designed to reinsure large single claims above the acceptable retention level. This can be arranged on either a treaty or a facultative basis.

(b) *Per event* – This is also known as catastrophe excess of loss. It covers losses arising from a particular event. This might be a series of liability claims arising out of the same accident, but is more commonly designed to cover a large number of property damage claims arising out of one event (such as a storm or a flood). Usually covering one class of business, it can also provide cover across multiple classes. First, a sizeable retention will be required of the insurer. The total claims attributable to the insured peril across all policies are then aggregated. If the aggregated total exceeds the retention, the reinsurance cover is triggered. It would be normal for such cover to include a coinsurance clause. This requires the insurer to pay a stated percentage (say, around 10 per cent) of losses above the retention with the balance being paid by the reinsurer. The purpose of the coinsurance clause is to encourage insurers to limit their exposure where possible.

Figure 7.6 shows the effect of this type of cover. Cover has been arranged up to £25 million in respect of any one storm. The insurers retain the first £5 million of loss arising from a single storm. The 1st layer provides £5 million in excess of the retention, with a 2nd layer covering a further £15 million of loss. Both layers contain a 10 per cent coinsurance clause. Storm A causes aggregate claims of £13.5 million, triggering both layers. The 1st layer pays £4.5 million after taking into account coinsurance, the 2nd layer pays £3.15 million, again after coinsurance. The insurer pays £5.85 million, being the retention plus their contribution under the coinsurance clause. Storm B causes £4.7 million in damage which the insurer must meet themselves.

Excess of loss ratio (stop loss)

The reinsurance policies discussed above cover individual policies or events. An alternative way of considering the problem is to reinsure the result on an entire class of business. An insurer may therefore reinsure their motor account not on the basis of reinsuring the individual claims, but rather on the basis of reinsuring the loss ratio experienced. They would meet all losses up to a stated loss ratio and then reinsure loss ratios above this figure.

Not for nothing is this called stop loss cover as the trigger for the reinsurance cover would be at a level where the insurer was already in a loss-making position. The policy is designed to limit loss, not to guarantee profit. Dependent on the efficiency of the insurer, the pure risk premium collected would typically be about 65–70 per cent of the total premium. The rest would be to meet the insurer's costs and commissions. Therefore, a loss ratio of 85 per cent of premium would be likely to lead to overall losses once costs were taken into account.

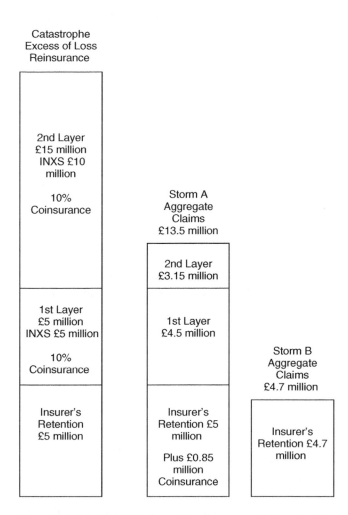

Figure 7.6 The structure of a catastrophe excess of loss reinsurance policy.

The cover will be limited by only offering to cover losses between two percentages. If losses exceed the higher percentage, no further losses are paid. Incorporating a coinsurance clause would also be standard practice. It would also be common for a monetary limit to be stated in addition in case the insurer writes far more business than expected.

The danger for the reinsurer with these contracts is moral hazard. Knowing that they are reinsured, the insurer might be tempted into a more adventurous underwriting approach. The reinsurance will be structured to ensure that the insurer feels the pain as well as the reinsurer. This is intended to encourage sound underwriting.

It is also possible to cover the aggregate loss above a specified sum as an alternative with the intent of achieving the same kind of protection. The problem here is that it cannot be known in advance how much premium income will be generated. If policy sales exceed expectations, naturally it would be expected that claims would also rise due to the increased exposure. A stop loss based on a finite sum rather than a ratio might have the unintended effect of compensating the insurer even though they have not actually suffered a loss as the increase in claims is more than offset by an increase in premiums. Nonetheless such policies are effected, usually with a clause excluding liability if the premium income proves to be greater than a specified level. So a policy covering aggregate claims of £50 million in excess of £100 million may be offered, with the proviso that premiums are no more than 115 per cent of the estimated sum at the commencement of the policy.

The policy is a derivative of excess of loss and is therefore non-proportional, indeed it is only indirectly related to any underlying policy, covering as it does the overall outcome on a large number of policies. As in the case of per event excess of loss, the nature of the cover means that it is only written as a form of treaty reinsurance.

As an example, a reinsurer may agree to cover 80 per cent of the insurer's claims between a loss ratio of 90 per cent and 120 per cent. If the premium income is £67 million and claims total £72 million, the reinsurance claim will be reconciled as follows:

Cover is triggered at a loss ratio of 90 per cent.

£67 million × 90 per cent = £60.3 million

The actual loss ratio is 107.5 per cent. The policy is triggered but not exhausted. The loss at the trigger point is deducted from the actual loss sustained and the coinsurance clause is applied:

£72 million − £60.3 million × 80 per cent = £9.36 million

In this example, the reinsurance recoveries reduce the effective loss ratio from 107.5 per cent to 93.5 per cent. Once costs and investment income have been accounted for, this will represent a loss-making year, however, disappointing rather than disastrous.

Retrospective reinsurance

Usually a principle of insurance is that it must be arranged before the event giving rise to a loss takes place. Reinsurance is, however, available to cover suspected future losses on policies already expired.

In liability insurance particularly, claims may continue to be made for decades after the policy period ends. The insurer may wish a measure of future certainty and may take out reinsurance against the risk that future claims may be higher than expected. Note that that cover would only be given in respect of unforeseen loss levels. The insurer would have to reserve against known and foreseeable losses themselves.

A good example of this is reinsurance to close, discussed with reference to Lloyd's in Chapter 6. By the time the next year's syndicate reinsures the previous year, the policies have already commenced. Of course the ultimate RITC policy was Equitas, reinsuring as it did policies going back over a number of decades. In the case of Equitas, National Indemnity have provided further retrospective reinsurance (or more correctly, retrocessional cover) on the Equitas liabilities. This is to cover against either more IBNRs occurring than are currently predicted or the cost of settling the anticipated number of claims rising beyond expectations.

The reinsurance market

Constructing as they do reinsurance pools comprising insurance company members, reinsurers are relatively rare beasts in comparison to insurance companies. The high risk nature of the business and the large capital requirements lead to a market with natural entry barriers. The international market is dominated by a handful of major players, mostly from Europe, but with significant US and Bermudan representation. The UK has no major reinsurance company, but Lloyd's syndicates collectively account for around 5 per cent of the global reinsurance market and a considerable amount of business is written in London by subsidiaries of the major reinsurance companies. To an extent, the limited number of market participants is the result of merger and acquisition activity.

In 2007, the global reinsurance premiums paid, according to Datamonitor's Global Reinsurance Report, amounted to $168 billion. The 'big six' reinsurers (Munich Re, Swiss Re, General Re, Hannover Re, Lloyd's and SCOR) accounted for over 50 per cent of this premium income. Munich Re and Swiss Re alone make up almost a third of the entire reinsurance market. It is perhaps surprising that the insurance process, designed as it is to achieve risk spreading should end up by concentrating so much of the most volatile risk in such a small number of risk pools.

High volume, small value policies offering cover against particular risks do not usually require very much in the way of reinsurance. This is why less than 5 per cent of general insurance premiums are passed on as reinsurance premiums. The percentage is lower for life assurance, higher for general insurance. A very large individual risk is very well spread via coinsurance, reinsurance and retrocession. But if the totality of insured risk is considered, hundreds of millions of policyholders insure with ten thousand or so insurance companies who pass the risk to around two hundred reinsurers and a disproportionate amount of this risk is delivered to the door of the 'big six'. Of course what is passed down the chain to the reinsurers is only a proportion of the total risk, but this proportion is the low probability, high impact, arguably fundamental risk. This is the risk that major natural or man-made disasters will occur or there will be a sharp increase in the number and/or cost of legal liability claims. Risks of this nature are reinsured because the insurers fear that if retained, their occurrence might seriously weaken or even bring down the ceding insurer.

Systemic risk?

The question then arises, does this process of concentrating the risk of catastrophe events or extremely adverse underwriting results endanger the insurance system? As discussed in Chapter 5, the retail banking system is vulnerable due to the fact that they borrow short and lend long. Available liquidity is never sufficient to meet possible demand, only likely demand. If confidence in a bank is lost and a bank run ensues, that bank cannot survive without assistance. There is also a danger that the panic will spread and the banking system will fail. For this reason, government-controlled central banks have been established to act as the lender of last resort.

This kind of systemic problem is not so apparent in the insurance system. If one insurer fails, policyholders cannot easily withdraw from their contracts with other insurers. Of course the policyholders from the failed insurer will become a new business opportunity for the survivors and with the reduction in supply, it is new business at enhanced premium rates. The loss of one insurer tends to strengthen the market. For this reason there is no Insurer of England operating alongside the Bank of England.

What though would be the effect of the failure of a major reinsurer? If this were to occur, it is possible that a number of insurers would fail in consequence. If a large reinsurer were to fail, it would be as a consequence of exceptionally poor trading conditions, probably as a result of an exceptional number of major losses combined with a prolonged soft market.

The insurers would in this situation already be weakened and the vast bad debt caused by the failure of their catastrophe reinsurance might be sufficient to cause insurer failures. As a major reinsurer would be covering a number of insurers, such consequences could be considered systemic failure.

Perhaps more pertinently, how likely is this scenario? Hollywood likes to regale us with tales of disasters of unparalleled magnitude: mega tsunami, massive earthquakes, volcanoes erupting in major cities and floods of Biblical proportions have all been featured in recent films alongside man-made disasters such as nuclear terrorism and the rapid spread of lethal diseases. While such events are all highly improbable within the short term, most have occurred in the past. More worrying is that similar if not quite so catastrophic events have occurred in the recent past.

In 2001, the World Trade Center attack cost insurers around $35 billion. The tsunami in the Indian Ocean in 2004 left an estimated 235,000 people dead. Hurricane Katrina in 2005 caused the flooding of much of New Orleans and cost insurers $49 billion. Most of the World Trade Center loss was insured (or was deliberately retained by the risk bearer); however, in the other two examples this was not the case. Most policyholders in New Orleans were not insured against flood and while the Federal National Flood Insurance Programme paid out a further $17 billion, this still means that of an estimated total loss of $144 billion only $66 billion was insured (Swiss Re: *sigma No. (2/2007)*). Remember that the global reinsurance premiums are only $168 billion, not much more than one Katrina. If the insurance cover is inadequate in the developed world, it is often almost non-existent in the developing world. Total insured loss as a result of the 2004 tsunami was around $2 billion and while accurate figures for the total damage are unavailable, most was uninsured. The insured cost was a tiny fraction of Katrina, despite the fact that the scale of the tsunami was very much greater, affecting many countries across a huge area.

According to the same report (*sigma No. (2/2007)*), of the 40 costliest catastrophes to the insurance market since 1970, 24 affected the United States, 10 affected Western Europe and 4 hit Japan. Only two (the 2004 tsunami and Hurricane Fifi in 1974) did not affect a G7 nation. Interestingly, of all man-made disasters, only the World Trade Center and the Piper Alpha oilrig fire make it onto this list, although if wars were to be included, many would dwarf any loss sustained from natural disasters. If the 40 most costly catastrophes during the period in terms of loss of life are listed, only two affected G7 nations and none affected the USA. From the insurance industry's perspective, it is not so much the magnitude of the catastrophe that matters but how many of those affected are insured. The cost of such events is growing (Table 7.2). The growing cost of catastrophe loss was highlighted in Chapter 6 as a contributory factor in the Lloyd's crisis. Since then the position has worsened.

So far, the major reinsurance companies have managed not only to survive but also to prosper (relatively) despite facing ever growing catastrophe losses. This is usually achieved by refusing to cover unacceptable levels of risk. Although in the UK, a standard home insurance policy will cover flood, storm, earthquake and terrorism, this is not the case elsewhere in the world. It should also be noted that the continuation of flood cover is by no means certain (see Chapter 1). While storm cover continues to be available for the present, growing losses in Southern USA and the Far East must cast doubt over the future of such insurance. Flood risks are excluded in many parts of the world and terrorism cover often requires special schemes. Most earthquake damage in high risk areas is largely uninsured.

Because reinsurers act as the conduit by which risks fundamental to insurers are arguably rendered particular when covered on a global scale, they must take care that they are not

Table 7.2 Cost of global catastrophes

Period	Average annual loss ($bn)
1973–1977	6.6
1978–1982	7.7
1983–1987	10.3
1988–1992	27.2
1993–1997	22.3
1998–2002	29.7
2003–2007	48.9

Source: Swiss Re Sigma Research (*sigma No .(2/2009)*)
Note: All figures are rebased to 2008 price levels.

accepting risks that might be considered fundamental even by their standards. They carefully model the outcome of likely catastrophes and seek to ensure that their exposure is limited to a level that can be afforded. The result is shortage of capacity as reinsurers refuse to offer further cover once their maximum exposure in a particular region is reached, even though they may have the capacity to write further reinsurance against the same risk elsewhere in the world.

As new problems emerge, it is often the case that reinsurers (and by extension insurers) restrict cover and wait to see how the problem develops. If it is deemed manageable, reinsurers will gradually begin to offer cover. If it is not manageable, it will become uninsurable. As evidence, consider how the risk of terrorism has been handled by the reinsurance market (see Chapter 13 for a fuller discussion of this issue).

Reinsurers face further difficulties due to the concentration of risk, often in less than desirable areas. Much of the world economy is highly concentrated in just a few countries and within these countries wealth is often disproportionately located in one economically dominant city or region. A catastrophe that only affects a relatively small area can, if it strikes in the wrong area, cause an excessive amount of loss. Insurance works on the principle of spreading the financial consequences of risk; if the underlying risks are not spread in the first place, the system is fragile. So while reinsurers report that the number and cost of catastrophes have risen sharply over the past 40 years, this may simply reflect the fact that the same events are occurring but humanity has placed large concentrations of valuable assets in areas where they are likely to suffer damage.

Although reinsurance has served the insurance industry well in the past, it has its limitations. The main reinsurers will continue to seek to limit their exposure to unacceptable loss levels and in so doing will inevitably be forced to refuse cover in respect of certain risks in certain locations. Although the resources of the insurance and reinsurance industries appear vast, they are finite and the insurance system can only do so much. Alternative solutions are necessary to deal with the excess risk that is beyond the capabilities of the insurance market. Possible alternative solutions are discussed in Chapter 14.

Conclusion

Reinsurance performs a key role in the insurance transaction although hidden from the policyholder, who is likely to be unaware of its existence. Insurance is as much about risk spreading as it is about risk transfer and reinsurance provides the means for risks to be spread throughout the global insurance industry. It is this that allows insurers to handle the huge commercial risks commonly insured and promotes greater stability in domestic insurance markets. The surprisingly small scale of the reinsurance market, accounting as it does for no more than 5 per cent of global insurance premiums, is a constraint on the ability of reinsurance to provide solutions to the really big problems.

8 Insurance intermediaries

Insurance intermediaries (or brokers as they are usually known) have been around since the earliest days of insurance. Even by 1575, the first intermediaries were recorded. As marine insurance developed, brokers developed as well, and by the beginning of the eighteenth century were a well-established part of the process. Although commonly termed 'brokers', not all intermediaries act as brokers as the term is generally understood. Although the term 'broker' used to possess a legal/regulatory meaning, since 2001, this has no longer been the case. The term 'intermediary' will be preferred in this chapter as this is currently the regulatory term used. Similarly, the policyholder is normally termed the client by intermediaries and both terms will be used in this chapter.

Intermediaries operate in both the general insurance and life and pensions markets, although many firms will have separate arms dealing in each market. It is also possible that an individual will be authorised to act in both areas. Intermediaries on the life and pensions side will usually be more investment advisors rather than insurance advisors, offering pure investment contracts and mortgages rather than limiting themselves to pure protection policies (see Chapter 10 for a further discussion of such contracts). Different kinds of intermediaries are:

(a) *Independent intermediaries* – Independents are firms or individuals established and operating independently of any insurer. The primary aim of an independent is the provision of advice and placing of insurance cover on behalf of the policyholder. The firm will enter into agency agreements with a number of insurers to permit such placement, being remunerated either by a commission on the premium or a fee payable by the policyholder. Even where operating on a commission, no single insurer is in a position to control their activities and the general rule is that insurers will not be expected to take responsibility for their activities. The firm may call themselves brokers but may operate under other titles such as consultant or advisor. The key identifying features are their ability to place cover with a number of different insurers and the independence to recommend insurers based on the best interests of the policyholder. When offering life and pension products, they are known as independent financial advisors (IFAs). Historically, individual brokers (sole traders, in other words) were common. As it has become harder for small businesses to maintain a wide range of agency agreements, many have either merged or become tied agents.

(b) *Tied agents* – These firms or individuals are established independently of insurers but do not operate independently. They enter into an agency agreement with a single insurer and only offer that insurer's products (and they should make this clear to the policyholder).

In many cases (e.g. solicitors and travel agents), the provision of insurance is not the firm's primary function. They may be remunerated on a fee basis, but it is far more probable that they will receive a commission on premiums. In this case, the general rule is that the insurer takes responsibility for their activities. They are still required to act in the best interests of the policyholder when making recommendations, but this requirement would only extend to the nature of the product rather than whether a particular product was competitive in the wider market. Nonetheless, if the insurer they are tied to does not offer the product best suited to the policyholder's needs, they should advise the policyholder accordingly.

(c) *Multi-tied intermediaries* – From 1988, polarisation was a requirement for firms offering investment advice. Intermediaries had to choose to become an Independent Financial Advisor or a Tied Agent. In 2005, depolarisation was introduced, creating a third category, multi-tied intermediaries. Such firms have a range of agency agreements, but do not claim to have access to the whole of the market. As a formal category this does not apply to general insurance intermediaries, however many independent intermediaries would effectively be multi-tied.

(d) *Coverholders* – Occasionally, an insurer may delegate many of their duties to a broker or tied agent (colloquially known as 'giving them the pen'). Although responsibility for the payment of claims remains with the insurer, the underwriting, policy documentation and claims negotiation functions are carried out by the broker. In this situation, the broker essentially becomes the insurer, with the actual insurer merely providing the financial backing to the broker's activities. This is especially common at Lloyd's, particularly where specialised bespoke products are offered to cover the requirements of certain customers. Such scheme products, as they are known, may be backed by a single insurer (a tied agent-type relationship) or by a number of coinsurers each responsible for a stated percentage.

The role of brokers

From the early days of insurance it was clear that the larger, more complex risks required the participation of a number of underwriters, each accepting a small percentage of the overall risk. The person seeking insurance would therefore need to discuss the proposed venture with all these underwriters with the consequent problems that they might not know where they were to be found and even then, they might not be able to discuss the proposal on equal terms. Brokers emerged to offer the following services:

(a) *Expertise* – A knowledge of policy wordings and standard practice, allowing negotiation with underwriters on an equal footing and speeding up the transaction. It also facilitates their service function outlined below.
(b) *Market awareness* – Knowledge of the location of suitable underwriters for particular risks, their capacity and reliability as well as the level of cover offered.
(c) *Price* – The placement of many policies gives intermediaries an awareness of current pricing, providing them with the market intelligence to negotiate better deals. This can also be viewed as a justification for their role. As they often control significant amounts of business, it can also be argued that this market 'clout' can be used to negotiate better terms for their clients.
(d) *Service* – Intermediaries can offer an advisory service, assisting policyholders with the preparation of risk details, recommending the type and nature of insurance which should be sought, reviewing the cover and formulating claims. Insurers generally rely upon

intermediaries to advise the policyholder of the extent of cover, relieving them of the responsibility. This is a sensible market efficiency; however, it is important that insurers remain aware that they should be providing this advice where no intermediary is involved (i.e. direct writing as it is known).

The use of intermediaries adds to the cost of insurance, whether remunerated by fee or commission. It is the case that some of these costs would be incurred in any event as the insurer would have to fulfil some of the functions habitually delegated to the intermediary, but by no means all. Intermediaries must then ensure that the value they add to the transaction exceeds the costs they add.

Intermediaries – agents of whom?

Normal principles of Agency Law assume that an agent is employed by a principal for that principal's benefit and will not act for other parties during a transaction (indeed this would generally be viewed as a breach of fiduciary duty). Insurance intermediaries could be viewed as an exception to this rule, being schizophrenic types, acting for both policyholder and insurer. In fact this is not strictly true. While they do indeed act for both parties, they do not do so simultaneously. It is not easy, however, to ascertain whose agent they are, as it depends not only on their status but on the nature of the task being performed. It should not be forgotten that irrespective of who they are acting for, they owe at least a duty of good faith to both parties at all times although there is no general duty of *utmost* good faith.

Preparation of proposals/risk details

The first stage of the chain is where the intermediary approaches the insurer for a quotation. The proposer obviously has a duty to disclose all the material facts. Where the proposer discloses to the intermediary but the intermediary fails to tell the insurer, a clear problem exists. Has the proposer disclosed to the insurer's agent? If so, their duty is discharged and the policy cannot be avoided. Alternatively, have they instructed their own agent to pass on the information? If so, they must accept the consequences of their agent's omission and the policy is voidable.

The general rule is that at this stage the intermediary is considered the agent of the proposer. Therefore, if the intermediary does not disclose a material fact to the insurer, the insurer will be entitled to avoid the policy, irrespective of whether or not the proposer disclosed the fact to the broker. If the fact *was* disclosed to the intermediary and not mentioned to the insurer, the intermediary would be in breach of their obligations to the policyholder and would be liable for damages, including the value of any claim that was not paid.

The key case is *Newsholme Bros v Road Transport & General Ins (1929)*. In this case, the intermediary was employed as an agent by the insurer, but had no authorisation to agree cover, permanent or temporary. The agent was deemed to have been acting as agent of the policyholder when assisting with the completion of the proposal, notwithstanding his relationship with the insurer. This was because he did so at the policyholder's request. The policyholder's position was badly undermined by the fact that they had then signed the proposal form which contained clear inaccuracies. English courts as a rule consider that you are bound by what you sign and with justification. The moral of the story is clear, intermediaries should avoid filling out proposal forms and policyholders should carefully check what they sign.

There are, however, exceptions to the *Newsholme* decision. In *Stone v Reliance Mutual Ins (1972)*, the facts were essentially the same as *Newsholme*; however, the agent in question was an inspector and was authorised to complete the forms. In view of his seniority and actual authorisation, the court held that he completed the form as an agent of the insurer. It is also worth noting that although the proposal form was incorrect in that a previous loss was not disclosed, the insurer had paid that loss and therefore knew all about it!

Coverholders would have to be considered the agents of the insurer as the policy will be underwritten without reference to the insurer. The insurer cannot then claim non-disclosure as they could not have been induced to enter into the contract by the non-disclosure. Similarly, FSA rules require that insurers assume responsibility for tied agents in the general insurance area and, notwithstanding the common law, insurers could not claim that the agent was acting as the agent of the policyholder in such circumstances.

In the life and pensions field, while IFAs would be usually be deemed the agents of the policyholder, the insurer must take responsibility for their tied agents (or appointed representatives as they are known) under the provisions of the *Financial Services Act 1986*, since subsumed into the *Financial Services and Markets Act 2000*. Therefore the common law view that tied agents are still agents of the policyholder is no longer relevant given the statutory duty. It appears responsibility extends to include the new multi-tied agents appearing from 2005 but this is not entirely clear.

Placement of cover

An intermediary, once instructed to place cover, is not under an absolute duty to place cover. There are circumstances where due to the nature of the risk or the record of the policyholder, the intermediary cannot find an insurer to take the risk. When placing cover, they will be acting as agent for the proposer. They cannot be considered agents for the insurer otherwise the instruction to place would be imputed to the insurer and they would be bound by the policy even though they might not know of the instruction. It is also worth noting that an instruction may be general rather than specific, i.e. to find an insurer to take the risk rather than to place with a named insurer.

If an intermediary fails to place cover they are not liable to the proposer unless:

(a) They have confirmed that cover was placed when it was not. Silence could constitute confirmation in some circumstances. If a proposer instructed a broker to arrange cover by a particular date and the intermediary did not notify them that cover had not been placed by the deadline or warn them that they might be unable to place, the proposer would be entitled to assume that cover was effective.
(b) They have been negligent, i.e., on the evidence, a court deduces that a reasonably skilled intermediary would have succeeded in placing cover given the nature of the risk and the time available. This argument would only be likely to succeed in rare circumstances.

The intermediary may, however, act as the agent of the insurer if they are authorised to confirm cover on the insurer's behalf. The obvious example would be coverholders who have specific binding authority. Additionally, if an intermediary issues a cover note on an insurer's behalf, the insurer will be bound by it. This would be the case even if the intermediary exceeded their authority under the principle of implied authority.

Payment of premiums

In the area of consumer insurances, increasing use of credit cards and direct debits means that much of the premium does not pass through the accounts of the intermediary, but goes directly to the insurer. Some payments are, however, still made to the intermediary, but this is far more common in commercial insurance. The usual method is that the premium is paid by the policyholder to the intermediary, who then passes on the premium to the insurer after deduction of any commissions owed. It is normal practice for credit terms to be arranged between intermediary and insurer, say, payment is due 60 days after the inception of cover. The question of agency is of crucial importance here due to the risk that the intermediary may go into liquidation before the premium is passed to the insurer, leading to the situation whereby the insurer does not receive the premium for the risk.

If the intermediary is the agent of the insurer, the insurer is deemed to have received the premium and must meet their obligations under the policy. If deemed the agent of the policyholder, the policyholder must pay the premium a second time if cover is to continue. In effect, who assumes the credit risk founded on the solvency of the intermediary?

When handling premiums, the intermediary is usually considered the agent of the insurer, therefore when premiums are paid to the intermediary, the insurer is deemed to have received them whether or not the broker actually passes them on. The policyholder's obligation to pay the premium is fulfilled and the insurer will be liable under the policy for any claims. The justification for this is that it is the insurer who has extended credit to the intermediary and authorised them to accept premiums on their behalf. They then bear the credit risk that results.

This principle extends only to the intermediary who actually places the business. Sometimes a sub-broker is involved whereby a broker is instructed by the proposer and then approaches another broker to place the business on their behalf. In this situation receipt of premium by the sub-broker is not imputed to the insurer as no contractual relationship exists between them and no credit terms have been extended. Only when the premium is received by the placing broker is the policyholder's obligation fulfilled.

It follows that before there can be any question of the insurer continuing cover following non-receipt of premium, that the policy must actually have been effected. In the event that a fraudulent intermediary collects a premium, falsely claiming to have placed cover with a particular insurer, the fictitious policy cannot be binding on the insurer. The same principle would apply if the broker was negligent rather than fraudulent, although this would extend to independent intermediaries only and not tied agents.

Submission of claims

In this instance, the intermediary is generally viewed as acting for the policyholder rather than the insurer. Where fraud by the policyholder is suspected, the position is difficult. A disclosure of such suspicions, if unfounded, could lead to an action for defamation and the safest route is probably to refuse to represent the policyholder. If despite clear evidence that fraud may have occurred the broker continues to act for the policyholder, they risk being held accountable as a participant. If, on the other hand, the insurer is unreasonably refusing settlement, representing the policyholder could not be viewed as contrary to any obligation owed to the insurer.

The intermediary may also be privy to the thinking of both parties as to the value of the claim which may lead to a conflict of interest if the insurers value the claim higher than the policyholder. The safest course here would seem to be to avoid acting for either party.

Payment of claims

Although claims payments are sometimes sent via the intermediary, in most instances this is by means of a cheque in favour of the policyholder, making it unlikely that any issue of fiduciary duty exists (other than passing on the payment within a reasonable space of time subject to fulfilment of contractual obligations by the policyholder). In the London market, a common practice is for the broker to collect claims payments (these are likely to come from a number of insurers), pay them into their accounts and then settle with the policyholder once the full sum is collected. Again the issue of agency arises. In such cases, the intermediary is deemed the agent of the insurer(s) and the claim is not considered settled until the payment reaches the policyholder. In the event of the broker's insolvency, the insurer will be required to resettle any part of the claim the policyholder does not receive.

Law Commission recommendations

The Joint Law Commission considered the issue of agency as a part of its 2007 recommendations for the reform of the law of insurance, limited to the problem of non-disclosure. The recommendations are lengthy and it is not proposed to reproduce them in full; however, in summary, the Joint Law Commission suggested:

As regards consumers

For independent intermediaries, they should be viewed as the agents of the policyholder and in the event of policy avoidance or partial claim settlement following non-disclosure, the policyholder should seek recovery from the intermediary. The amount recoverable would be reduced in the event of contributory negligence by the policyholder (for example, failing to check a proposal form properly before signing). Obviously any right of recovery would depend upon the policyholder establishing that the intermediary was aware of the material fact.

For tied and multi-tied agents, they should be viewed as the agents of the insurers. The insurer would not be entitled to avoid the policy if the policyholder made full disclosure to the tied agent. The insurer would, though, be entitled to claim contributory negligence if the policyholder was in part to blame for the non-disclosure. Again, any right of recovery would depend upon the policyholder establishing that the tied agent was aware of the material fact.

The Commission considered but rejected the possibility of making insurers responsible in all cases on the grounds of their ability to meet the loss (the 'deep pockets' argument). They found the argument persuasive, that independent intermediaries are now regulated and must carry professional indemnity insurance, in deciding that they should face the consequences of their default.

As regards businesses

The Joint Law Commission 'tentatively' proposed that small businesses (with a turnover less than £1 million) should be treated in the same way as consumers in that tied agents would be deemed the agents of the insurer, but proposed no change for larger businesses. It should be noted that it would be rare for a large business to deal with a tied agent for their commercial insurance requirements.

An intermediary's duty to the client

Performance and advice

Intermediaries hold themselves out to be insurance experts, so it follows that they must display such expertise in their dealings with their clients. Of course, they must follow the client's instructions and either arrange cover as required or at least warn the client if this proves impossible. However, they also offer an advisory service and should go beyond merely following orders and must consider the needs of the client. This may involve suggesting alternative cover and obtaining indicative quotes. Certainly they should warn clients of exclusions, warranties and special terms. They must make certain that the client is aware of the duty of disclosure and other relevant principles of insurance law. Therefore a general duty exists to recommend suitable cover and ensure as far as possible that the policy will operate as intended in the event of loss.

The extent of this duty will vary according to the circumstances. If the policy is a straightforward personal lines policy, printed in plain English and governed by a clear proposal form, the duty may be discharged by a standard warning letter. For complex commercial policies, the intermediary may have to go further, perhaps producing tailored reports on the benefits and drawbacks of the cover and drawing attention to important policy terms.

Selection of suitable insurers

Intermediaries also hold themselves out to be knowledgeable about the insurance market and suitability and reliability of insurers. This may extend to awareness of the breadth of cover offered by different insurers, perhaps warning clients that the cheapest quote is cheaper for a reason. They will need to consider the reliability of any proposed insurers, either avoiding recommending insurers known to be in financial difficulties or at least warning the client of the situation. This duty could certainly arise during the period of insurance as well as prior to placement. This is fraught with difficulty as such warnings could lead to an action for defamation from the insurer concerned. With the increasing use of credit ratings and greater regulation, the duty has become easier to discharge. Passing on information obtained from rating agencies or regulators cannot reasonably be considered defamatory and it is difficult to see how an intermediary could be expected to identify financial instability that evades the notice of such rating agencies and regulators. Nonetheless corporate clients will often specify a minimum credit rating for insurers, A+, for example. Given clear notification of this, the intermediary will need to monitor ratings and warn and seek instruction where an insurer's rating falls below the specified standard.

Fiduciary duty

Where acting as the agent of the client, an intermediary must not, as a matter of law, allow their own or the insurer's interests to conflict with the interest of the client. At least there should be full disclosure and the consent of the client obtained. In practice, this duty is frequently breached, particularly by coverholders. There have certainly been examples of coverholders purporting to represent the client regarding claims while simultaneously negotiating the claim on the insurer's behalf. The market, and it would appear the FSA, seem relaxed about this practice; however, it has been condemned by the courts on more than occasion. The scandals that engulfed the Howden and PWC syndicates at Lloyd's are further examples (see Chapter 6), although Lloyd's did of course subsequently prevent the conflict by divestment.

It goes without saying that a part of the fiduciary duty is a duty to deal honestly with the client. Any failure would also constitute breach of contract and would in addition be actionable under the tort of deceit.

Confidentiality

In the course of normal business, intermediaries obtain confidential information about their clients. This will include financial information and details of physical security. In the case of IFAs, they are specifically required to obtain financial information. Such information must be kept confidential except in the following circumstances:

(a) *Where disclosure is necessary to arrange cover* – A confidential fact is highly likely to be a material fact and must therefore be disclosed if the policy is to be valid. Similarly financial information may be need for the calculation of the premium. It goes without saying that an insurer covering theft will want to know the current security arrangements. The intermediary has an implied permission to reveal information incidental to the proper discharge of their duties. If a client specifically refuses permission for an intermediary to reveal information the intermediary knows to be material, the intermediary should refuse to act for the client (see duties to insurer below).

(b) *By permission of client* – In circumstances where the implied permission does not apply (for example, where revealing the information would not be incidental to normal broking), the duty of confidentiality can be expressly waived by the client. Also if the information has already been publicly released by the client, it would no longer be confidential.

(c) *Order of the court or the regulatory body* – There may be circumstances when the intermediary is ordered by the court or the FSA to release information. Where release is mandatory the intermediary would not breach their duty of confidentiality to the client.

An intermediary's duty to the insurer

In most cases the duty owed will be contractual as set out in the agency agreement. There are some duties which will apply in any event even if not mentioned by the contract.

A contract for intermediation is not a contract for insurance. The contract is not then one of utmost good faith. A common law duty of good faith is, though, obligatory, requiring that the intermediary be honest in their dealings with the insurer. This would also be implied into the contractual agreement.

An intermediary owes a fiduciary duty where they act as the agent of the insurer (see above). This is most likely to occur during the collection of premiums. Intermediaries must account to their principals for the full premium collected and may not make secret additional charges (a breach of their duty of good faith to the client anyway). They do not have to account for any fee charged to the client, however the premium and fee must be clearly separated in order that the position is clear to both insurer and client.

In the case of marine insurance premiums, specific duties are imposed by s53 *Marine Insurance Act 1906*. An intermediary is responsible to the insurer for the premium and to the policyholder for claims payments and return of premium. In effect this requires the intermediary to assume the credit risk.

S53 Marine Insurance Act 1906 requires that an intermediary must disclose any material facts known to them about a risk proposed to the insurer. Unlike s19, this provision is not limited to marine insurance. Hence the previous comment concerning a situation where the client orders the intermediary not to disclose. The intermediary should explain that they have a statutory duty to disclose, that the policy will be invalidated for a failure to disclose and that they must therefore refuse to act for the client.

The need for regulation of intermediaries

The basic intent of regulation is to ensure three things: honesty, expertise and solvency. The primary purpose is to provide protection to the policyholder, although insurers are secondary beneficiaries.

Honesty

One feature of the way that insurance operates is that the premium often passes through the accounts of the intermediary before reaching the insurer. As there may never be any need to claim on the policy or at least some time will pass before this happens, there is clearly scope for fraud. An unscrupulous intermediary may simply pocket the premium and fail to arrange the insurance. There also exists a risk that the unscrupulous intermediary will deliberately misadvise a client to obtain maximum commission, possibly in collusion with an insurer.

The problem of fraudulent intermediaries can exist across all insurance sectors, but is particularly prevalent in life and pensions. The long-term nature of the product means that such frauds may take some time to unravel and may take on the characteristics of a Ponzi scheme. The fraudster offers fabulous rates of return from apparently legitimate investments. For a period they appear to be fulfilling their promises, but are actually using funds from new investors to produce the 'returns' paid to the original investors. Robbing Peter to pay Paul, as the layman would put it. These frauds more commonly involve pure investment products (often fictitious), but insurance products have been used as the vehicle as well.

Recent examples in the area of general insurance include the Northern Ireland broking firm, Preston Whiteside who collected £880,000 in 'premiums' for policies supposedly placed with the insurer NIG when in fact their agency agreement with NIG had been cancelled. Consider also the £1.3 million fraudulently collected by the broker CFT Corporate Group Insurance Services for non-existent liability policies, mostly purporting to be placed with Iron Trades and Lloyd's. In both cases the insurers cited by the fraudsters had no knowledge of the transactions.

Expertise

The intent of insurance is to avoid financial catastrophe; it follows then that if the policy does not cover the risk the insured intends to transfer, such catastrophe will not be avoided. The role of the intermediary is to ensure that insurance is properly arranged and that the policyholder is advised of their duties both before and during the period of risk. The policyholder is entitled to expect that the intermediary possess the necessary expertise to discharge their duties.

Solvency

Both insurers and policyholders have an interest in the continued solvency of intermediary firms they do business with. It must be said that as regards the credit risk posed by the handling of premiums, the insurer is the party primarily exposed and is in a better position both to minimise the risk and to handle losses that do arise. It is, however, important to the policyholder that in the event that legal liability exists as a result of the intermediary's negligence, the financial means exist to meet such liability.

The road to regulation

The Insurance Brokers Registration Act & Industry Codes

Surprisingly, for many years, insurance intermediaries were entirely unregulated. Anyone could set up a brokerage and, if supported by agency agreements from insurance companies, trade without any regulatory constraints beyond basic company or partnership law. It was intended that this would be changed by the *Insurance Brokers Registration Act 1977*. This established the Insurance Brokers Registration Council, a statutory body charged with the regulation of the industry.

The Act provided for compulsory registration of all firms describing themselves as 'insurance brokers' by the IBRC, who had the power to ensure firms were managed by suitable persons and the discretion (never exercised) to require minimum professional qualifications. Registered brokers were expected to adhere to a code of conduct and to take out professional indemnity insurance. A compensation fund, known as the Grants Scheme, was established to compensate individuals and partnerships (but not limited liability companies). If a broker was insolvent and the professional indemnity cover was ineffective or exhausted, losses due to fraud or negligence would be met by the scheme. The Grants Scheme was funded by a levy on all registered brokers.

These measures ought to have considerably improved the protection available to policyholders, but the Act was fatally flawed. Instead of applying to anyone who acted as an insurance broker, it only affected individuals and firms who described themselves as an insurance broker. Any firm who didn't wish to be regulated simply described themselves as an insurance consultant or advisor and could ignore the Act with impunity. This compromised the code of conduct as the only sanction available for a breach of its provisions was removal from the register. A firm that was struck off could simply rename themselves and carry on trading. It can also be noted that reputable firms, both large and small, felt under a duty to register. Given that regulation has a cost, the effect was to put such reputable firms at a competitive disadvantage to unregistered firms.

The flaw was to an extent rectified by an industry solution. The British Insurers Association (soon to become the Association of British Insurers) introduced its own code of conduct in 1981. Designed to address the major deficiency of the Insurance Brokers Registration Act 1977, the code applied to all non-registered intermediaries, however they chose to describe themselves doing business with BIA member companies.

Once the ABI was formed in 1985, by the British Insurance Association, the Life Offices' Association, the Fire Offices Committee and the Accident Offices Association, the problem was revisited. The ABI subsequently developed a new code, introduced in 1989. This required a code of conduct and professional indemnity requirements that closely mirrored the IBRC regime. The registration process was irrelevant as the code continued to apply automatically to non-registered intermediaries. The ABI could not, however, enforce a compensation scheme as it lacked the statutory authority of the IBRC. The ABI membership wrote most of the business placed in the UK and it would be difficult, to say the least, to broke insurance in the UK without support from ABI members. The only significant area outside their control was Lloyd's of London. This, however, was not a problem as Lloyd's had firmly stated that all Lloyd's brokers must be registered with the IBRC. So 12 years after the original Act was passed, government and industry managed to muddle their way to something approximating regulation of insurance intermediaries, albeit with some noticeable gaps in the protection provided.

All of these schemes applied solely to brokers within the usual meaning of the term. The usual standard was that intermediaries had to have a minimum of six agencies in order to justify their independence. If this was not the case, they were considered tied agents (or possibly multi-tied although the term was not in common usage at the time) and fell outside the IBRC and ABI jurisdiction.

The Financial Services Act 1986

In the case of intermediaries in the life and pensions sector, reform had already been put in place courtesy of the *Financial Services Act 1986*. This applied only to investment business and therefore the pure protection contracts arranged by general insurance intermediaries were unaffected. The definition of investment included long-term (over 10 years) life contracts with a surrender value and pensions. Unit trusts and endowments, although not insurance products (albeit often linked with insurance cover), were often provided by life assurers and fell within the scope of the Act.

The Act was supervised by the SIB (securities and investments board) who delegated their duties to a variety of SROs (self-regulatory organisations) and RPBs (recognised professional bodies). The main SROs were LAUTRO (the Life Assurance and Unit Trust Regulatory Organisation), IMRO (the Investment Managers Regulatory Organisation), SFA (the Securities and Futures Authority) and the most relevant to intermediaries, FIMBRA (the Financial Intermediaries, Managers and Brokers Regulatory Association). This presented the non-expert consumer with a system of Byzantine complexity as they were expected to know which body they should complain to, without necessarily knowing whether the fault lay with the intermediary (governed by FIMBRA) or the provider (governed by LAUTRO, IMRO or possible the SFA). Not infrequently a complaint would take a tour of the regulatory bodies before finally being heard. It was also possible that all would deny jurisdiction!

The IBRC subsequently obtained RPB status for existing members for whom investment business constituted only a minority of income and did not handle client funds. This was of particular benefit to smaller firms who were relieved of the obligation to incur regulatory costs arising from two separate authorisations.

As mentioned above, the system required polarisation, with all intermediaries forced to decide whether to deal with a single provider as a tied agent or to maintain independence as independent financial advisors. Tied agents were the responsibility of the provider they were tied to and were not directly regulated. IFAs were required to adhere to a code of conduct drawn up by the SRO or RPB and not necessarily identical. Broadly, they all covered conduct of business, handling of client funds, advertising and disclosure. All monitored the financial position of regulated firms. A central Investor Compensation Scheme (ICS) was established by the Act with contributions drawn from the various SROs. The IBRC required compulsory professional indemnity insurance which was not a feature of the FIMBRA regime.

Possibly the most critical feature of the Act passed relatively unnoticed at the time, but it was to cause a damaging crisis for the life and pensions industry in the future. This was the principle that all regulated firms must offer 'best advice' based upon a thorough investigation of the client's financial position, the 'know your client' provision. The impact of this provision is discussed in greater depth in Chapter 11 with reference to the pension misselling crisis.

The Act was repealed in 2001 and its provisions subsumed within the *Financial Services and Markets Act 2000*. From 2001, the Financial Services Authority took over responsibility for the supervision of investment intermediaries.

The demise of the IBRC and ABI code

The fragmented nature of general insurance intermediary supervision was obviously unsatisfactory. Given that the investment side of the business was self-regulated, the insurance industry was invited to submit self-regulatory proposals which, if acceptable, would avoid the need for fresh legislation. The proposal put forward was the formation of the General Insurance Standards Council (GISC).

The intent was that this (a self-regulatory organisation) would replace the IBRC and ABI code, rectifying any defects along the way. The organisation was to encompass insurers (including Lloyd's syndicates) as well as intermediaries, which was particularly important given the rise of direct insurers since the *IBRA 1977* was passed. The early draft of the proposed GISC rules did include the following proposals:

(a) A move away from simple solvency requirements to a solvency margin calculation analogous to that introduced by the *Insurance Companies Act 1982*. This was only to apply to intermediaries as the ICA would continue to apply to insurers.
(b) Minimum levels of professional indemnity cover of £1 million or three times brokerage income, significantly higher than the IBRC limits which had never been reviewed since inception.
(c) Fines for members for breach of rules and the power to award compensation in the event of misconduct (up to £100,000). The IBRC and ABI had no such powers.
(d) The power to intervene in the event of misconduct or incompetence and prohibit intermediary members engaging in certain areas of insurance or even any areas at all.

What was clearly critical to the success of the GISC was that it must be compulsory. This is easily achieved with statutory authority, not so easy in the context of an SRO. The solution proposed was known as Rule F42. This required that no GISC insurer could do business with a non-GISC intermediary. As almost all UK insurers joined, this would have meant that any intermediary who chose not to join would find it all but impossible to trade.

Prior to the introduction of the IBRA 1977, the four main broker organisations had merged to produce BIBA (the British Insurance Brokers Association) allowing the industry to negotiate with a single voice. Due to a belief, justified or otherwise, that BIBA was dominated by the large broking firms, a rival association, the IIB (the Institute of Insurance Brokers) was founded in 1987. The IIB membership was drawn from smaller firms, with the major brokers remaining in BIBA. This split proved fatal to the GISC as BIBA and the IIB were incapable of reaching agreement. As BIBA stood solidly behind the GISC, the IIB adopted a hostile position. On the announcement of Rule F42, the IIB joined forces with ABTA (the Association of British Travel Agents) to strike it out. ABTA had a long tradition of opposition to any regulatory measure, which conflicted with the IIB's stance of seeking greater professionalism. ABTA members were also natural competitors of the IIB membership. Nonetheless these strange bedfellows joined forces to have Rule F42 struck down by CCAT (the competition commission appeal tribunal) as it was 'anti-competitive' under the meaning of the *Competition Act 1998*.

In a strange judgment handed down in September 2001, ABTA's assertions that Rule F42 would inhibit travel agents from selling insurance was upheld. ABTA claimed that the costs of regulation were unacceptable given the fact that, according to ABTA, insurance sales amounted to only 2 per cent of turnover (although they did not consider it necessary to mention that insurance sales accounted for a far higher proportion of profits). Of course the travel agent could avoid regulation by operating as a tied agent of an insurer, but it was claimed that this would prevent them from offering a range of policies to customers. In fact, it was almost unheard of for any travel agent to operate other than as a tied agent anyway.

It is probable that on appeal to the Director General of Fair Trading for exemption, this judgement would have been overturned. The issue was, however, overtaken by events very soon afterwards.

In the short term, this enabled the IIB to launch a rival regulatory body. It is difficult to see how a trade association, formed to protect the interests of its membership can be trusted to overcome the conflict of interest arising from having to protect the interests of clients at the same time. There was also the issue of two regulatory bodies competing for business. The less scrupulous firms who are the primary intended targets of regulation are likely to choose what they perceive to be the least rigorous option.

In any event, the GISC came into being in 2000 and in 2001 the IBRC closed its doors. The immediate impact of this was that the Grants Scheme came to end and was not replaced by any alternative. Generally compensation schemes require statutory authority, so had Rule F42 survived, the GISC might have been able to introduce a workable scheme. With the fragmentation of regulation, this possibility ended, and compensation awards made against an insolvent intermediary were then likely to be worthless.

Current regulation

It is arguable that the GISC would have had to come to an end or be put on a statutory footing in any event. On 26 November 2001, the European Council of Ministers passed draft legislation requiring statutory regulation of Insurance and Reinsurance intermediaries. The GISC was not a statutory body and the IIB were arguably not even a regulatory body, let alone on a statutory footing. The *European Directive on Insurance Mediation 2002/92/EC* was approved by the European Parliament in December 2002 and put an end to any self-regulatory systems. The government's response was to announce that the recently created Financial Services Authority would take responsibility for prudential and conduct of business regulation for insurance intermediaries and conduct of business regulation for insurance companies (they were already responsible for prudential regulation, of course).

From January 2005, general insurance intermediaries joined their life and pensions brethren in the all-embracing arms of the FSA. Due credit was given to former GISC members in the transition to FSA authorisation, easing the process and reducing costs. The government thanked the GISC for its efforts, but it is noticeable that no such thanks were extended to the IIB. Their opposition to Rule F42 meant that for four years the regulation of intermediaries was fragmented and it is doubtful that this stance won the IIB many friends in government.

The FSA regime: general insurance intermediaries

The FSA regime presented the following principles:

1   *Authorisation* – Compulsory for all firms carrying out 'regulated activities'. This would include dealing, arranging, assisting in the administration or performance or advising on a contract of insurance. Appointed representatives (tied agents) need not be authorised.

2   *Solvency* – The capital resource requirement for general insurance intermediaries is 5 per cent of the annual turnover generated from regulated activities, subject to a minimum of £10,000. These figures are halved if the firm does not hold client funds.

3   *Professional indemnity cover* – For general insurance intermediaries, the requirement, drawn directly from Article 4(3) of the Insurance Mediation Directive, is a minimum cover of €1,120,200 for a single claim and minimum cover in aggregate (all claims arising in a single year) of €1,680,300 or 10 per cent of annual income up to £30,000,000. If a significant excess is selected, the firm's capital requirement will increase on a sliding scale based on the size of both the firm and the excess.

4   *Conduct of business* – The FSA's *Insurance Conduct of Business Sourcebook* (ICOBS) applies to all authorised intermediaries. Additional codes specify requirements concerning both client funds and training. ICOBS has eight chapters and applies equally to insurers and Lloyd's syndicates, meaning that not all provisions will be relevant to an intermediary. The following are the main points:

    ICOBS 1 – Confirms the sourcebook is applicable to intermediaries, insurers and Lloyd's syndicates.

    ICOBS 2 – Covers general matters such as client categorisation, communications to clients and financial promotions, inducements, record-keeping and the exclusion of liability and reliance on others.

    ICOBS 3 – This governs distance communications, including e-commerce.

    ICOBS 4 – Covers the provision of information about the firm, including disclosure of fees and commissions.

    ICOBS 5 – This is concerned with the identification of client needs and advice provided.

    ICOBS 6 – Refers to the provision of product information, mostly applicable only to personal lines policies, but there are general duties applicable to all policyholders. The primary duty lies with the intermediary, but the insurer must comply where there is no intermediary.

    ICOBS 7 – This sets out the consumer's right to cancel the policy without penalty and without providing reasons within a specified period.

    ICOBS 8 – Refers to intermediaries and in limited cases insurers and deals with conflicts of interests arising from claims negotiations. In particular, where the intermediary knows the policyholder is prepared to settle for less than the insurer is prepared to pay, where the recommendation is that they should refuse to act for either party.

5   *Compensation* – Intermediaries now fall within the provisions of the Financial Services Compensation Scheme (see Chapter 12).

6   *Disciplinary sanctions* – Serious sanctions do exist. The FSA have wide powers to issue fines and order compensation. The FSA have issued frequent fines and are clearly prepared to bare their teeth. They can also remove the firm's authorisation in part or in its entirety. This would prevent the firm from trading. This can also involve banning

individuals from carrying out regulated activities, either in addition or as an alternative to, banning the firm.

IFAs and the FSA

The basic requirements regarding authorisation, compensation and disciplinary sanctions are the same. It should be noted that IFAs can fall into a number of different authorisation categories depending upon the business they arrange. The four authorisations exist depending upon the mix of investment, mortgages and non-investment insurance that is undertaken:

Insurance and Investments
Investments only
Investments and Mortgages
Non-Investment insurance, Investments and Mortgages

Other principles regarding IFAs and the FSA are:

(a) *Solvency* – The capital requirement for IFAs selling insurance is the higher of: (i) the requirement for insurance intermediaries; or (ii) the financial resource requirement which is applied by the *Interim Prudential Sourcebook for Investment Businesses*. The calculation of the requirement is complex and is beyond the scope of this book, which is concerned only with insurance products.

(b) *Professional indemnity cover* – Any firm that sells insurance will have to arrange the limits specified by the Insurance Mediation Directive stated above. Additional limits may be required if the firm engages in other types of investment business, depending on the nature of the business and the size of the firm.

(c) *Conduct of business* – ICOBS will apply as outlined above. In addition a further conduct of business sourcebook (COBS) will apply to the investment functions of the firm. This adds a further 19 chapters of requirements. Analysis of this sourcebook is beyond the scope of this book.

As of 1 January 2009, the long drawn-out fight by travel agents to evade regulation was lost. Travel agents selling 'connected' travel insurance (i.e. packaged with a holiday) came within the FSA's regulatory control. Unconnected sales were regulated from 2005. This was the last noteworthy area outside FSA control and it is now fair to say that virtually all insurance sales within the UK are covered by the rules governing either independent intermediaries or tied agents.

Summary

The statutory regulation (IBRA 1977) was swept away in the expectation that a market solution was ready to take its place. Not only was this solution distinctly unready, within a matter of months, internal faction fighting cast doubt on the entire process. The European Union offered the government a way out and this was grasped with both hands. It would appear that all the expenditure by insurers and intermediaries has been wasted. In addition, intermediaries are probably now perceived by government as fractious and difficult to deal with. The result has been that the new regime was to a large extent imposed.

The firms most likely to be prejudiced are the small firms, in other words the IIB's core membership.

In so far as there may have been gaps in regulation in the past, this problem can probably be regarded as fixed. Whether it should have taken 28 years is another matter. The question remains as to the long-term impact on insurance intermediaries and in particular the smallest firms.

The impact of regulation on brokers

According to their own figures, as of June 2009, the FSA regulated 6751 primary category general insurance brokers (firms whose main business is insurance broking). This appears an impressive number; however, in January 2006, (one year after regulation came into effect) they were regulating 9918. It appears, although the FSA figures are not clear, that 10,275 were regulated as at March 2005. Numbers have fallen every single quarter between January 2006 and June 2009. What these figures do not show is the firms who applied for registration but failed to meet the FSA requirements (35), the firms that applied for registration but withdrew prior to the FSA's decision (566) and the firms that switched from seeking authorisation as an independent intermediary to appointed representative status (not quoted by the FSA but it is unlikely that many specialist general insurance intermediaries would have taken this route). What is also not known is how many firms did not apply at all, closing their doors or selling out. So of 10,876 specialist general insurance intermediaries which appear to have been in business in January 2005, 38 per cent are no longer trading. The true reduction is certainly higher, taking into account mergers and acquisitions in the run-up to the FSA regime.

Intermediaries like Towergate and Oval have aggressively expanded, buying out large numbers of smaller firms (Towergate, for example, had made 139 acquisitions by August 2008, Oval have completed 32 to date). Some firms continue as branch offices of the big broker chains, others sold their book of business and disappeared altogether.

The bulk of the casualties have been among the smallest firms, those with less than 10 employees. Certainly, they face greater compliance challenges. The large national and international brokers can afford to have full-time compliance officers to oversee the process and the regulatory cost is supported by significantly higher income. The regulatory cost as a percentage of income is not evenly distributed. In 2007, the ABI estimated the regulatory cost to largest firms (income in excess of £100 million) as 1.13 per cent of income. The cost to the smallest (income less than £100,000) was estimated at 5.2 per cent of income. The problem is exacerbated by the fact that the principals of small brokerages have to devote time to compliance rather than developing the business. The ABI also dispute the FSA's estimate of the cost of regulation of £160 million a year. They feel that once the indirect costs are properly accounted for, the true figure is nearly £400 million.

It is difficult not to conclude that the regulatory regime has made it difficult at best for the smaller intermediary to remain in business. Is this necessarily worrying? From the consumers' perspective (and this is the FSA's primary concern), there seems no evidence that the competitiveness of the market has been affected. Some 6,751 intermediaries still represent very considerable consumer choice. Maintaining vast numbers of agencies, often producing minimal premium income, was expensive for insurers and the reduction in numbers is likely to improve efficiency in the insurance industry. Nonetheless it is difficult not to feel sympathy for the small intermediaries who have lost their independence by being forced to sell their business or take early retirement.

Direct writing

It would be wrong to identify the FSA as the sole cause of the demise of the small broker. They have been under pressure for many years from the direct writers, most noticeably Direct Line. Founded in 1985, Direct Line were the pioneers of a new marketing strategy based upon telesales and heavy advertising spend, and a refusal to use intermediaries. This was a departure from the traditional methods of the existing insurers who largely relied upon an intermediary network to market their products. The arrival of e-commerce then provided further opportunities for direct marketing.

The success of the newly established direct writers led to the existing, previously broker-orientated insurers, to set up direct writing arms. Again this is a process that has accelerated with the growth in e-commerce.

Initially concentrating on motor insurance, the direct writers then moved into household, travel and life and now are beginning to target small commercial business. These are the core businesses for small intermediaries and the growth of the direct writers' market share has long been a major concern for them. Indeed, the split in the ranks of BIBA that led to the formation of the IIB was to a large extent caused by dissatisfaction with BIBA's response to the threat posed by direct writing.

As of 2007, according to ABI figures, Royal Bank of Scotland (owners of direct writers such as Direct Line, Privilege and Churchill) were the largest UK motor insurer and the second largest home insurer. They were the second largest general insurer overall with nearly 14 per cent of the total UK market excluding Lloyd's. Add to this the smaller direct writers and the direct activities of insurers who also deal with the intermediary market and the loss of business suffered by intermediaries has been massive.

Once an intermediary-orientated market, intermediaries now control less than half of UK insurance business, with the proportion continuing to fall. Although a well-run intermediary can continue to prosper, particularly if they are adept at identifying a niche business poorly served by mass market insurers, conditions have got much tougher. In a Darwinian process, the weakest have been ruthlessly culled.

The contingent commission and bid rigging scandal

Small intermediaries have clearly been under pressure. Their bigger brethren have had their share of woes as well. In 2004, Eliot Spitzer, the New York Attorney General, launched an investigation into the activities of Aon, Marsh & McLennan and Willis, the three largest international brokers. The investigation concerned contingent commissions. These are deals whereby an insurer offers an enhanced rate of commission if a broker introduces more than a specified amount of premium income to the insurer. The accusation was that this would influence the broker in the advice offered to clients, inflate premiums and stifle fair competition. Given that a broker is large enough to control a significant share of the market, this risk unquestionably exists and the major brokers cited did indeed have a sizeable market share. Spitzer's implication was that this was a secret, underhand process known only to a few senior executives. In fact, the existence of contingent commissions was well known in the industry and was widely discussed within the firms. Indeed, there was pressure placed at times on staff to steer business to certain insurers with the intent that contingent commission thresholds would be reached. The result was that all three brokers paid large settlements as fines and compensation, reported as $50 million by Willis, $190 million by Aon and $850 million by Marsh. The market as a whole undertook to end contingent commissions.

Although this was a US-based investigation, these brokers (and others) were also negotiating contingent commissions in the UK, a practice that hopefully has now ended.

The reason why the Marsh settlement was so much larger was because they were additionally charged with rigging insurance bids. The allegation was that Marsh encouraged insurers to submit artificially high quotes to make their recommended insurer's quote appear competitive. The co-operation of insurers was secured by the promise of similar support when their policies fell due for renewal. Unlike contingent commissions, this was not an open secret in the wider market and it is difficult to gauge the extent of the practice. The then Chairman of Marsh, Jeffrey Greenberg, resigned in 2004 apparently to avoid criminal charges against the firm. In 2008, two senior Marsh executives were convicted under US anti-trust legislation (but acquitted of fraud and larceny charges) over this practice.

Contingent commissions were not illegal although they could be considered to distort fair competition and as such should be prohibited. Bid rigging involves active dishonesty and cannot be justified under any circumstances.

9 Claims handling

Claims handling is often described as the acid test of an insurance company. Certainly the policyholder, when judging the quality of a company, will give greater weight to how claims are settled than to any other factor. In some cases the availability of an insurance indemnity is all that stands between a policyholder and bankruptcy or insolvency. As Cuthbert Heath put it, the role of an insurer is 'to get a man out of trouble, that's what he's paid you for'.

Although an insurance contract is based upon mutual trust, all too often both insurer and policyholder negotiate claims in an atmosphere of mutual suspicion, both equally convinced that they are being defrauded. At times such paranoia is justified.

The legal position of the parties

It is for the party seeking to rely upon a contractual term to prove their case. Therefore as the policyholder is seeking to claim an indemnity based upon the cover offered by the policy, it is for them to prove on the balance of probabilities that the loss occurred as stated. They must then establish that the loss that occurred was actually covered by the terms of the policy. They then have to demonstrate the amount of loss in order to claim an indemnity. At this point, *prima facie*, they have a valid claim.

If the insurer wishes to avoid the claim once established, they may seek to claim non-disclosure, breach of warranty or fraud, for example. Alternatively they may argue that a policy exclusion operates. Either way they will be relying on an express or implied term of the contract and the burden of proving the applicability of the term lies with them.

The conduct of the policyholder

The policyholder must of course be honest. Fraud defeats a claim and is discussed in greater depth below, but briefly if a policyholder intentionally causes a loss with the intention of claiming an insurance indemnity, that would *prima facie* constitute fraud. The question does still arise as to the extent that the policyholder can be the agent of their own misfortune and yet still validly claim an indemnity.

An insured loss must be fortuitous. Insurance covers against unexpected and unwelcome events and it is a fundamental assumption of the common pool concept that its members do not wish the loss to occur. This is reinforced by a common clause in all classes of cover that the insurer is not liable if the policyholder fails to take reasonable care. The intent is to reduce moral hazard by requiring the policyholder to act as if they are not insured and facing the financial costs of any loss.

Property insurance

The policyholder is expected to safeguard their property, however a claim is not necessarily repudiated if they fail to do so. First, no policyholder can be expected to risk their own or other people's lives in the defence of property. If property is voluntarily surrendered following a threat of violence, that is not unreasonable and would not invalidate a theft claim. No fire insurer would expect a policyholder to enter a blazing building to salvage any part of the contents. If property is lost or damaged due to the negligence of a party other than the policyholder, the loss would remain fortuitous from the policyholder's perspective and would be covered. Indeed the insurer may well be able to recover their loss due to the principle of subrogation. The next question to consider is the extent to which damage caused by the negligence of the policyholder will be covered.

It is common practice for the policy to contain a condition stipulating that the policyholder will 'take all reasonable steps to protect the property' or 'take all reasonable precautions to prevent the loss'. In the real world losses frequently arise because the policyholder has left a bath running or a door unlocked, unquestionably negligent acts. The courts, however, take the view that one of the risks that a policyholder insures against is their own carelessness and have interpreted 'reasonable precautions' clauses as requiring that the policyholder is reckless rather than negligent before the insurer is entitled to avoid liability. The distinction is that the negligent policyholder *ought* to have realised that their act or omission created a risk of loss. A reckless policyholder *actually does* recognise that the risk exists and carries on regardless, not caring whether it is averted. By way of example, in *Sofi v Prudential Assurance (1993)*, the policyholder left £42,000 of jewellery locked in the glove compartment of his car for a brief period. The court held that although this might be careless, the fact that the property was locked away out of sight of a thief meant that it could be inferred that the policyholder did take steps to avert the risk. Their conduct did not therefore amount to recklessness and the claim was covered.

The clear message to insurers was that if they wished to exclude certain types of conduct, it was for them to introduce clear policy conditions or warranties spelling this out to the policyholder. In the example of *Sofi* the insurers might have excluded theft from an unattended vehicle. The exclusion would clearly have been upheld and the policyholder would have been forewarned.

Liability insurance

The question of intent is an issue in liability insurance. As the policyholder does not receive the benefit of the policy, causing intentional harm to a third party would not be fraudulent in the absence of collusion. The question does though arise as to how far the policyholder is entitled to recover in respect of liability claims arising from their intentional act. The controversial case of *Gray v Barr (1971)* creates significant difficulties. Here a man, suspecting that his wife was having an affair, went to her lover's house with a loaded shotgun to confront them. In the ensuing struggle the wife's lover was shot dead. Although acquitted of murder and (astonishingly) manslaughter, he was liable to compensate the widow of the deceased and claimed on his liability insurance. Had he been convicted of a criminal offence, the court could have found that he was not entitled to recover as a matter of public policy. As he was acquitted, the leading judgment found that the death was a foreseeable consequence of an intentional act, and therefore what had occurred could not be described as accidental. This decision is problematic as foreseeability is a crucial ingredient of negligence. Is it then the case that if a court finds against the defendant, the consequences were foreseeable and the defendant's insurer is not liable to indemnify them?

An alternative interpretation of this case is that the insurers were not liable on public policy grounds. There are problems, however. First, Barr was not convicted of a criminal offence. Second, the commission of a criminal offence frequently precedes an incident which gives rise to liability. It is usual for a motorist causing an accident to be guilty of driving without due care and attention at least or for an injury to an employee to be brought about by a breach of health and safety legislation. It is hardly in the public interest for the insurers to be relieved of liability in these examples where of course compulsory insurance is required. In *Hardy v Motor Insurers' Bureau (1964)*, those convicted of manslaughter in motoring cases were held to be entitled to be indemnified by their insurers unless their conduct was wilful (i.e. intentionally running someone down). It is respectfully suggested that a more sensible test is not whether the harm was foreseeable, but whether it was actually foreseen or even that it was intended. Certainly in practice this appears to be the test.

Applied literally, a reasonable precautions clause inserted into a liability insurance creates an absurdity. One of the main reasons the policy has been taken out is in case the policyholder is sued in the tort of negligence. Negligence is based upon a lack of reasonable care and if such conduct invalidated cover the policy would lose much of its commercial purpose. Again the test is that of recklessness rather than mere negligence. In *Fraser v BN Furman (Productions) Ltd (1967)*, an employee suffered serious burns to both hands from an arc welding machine. In order to prevent such accidents the machine was initially operated by two buttons on either side of the machine making it impossible to operate unless both hands were clear of danger. The employer later modified the machine to allow it to be operated by a foot pedal. The employee inadvertently triggered this pedal while loading the machine, thus causing the injuries. Although the employer had acted stupidly, they had not acted recklessly and were therefore entitled to be indemnified. It is worth noting that today due to the *Employers Liability (Compulsory Insurance) Regulations 1971*, insurers must meet the claims of injured employees even if the policyholder has been reckless, although they may then recover the sum from the policyholder.

Life assurance

Surprisingly, life assurers do not necessarily refuse to pay in the case of suicide. Most would impose a moratorium of, say, two years from the date of inception, during which death due to suicide would be excluded. After this period has expired, it will be covered. The thinking is that after a reasonable period of time, suicide cannot be said to have been in the mind of the policyholder when they took out the policy and therefore there was no fraudulent intent. It is deemed that some new and intervening cause has operated (depression perhaps) which has brought about the loss.

A common exclusion in personal accident policies is that cover will not operate if the policyholder wilfully exposes themselves to danger. This is always qualified by the comment 'except in the attempt to save human life' or words to that effect. Once again the test would be one of recklessness rather than mere carelessness. In order for the act to be 'wilful', the policyholder would have to have recognised that their act exposed them to the risk of serious harm.

Notification

It is normal practice for insurers to impose conditions concerning the period during which a claim must be notified. This can to an extent be justified by the fact that where the notification of a claim is delayed, they may not be able to properly investigate or in the case of a liability claim they may no longer be able to defend the claim. Unfortunately the clause can be misused as the letter of the clause may be applied even though the insurer has suffered no prejudice. Where the clause merely requires notification 'as soon as possible', the state of knowledge of the policyholder will be relevant and notice long after the accident may be acceptable if there are circumstances that make the late notification reasonable (for example, where the policyholder is unaware of the existence of the policy or if they were also injured in the incident and are in hospital receiving treatment). If the clause specifies a set period of, say, seven or fourteen days, this becomes more problematic, although it is arguably open to the courts to find an implied term modifying the clause to run from the moment that the policyholder is reasonably able to notify. This, it is suggested, would certainly be the Financial Ombudsman's view.

Fraud

Surprisingly, for centuries, there was no precise legal definition of what constituted fraud in English law. This has been remedied by the Fraud Act 2006 which defines the offence as:

A dishonest intent to gain or cause loss to another facilitated by:

(i) making a false or misleading representation
(ii) failing to disclose information when legally obliged to do so
(iii) abusing a position of trust.

For many years, deception was a key element in fraud; this is no longer the case as it is the intention that is important not whether anyone was in fact deceived. This arises out of the legal technicality that a machine (for example, a bank cash point) cannot be deceived. In insurance claims it will almost always be a false or misleading representation that is the basis of an allegation of fraud.

There can be no doubt that there are large numbers of fraudulent claims submitted. Some are conceived as entirely fraudulent claims in that the alleged loss did not happen or alternatively the loss was deliberately caused by the policyholder. More commonly, a genuine loss has occurred but the policyholder overstates the amount of damage or claims non-existent property has been lost or stolen. It can even be fraud when the policyholder lies to improve their chances of recovering in respect of a genuine claim.

More controversially, there is the question of exaggeration of the amount claimed, where the cause of loss and the description of the items lost or damaged are stated truthfully. In *Ewer v National Employers Mutual (1937)*, claiming the replacement cost of goods when the policy only covered their second-hand value was held to be a bargaining position rather than fraud. It would seem that this may continue to be the position, particularly as the policyholder may not realise how an indemnity is to be calculated. However, if an opinion as to value is offered and it is clear that the policyholder had no honest belief in that opinion, modern cases would indicate that this would constitute fraud if the intent is to recover more than the policyholder believes they are entitled to.

Merely making a claim for a loss that is not covered is not fraudulent in the absence of any falsehood. There seems no reason why a policyholder should not submit the claim for the insurer to determine. Policyholders should not be expected to be experts in the interpretation of insurance contracts.

The burden of proof is on the insurer in such cases. As this is argued in front of the civil courts, the court will require that fraud is proved on the balance of probabilities. For a criminal conviction, the proof must be beyond reasonable doubt. Although the insurer may make a complaint of fraud, it is the decision of the Crown Prosecution Service whether or not the policyholder is charged.

The effect of fraud is to disallow the entire claim. In *Galloway v Guardian Royal Exchange (2000)*, the policyholder, having fraudulently claimed for an item that was not stolen in a burglary, could not recover in respect of other items which had genuinely been stolen. It can be argued that this is due to the operation of the duty of utmost good faith; however, it is more likely that the insurer will rely on a common clause inserted in policies to the effect that the policy will become void in the event of fraud. In the case of Galloway, no such clause was in effect, but the Court of Appeal still found a common law principle entitling avoidance of the entire claim.

The right to avoid the claim does not operate retrospectively. Previous claims payments made under the policy cannot be recovered by the insurer. Neither can interim payments made prior to the fraudulent act. Whether the policy survives fraud depends upon the nature of the fraud. In *Agapitos v Agnew (The Aegon) 2002*, the court distinguished between 'material fraud' where the claim was false or exaggerated and 'fraudulent devices' where a fair claim was fraudulently embellished (for example, submitting a forged receipt for an item genuinely stolen). Material frauds permit avoidance of the contract from the date of the fraud, but fraudulent devices merely permit avoidance of the claim without cancelling cover for the future. It should be noted that insurers could invoke the cancellation clause in any event but would be bound by any period of notice specified.

The fight against fraud

In July 2009, the ABI estimated that general insurance fraud costs £1.9 billion equivalent to 6 per cent (or £44) of the average individual's annual insurance cost. As many as 13 per cent of claims were estimated to be fraudulent. These of course are the undetected (or possibly unproven) frauds. Where fraud was detected, insurers repudiated liability in 1.6 per cent of all claims, the aggregate value of such claims being £730 million. Both detected and estimated frauds have risen sharply in recent years, perhaps unsurprising at a time of economic recession. The effect of fraud in the long term is that the costs are added as a charge on the common pool and met by the pool members by way of increased premiums. The apparently widely held view that fraud is a victimless crime as it is the insurer who pays and they can well afford to, is erroneous.

What may worry insurers is the attitude towards insurance fraud shown by the general public. In three ABI surveys between December 2008 and June 2009, almost 45 per cent did not see anything wrong in overstating the value of an item when claiming and almost 40 per cent thought overstating the damage was not dishonest. About 25 per cent considered adding items that were not lost or damaged to the claim was normal behaviour and astonishingly around 5 per cent thought it acceptable to cause deliberate damage in order to claim. One in five stated that they would consider making an exaggerated or entirely fabricated claim in the future. Either the insurer's message that insurance fraud is not a victimless crime does not seem to be getting through or policyholders are taking the view that if they have to pay for insurance fraud they may as well partake of its proceeds by way of compensation.

The insurance industry has established a number of initiatives in an attempt to limit the losses caused by fraud. In 1994, the Claims & Underwriting Exchange (CUE) was set up by a consortium of insurers. The aim was to maintain a central database of claims information from the member insurers. This would enable an insurer to check the previous claims history of a proposer, but more importantly enables an insurer to check whether multiple claims are being made in respect of the same incident. One easy way to maximise the benefit of an insurance fraud is to take out cover with a number of companies, invent or stage a loss and then submit a number of fictitious claims. Fraudsters are well aware that large losses are likely to be investigated but small claims probably won't be queried. This is a means of claiming a large sum with a low risk of detection.

In 2006, the Insurance Fraud Bureau (IFB) was established by a group of insurers specifically to fight organised insurance fraud in personal lines insurance. A particularly common problem is the staged accident where the fraudsters brake suddenly to cause an innocent motorist to crash into the back of them (often with the brake lights temporarily disabled). Particularly large-scale frauds will involve the fraudsters hiring accomplices to actually crash while remaining behind the scenes themselves to avoid detection. Claims are then submitted for personal injury by the driver and passengers, as well as inflated claims for the damage to the vehicle, recovery charges and car hire. Garages and vehicle recovery firms are usually part of the fraud and it is suspected that even doctors and solicitors have been involved. One way this can be detected is by a sharing of information between insurers, looking for common links between apparently unrelated incidents.

Although the primary intent is to combat organised fraud, the IFB has certainly investigated individual frauds where it appears that the fraud is a one-off occurrence. An example would be fraudulent life assurance claims where the 'deceased' is in fact alive and well (and usually living abroad). This type of fraud hit the headlines recently in the UK when John and Anne Darwin were convicted of fraud in 2008 after John Darwin faked his death in a canoeing 'accident' and moved to Panama.

Fraud by insurers

Although insurers are more sinned against than sinners when it comes to fraud involving single insurance claims, they are not entirely innocent. It is well established that if a policyholder knowingly claims more than a fair indemnity that is fraud, see *Galloway v Guardian Royal Exchange*. It is difficult to argue against the proposition that if an insurer knowingly offers less than a full indemnity, that too is fraud. For example, an insurer who knowingly represents to a policyholder that a particular loss is not covered when they know full well that it is, commits fraud. Again the distinction between a bargaining position and a deliberate misrepresentation with the intent of financial gain discussed in *Ewer* arises. There do not appear to be any examples of such a case appearing before the criminal courts; however, it is more probable that the matter would be dealt with by the Financial Ombudsman Service and/or the FSA.

What is far more likely is for economic duress to be used to force a policyholder to accept a settlement offer below a fair indemnity. This problem is mainly confined to small commercial insurance where a relatively large loss has occurred. By withholding payments an insurer can place the policyholder in such a position that their cash flow is badly interrupted and they may be left with no choice but to accept a low offer as a full and final settlement. If they argue, the insurer simply closes the chequebook and the business fails for lack of liquidity.

An alternative scenario arises where an insurer agrees that property may be replaced but refuses to pay on production of the invoices unless the policyholder also agrees to accept the insurer's position on other elements of the claim. In this situation the cash flow crisis is engineered by the insurer.

The problem is that if an insurer delays payment on spurious grounds and the business collapses as a result, the policyholder cannot claim additional damages over and above the value of the claim, plus interest on the amount for the period of delay. In *Sprung v Royal Insurance (1997)*, an unjustified delay in settling a claim of more than three years did indeed cause the policyholder's business to fail. Nonetheless the Court of Appeal ruled that no entitlement to additional damages arose. This is because the claim itself is seen as an action for damages and an action for damages arising out of a failure to pay damages is not permitted. It is arguable that the FOS (see Chapter 12) has the power to award compensation in such circumstances. The problem is that their decisions are only binding on the insurer up to £100,000.

Loss adjusters

Although small value claims will typically be investigated by the insurer's own claims handlers, the negotiation of larger losses will usually be delegated to a loss adjuster. Loss adjusters are independent firms who carry out claims investigation and negotiation on behalf of the insurer for a fee. It is the insurer who pays this fee. The cost of employing a loss adjuster means that it is far more likely that they will be instructed to investigate commercial claims rather than personal lines claims.

Loss adjusters probably first appeared in the eighteenth century on an ad hoc basis, being lawyers, valuers or surveyors appointed to investigate losses as a sideline to their main profession. By the early nineteenth century specialist firms had begun to emerge in the London marine market known as 'average staters', average meaning loss in this context of marine insurance terminology. This title was subsequently amended to average adjusters and confirmed as such when the first professional body, the Association of Average Adjusters was founded in 1869. The profession appears to have developed more slowly in the field of fire insurance. It was not until 1941 that the Association of Fire Loss Adjusters was founded, which later became the Chartered Institute of Loss Adjusters. The CILA introduced professional exams in 1971 as a means to ensure a minimum standard of expertise within the profession.

As stated above, loss adjusters are appointed by the insurer to investigate the loss and report back to the insurer with a recommendation of whether any claim should be paid and, if so, how much. The insurer is not bound to accept this recommendation and may settle or decline the claim against the loss adjuster's recommendation. The policyholder cannot therefore compel the insurer to pay even when their position is supported by the loss adjuster. It is probable, however, that a court would in this situation, place considerable weight on the loss adjuster's opinion.

For many years, loss adjusters have proclaimed themselves as entirely independent of their instructing insurers, acting on the behalf of both insurer and policyholder. There are no doubt many excellent loss adjusters who consider it their duty to ensure that the policyholder receives a fair claim settlement in compensation for a fair claim. However, they are often viewed with suspicion by the policyholders as they are appointed and paid by the insurer and the policyholder has no say in the matter. It is inferred that loss adjusters who wish to receive further instructions from the insurer may be biased in that insurer's favour in order to gain a reputation for minimising the cost of claims. Unfortunately there are certainly adjusters of that type operating alongside their more honest brethren.

Loss adjusters will of course first consider the basic validity of the claim, seeking to confirm that the loss as claimed, first, is honest and, second, was actually covered by the policy. Assuming these fundamental requirements are met, there are then two approaches that may be taken.

Disaster recovery consultants

An adjuster should have considerable experience in dealing with major losses, but most policyholders do not have one. The adjuster can 'add value' by advising the policyholder as to how they can recover from the loss efficiently. This might include measures taken to reduce further damage or speed up the repair process. This will minimise the losses that arise in consequence, predominantly in commercial insurance by reducing the interruption to business and therefore the consequential loss of profits. Even in consumer insurance, this can be of benefit, as home insurance policies cover the cost of renting alternative accommodation. They should also be in a better position than the policyholder to spot that a contractor is trying to take advantage of the fact that an insurer is paying by inflating their estimate. These measures will reduce the cost of the claim to the insurer while causing no detriment to the policyholder and indeed benefiting them, if the damage is repaired faster.

Insurer watchdogs

An alternative approach is for the adjuster not to intervene in the disaster recovery process as an active consultant, but rather to criticise the process after the event. This would leave the inexpert policyholder to attempt to resolve the crisis, often in a less that optimal fashion even if well intentioned. The overall cost of the loss may be unnecessarily inflated as a result. This type of adjuster will then consider that their role is to try to avoid paying as much as possible of the policyholder's claim by criticising their actions, for example, claiming that they are not entitled to claim certain sums because they have failed to minimise the loss. The use of economic duress, discussed above, is another tactic. To the insurer it may well appear that the adjuster has done a good job on their behalf by reducing the settlement figure by x per cent, without stopping to consider that the original figure was unnecessarily high and the claim might have been settled at a lower cost without causing detriment to the policyholder.

The first category of adjuster may be considered to be genuinely independent. Adjusters in the second category are unquestionably the agents of the insurer. The FSA does not require loss adjusting firms to be directly regulated and specifically states that they are viewed as the agent of the insurer. The insurer is then required to ensure that their agent follows the relevant insurance conduct of business rules (ICOBS), in particular ICOBS 8 which sets out general principles governing claims handling. Any failure on the part of the adjuster would be imputed to the insurer, who may face sanctions for failing to supervise their agent. A protocol has been agreed between the CILA and the ABI setting out the duties owed by loss adjusters to their insurer principals relating to the insurer's regulatory duties.

Loss assessors

Loss assessors are appointed by the policyholder to negotiate claims settlements on their behalf. They are remunerated on a fee basis, possibly a specified sum but more commonly a percentage of the claims payment. Loss assessors do not pretend to be independent as they are agents representing the interests of the policyholder and are appointed to recover the maximum indemnity possible consistent with the obligation of the policyholder (or in this case their agent) to act with good faith. As they are the agents of the policyholder, they are required to be authorised by the FSA as they are 'assisting in the administration or performance of an insurance contract'.

In the event that a loss assessor is appointed, this may change the position of the loss adjuster. The loss assessor is not pretending to do other than represent the best interests of the policyholder. The loss adjuster will by default be cast as representing the interests of the insurer. Loss assessors would claim that that is what they do anyway and that no substantial change arises. Some loss adjusters would dispute that view, claiming that it is their intent to act as an unbiased consultant.

International disaster response: the capabilities of the adjusting industry

One problem faced by loss adjusters is that at times there are not enough of them. Particular risks such as fire or legal liability claims usually occur in reasonably predictable numbers and there is a steady stream of such losses. Loss adjusters can assume that each month a number of claims will arise while a similar number will be resolved, leading to a more or less constant drain upon their key resource, the time demands on the adjusters.

Fundamental type losses such as storm or flood can cause large numbers of serious claims within a few days or even a few hours. The 2007 summer floods in the UK, for example, caused 160,000 losses within a short space of time, leading to a massive increase in the demand for loss adjusters. As loss adjusting firms cannot afford to have more than a limited amount of spare capacity, this immediately creates problems. Although localised disasters can be handled by the temporary transfer of staff from other parts of the country and indeed loss adjusters do keep insurers updated as to their spare capacity at all times, in 2007 the losses were so widespread that the spare capacity from the unaffected areas was soon used up. It is not uncommon for loss adjusters to be brought in from abroad in such cases and certainly British loss adjusters have frequently been deployed abroad to negotiate claims arising from natural disasters. The problem with this approach is that the incoming adjuster may have little idea of local insurance practice or the usual cost of goods or services.

Insurers may of course raise the limit at which an adjuster will be appointed in order to reduce the number of instructions. Their difficulty is that fraudsters are well aware of this and will seek to make fraudulent claims just below the limit at which they anticipate that the claim will be investigated. It is also the case with flood claims, that a high percentage of them are serious. Unless the limit triggering the instruction of an adjuster is raised sharply, the number of investigations will not be reduced to any great degree.

Even when a loss adjuster is appointed, they may find it difficult to manage the claim. Building contractors will be inundated with flood repair work, if the pun may be excused, and even when their services are available, prices will be commensurately higher. They of course are not immune from the effects of the flood and may not be able to work at maximum efficiency themselves as their stock, plant and premises may also have been damaged. Installing dehumidifiers in a building to speed up the drying process is a common technique; however, there are a finite number of dehumidifiers and they will rapidly be deployed. There were many complaints from policyholders that the insurers took too long to resolve claims; however, in many cases, repair work could not commence until the building had dried out and the loss adjusters had no means to accelerate the process. There were also queues for the services of contractors.

As the industry cannot afford to have more than a small amount of excess capacity, which will after all only be utilised in exceptional circumstances, it appears that the solution lies in greater internationalisation of spare capacity for disaster recovery. Although the small amount of excess capacity in a single country cannot be an adequate solution to the problem, the aggregation of such facilities from a number of territories may well be sufficient.

10 Life assurance

As already established, the insurance industry is divided into two branches, short-term business (usually annual contracts for fire, motor, marine, etc.) known as general insurance, and long-term business (life and pensions contracts stretching over a period of many years). This chapter will concentrate on the life assurance aspects of long-term business.

Note that it is usual to talk in terms of assurance, assurer and assured when referring to life cover, as opposed to the terms insurance, insurer and insured used in general insurance. The common explanation is that assurance refers to a protection policy covering a single risk, the timing of loss and insurance refers to a protection policy covering the dual risk of both timing and occurrence. Hence because death is certain to occur, we refer to life assurance rather than life insurance. This is indeed the common usage, although in fact both terms can be used interchangeably and analysis of older legal decisions reveals that the courts frequently did. This chapter will follow common usage and use the terms assurance and assurer.

It is important to note that while general insurance is concerned solely with providing protection, life assurance has two functions. Pure protection policies (term assurance, for example) and investment-based policies (e.g. pensions and endowments). These branches are not, however, distinct as some policies contain an element of both protection and investments (e.g. whole life and endowment assurance).

Just to confuse matters further, protection of life and limb is not the exclusive preserve of the life assurers. General insurers cover accidental death and injury (not including death from natural causes) giving the lie to the oft quoted statement that the only thing Lloyd's will not insure is life.

Life assurance

Although death is certain, people have for centuries sought to prepare financially for the uncertainty surrounding the timing of death. The basic premise behind life assurance is simple. A reasonably large group pool their collective risk and pay regular premiums into the pool. These premiums are invested. The members of the pool collect a set benefit on death, with the premiums of the long-term survivors compensating for any shortfall between the premiums paid and the benefit received by the early deaths (and presumably the long-lived policyholders are delighted to be in a position to do so).

Although an individual's death is unpredictable, the mortality rate of a large group of people is in fact highly predictable in a stable society. This was recognised by the third-century Roman mathematician Ulpian, leading to the production of an early form of what we now know as mortality tables (or life expectancy tables if you feel in a more positive frame

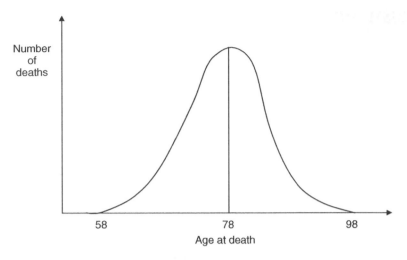

Figure 10.1 An illustrative mortality curve.

of mind). Burial societies were common in Roman times whereby the purpose of the fund was to pay for funeral expenses, thus prompting Ulpian's study.

As discussed in Chapter 4, the development of mortality tables was the beginning of actuarial science, ultimately influencing all forms of insurance. The work of Halley and Dodson had more direct and immediate effect on life assurance. They demonstrated that the distribution of age at death could be mathematically modelled and therefore the life expectancy of an individual could be modelled. In Figure 10.1, the mortality curve for a group of 58-year-old policyholders is shown (note this is illustrative only and is not based upon real-life data). Although the assurer cannot know when any given individual will die, they do know that most will die within a few years of the median age of 78. They can then use that median age as a starting point for the calculation of the premium.

Initially life assurance was sold on an annual basis, often without regard for the policyholder's age. Life assurers rapidly worked out that the old were more likely to die than the young. However, if annual premiums are calculated on an equitable (or natural as it is termed) premium basis, a problem emerges. The cost of the premium steadily rises each year until the point is reached where the policyholder can no longer afford to continue to insure. If after many years of premium payment, a policyholder was forced to allow a policy to lapse shortly before death, the dependants of the deceased might reasonably feel aggrieved.

By way of example, in the UK, the risk of a 30-year-old dying before age 31 is roughly one-tenth the risk of a 60-year-old dying before age 61. Therefore, under a natural premium system, the pure risk premium charged to a 60-year-old would be 10 times greater for a given sum insured.

James Dodson's great contribution was the level premium concept. This used estimated life expectancy as its basis, i.e. the median survival rate for a person of that age (more crudely the age at which 50 per cent of that age group will have died). The risk could then be priced on the basis of the premium required from inception to expected death. This could in turn be separated into annual instalments (and today into monthly instalments). Even though the risk steadily increases throughout the policy, the premium remains unaltered and the risk that the policy may lapse due to the impecuniosity of the policyholder is minimised (Figure 10.2).

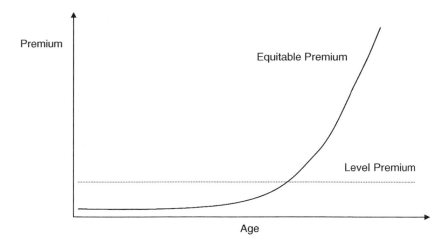

Figure 10.2 The level premium concept.

The beauty of this arrangement for the insurer is that the policyholder overpays in the early years as the annual premium exceeds the equitable premium for the year. As the policyholder ages, the annual premium and equitable premiums converge, until the equitable premium exceeds the annual premium and the premiums diverge. Therefore in the event of early death, the policyholder will have paid more in premium than the risk justified, mitigating to some extent the assurer's loss.

Life assurance has long been regarded as the most stable form of insurance. All insurance is governed by the law of large numbers (see Chapter 4). The prevalence of life assurance in the UK is such that the insurer can underwrite with a considerable (if not total) degree of certainty.

There is, however, another reason why life is regarded as a lower risk business than general insurance. With most classes of insurance, changes in loss profiles can cut both ways, so loss rates can improve or deteriorate. It would be going too far to say that life expectancy is a one-way bet, but throughout the twentieth century life expectancy has steadily increased. In 1900, male life expectancy at birth was 45. In 1999, this had risen to 75 (and continues to rise). Women survive for four to five years longer though the gap is beginning to narrow.

Note, however, there is a difference between life expectancy in the general population and life expectancy in the insuring population. First, the greatest medical improvement of the twentieth century has been a massively reduced infant mortality, from 140 per thousand to 5.8 per thousand. As newborn babies do not buy life assurance, then no benefit accrues to assurers. Nonetheless life expectancy at all ages has improved significantly. Therefore for more than a century, life assurers have been underwriting against a background of steadily improving risk. This is emphatically not the case in general insurance!

Note that not all proposers are treated the same; life is underwritten just as any other class of insurance, based upon the hazard factor of the risk proposed. Normal rates will be applied to what are termed 'standard lives', i.e. proposers with no adverse health features. However, substandard proposers will pay more. So smokers, the seriously overweight or underweight and those with previous health problems will face higher premiums or a refusal of cover.

Medical examination will be required once the requested benefits exceed a certain level. Women are less likely to die than men at all ages and so pay lower premiums. This is the familiar equitable premium concept, with the modification of the level premium.

Major classes of cover

Whole life cover

This is life assurance in its traditional form. Originally level premiums were paid from inception throughout life with a set benefit paid upon death when it occurs. In the modern era premiums usually need only be contributed to a pre-determined age (usually retirement age). At this point the policy is described as 'paid up' having reached 'maturity' and although the policy remains in force, no further premium need be paid.

Policies paying a set benefit are certainly sold, however investment-linked benefits are more common. Policies may be 'with profits' (also termed 'participating'), in which case a 'with profits' fund is created into which a proportion of the assurer's profits is paid. This is then distributed to the policies by means of annual and (more valuable) terminal bonuses on maturity of the policy or death.

Another variation is unit-linked cover. In this case the premium purchases units in an investment fund. The value of each unit is variable according to investment performance. Once they know the number of units possessed, the policyholder can quickly value the policy as the unit price is usually publicly quoted. The policy would provide a minimum benefit on death, the original sum insured. The intent would be for the value of the policy to exceed the sum insured at maturity.

One important feature of whole life assurance is that because a loss is certain, the policy has a monetary value. The policy can be surrendered at any time and a proportion of the benefit paid. In the early years, the surrender value will be zero, but with the passage of time and given good investment returns, the policy will increase in value. Therefore, a policy can be taken out to provide protection for lost earnings should the policyholder die in their working years and then be surrendered on retirement when the need for protection has ceased, thus providing additional retirement funds. As the majority of policyholders survive to retirement, most whole life contracts offer investment rather than protection. Of course, there is no way of knowing this in advance.

As insurable interest is only required at inception and not at the time of claim, whole life policies are marketable. As an alternative to accepting the surrender value offered by the assurer, which is usually well below the value of the policy, the policy may be sold to a third party offering more than the surrender value. The vendor will assign the benefit of the policy to the purchaser, who will take over responsibility for premium payment and collect when the policyholder dies, having no doubt named themselves as beneficiary. This arrangement is unique to life assurance as the requirement of insurable interest at time of loss applicable to other forms of insurance would render the policy worthless to the uninterested third party. Even within life assurance, this practice requires that the policy has a surrender value.

It used to be the case that premiums paid for life assurance were tax deductible so long as the policy met certain criteria (what was termed a 'qualifying' policy). This made whole life policies very tax efficient investments. This tax relief was removed by the *Finance Act 1984* which came into effect on 14 March 1984. However, any policies taken out before this date are still entitled to Life Assurance Premium Relief (LAPR) as it was known. Of course their numbers are now dwindling, but qualifying policies are no doubt still around.

The effect of the removal of LAPR was that it made whole life policies much less attractive as an investment vehicle. As pension contributions *are* tax deductible, the use of whole life policies as a means of providing for retirement is unviable.

Today there are a number of large life assurers who no longer offer whole life cover and while it would be wrong to suggest such policies are no longer of relevance in the modern life market, they now account for only a small percentage of policies.

Industrial life assurance

This is a once common form of life cover that after many years of decline could be viewed as having reinvented itself and re-emerged in a different form in recent years. Whole life cover used to require the payment of annual premiums or in some cases might even be funded by a large single premium paid up front. Those on lower incomes would find it difficult to meet large annual premiums. Industrial life assurers maintained large networks of agents, full- and part-time, who called on the policyholder weekly to collect the cash premium on policies that were on average far smaller than ordinary life assurance policies. In most cases the industrial life policy was designed to provide for funeral costs or leave a small legacy. The sums insured were insufficient to fully compensate the dependants for the early death of a wage earner. As more and more people began to have bank accounts and, with the introduction of direct debits, personal collection of premiums was rendered hopelessly uneconomic, true industrial life cover has become almost extinct.

In recent years a number of companies have introduced over-50s plans designed for policyholders of advanced years. These are simple, low-value whole life contracts with no surrender value which like industrial life are designed to provide for funeral expenses or small legacies. Of course the premiums today are collected monthly by direct debit and no assurer would use such an antiquated term as industrial life to describe such policies. Nonetheless they are distinct from ordinary whole life contracts as their purpose is not to offer significant protection to dependants or to provide additional retirement funds.

Term assurance

By far the most common form of life assurance, term assurance provides cover for a set period of years. If the life assured dies during the period, then the benefit is paid. If the life assured survives, no benefit is paid. It follows that this is the cheapest form of life cover as there is no certainty that any payment will be made. This is a pure insurance contract, not an investment. Term assurance policies have no surrender value and are not marketable.

The usual reason for purchase is to secure a mortgage. The standard practice of mortgage lenders is to require the borrower to insure their life for the value of the loan. Term assurance is the cheapest means of providing such cover, an important consideration as for many money will be tight in the early years of a mortgage.

Endowment assurance

An endowment is an investment plan and cannot be considered an insurance policy. Regular sums are paid into the plan, they are then invested and the premiums plus investment returns are returned to the investor at maturity. In the event that the investor dies before maturity, contributions plus investment returns will be paid back, but there will be no additional death benefit as would be the case in a life assurance contract.

However, in the 1980s and early 1990s, endowment assurance was a popular variation. This is a combination of term assurance and endowment, issued for a fixed term. If the policyholder dies during the term, the death benefit offered under the term assurance element is paid. If the policyholder survives,they receive the maturity value of the endowment. The reason for the popularity of these plans was their use in connection with mortgages. The borrower would only pay the interest on the loan. The intent then was that the endowment would provide the means to pay off the mortgage at maturity, while the term assurance would provide the required life assurance. In fact these were often sold on the basis that the endowment would not only pay off the mortgage but produce a healthy surplus for the policyholder in addition. These policies are rarely if ever sold today, and the reason for this is discussed in Chapter 11.

Group life

It is common for larger companies to provide their employees with life cover as a part of their employment benefits, usually termed 'death in service' benefit. Schemes can require contribution from the employee or be fully funded by the employer. They either offer a set benefit or a stated multiple of salary. The policy will cover present and future employees, therefore cover will cease when an individual leaves the companies' employ. It would also be normal for employees to be covered only up to normal retirement age. The advantage is that economies of scale allow the company to provide cover at a much lower cost than the individual could arrange. Indeed, for the very largest companies with many thousands of employees, the policy can take on the characteristics of the common pool in itself.

Life assurance: legal aspects

The following are the legal aspects of life assurance:

(a) *Involved parties* – In life assurance there are three categories of involved parties: the policyholder, the life assured and the beneficiary. There may be more than one individual in each of these categories. It is perfectly legal to effect joint names policies, joint life policies and to name multiple beneficiaries if the requirement of insurable interest is satisfied.

The policyholder takes out the policy, the life assured is the life covered by the policy and the beneficiary receives the benefit of the policy. The number of individuals involved can range from one to a theoretical infinite number. The number is not limited by law, but will be limited in practice. Therefore, an individual may take out a policy on their own life, naming their estate as beneficiary. Alternatively, policyholder, assured and beneficiary may be three different persons, for example, a wife insures her husband's life for the benefit of their child. The policyholder can freely assign the benefit of the policy and may therefore change the named beneficiary at any time.

(b) *Insurable interest* – As discussed in Chapter 2 and above, the key case of *Dalby v India & London Life Assurance (1857)* settled definitively that insurable interest is only required at the inception of cover. There seems little evidence that the policyholder is required to value this interest given a presumption that some interest exists.

(c) *Beneficiaries* – The policyholder must have an interest in the life assured. The beneficiary if different, need not. The beneficiary must, however, be named in the policy as required by s2 *Life Assurance Act 1774*. This requirement was amended by s50 *Insurance Companies Amendment Act 1973* to permit groups or classes of beneficiary if stated 'with sufficient particularity to make it possible to establish the identity of all persons who at any given time are entitled to benefit under the policy'.

It used to be the case that due to privity of contract a beneficiary could not enforce a policy against the insurer, unless they were a joint policyholder. It would seem that a statutory right now exists under the *Contracts (Rights of Third Parties) Act 1999*, given that they are both identified by the contract and the contract unquestionably confers a benefit upon them. The assurer can though insert an express clause in the contract excluding such rights. As the deceased's executors can enforce the policy on the policyholder's behalf, most assurers would insert such a clause excluding statutory rights.

(d) *Trusts* – A life policy can be held by the policyholder in trust for the beneficiary. This avoids the problem of privity of contract, but more importantly the proceeds are not considered a part of the deceased's estate. The benefits would also evade any claims by the policyholder's creditors. The most common trust is formed under s11 *Married Women's Property Act 1882*. Such policies are taken out by the husband or wife for the benefit of their spouse and/or children. Group life policies effected by companies on the lives of their employees have been held to be trusts, critically important if the company goes into insolvency. This is not an automatic process, however, and will depend on the wording of the contract.

(e) *Assignment* – The *Policies of Assurances Act 1867* permits legal assignments. Under this Act an assignee can enforce a policy as if they were the original policyholder. Hence the second-hand market for life policies.

(f) *Indemnity* – Insurances of the person are not indemnity policies, even where they may appear to operate as such, for example, life cover arranged by a creditor on the life of a debtor. This is despite s3 *Life Assurance Act 1774* which states 'no greater sum shall be recovered or received from the insurer or insurers than the amount of value of the interest of the insured in such life or lives'. Any individual can take out as many policies as they like and recover in full on all policies. It should be noted though that the existence of other policies is considered a material fact by assurers and if not disclosed will render the new (but not the original) policy voidable.

Other coverage

The most important policies offered by life assurers outside their core life business are pension schemes which are discussed in Chapter 11. Life companies usually offer a range of pure investment products which lie beyond the scope of this book, concentrating as it does on insurance. However, there are other insurances of the person offered beyond traditional life cover.

Permanent health

This is a long-term income protection cover. Contracts must be for at least five years but would normally extend to the policyholder's normal retirement age (policies of shorter length would be considered a general insurance cover). These contracts may not be terminated by the insurer save for breach of contract on the part of the policyholder.

Premiums can be guaranteed, and the same premium is paid on a level premium basis for the duration of the policy. Alternatively they can be reviewable, based not upon individual experience but upon overall results. This allows an insurer to review their claims experience every few years and increase premiums. Naturally reviewable premiums will initially be cheaper. Insurers have constructed their mortality tables over many years, so some will have data going back for over 100 years. Morbidity tables estimating the risk of serious illness are a much more recent innovation and cannot be viewed as being as reliable. The right of insurers to tinker with the premium in the event that they miscalculate is of value.

The policy provides a specified weekly or monthly benefit in the event that the policyholder is unable to work due to a medical condition. It is probable that this will be due to illness, but accident is not excluded. Generally, the policy covers an inability to engage in the policyholder's usual occupation. Premiums are usually paid monthly and depend on risk factors such as the occupation of the policyholder, previous medical history, as well as the well-established hazards of smoking and obesity. It would be normal for the policy not to pay for the first four weeks of disability and discounts will be offered for longer excess periods.

Claims payments will then continue until recovery, death or the policyholder reaches a specified age (again normally expected retirement age). To avoid malingering, assurers usually refuse to cover full normal salary (covering say, 60 per cent of the full salary) reduced to take account of any welfare benefits the policyholder might receive.

Critical illness

This is a recent addition to the life assurer's portfolio, drawing on the morbidity experience gained from writing permanent health insurance. The policy pays a set benefit in the event that the assured is diagnosed with a specified disease or is permanently disabled.

The problem with these policies has been the way that the specified diseases are defined. Cancer would of course be covered by such policies, but there is a considerable difference between advanced lung cancer and early stage prostate cancer. Heart attacks vary considerably in magnitude. There are obscure conditions which might not be specified but fall within the kind of conditions that are covered. There are conditions which might have a serious effect on some, while leaving others with only mild symptoms. Being within the broad heading 'life', critical illness cover is not a form of indemnity insurance, relieving the policyholder of any obligation to prove financial loss. The problem is that the policyholder could all too easily misunderstand quite what cover they have bought.

Given the difficulties in establishing the occurrence of an insured event, the ABI are presently seeking to intervene by producing best practice guidelines for critical illness cover. It is perhaps inevitable following the introduction of new types of cover, that for a time some uncertainty exists. The danger for insurers is that the reputation of this type of policy could be irreparably damaged before these issues are resolved.

Fundamental risk in life assurance

The entire life assurance concept works on the basis that only a small number of policyholders will die young. Despite the fact that the level premium system means that the policyholder will pay more than the risk truly warrants in early years, this discrepancy will not protect the assurer from loss in the event of early death. Although all are at risk from accidental death, despite our perceptions the great majority of deaths occur due to disease and the majority of these diseases strike principally at the elderly. Therefore the majority of claims only occur after premiums have been paid for a good few years. Indeed the majority of whole life policies never result in a claim as the policy is surrendered prior to death.

Any development that threatens this stable system is going to be of concern to assurers. Back in the 1980s the emergence of AIDS caused something close to panic among life assurers. AIDS being predominantly a sexually transmitted disease, it tends to affect the young. Promiscuity was and remains a key hazard factor in the risk of contracting the disease and usually it will be the young who are at risk. Suddenly the prospect of large numbers of young policyholders dying unexpectedly loomed large. As a new disease the assurers' carefully constructed mortality tables containing decades of accumulated knowledge were of no assistance and they were left with three courses of action.

They could take the view that losses would be manageable and that with the passage of time the impact of AIDS would feed through to the mortality tables allowing a review of premium levels. This would have been extremely imprudent and could have placed their business at risk to the detriment of all policyholders.

They could have simply excluded death resulting from AIDS. This would have been problematic as well. The noticeable feature of life assurance is specific causes of death are not excluded (other than suicide in the early years of a policy). It is important that policyholders can be certain that their policy would be valid in the event of death if policy conditions are met. There would also have been resistance from mortgage lenders who would have faced the possibility of loss where borrowers were dying uncovered with large loans outstanding.

They therefore responded by seeking to improve underwriting by identifying high risk applicants. 'lifestyle' questionnaires appeared as a part of life assurance proposal forms. As in the 1980s the prevalence of AIDS was greatest among gay and bi-sexual men, these questionnaires sought to identify sexual orientation and promiscuity with varying degrees of subtlety (or in some cases with no subtlety whatsoever). Cover was refused or additional premiums imposed on the basis of this questionnaire. This approach was controversial as it made mortgages difficult to obtain for gay men. It is a matter for conjecture as to whether such an approach could have been introduced in the politically correct twenty-first century. Indeed, in 2004, new ABI guidelines prohibited the use of lifestyle questionnaires and the imposition of premium loadings based upon sexual orientation at all. Neither can assurers request an HIV test based solely on the applicant's occupation, it being well known that certain occupations attract a high proportion of gay men. However, disclosure of high risk factors is still required, applicable to all applicants. Even this can cause problems if the proposal is for joint lives, common when couples are arranging a mortgage. It is easy to imagine the reluctance of an applicant to disclose prior indiscretions when they know that the form will be jointly completed by their spouse.

As it happens, the numbers of deaths from AIDS in the UK were vastly fewer than was predicted in the mid-1980s. Some commentators estimated a death toll running into tens of thousands a year by 2000, in part influenced by the belief that contracting the virus would prove terminal within a few years. Since the late 1990s, AIDS has actually caused a fairly predictable 500 deaths a year, a rate of loss that the large and well-funded UK life assurance industry can handle without difficulty. Infection rates were far lower than predicted and new drugs significantly extended life expectancy. Had the doomsday predictions of the 1980s proved accurate, there is little doubt that the assurers would have been forced to consider excluding cover for this disease. This in turn would in all probability have provoked government intervention to provide a government-sponsored pool in much the same way that a pool was created to handle terrorism risk in the area of property insurance. The particular risk of individual early death could have become a fundamental risk of early death by AIDS, causing an increase in exposure that could not be handled by the hitherto stable private sector common pool arrangement. At present, however, AIDS could not be considered a fundamental risk or even approaching such a description. Assurers are right to remain concerned, but more on the basis of underwriting high value policies with care rather than seeking to impose draconian terms on large numbers of ordinary policies.

At the time of writing, there is concern over the H1N1 flu strain or swine flu as most would refer to it. This follows previous alarm over avian flu strains. Normally flu is most likely to cause deaths among the very young or the elderly. Callous as this may sound, this is actually beneficial to assurers as any life claims will be more than offset by savings in pension payments. Obviously infants will not be insured. However, deaths from swine flu have been evenly distributed across all age groups (although fortunately in such small numbers as to prevent reliable statistical analysis).

Consider the notorious Spanish flu pandemic of 1918/19 (a variant of the H1N1 strain) which claimed tens of millions of lives around the world, including perhaps 250,000 in the UK. In this case more than half the dead were adults aged 20 to 40 years old, while death rates among the elderly were little more than would be expected from ordinary flu epidemics. Life assurers incurred heavy losses, but none appear to have failed as a result. Relatively few individuals carried significant amounts of life cover in 1918.

The population of the UK in 1918 was only two-thirds of the present figure. Were a similar pandemic to strike today, life assurers might face 100,000 or more claims from 20- to 40-year-olds. It is fervently hoped that modern drugs would prevent a catastrophe of such proportions, although hospitals might be unable to deploy these drugs if too many of their own staff succumbed. Such loss rates would imply claims exceeding £10 billion based on the fact that in this age bracket many would have bought life assurance to secure a recently arranged mortgage. Life assurers might rely upon a natural 'hedge', that losses on life assurance are offset by reduced pension payments. If mortality follows the 1918 pattern, this will be ineffective as the vast increase in early deaths will not be balanced by similar increases in mortality among the elderly. Life assurers can and do reinsure. However, in the event of a global pandemic, reinsurers would be under extreme financial pressure due to claims from insurers in other countries, claims received from general insurers and the economic recession that would inevitably accompany such an event. There is some possibility that they may fail, throwing the loss back to the insurer. Trading conditions for UK life assurers have been relatively benign for decades, certainly they have not had to handle the frequent catastrophe losses faced by general insurers. A global pandemic with high mortality rates is the life assurer's nightmare scenario, as the ability to meet such losses is finite and government assistance may be necessary. Fundamental risk is uninsurable and a true pandemic is certainly a fundamental risk.

Underwriting issues raised by the use of genetic testing in life assurance

Assurers have been underwriting life assurance on a modern basis since the mid-eighteenth century. Over 250 years they have picked up a thing or two. Nonetheless the information they have to work with has been fairly rudimentary. If a proposer smokes, is seriously overweight or underweight or drinks heavily, an increased premium will be applied. Assurers investigate family history as it has long been known that illnesses can run in the family. Now with the introduction of DNA testing they have an exciting new underwriting tool which can enable them to predict the probability that a particular individual will die before a given age with much greater accuracy.

So is this a bright new dawn for the life assurance industry? Well, perhaps not. The ABI has agreed a moratorium with the government which all but eliminates DNA testing from life assurance underwriting. Under the terms of this moratorium, life assurers cannot require a proposer to be tested. Proposers are not required to disclose the results of any predictive DNA test they may have taken unless they require cover of more than £500,000 and only a small percentage of proposers would seek cover for that level. Even if you have taken a test and are seeking cover over £500,000, all that must be disclosed is a predisposition to Huntington's disease. The prevalence of the disease is 70 per million among the white population, lower for other racial groups. So why is the latest scientific knowledge not being deployed?

First, there is the issue of politics and public relations. Consider the effect of automatic genetic testing. This would reveal whether a particular individual has a predisposition to variety of life-shortening ailments. The result would be that some proposers would face increased premiums, others might not be accepted at all. Quite apart from the fact that those deemed unacceptable would be unable to shield their families from the consequences of early death, in the absence of life assurance it would be far harder for them to raise a mortgage. This prejudice would arise due to circumstances entirely outside their control. If a motorist renders themself unacceptable to a motor insurer it is due to their poor driving record and/or convictions. Few would have any sympathy for them as it is their own fault. There would though be considerable sympathy where a refusal to insure arose due to an adverse genetic test unaffected by the conduct of the proposer. This is certainly a factor influencing the government in seeking the moratorium from the industry.

However, it is worth considering if it is in the best interests of life assurers to ignore genetic testing anyway. The effect of mandatory genetic testing would increase the underwriting cost. It is difficult to know how much because economies of scale would lead to a reduction in the current cost of several hundred pounds per test. Therefore life assurers should only consider the tests if a benefit exists that would outweigh this cost.

The existing questions about family history will often reveal the required information anyway, e.g. a history of Huntington's disease in the family. Questioning is obviously not as precise but on the other hand it is considerably cheaper.

The effect on the pool would need to be considered. Certainly the worst risks could be excluded from the pool, which would lower the premiums for the remaining members. This would not leave the life assurers any better off as the reduced claims level would be funded by fewer and lower premiums. The reduction in income would leave the company facing either reduced profit or a need to cut administrative costs.

A further possibility is that proposers in receipt of a highly favourable report might have an incentive to take the risk and not take out insurance. This is the risk thermometer theory discussed in Chapter 1. This would be a dubious decision as even the most perfect genetic profile would not shield you from the impact of a bus. However, it is possible that the impact of genetic testing would be to remove the extremes from both ends of the probability curve. The overall claims result of the insurer might be similar. Of course the demands of mortgage lenders would force the purchase of cover irrespective of any genetic profile, but the purchase of voluntary cover might be curtailed.

One argument in favour of testing is the possibility that a proposer might arrange a test, discover that their life expectancy is considerably lowered and then arrange insurance solely because of this discovery, a process known to insurers as selection. This would obviously prejudice the insurer's position given that they are not obliged to disclose this information. It is suggested, however, that such a scenario would be rare and certainly not sufficiently widespread to have a noticeable effect on the life assurer's results. In most cases those tested would have bought cover anyway, again due to the demands of mortgagors and would have been accepted at standard terms. It is also worth noting that despite a raised disposition to disease, many would live a perfectly normal lifespan. Should it be established though that selection was occurring to any acceptable degree, life assurers would have a sound argument for the introduction of mandatory testing, perhaps above a certain benefit level to minimise the cost implications.

Finally, it should be noted that life assurance has flourished for centuries in the absence of such tests. For the present at least, there seems no compelling reason to introduce them.

11 Pensions

A pension plan might not at first glance appear to be an investment product rather than a form of insurance. Most people associate a pension with a regular payment for the life of the pensioner. Known as an annuity, this is certainly an insurance product.

UK pension options

Although pensions have been offered for centuries, this was historically a product for the middle classes, particularly the professional classes. The upper classes with their wealth founded on land ownership had private means and did not require pensions. The working class simply could not afford them.

The basic principle is simple, the policyholder contributes premium on a regular basis up until the intended retirement date. The contributions are invested, thus building up a fund. This fund is then used at maturity to purchase an annuity (a regular payment made until the death of the annuitant), thus providing retirement income. Clearly, the greater the contributions and the longer the period available for investment, the greater the resulting annuity is likely to be.

Modern UK pensions are obtained from three main sources: state provision, occupational schemes and personal pensions. State provision is universal, but may be augmented by either or both alternatives.

State provision

The first state provision was introduced in 1909 and soon became part of the new National Insurance scheme. The maximum entitlement was 25p (worth around £20 today, in comparison to the 2009 payment of £95) for a single pensioner payable from age 70 (payable at 65 for a man today). It was also means tested, therefore only the poorest could collect the full amount and indeed no more than 40 per cent of over-70s qualified. Many of course did not survive to collect as at the time, overall male life expectancy at birth was under 50 and life expectancy among the working classes was even lower. Prior to this, the vast majority of the population had no pension (although, as stated, most of the working class did not expect to survive to pensionable age!).

The state pension, as it was known, was funded by contributions from employees, employers and the state and guaranteed a flat rate pension to contributors. Initially it was offered to anyone who had lived in the UK for 30 years as there were no prior contributors. In the early days it was not paid to anyone who had refused work or had been in a workhouse or prison, a robust approach that might interest certain tabloid newspapers today!

From 1945, it became the basic state pension, a non-means-tested benefit available to all, with the entitlement dependent on the number of years contribution had been made. The pension is payable at aged 65 for men and 60 for women, with men having to work for 44 years to qualify for the full amount, women only 39 years.

The basic state pension was, however, never intended to be anything other than a 'safety net', providing sufficient to cover basic necessities. It was also noticeable that the flat rate payment meant that benefits were unrelated to contributions. Higher tax contributions during working life did not obtain any extra pension.

The Labour government of 1974–79 attempted to address these deficiencies via the State Earnings Related Pension Scheme (SERPS) introduced in 1978 by the *Social Security Pensions Act 1975*. This scheme was intended to work on similar principles to private pensions in that the value of the pensions would be dependent upon the contributions paid in. As the contributions were based upon additional National Insurance payments (by both employer and employee) and therefore a percentage of earnings, the pension payable would be a function of earnings. Initially the maximum available was 25 per cent of average earnings between the upper and lower NI contribution levels over the highest 20 years of contribution. This would usually be the last 20 years, in which case a pension of 16.36 per cent of final earnings would be paid, on the assumption that pay increased by the same percentage each year over the 20-year period. SERPS was paid in addition to the basic state pension, but any earnings above the upper limit would be ignored for the purpose of calculating SERPS entitlement. The original scheme offered a full pension to a surviving spouse on the death of the pensioner.

SERPS was compulsory for all employees unless the employer offered a pension scheme offering benefits comparable to SERPS.

State pensions are non-funded. The contributions made by today's workers are not invested for their future benefit, they are used to pay the pension costs of today's pensioners. Workers today are reliant on the tax contribution of those in work in the future for their pension when they come to retire. This can, however, lead to problems if contributions and expenditure are not in equilibrium.

Initially though, SERPS was a good source of revenue for the government in the financial crisis of the late 1970s. Enhanced contributions were collected, but payments remained unchanged as SERPS liabilities would not have to be paid until years into the future. So SERPS contributions were treated as current revenue, they were not invested to meet these future liabilities. In the future, more and more scheme members were scheduled to retire, leading to an ever increasing cost. Only with favourable demographics can such a scheme work. What is required is static life expectancy combined with a steady birth rate. The number of pensioners would not then increase and the number of persons of working age (who have to fund the cost of pensions) would also remain unchanged.

Of course what has happened is that life expectancy has increased leading to more pensioners, who survive longer, while at the same time birth rates have fallen. If SERPS had remained as the cornerstone of UK pension provision (as was intended), it would have swallowed an ever increasing proportion of government revenue, putting the provision of other services at risk. This was entirely predictable as life expectancy had been rising steadily throughout the twentieth century and by the mid-1970s the birth rate had fallen sharply in comparison to the rates of 1945–1965.

In the face of projections predicting a sharp increase in SERPS costs in the future, the incoming Conservative government chose to reduce the future liabilities of SERPS.

The scheme was not cancelled, but members were encouraged to leave and new members deterred. This was achieved by the *Social Security Act 1986*. First, this reduced SERPS benefits to a maximum of 20 per cent of average earnings, calculated not over the highest 20 years of contribution but over the whole working lifetime. The likely effect was to cut the value of SERPS from around 16.36 per cent of final salary to about 9 per cent of final salary (again on the entirely unrealistic assumption that salary increases by a similar increment each year).

Furthermore, a surviving spouse's pension would be cut from 100 per cent to 50 per cent of the pensioner's entitlement. This was intended to be deferred until 2000; however, this was put back until 2002 and then introduced incrementally as the government failed to properly advise SERPS pensioners of the change.

It was intended that SERPS would appear to be poor value for anyone under 40 years old, thus encouraging the younger generation to leave the scheme. It could be argued that the Social Security Act 1986 signalled a reversal in government policy, away from a system increasingly based upon the state and back towards a system of private provision with the state providing little more than a safety net.

This philosophy was strengthened by the introduction of the State Second Pension in 2002. This replaced rather than supplemented SERPS and in fact operates on a broadly similar way. However, entitlements are not earned evenly but are skewed towards lower levels of earning. This has the effect that the more you earn, the less attractive the scheme becomes. The aim is that people are encouraged to make private provision, unless they are on such low earnings that this is not a practical proposition.

Of course, this strategy of steering people into private pension provision requires this alternative to be developed. This is where the UK insurance industry comes in.

Occupational schemes

Government pensions (or superannuation schemes)

Technically not 'private', these pensions are available to employees of central and local government and do not involve private sector life and pensions assurers. They pay a fixed percentage of final salary dependent upon length of service. Usually they require some contribution from the employee, but this contribution is almost certainly less than would be required to fund the same level of pension privately. There is then a significant level of contribution from the employer. The benefits under the scheme are guaranteed and sufficient contributions have to be made to ensure payments can be made. They can be distinguished from the state provision as they are individual pensions within a group scheme and form a part of the contract of employment.

Like the state pension, these schemes are not funded. The annual cost of paying pensions, over and above the employee's contributions, is met from current budgets. The result is that pension costs represent an increasing proportion of government salary costs.

Government pensions represent some of the best pension schemes available, particularly central government schemes where the benefits are index linked to preserve their value from the effects of inflation.

However, the schemes are so costly that government is seeking ways to reduce pension expenditure. This must inevitably mean cutting benefits or increasing staff contributions. Needless to say, union opposition has been encountered.

Private sector occupational pensions

These are arranged via a company scheme, but on an individual basis. They may be non-contributory (funded entirely by the company and rare today) or contributory (funded by both the employee and the company). They may be defined benefit or final salary based (a fixed percentage of final salary is paid according to length of service). Alternatively they may be defined contribution or money purchase schemes (a fund is built up which is used to purchase an annuity on retirement). The difference is that in a final salary scheme the investment risk lies with the employer, in a money purchase scheme, it is with the employee.

These are funded schemes, with substantial investment pools built up to meet future liabilities. The guaranteed value of final salary schemes makes them considerably more attractive, particularly as the maximum benefit may be as high as two-thirds of final salary. They have the advantage that not only is the company contributing, but the unit administration costs are lower than would be the case if individually purchased.

Larger companies often administer their own scheme, smaller company schemes are arranged on a group basis with life and pensions assurers.

Personal pensions

These are arranged by an individual and funded entirely by that individual. They are then money purchase schemes. Although there is no government or company contribution, tax relief is provided on contributions (up to 17.5 per cent of total earnings, the percentage increasing as retirement approaches). The accrued fund is then used to purchase an annuity on retirement.

Although already well established, this sector grew significantly in the aftermath of the Social Security Act 1986. As discussed above, this Act was introduced to counteract the probable demographic time bomb of the State Earnings Related Pension Scheme (SERPS). Personal pensions were seen as providing an alternative to state provision and the aim of the Act was to promote their use, thus steering individuals away from SERPS. As will be seen, it could be argued that this measure was far from successful.

Annuities

Although the investment experience of life assurers is valuable in the provision of personal pensions, their main role is as the providers of annuities. An annuity can be seen as the reverse of life assurance. Life assurance covers against the risk of early death, an annuity protects against long-term survival.

On retirement, in the absence of any occupational scheme, an individual will have to live off their savings for the rest of their life. The problem is that they cannot know how long that life will last. By handing over their fund to an annuity provider, a guaranteed monthly payment for life is secured. Although an individual death is unpredictable, the distribution of age at time of death for a large group is predictable given a well-constructed mortality table. In exactly the same way as life expectancy is estimated in life assurance, it forms the basis of the calculation of an annuity. Some annuitants will survive beyond the expected age at death, but this will be balanced by those who feel the scythe of the grim reaper at an earlier age than predicted.

A proportion of the fund is returned each year, but the balance is reinvested thus 'topping up' the fund each year. The annuity is set at a level that is intended to return the fund plus investment income to the annuitant by the expected age at death, less an amount to represent the assurer's margin on the annuity and an allowance for contingencies. There are two major risks for the assurer. First, if life expectancy is greater than anticipated, the annuity will be paid out for longer. Second, the assurer may not generate the level of investment return that they predict or even see negative returns.

Assurers seek to minimise the investment risk by buying long-term fixed interest investments, usually long-dated government securities (gilts). Offered for 25 years or more, a holding of long-term gilts shields the assurer from short-term market fluctuations as the return is fixed and is as guaranteed as it is possible for an investment to be, it being unthinkable that the UK government would default on its debt. Hence the reason that gilt rates are commonly referred to as a risk-free rate. There is therefore a close correlation between long-term gilt yields and annuity rates.

Annuities are quoted as a percentage of the fund value, this being the annuity paid each year, usually in monthly instalments. The percentage offered will increase for older applicants, so deferring retirement will lead to a bigger pension. In all cases the percentage is primarily determined by life expectancy and anticipated investment returns. In recent years a degree of underwriting has been introduced, so-called impaired lives annuities. Smokers, having paid extra for life cover, can now reap the benefit by collecting enhanced annuities based upon their lower life expectancy. Similarly, applicants with serious medical problems that would result in a refusal to offer life cover, can obtain significantly higher annuities.

On the other hand women, whose longer life expectancy means they pay lower life assurance premiums than men, receive lower annuity payments.

Note that s45 of the *Sex Discrimination Act 1975* permits such discrimination in the case of life assurance, annuities or accident insurance if the differential rates are actuarially justified. The *Sex Discrimination Act 1975 (Amendment of Legislation) Regulations 2008* now require insurers to publish the data. This is due to the *EU Gender Directive 2004* requiring that discriminatory rates are 'based on relevant and accurate actuarial and statistical data' and that this data is 'compiled, published and regularly updated'.

Annuity rates can vary between annuity providers. There is no obligation to purchase an annuity from the company that provided the pension plan that was used to generate the fund, the applicant is free to compare offers and purchase from any authorised provider.

Issues affecting pension provision in the late twentieth century

The pension mis-selling crisis

The aim of the Finance Act 1986 was to encourage personal pension provision to reduce the burden on SERPS. With that in mind, the government reduced the benefits offered by SERPS as discussed above. They also offered incentives in the form of discounted rates of National Insurance contributions if an individual left SERPS, but such discount could not be taken in cash and had to be paid into an approved pension scheme, occupational or private.

As planned, the number of personal pensions taken out after the provisions came into force in April 1988 soared. The Act appeared a great success, government liabilities were being reduced and life and pensions assurers together with their associated intermediaries were booming.

However, within a few years, criticism began to emerge regarding the suitability of personal pensions for many of these new policyholders and the manner in which they were sold. Such criticism identified two major areas of poor advice.

First, many individuals with access to final salary occupational schemes were advised not to join the scheme or even to leave if already a member. A personal pension would be highly unlikely to produce a better pension and of course the investment risk would lie with individual.

Second, many with existing SERPS entitlement were advised to leave and take out personal pensions, even thought they were already so close to retirement that they did not have time to build up any decent pension fund. A personal pension is a long-term product, as unless it runs for at least 15 to 20 years, it would be unlikely to offer better value than SERPS. A man under 45 might have been better off with a personal pension but beyond that age it became increasingly less likely. Even at 45 a woman would probably have been better off in SERPS.

It could be said that any such sales would have been negligent. However, due to a provision of the *Financial Services Act 1986* establishing negligence was not necessary. Under the Act, insurers and intermediaries were required to offer 'best advice', not merely reasonable advice. The onus was placed on the seller to demonstrate that they had offered best advice, not on the policyholder to prove that they hadn't.

The reasons for such poor advice being offered were varied. Certainly a sales culture pervaded the industry to which the provision of sound advice could be considered subsidiary. Sales staff were usually remunerated primarily by a commission on sales, creating an incentive to sell at all costs. Companies were clearly turning a blind eye to dubious sales and the various self-regulatory organisations, principally FIMBRA and LAUTRO, were not effectively policing sales practices. The expansion of the sector caused by the Finance Act 1986 inevitably led to a shortage of experienced professional salespeople and it can also be argued that the new recruits lacked the necessary knowledge and training. This was exacerbated by a high turnover of staff.

The government must also share the blame for not making it absolutely clear, both to industry and the public at large, the intent of their initiatives regarding personal pensions. They were aimed at the self-employed and those working for smaller companies without access to an occupational scheme and this could have been highlighted together with the advice that occupational schemes were likely to be the better option where available. They might also have stressed that those close to retirement would probably be better off staying in SERPS.

Had the issue been recognised early, firm action by the government and regulators could have limited the damage. Unfortunately these sales practices were widespread up to 1994 (and persist on a smaller scale to this day). The problem mushroomed into a major crisis that was not substantially resolved until December 2002 under the control of the FSA.

Assurers and intermediaries were liable to pay compensation where it was clear that the advice offered did not constitute best advice. However, in many cases compensation resulted from the inability of the firm to justify their advice. Due to poor record keeping many were unable to ascertain what the customers' financial position was when the advice was given and therefore could not discharge the burden of proof that lay upon them.

Ultimately, according to the FSA, close to one million were compensated at a total cost of £9 billion. The FSA also estimated that the administrative cost to the pensions industry was around £2 billion. What was more difficult to estimate was the impact of the loss of confidence in the industry.

No sooner had the mis-selling crisis started to subside, when a new problem emerged. In this case, the product involved was endowment assurance (or endowment mortgages as they were often erroneously termed). Huge numbers of these policies were sold in the 1980s and

1990s with the intention that they would produce a fund sufficient to pay off a mortgage at the end of the term. At the time assurers based contributions on an apparently conservative 8 per cent annual return, well below prevailing returns at the time the policies were written. In fact, many were sold on the basis that significantly higher returns would be generated and cash surplus would result. All too often, returns of 12 per cent or more were implied. Of course a straightforward repayment mortgage could have been offered which would have guaranteed that the mortgage would be paid off if payments were maintained.

However, a fall in investment returns since the early 1990s has meant that many policies have failed to return even 8 per cent, many failing to do so by a wide margin. This has left borrowers needing to fund any difference between the plan value and the outstanding mortgage, a sizeable sum in some cases. Life assurers cannot be held responsible for the state of the investment market, however complaints were made on the grounds that the policyholders were not adequately warned of the risk of poor investment performance.

Although refusing to launch a full investigation as was the case with pension mis-selling, the FSA required all companies to issue warnings to those likely to be affected. Furthermore, those companies who could not demonstrate that the policyholder was clearly warned of the investment risk could be required to pay compensation. In addition, a number of companies received large fines for mis-selling.

It is arguable that recommending an endowment in 1988 was not at the time poor advice, given adequate warning of risk. Expecting an IFA or tied agent to accurately predict economic performance over a 20-year period is hardly fair. What was unacceptable was that many companies continued to market endowments aggressively into the late 1990s and beyond, by which time it was obvious to the industry that they were underperforming and that this underperformance was likely to worsen.

However, endowments paid high commission, while there was little to be earned from repayment mortgages. Once again, the sales-orientated culture bolstered by upfront commissions led life assurers into difficulties, in just the same way as the sale of personal pensions had done only a few years before.

In all, around 2.2 million endowments ran into varying degrees of problems, with the FSA reporting in 2005 that the average shortfall was £7,200, a position that is unlikely to have improved since then. In a 2009 report to the Treasury Select Committee, the FSA stated that 436,000 customers had received £673 million in compensation over the endowment mis-selling issue.

Pension mis-selling was a far greater problem for the industry; however, the very last thing assurers needed was the growing public perception that they could not be trusted to be reinforced.

It is worth noting that endowment assurance does not appear to be offered by life assurers any more, although it could be said that this decision was delayed for far too long.

Robert Maxwell and the Mirror Group pension scheme

In 1991, the Mirror Group Chairman Robert Maxwell drowned in unexplained circumstances. After his death it transpired that he had authorised the loan of £350 million of pension fund assets to the Mirror Group to use as collateral to secure loans to the Group, Maxwell having appointed himself as trustee of the fund. Maxwell then authorised the sale of this collateral without reimbursing the fund. On the insolvency of the Mirror Group immediately after Maxwell's death, the pension fund lost most of its 'investment'. With assets of just £170 million and liabilities of £370 million, by early 1992, the fund that had been in surplus at the beginning of 1991, was unable to meet its obligations. Some recoveries were subsequently made from various financial institutions involved in the loan deals, but these were not enough to fully rescue the fund.

As a response, the *Pensions Act 1995* was passed, intended to regulate the governance of occupational pension schemes and to govern how such schemes should be wound up. As a result, the serious irregularities that characterised the Maxwell scandal are less likely to re-occur. Maxwell was responsible for damaging confidence in occupational schemes. The scheme was not managed by a life assurer, nonetheless they have a vested interest in the maintenance of confidence in occupational schemes and this highly public scandal was damaging to the reputation of such schemes.

Equitable Life

Founded in 1762, Equitable Life was the first ever modern life assurance company. Backed by more than two centuries of tradition, they enjoyed a good reputation in the market and were a sizeable presence in the UK life and pensions market, the sort of company that one could fairly trust with one's life savings. However, in a few short years, their reputation for financial probity was destroyed, along with the retirement plans of tens of thousands of policyholders. The regulatory failures surrounding the Equitable Life crisis have been explored in Chapter 5. Equitable Life's woes were, however, caused by the company itself.

The problem stemmed from the 1970s and 1980s when high interest rates introduced to counteract high inflation led to apparently high investment returns. Gilts (government securities) need to offer a yield slightly over base rates, corporate securities, being riskier, have to offer a higher return to attract investors. Equities do not offer a fixed return, but should offer potentially higher returns than securities to compensate for the additional risk. UK base rates were rarely less than 10 per cent from 1973 to 1991, peaking at 17 per cent in 1979 and reaching almost 15 per cent in 1989. The yield from gilts rarely dropped below 10 per cent from 1973 to 1991. During this period a double digit return could be achieved with minimal risk by investing in gilts or good quality corporate securities. As the UK was battling high inflation throughout this period, real returns (the actual return minus the rate of inflation) were not so impressive.

As a promotional tool, many life assurers attracted new personal pension holders by offering a guaranteed annuity rate (GAR) when they took out the pension, which guaranteed that the assurer would offer a minimum annuity on maturity. Alternatively the policyholder could opt to take the current annuity rate (CAR). The GARs offered were below annuity rates at the time and the assurers clearly did not expect them to actually be invoked. Guaranteed annuity rates as high as 13–14 per cent for a 65-year-old man were offered. As CARs in the late 1980s tended to be higher, touching 16 per cent or more at times, it was unlikely that the GAR option would be selected and, if it was, the differential between the two rates would not be significant.

Annuity rates, although linked to gilt yields, do not follow them absolutely as life expectancy is also an important determinate. Life expectancy rose throughout this period and continues to do so. This put downward pressure on the rates offered, however while investment returns remained high, the effect was counteracted.

By 1992, the economic situation had changed. Falling inflation saw base rates fall below 10 per cent in May 1992 and within a year below 6 per cent, which had not been seen since 1971. Gilt yields fell accordingly from 11 per cent in 1990 to less than 8 per cent in late 1992. Current annuity rates fell as well, but at a slightly greater rate as rising life expectancy influenced the calculations. From around 14 per cent in 1991, CARs fell to just over 10 per cent by 1993. GARs now exceeded normal rates by a noteworthy margin and assurers faced the prospect of paying well over the market norm to holders of GARs.

In the short term, this would have been manageable, but not only did CARs remain depressed, they fell further throughout the 1990s, following a steady decline in gilt yields. This widened the differential between the GAR and the CAR and therefore increased the assurer's loss. The downward trends have continued up to the present day, raising the possibility that the GAR could be double the CAR.

Most life assurers stopped offering GARs by the early 1990s; however, there were an estimated 450,000 past GAR policies which had not yet matured, dating back to 1957. Equitable Life had written some 90,000 of them, a disproportionate exposure in comparison to their overall market share.

The insurance market convention is (or certainly should be) that it is the insurer's decision to make a promise. If they get it wrong, they must honour that promise and try to look as cheerful as possible while they do it. Accordingly, many life assurers started to set aside reserves against these future GAR liabilities from the early 1990s onwards. Equitable Life, however, were the exception, in that as late as 1996 they were valuing their future liabilities on GARs at nil even though the CAR had fallen well below the GAR and they had recognised the problem as early as 1993. This calculation was accepted by the regulatory authority (from 1993 until the end of 1998, this was the Treasury).

The problem was the way that policies had been marketed. For many years investment performance had been a major sales tool. Sales staff were armed with impressive-looking graphs showing how their company had produced superior returns in comparison to their competitors. As all companies appeared to use this technique, the veracity of these graphs would appear to be doubtful at least! Included in this was information about the impressive bonuses offered to participating or 'with profits' policyholders over and above the standard returns. Any cut in bonuses would be seized upon by the competition and might lead to a fall in sales. Had Equitable Life reserved for GAR liabilities, that reserve would have had to come from funds otherwise available to the with profits funds. In other words, bonuses would have had to be cut. As Equitable Life were over-exposed to GARs, if they had cut bonuses, this might well have been at a level that would be particularly noticeable.

By 1998, Equitable Life faced a serious problem. Their failure to build up a reserve against future GAR liabilities meant that it was no longer possible to spread the pain over a number of years. Savage cuts to bonuses would be needed to balance the books and their over-exposure to GARs might even have rendered this ineffective. Their response was to attempt to renege upon the guarantee. Clearly they could not avoid paying the guaranteed rate, but they could manipulate the size of the fund to limit the loss.

The majority of GAR policies are 'with profits' policies. As stated above, the life assurer distributes a proportion of profits each year to policyholders (in the case of mutuals like Equitable Life, all of the profit not added to reserves). This distribution takes the form of an annual percentage bonus added to the value of the fund. The most valuable bonuses are the terminal bonuses, a final bonus paid as the policy matures. By the late 1990s, the terminal bonuses offered by Equitable Life constituted around 40 per cent of the total fund value. Equitable Life planned to offer a two-tier bonus. One bonus rate would be paid on ordinary pension plans and other with profits policies and a second much lower bonus for policyholders who insisted upon their GAR. The effect would have been to reduce the value of the GAR. The GAR percentage would have been paid but on a smaller fund value. The regulator (the Treasury and subsequently the FSA) went along with this little scheme and a further two years went by without any provision for GAR liabilities.

Unsurprisingly GAR policyholders were somewhat upset. They sued, insisting that they were entitled to the same level of bonus as everybody else. Although Equitable were victorious in the High Court, the policyholders won where it counts, in the Court of Appeal and the House of Lords in the case *Equitable Life v Hyman (2000)*. Equitable Life's argument that the policy allowed them full discretion as regards bonus allocation, including applying discriminatory bonuses, was rejected as nowhere did the policy state clearly that they could. The action was contrary to the policyholders' reasonable expectations. If a life assurer wishes to reserve such power, the onus is on them to make this clear from the commencement of the policy. As discussed in Chapter 5, the FSA-sponsored attempt to find a buyer for Equitable Life failed and it was subsequently closed to new business.

The existing policies still had to be run off and the Equitable Life with profits fund could not meet its liabilities. In the end, a compromise was put to policyholders in September 2001, which substantially reduced the value of policies held by all GAR and with profits policyholders. GAR policyholders received a bonus of 17.5 per cent on the by then much reduced value of their fund for foregoing their GAR. Other policyholders received a 2.5 per cent bonus on their (much reduced) fund value for agreeing not to sue. This deal was approved following a vote, claimed by Equitable Life to have been 97 per cent in favour.

Many policyholders cut their losses and transferred their reduced fund to another company. Not only was the fund value reduced but Equitable Life imposed a penalty of up to 20 per cent of fund value for such transfers.

Today, Equitable Life remains in run off. Equitable Life no longer have any ongoing business and are attempting to meet liabilities from the funds available in December 2000 plus investment income less claims and transfers. The policyholders can, however, expect a below average performance from the funds.

The effective collapse of a prominent life assurer, especially in such controversial circumstances was unhelpful when considered together with pension mis-selling and the Maxwell fraud.

The current pension crisis

Despite this apparently adequate arrangement, based on a combination of private and state provision, serious concerns are being raised about the viability of the pension system and the adequacy of future pensions. These problems arise from a number of causes.

Damage to industry reputation

The pensions industry entered the twenty-first century with its reputation severely damaged by a decade of very public scandals. In order to convince policyholders to commit to a long-term investment which will determine their financial well-being in old age, it helps if the public have broad trust in the industry and their products. Although it is impossible to establish with precision how many individuals were deterred from arranging a pension, loss of confidence can be predicted to reduce take-up.

Table 11.1 Replies to survey questions on pensions

Reply	(%)
Myself	36
Employer	26
Government	11
Insurance company or bank	14
Don't know or none of the above	14

By way of illustration, in response to a 2008 survey by the National Association of Pension Funds, asking the question 'Who do you most trust to provide a pension?' the following replies emerged (Table 11.1).

Of course this is only one survey and the results should not be considered conclusive. Nevertheless, this is a worrying outcome not only for life assurers, but also for government. Only 50 per cent of respondents expressed confidence in the three official sources of pensions. In response to a separate question, only around 40 per cent felt that a pension was the best way to save for retirement anyway.

Policy charges

The value of a pension fund can be eroded by the policy charges made by the assurer. Life assurers have long been criticised for failing to make charges clear in advance, complicated by the fact that it is not uncommon for a number of separate charges and possibly flat fees to be levied on the pension plan. This is an area that the FSA has sought to address in recent years, with a view to making charges as transparent as possible. The problem remains in that many plans reserve the right to alter charges.

Although the level of charges varies significantly from company to company and for different pension plans within the same company, annual charges of 2–3 per cent would not be unusual. When investment returns of more than 10 per cent could be generated with confidence, their impact was hidden. As investment returns have fallen, charges have eaten up an ever increasing proportion of returns, sometimes leaving little left for the policyholder. If assurers wish to levy high charges, the returns offered must be sufficient to justify their imposition. All too often that has not been the case, leaving the policyholder disappointed with the performance of the fund.

The position has been improved somewhat by the introduction of stakeholder pensions in 2001. These are intended to be simple low cost plans for the lower paid and charges are capped at 1.5 per cent of fund value for the first 10 years and 1 per cent thereafter. There is evidence that they are having a competitive effect in that charges on other plans have been reduced since their introduction, but much higher charges are still commonplace.

Demographic changes

The stability of non-funded state pensions has always depended upon the existence of an approximate equilibrium between taxpayers and pensions. This equilibrium has been disturbed in recent decades by demographic change.

First, life expectancy has risen, in particular the key indicator of male life expectancy at age 65. This determines the number of years a pension must be paid. This rose gradually throughout the twentieth century from about 10 years in 1900 to approximately 12 years in 1970. Since then, according to the Government Actuaries Department, the rate of improvement has accelerated:

1981	13 years	1997	15 years
1990	14 years	2006	17 years

Women currently survive about three years longer, although there is evidence that the gap is narrowing as this was four–five years in the 1970s and 1980s.

In comparison to the early 1980s, pensions are being paid for 30 per cent longer, significantly increasing costs for government and private sector providers alike. It is projected that this trend will continue. By the time the male 'baby boomers' of the 1960s reach 65 in 2025, their remaining life expectancy is projected to be 21 years and more.

The second factor is the birth rate or more specifically the effect that this has on the working population in the future. A total fertility rate of around 2.1 is required to keep the population stable (i.e. the number of children each woman will on average produce). In the mid-1960s, this rate approached 3. This fell sharply over the next decade to around 1.6 to 1.7 where it stayed for 25 years before recovering slightly to 1.9 in the last few years. The demographic profile of the UK has a distinct bulge, representing the baby boom years of the early 1960s. There are significantly more 40-somethings than 30-somethings or 20-somethings. When they retire, the ratio between workers and pensioners is likely to reduce sharply.

The number of over-65s expressed as a percentage of the working age population (the aged dependency ratio) rose slowly from 28 per cent in 1970 to 30 per cent today. Projections estimate that this will reach 40 per cent by 2025 and 50 per cent by 2053 due to a combination of reduced mortality and lower birth rate. This would significantly increase the tax burden on the working population. Remember also that not everyone of working age actually works!

Investment returns

In addition to the impact of demographics, funded private pensions are dependent upon investment returns. After a long bull run from 1982 to 1999, the UK stock market has performed poorly in the twenty-first century. The FTSE 100 index stood at 6,930 as at 31st December 1999. It fell sharply to 3,287 by 2003 and while it rallied to hit 6,500 in 2007, in January 2009, it had fallen back to 4,500. Nine years of overall poor performance have made it difficult to produce consistent growth. The effect of this reduction in returns is that either contributions to funds have to be increased or a reduced fund must be accepted. The costs of running final salary schemes have increased accordingly, while money purchase and private pension schemes buy annuities with a smaller fund value.

The annuity rate is also affected. This is historically linked with the long-term gilts (UK government securities) price as a conservative investment policy is required due to the contractual obligation on the annuity provider to pay a fixed (perhaps index-linked) sum. Since the early 1980s, falling inflation has led to falling interest rates and in turn to a reduction in gilt yields. In 1990, the yield from 15-year gilts was around 14 per cent. In 2009, the yield has been not much more than 4 per cent.

Annuity rates

Annuities are quoted as a rate percentage. This percentage is then applied to the value of the fund and paid annually for life. Falling investment returns limit the size of the fund in the

Table 11.2 Annuity rates for a single male aged 65
(no widow's pension)

Date	Approximate rate (%)
1990	14
2000	9
2009	7

first place. Rising life expectancy leads to a fall in the annuity rate as the sum will on average be paid for longer.

Of course the balance of the fund will be re-invested. This re-investment will be in gilts, preferably medium to long term. The fall in yield from this investment has also caused a fall in annuity rates (Table 11.2). This is the level rate (the annuity is fixed for the duration). If the annuity is index linked , the rate is now about 4.5 per cent. A lower rate on a smaller fund equals a greatly reduced pension in comparison to that available in the past.

Final salary schemes

Historically a significant percentage of the population had access to a company (or government scheme) that guaranteed a pension equivalent to a percentage (up to 66 per cent) of their salary at time of retirement, the defined benefit or final salary scheme. Although a contribution was usually required, this contribution was less than the long-term cost of providing the pension and the risk lay with the provider not the scheme member.

However, there has been a growing trend in the private sector towards closing these schemes to new entrants (and even existing members) and offering defined contribution (money purchase) schemes instead. Beginning in the late 1990s, this trend has continued at varying rates of decline. In 2002, according to the National Association of Pension Funds, 70 per cent of Defined Benefit schemes remained open to new members. By 2009, only 28 per cent were still open. There are fears that the current economic crisis may cause re-acceleration in the demise of these pensions in the private sector, although most public sector final salary schemes remain open for the present at least.

Obviously increasing life expectancy and reducing investment returns (both equities and gilts) have played a major part in this decline. However, other factors are apparent:

1 *Cancellation of dividend tax credit* – Dividends received from shares were free from tax. Given the high percentage of funds invested in equities (60–70 per cent would be the historical norm), this was a useful tax break. Its abolition in April 1998 forced an increased contribution from employers to compensate for the reduced earnings. The reported increase in revenue for the government was £5 billion. Either funding would have had to increase by this amount or funds would risk falling into deficit. It should be noted that this controversial measure also affects money purchase schemes, however, in this case it is the employee who suffers not the employer.

2 *FRS17* – This is a new accounting standard, introduced in 2001, requiring any pension scheme deficit to be declared in the balance sheet. Broadly speaking, FRS17 requires the market value of the assets to be compared with the value of the liabilities, calculated using bond yields. This means that for the majority of pension schemes, the value of assets will move in line with equity markets while the value of liabilities will move in line with bond yields.

In 2007/08, the stock market fell sharply, reducing asset values. At the same time, bond yields have also fallen, increasing liabilities. The result has been a general increase in pension scheme deficits, all of which have to be recorded on the balance sheet.

The liabilities would not, however, arise for many years, leading to the possibility that a stock market recovery in subsequent years might eliminate the liability without any action on the part of the company. Even if this is not the case, increased company contributions could probably be spread over a number of years. The argument exists that by utilising a short-term 'snapshot' when valuing a long-term liability, FRS17 could provide a misleading picture of the balance sheet. It can also be argued that it is a direct disincentive to offer a final salary scheme, as money purchase schemes cannot be in deficit, offering as they do no guarantee.

3 *Increased regulatory burden* – The new Pension Protection Fund (PPF) introduced by the Pensions Act 2004 is a case in point. Coming into effect in April 2005, it is designed to compensate the members of private sector final salary schemes. Funded by a levy on all such schemes, it will offer: (a) 100 per cent of the pension benefit to those already receiving a pension; and (b) 90 per cent of the promised benefit to those who have not yet started to collect their pension. The levy will not be based entirely on the size of the scheme, but will be '80 per cent risk based'. This means that a well-run fund with sufficient assets on conservative projections should pay a lower contribution to the scheme than a fund already in deficit, possibly based on 'adventurous' projections. This is certainly equitable, but is it sensible to load additional costs onto a scheme that you have already identified as being in difficulties?

Crucially, the PPF only covers final salary (defined benefit) schemes. Defined contribution schemes are not covered as no guarantee is offered. Therefore, while employees will receive valuable protection from the PPF, the cost of providing final salary schemes will increase. By switching to money purchase, company schemes can avoid paying a hefty levy to the PPF.

Current pension provision

According to the Family Resource Survey by the Dept of Work and Pensions (DWP), as of 2005/06, the position is as shown in Table 11.3. Even in the age category 55–59 years, 37 per cent have no pension. Clearly a significant percentage of the population is relying on the generosity of government provision. The question then arises, is this wise?

State pension in the future

The Pensions Acts 2007 and 2008 introduced a number of reforms based upon recommendations of an independent commission and two government White Papers.

Table 11.3 Pension provision, all adults, 2005/06

Status	(%)
Members of occupational schemes	42
Contributing to a personal pension	9
Members of an occupational scheme and have a personal pension	2
No pension provision other than the state provision	47

The Pensions Act 2007

The stated aim was to make 'the state system more generous, fairer to women and carers, and more widely available'.

1　The qualifying period for the full basic state pension was reduced from (44 men/ 39 women) years' contribution to 30 years for all.
2　Contribution credits introduced for those who do not work due to care of children or the disabled.
3　The Act promised in future to link the basic state pension increases to increases in average earnings rather than increases in retail prices, the increase in earnings tending to be higher than inflation. Pensioners would also be kept in much the same financial position relative to the working population. This is, however, only scheduled to start in 2012 and is subject to affordability. It is worth noting that prior to 1980 the average earnings index was the basis and the state pension was worth about 25 per cent of average earnings. Given that median earnings were £479 per week in 2008, the basic state pension would be around £120 had this link been maintained.

However, there was a price to pay:

1　The state pension age for women will gradually rise from 60 to 65 between 2010 and 2020.
2　For men and women, the state pension age will rise from 65 to 68, between 2024 and 2046. It is anticipated that this will reduce the aged dependency ratio in 2053 from 50 per cent to around 35 per cent.

The Pensions Act 2008

This Act is intended to deal with those not making any pension provision. As from 2012, all employed workers over 22 are to be enrolled in a workplace pension scheme. Therefore, if a company scheme is in existence, enrolment is intended to be automatic. This merely returns to the system in place before the Finance Act 1986 when joining the company scheme could be made mandatory.

If there is no company scheme, they will be enrolled in a new Personal Account Scheme. It is intended that these will be administered by the private sector, but with statutory limitations on terms and conditions, crucially a proposed cap on management fees of 0.3 per cent p.a. Whether the private sector will support the initiative at these fee levels remains to be seen.

The employee will contribute a minimum of 4 per cent of salary, the employer 3 per cent and the government about 1 per cent in the form of tax relief. Higher contribution levels from both employees and employers will be permitted.

Absolute compulsion was considered, however in the end employees were permitted to opt out (and this means actively deciding to opt out). Employers may not opt out, although of course there is the danger that they may put pressure on employees to opt out.

The future

The government response to the looming crisis has been to move further towards a system that is mostly privatised, other than the basic state pension which is little more than a safety net and the residue of the state second pension, which is a shadow of what SERPS was intended to be. This contrasts sharply with the position in most of Europe, where government provision dominates and the private sector plays a relatively minor role. In Germany, for example, almost all workers bar the self-employed are covered by a mandatory state scheme paying around 60 per cent of final salary for the average worker. Generous state provision is also available in other major European countries such as France and Italy. However, doubts are being expressed as to how long these admittedly attractive schemes can be maintained. Germany, France and Italy all face the problem of increasing life expectancy, exacerbated by the fact that the birth rate is below that of the UK. Pension costs are predicted to swallow an ever increasing proportion of government revenue in these countries, perhaps to the point where sacrifices in other key areas such as health and education may have to be made. It is worth noting that an ageing population will be making greater demands on the health service, leading if anything to increases in health spending.

Not so long ago, the UK system was widely admired. Government liabilities were minimal by EU standards. A high proportion of the workforce were members of good quality pension schemes and the future looked to be well under control. Now there is talk of crisis. Dependence upon private sector provision is out of step with most of the rest of Europe, but may prove to be a sound measure if the demographic problem continues to worsen. However, the policy relies upon a strong private pensions sector, capable of securing the trust of policyholders and maintaining that trust by delivering adequate pensions.

12 Policyholder and third party protection

Policyholder protection

The aim of policyholder protection should surely be to:

(a) Protect policyholders against losses arising from fraud or insolvency of insurers or intermediaries.
(b) Ensure that policyholders are not misled as to the nature or suitability of the policy due to the insurers'/intermediaries' greater expertise.
(c) Prevent insurers from unfairly avoiding claims.
(d) Provide compensation for policyholders who suffer loss due to negligent advice or performance.

In the first case, the firm responsible is no longer in any position to settled valid claims. The policyholder's interest can only be protected by an alternative source of funding.

In the other three cases, it is not a matter of the firm being unable to meet their responsibilities but unwilling. This can be resolved by the courts in many cases, but in view of the huge number of policies written each year, it is certainly desirable that a quick, cheap forum is available for any disputes to be settled.

Solvency and fraud

These two issues can be considered in conjunction as fraud almost always results in insolvency, although of course insolvency can occur in the absence of fraud

The Financial Services & Markets Act 2000

As discussed in Chapter 5, the current *FSMA 2000* is derived from the *Insurance Companies Act 1982*. This in turn was in part introduced by the string of insurance company failures in the 1960s and 1970s: Fire, Auto & Marine in 1965, Vehicle & General in 1971 and Nation Life in 1974. Many policyholders suffered as a result, either because claims were unpaid or investments lost or at best they had to reinsure and pay a second premium.

The aim of this Act was to ensure a basic level of solvency and provide for continuous monitoring of the financial position of insurers. This is intended to reduce the likelihood of insolvency and large-scale fraud. At the very least it should operate as an early warning system, allowing action to be taken while assets nominally exceed liabilities. The idea is that the company should be put into run off at a point where it is hoped that most of the liabilities will be met. Practice has shown that this is often not the case. Asset values can be unreliable when they are sold in a hurry, perhaps at 'fire sale' prices. In the event of fraud, there is the risk that assets have been overstated and/or liabilities understated. The case of Independent Insurance is an example (see Chapter 4). Initially applying only to insurers, intermediaries were included in the prudential regulation scheme from January 2005.

The effect of the Act is indirect. It does not give any rights to policyholders, however the policyholders' interests are protected to the extent that insurer insolvency is less likely. The problem is that even if insolvency is less likely, absolute solvency of insurers is not and cannot be guaranteed. No direct protection for the policyholder is provided by prudential regulation and alternative measures had to be put in place.

Policyholder protection schemes

Despite the undoubted improvements in the prudential regulation brought about by the Insurance Companies Act 1982 and the FSMA 2000, no direct compensation was available to policyholders who suffered loss as a result of insurer insolvency. The contractual right to recover claims payments was near worthless in the event of insolvency. Insurance, as opposed to investment, policyholders rank as ordinary creditors and line up behind secured creditors and the Inland Revenue when the remaining assets of the insurer are distributed. In all probability, the best that the policyholders could hope for is that they would receive a percentage of the value of any claim. If the claim was for the total loss of the policyholder's home or for the death of the main wage earner in the family, severe financial distress would result and possibly personal bankruptcy. The government accordingly determined that statutory protection would be put in place.

The Policyholder Protection Act 1975

This established the Policyholders Protection Board (PPB) with powers to raise levies from insurers to provide compensation in the event of the insolvency of an insurer. Such levies could also be raised from intermediaries who had introduced business to an insolvent life assurer. This was limited to insurers (UK or foreign) authorised to transact business in the UK and where the insurance was actually effected within the UK. The Act did not apply to commercial marine, aviation or reinsurance policies.

This protection was extended only to 'private policyholders' defined as 'individuals, partnerships or other unincorporated bodies of persons, all of whom are individuals'. These individuals did not have to be resident in the UK, they did not have to be insuring risks located in the UK and the risks covered did not need to be private in nature. Therefore, a large UK law firm established as a partnership would be protected by the Act in respect of their commercial insurance cover so long as the cover was purchased from a UK authorised insurer. No limited liability company would be protected irrespective of the size of the company.

The protection offered was that:

(a) Where the insurance is a compulsory class, the Board would meet the insurer's liabilities in full. The only major classes of compulsory cover are third party motor risks and employer's liability.
(b) For other general insurance policies, the Board would meet 90 per cent of liabilities.
(c) In the case of long-term insurances the Board would first try to transfer the policy to another assurer. Failing this, the Board was required to provide 90 per cent of the benefits

offered by the policy, but if in the opinion of an independent actuary the benefits offered were excessive, then they could offer such lower sum as the actuary recommended. This cover would only extend to claims the assurer was legally liable to pay (for example, the guaranteed death benefit on a life policy) and claims arising from disappointing investment returns would not be met.

The aim of limiting compensation under the Act was twofold. First, it was to reduce the risk of moral hazard. If full compensation was offered, policyholders might accept a ridiculously low quote for cover, not caring whether the company was reliable, safe in the knowledge that claims would be met in full by the PPB. Given that most policyholders' knowledge of the operation of the PPB is sketchy at best, it is questionable how effective the part compensation provision is in deterring such conduct in practice.

Second, there is the risk that a fraudulent or incompetent life assurer might offer fabulous benefits that could not reasonably be delivered, in order to attract large amounts of business in as short a time as possible. It could be viewed as unfair to expect other insurers to meet the possibly high costs of meeting these unreasonable promises where they exceeded the benefit a policyholder might reasonably receive under such a contract.

Although protection was extended to individuals only, this was extended to cover limited liability companies in respect of compulsory insurance only. Of course the true beneficiary of such cover will be an employee or a road accident victim, although the company also benefits as the insolvency of their insurer obviously does not relieve them of liability. This provision did not extend to non-compulsory liability policies.

Protection was not limited to private individuals in the case of long-term insurances. This was because most firms arranging cover on behalf of employees do so as a part of employee benefit schemes. The individual employees are the true beneficiaries of the policy rather than the company and were therefore covered by the Act.

The Board had wide powers to intervene where an insurer ran into difficulties, entered provisional liquidation or entered into a compromise with creditors. The Board could transfer business to another insurer (if one was willing) or 'prop up' the insurer to allow it to continue, possibly with a reduction in its liability. Such measures could not, however, be taken with life and pensions assurers if it would have been cheaper to settle at 90 per cent of the liabilities.

The Board was funded by a levy on all authorised insurers up to a maximum of 1 per cent of the preceding year's premium income. The cap was introduced to avoid a 'snowball effect' whereby a huge levy imposed, due to a major insolvency, threatened the financial position of other insurers. In practice, the Board built up a surplus rather than seeking to respond to individual insolvencies, by continuing to raise a levy in years of low expenditure. This minimised the risk that the Board's liability would exceed the maximum levy in any one year.

The Act had a retrospective effect as far as compulsory insurance went. In practical terms, this would only affect employers' liability insurances today. The Act covered all employers' liability policies written after compulsory legislation came into force on 1 January 1972.

Following a number of cases where long tail claims arising on policies issued by insolvent insurers prior to 1972 were not compensated by the PPB, the issue became a minor political cause. After considerable argument between the government and the ABI, the result was a voluntary agreement by the ABI to provide compensation via the PPB where the injury occurred prior to 1972, the employer was insolvent and their insurer was also insolvent. There was a proviso that no compensation would be paid if the employee was employed by a nationalised industry where it was felt that the government could fairly be expected to take responsibility. As the insurance was not compulsory, only 90 per cent of the liability would be paid. Of course recovery would then depend on identifying the insurer, no easy task after a period of, say, 40 years, particularly if the employer had been wound up many years ago. The ABI do maintain a database intended to identify the insurers of historic employers' liability insurance policies, but this database is not comprehensive as some insurers were wound up long before its creation. Unfortunately, if the claimant employee is unable to identify the existence of insurance covering the period during which the harm was caused, they may not claim from the FSCS.

The Policyholders Protection Act 1997

The PPA 1975 did not require that the risk was domiciled in the UK or that the risk was private in nature. All that was required was that the policy was issued by a UK insurer and that the policyholder was an individual not a limited liability company. This caused controversy when a number of subsidiary companies of London United Investments plc, Kingscroft, Walbrook, El Paso, Lime Street and Mutual Reinsurance (collectively known as KWELM) failed. These companies wrote US liability business in London, including significant amounts of professional indemnity business covering doctors, engineers, architects and lawyers, trading as individuals and partnerships, not as limited liability companies. Although it was never the intention that the PPB would meet claims on overseas commercial policies, the policyholders fell within the scope of the Act and a liability amounting to several hundred million pounds was met by the PPB.

UK insurers duly paid the required levy but the howls of protest were heard at the Palace of Westminster. Partially as a result of the KWELM payout the original Act was amended by the *Policyholders Protection Act 1997*. At the same time, the government needed to consider the *3rd EU Non Life Insurance Directive (92/49/EEC)*.

The PPA 1997 did not change the basic intent of the Act, however it did alter its application. The Act was limited to covering UK risks in its narrow sense. This meant a UK authorised company writing a policy on a UK situated risk. There are, however, three exceptions. Surprisingly perhaps, the EU does not at present require universal policyholder protection schemes to be in force. The UK, along with Latvia, Malta, Romania and Spain, offers such cover. Other states may offer partial coverage, but 14 have no scheme at all. However, with the introduction of an EU single insurance market, the scope of PPB protection was reconsidered.

The Act was extended to cover:

1   Risks written by UK authorised insurers where the risk is situated in the EU.
2   Risks written by EU subsidiaries of UK authorised insurers where the risk is situated in the UK.
3   Risks written by UK authorised insurers operating in the Channel Islands or the Isle of Man where the risk is situated in the UK, the Channel Islands or the Isle of Man. This is to clarify that the Channel Islands and Isle of Man fall within the Act although not part of the UK.

The Act did not cover risks written by insurers authorised elsewhere in the EU even if the risk is domiciled in the UK. In such circumstances the policyholder would have to look to the scheme offered by the EU state where the insurer is domiciled (if any).

Therefore, the UK insurance market via the PPB would be obliged to compensate a German domiciled policyholder, insuring their house with a UK authorised insurer, if the insurer was to fail. Were a UK policyholder to insure with a German authorised insurer, the policy would not be protected. Such scenarios would have been unlikely a few years ago, but with the increasing number of policies being purchased online, it is entirely possible that a consumer could purchase cover from an overseas insurer without even realising.

The Act ended the exposure of the PPB to huge US professional liability claims; however, as the Act does not have retrospective effect, there will be a run off period as liability for policies written prior to 1997.

The Financial Services Compensation Scheme

As of 1 December 2001, the FSA assumed responsibility for the payment of compensation. A new body, the Financial Services Compensation Scheme, was brought into being by the *Financial Services and Markets Act 2000* and took over from a number of pre-existing organisations, including the PPB. The scheme applied to policies effected after 1 December 2001, but the FSCS is responsible for settling compensation claims arising from policies written before that date under the rules of either the PPA 1997 or the PPA 1975. The date the policy commenced determines which rules apply. Therefore although both Policyholder Protection Acts are repealed, they remain relevant, although it must be said that claims under the PPA 1975 are not likely to occur very often.

The FSCS is also responsible for other guarantee schemes, including deposit takers (banks), investment firms and since 2004, home finance. The FSCS rules governing insurance are based on the well-established PPB approach; however, there are some changes:

1 The compensation payable has changed marginally. 100 per cent compensation remains payable in respect of compulsory insurance classes. Non-compulsory compensation is now 100 per cent of the first £2,000 and 90 per cent of the balance.
2 The principle of levy funding is unchanged from the provisions of PPA 1997. There may, however, be an element of cross-subsidisation as banks, investment firms and building societies have all joined and the FSA have indicated that it will not be cost effective to ring fence every category of business.
3 The scheme now covers 'small businesses' within those eligible for compensation on policies written after 1 December 2001. The definition of 'small' is a turnover of less than £1m, which would include the great majority of UK businesses. Note that this does not affect policies written before December 2001 which remain governed by the old PPB rules which provide no protection for limited liability companies. At the same time the cover extended to partnerships, mutual associations and unincorporated associations but is limited to those organisations who meet the small business definition of a turnover less than £1 million.

The operation of the scheme

Often the insolvency of an insurer can only be definitively established after the run off of its business has unravelled, a process that may take many years. The FSCS, though, intervenes as soon an insurer or intermediary is declared in default. This is defined as being 'unable to satisfy protected claims against it or likely to be unable to satisfy protected claims against it'. In practice, this is likely to follow shortly after a decision by the FSA that the firm must cease accepting new business, although there may be circumstances when the declaration that the firm is in default is delayed as it is initially believed that the firm may succeed in meeting its obligations.

Once an insurer is declared in default, the FSCS will initially concentrate on maintaining cover for affected policyholders. This might be achieved by another insurer taking over responsibility for the policies, but they would be unlikely to receive the full premium, making this scenario unlikely. It is more probable that another insurer would take over the policyholder base, issue their own policies to them and charge normal premiums. They would then pay an introduction fee to the receiver for the transfer of the goodwill of the business which can be added to the funds available to meet outstanding claims.

The FSCS would then deal with the claims from the policyholders. This would include claims in the normal insurance sense, but would also cover return premiums due following the cancellation of the now worthless policies. The actual negotiation of the insurance claims would not be conducted by the FSCS but by the original claims team at the failed insurer or more commonly a specialist firm appointed to manage the run off of the company's business. The FSCS would be responsible for payment once the claims were agreed. Having settled the policyholders' claim, they would require that the policyholder assign their rights to the FSCS. The FSCS can then recover what it may of the loss. This would include their share of any assets that the defaulting firm may distribute on the basis that the FSCS would stand as an ordinary creditor. It would also include any subrogation rights available (see Chapter 2). Any recoveries made would be offset against the compensation payments made, thus reducing the required levy.

Levy funding

Under the current arrangements introduced in April 2008, the FSCS split the levy funding arrangements into five broad classes: Life & Pensions, Fund Management, General Insurance, Deposits and Home Finance (Figure 12.1). With the exception of Deposits, these broad classes were further divided between providers and intermediaries. A cap was placed on the contribution of each subclass and each broad class.

Once the subclass has contributed to the maximum amount, responsibility then passes to the broad class concerned. Once the broad class has also contributed to the maximum amount, the general retail pool becomes responsible for any shortfall, although Home Finance providers are exempted from contributing to the general retail pool.

Therefore once the losses in a single year arising from the insolvency of General Insurance intermediaries exceed £195 million, General Insurance providers must meet the surplus. When the total losses of the General Insurance class exceed £970 million, other financial firms (except Home Finance providers) will meet the surplus via the General Retail pool.

When the FSCS began, it was expected that the banks might be subsidising the insurance industry, due to the relatively greater perceived risk of insurance company failure. Indeed in the early years of the scheme, costs due to insurance insolvencies (principally Independent Insurance) far exceeded the costs due to the failure of deposit takers which were comparatively trivial. However, it should be noted that insurance compensation never reached the level at which the insurers were unable to meet it from their own levy. As a result, the funds accrued by the FSCS to meet immediate claims reflected this imbalance.

Following the review of funding carried out in April 2008, resulting in the new levy model, these figures were: Deposit Takers funds, £1.8m and Insurance funds (almost entirely

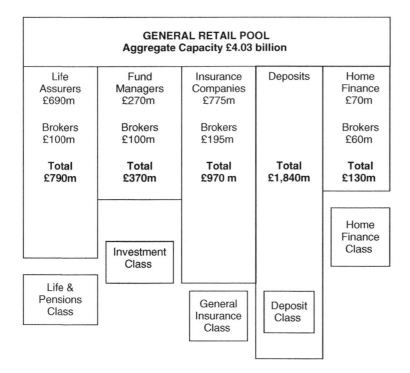

Figure 12.1 The FSCS levy funding arrangements.

general insurance) £72.4m. Over the next year, compensation in the Deposit Takers class totalled £19.77 billion (no, that is not an error, *billion*) following the failure of a number of banks (Bradford & Bingley being the chief culprit). This was far in excess of the FSCS's levy-raising capacity and was primarily funded by a loan from the Bank of England. The Insurance funds had shrunk to £34.4 million by April 2009 due to net compensation being paid under this class during the year of £40 million. Taking into account administrative costs, insurers were not in fact required to directly subsidise the banks despite the creation of the Retail General pool.

Nevertheless, is it reasonable to expect firms in one financial sector to contribute large sums to compensate the customers of another financial sector? It could be argued that it is in the general interest of insurers to compensate when one of their own fails, on the grounds that this maintains consumer confidence in insurance. The argument becomes less persuasive when a motor insurance intermediary is asked to pay for the collapse of the UK subsidiary of an overseas bank. The FSCS model appears clear, however. UK insurers and intermediaries could be asked to pay up to £970 million in the future towards the compensation costs arising from failures outside the insurance sector.

Excluded policies

The FSCS does not provide compensation for policyholders' losses arising from commercial marine, aviation, transport, reinsurance or credit contracts. With the exception of credit insurance, it is unlikely that many policyholders would meet the 'small business' test in any event. In addition, the FSCS does not cover any policies issued by Lloyd's underwriters. The insolvency of a Lloyd's syndicate is compensated by the Lloyd's Central Fund.

Summary

As far as the insurance market is concerned, the scheme has been so far been successful. It is probably the best scheme in the EU in terms of the protection available to policyholders and although insurers are no doubt unhappy at having to meet the contributions levied, the scheme has met its insurance liabilities without causing financial instability in the insurance market as a whole. The banking crisis of 2007 to 2009 has exposed the limitations of the scheme as it cannot cope with systemic risk. Operating in much the same way as an insurance pool, the scheme relies upon the existence of sufficient numbers of relatively financially healthy contributors to compensate for the default of a minimal number of failed firms. The FSCS can handle the failure of a single financial firm, it cannot handle the failure of a financial system. The sheer number of banks facing difficulties meant that government intervention was necessary if the scheme was to meet its obligations. The risk of systemic failure in the insurance system is lower than in the banking system as it is not rooted in customer confidence (see Chapter 5). Only if an insured catastrophe event were to occur, of a magnitude unparalleled in recent history, would the insurance system be likely to fail. In such circumstances it would appear that government intervention would be the likely solution.

Misleading advice, negligence and the unfair avoidance of claims

Assuming that the intermediary or insurer is solvent, the issue here is one of dispute resolution. It is of course the case that many complaints in this area are unjustified; however, the policyholder will rarely accept the word of the firm that they have no valid claim or that they have been properly advised. On the other hand, no policyholder should be deterred from pursuing a genuine grievance due to the lack of an appropriate forum.

Although the *Financial Services Act 1986* requires 'best advice' to be provided in relation to investment business, no such requirement is imposed upon insurers when it comes to general insurance business. Although all insurance policies are contracts of utmost good faith and this duty is imposed upon the insurer as well as the insured, doubt exists as to how far this duty extends. The law does not impose any duty on insurers to investigate a proposer's requirements before offering cover. That being said, deliberately or even inadvertently misleading *statements* not only would breach the requirement of utmost good faith, but would constitute fraudulent or negligent misrepresentation in the ordinary law of contract. Equally it is doubtful whether silence would protect an insurer if a proposer specified that the policy cover a particular risk, and the insurer knew that this was not covered by the policy but still offered it.

The relationship between intermediaries and their clients certainly gives rise to a duty of care (explored in greater detail in Chapter 8). Authorised brokers are required to hold professional indemnity cover as a condition of such authorisation. Tied agents are the responsibility of the insurer concerned and as such may or may not have professional indemnity cover, but it is probable that most insurers would insist that they do. In clear-cut cases, it is probable that the professional indemnity insurers would settle the claim without the need for legal proceedings. However, if a genuine dispute exists as to liability, the claim will be defended requiring the matter to be brought before the courts.

The courts will uphold the policyholder's contractual rights. The problem is twofold. As has been discussed in Chapters 2 and 3, the law of insurance is biased in favour of the insurer in a number of areas. Although the courts recognise that such bias exists and will often seek to minimise the impact on the policyholder, in the end the law is the law and must be applied by the judge. There is also the question of representation. Many policyholders would be unable to prosecute their own case in court. They can of course employ a lawyer, but even if successful are unlikely to recover more than two-thirds of the costs, leaving them with less than the true value of the claim. Any claim for less than £5,000 would be allocated to the small claims courts in all but exceptional cases. The small claims court rarely makes costs awards, leaving the claimant to pay legal fees that might eliminate most of the sum they have been awarded. If the claim is more than £15,000, it will be allocated to the High Court and the costs and therefore the risks to the claimant increase dramatically. A large insurer can generally shrug off defeat in the High Court as just one of those things. A claimant may face bankruptcy if the decision goes against them.

Many policies contain arbitration clauses preventing the policyholder from bringing the matter before the courts in any event. The ABI and Lloyd's have undertaken not to invoke such clauses where liability is refused, but of course many disputes will arise regarding the amount of the claim and these can be and are taken out of the courts' jurisdiction by arbitration clauses. The justification for such clauses is that arbitration is cheaper, but given that insurers will often employ a full legal team to represent them, this has to be open to question. A more cynical explanation would be that arbitration hearings are private and the decisions do not create binding precedent, thus avoiding the negative publicity of an open court hearing with the added danger that the insurance industry may face an unwelcome change in the law. Even if costs are reduced, the claimant still finds themselves forced to accept the risks of litigation which may be out of all proportion to the amount in dispute.

Seen from the other perspective, insurers are sometimes faced with frivolous or ill-founded claims. Even if they are certain to succeed in court or arbitration, they will not be awarded all their costs and may in practice find it difficult to make any costs recovery. A low-cost method of dealing with such claims is greatly to their advantage.

A final consideration is the limitations of the court system. There is a practical limit to the number of cases that can be heard each year and of course there are many other types of dispute that also need to be determined. The system simply does not have the capacity to hear all the disputes that might arise on the tens of millions of policies written each year. As the prevalence of insurance grew in the latter half of the twentieth century, so did the need to relieve the pressure on the courts by removing from their jurisdiction as many as possible of the mundane complaints. Making the legal process so costly and intimidating that policyholders are deterred from bring the complaint in the first place is not a reasonable response to the problem.

The Insurance Ombudsman Bureau

In recognition of these problems, in 1981 an ombudsman scheme was set up, instigated and established by the insurance industry. It might be said that this was to forestall statutory intervention, but it could equally be argued that many within the industry recognised that there was a need to resolve the inevitable disputes that arise from insurance contracts in a more efficient manner. Initially a Swedish concept, an ombudsman is an independent arbitrator appointed to arbitrate disputes arising within a defined sphere of competence, where no other forum exists or other forums are deemed unsuitable.

The Insurance Ombudsman Bureau (IOB) heard complaints brought by 'natural persons' (so excluding limited companies or partnerships). These complaints could relate to either life or general insurance, but the risk had to be private in nature. The procedure was that a complaint must have been referred to the insurer's Chief Executive for a final decision (in practice delegated back down the chain of command) and rejected. The complainant then had six months from this final decision to refer the matter to the IOB. Any complaints related to an insurance policy would be heard, but in practice most of these related to claims.

The Ombudsman's jurisdiction was, however, limited and no complaint would be heard if it related to:

(a) Investment business where the complainant did not effect the policy (i.e. they were a beneficiary or the policy was assigned to them).
(b) Claims by third parties against 'insurers' as in fact such claims are of course made against the insurer's policyholder and not against their insurers.
(c) Actuarial disputes involving long-term policies, due to the sheer complexity of such disputes and the need to employ highly skilled and therefore expensive adjudicators.

The scheme was then limited to contractual disputes between the actual parties to the contract and accepted that certain disputes were beyond the competence of the IOB. Note that in 1994 the scheme was limited to general insurance only, when responsibility for complaints about life assurers was passed to the Personal Investment Authority ombudsman.

The IOB had the power to order payments of up to £100,000. This award was binding on the insurer and payment was a prerequisite of continued membership of the scheme. Awards of higher amounts could be made, but only the first £100,000 was binding, the balance was a 'recommendation' and the insurer was not bound to pay. In fairness, many insurers have made a point of paying the recommended amount irrespective of the lack of compulsion. This practice is not, however, universal. The IOB decisions were not binding on the policyholder. There was no right of appeal, however by approaching the IOB, the policyholder did not lose the right to bring the matter before the courts in the future.

Membership of the scheme by insurers was voluntary and only complaints brought by the policyholders of members would be heard. That being said, all major personal lines insurers and all Lloyd's syndicates offering personal lines were members. The scheme was funded entirely by the participating companies, there being no fees or costs for the policyholder to pay. The IOB did not hear complaints against insurance intermediaries.

The approach of the IOB

As the IOB was an insurance industry creation owned by its member insurers, there were entirely legitimate fears that it would be controlled by the industry and ineffective when asked to act against the interests of its paymasters. In fact, the IOB commanded considerable respect and proved perfectly capable of championing the cause of the policyholder where it was considered justified. From the start a number of consumer groups were involved in the establishment and operation of the IOB. Although the insurers who 'owned' the IOB comprised the Board, the consumer groups formed the Council which actually appointed the ombudsman. The very first ombudsman, James Haswell, had no insurance industry background whatsoever, joining the IOB from the Army Legal Corps.

His brief was to consider complaints on the basis not just of the law, but on the basis of 'good insurance practice'. This might of course be what good insurance practice should be rather than what insurers themselves might consider to be good practice. This subsequently became an approach based upon what was 'fair and reasonable' given the particular circumstances of the case. Ideally the law, good insurance practice and 'fair and reasonable' should dovetail so neatly that the joins are invisible. Sadly we do not live in an ideal world.

Therefore the approach taken by the IOB was very different to that taken by the courts. Although legal principles are considered by the IOB, so are relevant codes of conduct, originally the Statements of Insurance Practice, ICOBS, today. If the application of the code of conduct led to a more favourable outcome for the claimant than the strict application of the law, the code of conduct prevailed. The courts could not adopt this approach, being bound by the doctrine of precedent. In certain areas, particularly non-disclosure and warranties, this significantly improved the claimants' prospect of a successful claim, often in circumstances where the courts, however reluctantly, would inevitably have found for the insurer. (The precise requirements of the codes in these areas are discussed in greater detail in Chapters 2 and 3.)

Approximately one-third of all complaints were upheld by the IOB. Of the remaining two-thirds, although it was still possible for legal action to be commenced, in practice, this has been rare. Having failed at the IOB it was unlikely that a court action would succeed. Therefore both policyholders and insurers were able to resolve their differences at a fraction of the cost of the formal court system.

The IOB should not be viewed as the consumers' champion, as that was never its intention and indeed it would have failed swiftly had this been the case. Its aim was to allow a claimant to voice their complaint and have it heard fairly and impartially without risk or prejudice to the claimant. At the same time, insurer membership was voluntary. The IOB had to maintain the confidence of the claimants who could and would have elected to use the courts if the IOB had been perceived as lacking the necessary independence. On the other hand, if the IOB had leant too far in favour of the claimant, in the early days at least they might have seen insurer resignations which could have caused the scheme to fail ignominiously. The insurers could even have closed the scheme down. It must be said that after the first few years of operation, once policyholders had got used to the new scheme, resignation by a member company might have had serious public relations consequences and for the insurance industry as a whole to close it down would have been unthinkable.

The philosophy and practice of the IOB continue to this day, even if they were overtaken by other developments. This can be considered evidence that the IOB got it about right. As the first scheme to be established, the IOB became a template for a number of financial services ombudsman schemes set up in their wake. It is unlikely that this would have been the case unless the IOB was broadly considered to be successful.

The Personal Insurance Arbitration Service (PIAS)

This was set up by a partnership between insurers who did not wish to subscribe to the IOB scheme and the Chartered Institute of Arbitrators. A less formal forum than a full court of law, again codes of conduct and accepted insurance practice were to be taken into account. This forum, however, was governed by the *Arbitration Acts 1950–1979*, therefore the decision of the arbitrator was binding on both parties, with limited grounds for appeal. The PIAS could only award up to £50,000 and the arbitrator was bound by the law, rather than good insurance practice. 'Fair and reasonable' was certainly not a consideration in itself.

The scheme applied to all policyholders resident in the UK in respect of policies arranged in their private capacity, but excluded life assurance and any cover arranged by an employer for the benefit of employees. As the majority of such policies were issued by members of the IOB scheme, the arbitration route was rarely adopted. The decision as to which forum was to be used was determined by the membership of the insurer in question, the policyholder not having a free choice unless the insurer was a member of both. The PIAS did partially plug a gap, as only the policyholders of life assurers who were not members of the IOB scheme were denied a forum as an alternative to the court system. Nonetheless the number of member insurers was low and the PIAS never handled anything close to the number of complaints dealt with by the IOB.

The Financial Ombudsman Service (FOS)

The IOB did not succeed in resisting the gravitational pull of the FSA. In common with so many other bodies operating in the field of financial regulation, it too was absorbed in 2001, alongside seven other financial ombudsman schemes (including the Personal Insurance Arbitration Service). No longer an industry scheme owned by the industry itself, the IOB is now one division of one function of the large government-run organisation that is the FSA.

The resulting Financial Ombudsman Service is designed to be a single, all-embracing body to deal with all consumer complaints from the finance sector. This arguably ended the problem of a claimant being passed from one ombudsman to another while it was decided which jurisdiction the case fell under. This was rarely a problem with general insurance, but complaints against life assurers could fall under the auspices of several schemes dependent upon the nature of the product. It is no longer correct to talk of membership as all authorised insurers and now authorised intermediaries as well, are bound by the FOS scheme as a condition of authorisation. Exemption is only permitted if the firm does not do business with eligible complainants. Specialist reinsurance brokers would be an example as reinsurance policies cannot be the subject of a complaint to the FOS.

On the other hand voluntary jurisdiction is possible where the firm is not regulated by the FSA but nonetheless would like to use the FOS as a dispute resolution service. In the insurance area the obvious example would be an insurer authorised elsewhere in the EU that has a number of UK policyholders.

Authorised firms are provided with guidance as to what is required of them by the Dispute Resolution section of the Redress chapter of ICOBS. This confirms the role of the FOS as stepping in as arbitrator only once the insurer and policyholder have been unable to settle the matter between themselves. Within eight weeks of receiving a complaint, the insurer (or intermediary) must send a final response or explain why it is not in a position to make a final response. The quality of such response is subject to scrutiny by the FSA and it must therefore deal with the substance of the complaint and not merely take the form of a standard rejection letter. Equally the reasons provided for additional delay must be reasonable. The final response must draw the complainant's attention to their right to take the matter to the FOS if they remain dissatisfied. The FOS will refuse to accept a complaint unless either a final response has been sent or more than eight weeks have elapsed since the complaint was made. Where the policy has been issued by a Lloyd's syndicate, the complaint must first be made to the Lloyd's Complaints Department. Again the eight-week response period will apply.

The clear intent is that the volume of claims received by the FOS is minimised. As will be seen, it is in the financial interests of the firm to resolve complaints internally where possible.

Jurisdiction

Once the claim has passed to the FOS, it is governed by statute, specifically Part XVI and Schedule 17 of the *Financial Services & Markets Act 2000*. Part XVI confirms the powers of the FOS where either compulsory or voluntary jurisdiction applies. These powers include the power to make awards, enforceable by injunction, to recover the FOS's costs from the respondent firm (but not the claimant) and to raise general funding from industry. Schedule 17 confirms the constitution of the FOS and provides greater detail regarding the application of the broad powers granted by Part XVI. Still more precise details are set out in the Dispute Resolution section of the *FSA Handbook*.

Some of the jurisdictional powers are lifted straight from the old IOB rules. Awards are binding up to £100,000 and recommendatory above this figure. The decision remains binding on the firm but not the complainant.

Other provisions are new. For example the complainant need not necessarily be a policyholder. The FOS will hear complaints where 'the complainant is a person for whose benefit a contract of insurance was taken out'. This may include members of group life, accident or health schemes taken out by their employers, so long as the intent was that they should receive the proceeds of any claim. It might seem to extend to include third party claimants in dispute with liability insurers, motor insurance being the prime example. The FOS have, however, clarified that this is not the case, presumably as the intent of the policyholder is not to confer any benefit on an unknown individual who might sue them at some future date. Complaints will though be heard from persons who, although not the original policyholder, have a legal right to claim under the policy due to assignment, subrogation or contract.

The FOS can refuse to hear a claim. Part 3.3.4 of the Dispute Resolution chapter of the *FSA Handbook* lists 17 reasons that the FOS can cite for such refusal. Some are entirely sensible, for example, where the complaint has no reasonable prospect of success, is the subject of current court proceedings or the subject matter has previously been considered and rejected by the FOS. Others limit the jurisdiction of the FOS. They will not, for example, hear a dispute purely regarding the investment performance of a policy. Neither will they hear a complaint if the subject matter has already been heard by the courts and a decision made. The FOS cannot be seen to overrule the courts, so a complaint can be brought to the FOS before court proceedings but not after the court has reached a decision. Some reasons can be open to question. For example, the FOS can refuse to consider the merits of a complaint if they deem that a reasonable settlement offer has been made by the respondent firm and this remains open. Deciding that an offer is reasonable may be difficult if the merits are not considered. The FOS also has a catch-all clause permitting refusal where there 'are other compelling reasons why it is inappropriate for the complaint to be dealt with under the FOS'.

In addition, in very rare circumstances, the FOS can refuse to consider a complaint on the grounds that it raises an important or novel point of law that ought properly to be considered by the courts as a test case. This can also be invoked where the respondent firm requests that the FOS step aside to allow a test case and undertakes to meet the legal costs of the complainant. If this provision did not exist, important areas of consumer finance law could be removed from the jurisdiction of the courts and the law could not develop. It is noticeable that since the IOB commenced in 1981, very few significant cases involving consumer insurance have reached the superior courts.

Finally, claims must be brought within six months of the respondent firm's final response, which must draw the complainant's attention to the six-month limit. Claims will not in any event be heard if the event complained about occurred more than six years before the complaint or three years from the time the complainant knew they had cause to complain, whichever is the later.

Determination

The FOS has adopted the approach taken by the IOB in the determination of complaints. This is given statutory weight by s228 *Financial Services & Markets Act 2000* which states that complaints are 'to be determined by reference to what is, in the opinion of the ombudsman, fair and reasonable in all the circumstances of the case'. This gives the ombudsman not merely the power but the obligation to rule contrary to law where the application of the law would produce a result that is unfair.

The approach of the FOS to the issue of non-disclosure and warranties has been discussed in Chapters 2 and 3. Of particular note has been the refusal to permit automatic avoidance in the case of non-disclosure and the substitution of proportionality unless the insurer can establish that they would never have offered cover at all. The concept of a breach of warranty extinguishing all liability under the contract is not a feature of FOS thinking which only considers the claim, not the continuation of cover. Even here, the impact of breach of warranty has been lessened by the requirement that the breach be causally connected to the loss.

This power, however, permits the FOS to go beyond these well-established areas of controversy and disregard any policy term that is deemed unfair. The result has been the effective overruling of many areas of English law and the importation of ideas from other legal jurisdictions. Of particular importance has been the Australian *Insurance Contracts Act 1984* which had long influenced IOB thinking. Of course, this informal law reform can only affect policies taken out by eligible claimants; however, the scope of the FOS has widened to the point that this in practice means the vast majority of policies issued in the UK.

Funding

Like the IOB scheme, the FOS is entirely funded by the financial firms appearing as respondents in their adjudications. There is no cost to the complainant, although neither would there be any award as regards the legal costs incurred by either side, save in exceptional circumstances. All authorised firms not exempted pay an annual levy based upon the size of the firm. Currently this ranges from a minimum of £100 per annum for the smallest firms to several hundred thousand pounds for the big 'household name' companies. This levy is payable regardless of whether any of the firm's customers use the FOS service. The actual amount is variable as the FOS will allocate charges to various financial services sectors based upon the number of complaints the sector is generating and therefore the amount of the FOS staff resources that needs to be allocated to that sector. Therefore, when endowment assurance was generating large volumes of complaints (63 per cent of all complaints in 2005), the life assurers were paying additional levies. Now that the focus has switched to complaints regarding payment protection insurance (PPI) and bank charges, the banks will be the largest contributors (although an insurance product PPI is largely sold by banks rather than insurance companies). No doubt in future another financial product will pick up the mass complaints baton and the relevant sector will be paying accordingly.

The basic levy buys three free adjudications under current rules. The fourth and subsequent adjudications are charged at a rate of £500 each. Therefore, the more complaints made, the higher the fees. It is in the interests of the insurer or intermediary to resolve the dispute without reference to the FOS if possible. However, as the FOS quite fairly point out, £500 is significantly less than the legal costs that would be incurred if the matter proceeded to court.

Box 12.1   Analysis of the FOS

In 2001, the first annual review was published, covering the period April 2000 to March 2001. During 2000/01, the FOS recorded the following data:

Enquiries made	414,722
Investigations commenced	31,347
Insurance investigations	5,654 (18 per cent of the total)
Staff	450

84 per cent of cases were less than 6 months old, 12 per cent between 6 and 12 months and 4 per cent remained undetermined for more than a year.

The largest number of complaints concerned endowment mortgages with 9,067 recorded, 29 per cent of the total. In addition, there were 711 complaints about payment protection insurance which are not included in the insurance investigations figure above as the product is offered primarily by banks rather than insurers. During 2008/09, the figures were as follows:

Enquiries made	789,877
Investigations commenced	127,471
Insurance investigations	19,102 (15 per cent of the total)
Staff	793

Some 56 per cent of cases were resolved within 6 months and a further 32 per cent within 12 months, leaving 12 per cent taking more than a year to determine, a slightly different reporting format from that used in 2001. Dependent on the class of insurance, between 31 per cent (health insurance) and 50 per cent (motor insurance) of complaints were upheld.

Endowment mortgage complaints continued to reduce in the 2008/09 year with 5,798 new complaints, well below the peak of almost 70,000 a year. However, as has been the case for many years, as soon as disputes over one type of financial product are resolved another class of product comes under fire. In 2008/09, payment protection insurance was the culprit, with 31,066 complaints made. Again payment protection insurance is not included in the figure for insurance investigations above.

Criticisms of the FOS

The large increase in the number of complaints made would seem to indicate that the public have broad confidence in the FOS for which they deserve credit. However, there are a number of criticisms that can be made.

Speed of service

One of the purposes of an ombudsman scheme is that it should be a means of resolving disputes faster than the court system. As can be seen from the data above, the length of time taken to resolve disputes is increasing and many thousands of complaints go unresolved for more than a year. In part, this can be explained by the increase in the volume of complaints, however in some areas delay can have serious consequences. This is particularly the case when it comes to commercial insurance claims. Although record numbers of complaints were received during 2008/09, staff numbers actually reduced over the year from 897 to 793 following a voluntary redundancy programme.

The maximum award

Binding awards can only be made up to £100,000 although, as previously mentioned, many insurers do consider themselves bound as a matter of honour to pay any higher recommendatory award. This £100,000 limit has remained unchanged since the establishment of the IOB in 1981. It may have been reasonably adequate then, but had the limit moved in line with inflation it would stand at about £290,000 today. While the limit would have exceeded the sum insured on the majority of consumer policies 28 years ago, in 2009 many complaints will be brought on policies with a sum insured far in excess of the FOS limit. Consider, for example, the rebuilding cost of the average home and the value of the contents. This could comfortably exceed £100,000. Since 2001 the FOS have handled complaints arising on commercial insurance policies for businesses with a turnover up to £1 million. Major losses on such policies would be likely to involve far greater sums than on consumer policies. Of course, disputes over sums in excess of £100,000 will be few, but the possible effect of non-payment of awards over the limit on the policyholder would be bankruptcy or insolvency. There is a persuasive argument for reconsidering the limit.

The method of adjudication

Most cases are resolved informally by the provision of written evidence and statements and often this is a suitable and cost-effective method. However, although suitable where the dispute turns on a single issue, the approach becomes more problematic when the FOS is presented with a more complex complaint. The FOS does not always disclose the insurer's defence to the complainant who may then be denied the possibility of refuting some of the insurer's statements. There is also the possibility that where the dispute has gone on for some time, a considerable volume of paper will have built up. Given the pressure to settle swiftly (and adjudicators rule on an average of almost five cases a week), it is easy to conclude that crucial evidence may be overlooked or misinterpreted by the adjudicator. The FOS has the power to convene a hearing, but this is very rarely exercised. Only 20 hearings took place in 2008/09. Although there are cost implications, it can be argued that the interests of justice might be better served if this route was taken more often.

Lack of transparency

As previously discussed, the FOS is obliged to ignore the law in pursuit of their obligation to settle on the basis of what is fair and reasonable. By producing the Statements of Insurance

Practice (see Chapters 2 and 3) the insurers have indicated that they accept this. However, the general powers conferred on the FOS raise the issue of transparency. Although the FOS, and previously the IOB, issue regular reports advising insurers of the general approach they are taking which cite examples, individual decisions are not published. The degree of consistency in FOS adjudications is consequently a matter of conjecture. This is particularly the case as the FOS admits that the standard will vary according to the status of the complainant.

Consumers will receive the full benefit of the FOS powers. In key areas such as non-disclosure and warranties, the FOS will apply its own thinking, based upon but not constrained by ICOBS and the Statements of Insurance Practice. In the case of commercial policyholders, however, the position is far from clear. The Statements were intended only to apply to consumer policies and ICOBS has followed that lead when incorporating part of the Statements. The FOS has, though, indicated that they might apply principles similar to those applied to consumer policies. They are more likely to take this approach in the case of sole traders than limited companies and the policyholder's knowledge of financial and legal matters will be relevant. The FOS seem also to consider that, if the policy has been bought through a broker, the policyholder will have the benefit of expert advice, although how much advice will be provided at the point of sale on a small commercial policy is questionable to say the least if the commission is only a hundred pounds or so. The size of the business will be relevant but not decisive. This is all very unsatisfactory. The insurers are left uncertain as to what will be considered good insurance practice and therefore how to deal with complaints and the degree of imprecision in the FOS thinking raises the risk of inconsistency.

The lack of appeal

The decisions of the FOS cannot be directly appealed externally by insurers or intermediaries, although of course the complainant is free to take the matter to court. The decisions of IOB were not susceptible to judicial review, confirmed in the case of *R v Insurance Ombudsman Bureau ex parte Aegon Life (1994)*. This was because the IOB was not deemed a public body. The FOS is a public body and their decisions are subject to judicial review, but in practice such an action is very unlikely to succeed. In *R v Financial Ombudsman Service Ltd ex parte IFG Financial Services Ltd (2005)*, the power of the FOS to adjudicate contrary to law was confirmed. It was also confirmed that they did not have to justify their decision to depart from the law. An insurer would therefore need to demonstrate either that the decision made by the FOS was irrational or that the FOS had failed to consider their own procedural rules.

This lack of transparency and effective appeal is a cause for concern. When the IOB was established, its membership was comprised solely of insurance companies to who could comfortably meet an award of £100,000. Today the FOS has jurisdiction over large numbers of small intermediaries to whom £100,000 would constitute a serious loss if uninsured by their professional indemnity cover. They cannot protect themselves by following the law, they must follow good insurance practice. It is far from clear in some circumstances quite what good practice would be. The intermediary then has no effective appeal against a decision that might cause the failure of their business.

Commercial insurance

The area most affected by the above criticisms will be commercial insurance complaints. Such policies are more likely to involve sums insured way above the £100,000 limit.

The claims are often complex, frequently involving multiple sections of a policy and can rapidly generate large volumes of correspondence. In such circumstances it may be difficult to resolve without a hearing, yet, as previously noted, that rarely happens. Commercial insurers are left in the dark to an extent as to the standards expected of them by the FOS, in particular as to whether the ICOBS or Statements applicable to consumers will be applied. Many complainants might reasonably conclude that the FOS offers no better forum than the courts if the FOS does not apply ICOBS. Although the FOS do not provide details of the qualifications or experience of their adjudicators even when such information is requested by the complainant, it would be surprising if many had any significant experience of commercial insurance claims. Slow processing of complaints is likely to be a major concern to many complainants. Where a commercial insurance claim is disputed, the future of the business must be in doubt if the claim represents a sizeable proportion of the firm's turnover. Even if the insurer is subsequently forced to compensate, the business may by that stage have already failed due to cash flow problems or loss of market share. Speed is of the essence if the business is to properly recover from the loss.

Although commercial policyholders could complain to the FOS from 2001, take-up was slow. In 2002/03, only 29 complaints were made. Since then the number of complaints has steadily risen, reaching 493 in 2008/09. This still appears low, being just 2.5 per cent of general insurance complaints. Unfortunately, the FOS does not release details of the number of commercial insurance complaints that are upheld. It would be hard to conclude that the FOS is established as the natural forum for commercial insurance dispute resolution in the same way that it is for consumer insurance.

Third party protection

It is a common misconception made by third party claimants (particularly in motor insurance) that they are making an 'insurance claim'. They are not, they are suing the policyholder and it is the policyholder who makes the insurance claim for indemnity against sums they may be liable to pay. Nonetheless they have a legitimate (if not legal) interest in the outcome of the claim. Most legislation in the insurance area regulates relationships between insurers and policyholders. In some circumstances, however, there has been statutory protection for third parties.

Third Parties (Rights Against Insurers) Act 1930

Even in back in the 1930s, the long tail nature of liability claims was recognised. The period elapsing between the incident and the third party discovering the harm could be years. The injured third party might not be able to recover due to the changed position of the policyholder, even though the insurance cover remained valid. One risk would be that the defendant was bankrupt or insolvent, so the third party would merely stand in line as an ordinary creditor and the indemnity paid by the policy would go into a general pool of assets from which the third party could only claim a share, possibly receiving very little of the compensation awarded. Second, if a company had actually been wound up, no legal action could be commenced as they no longer possessed a legal identity.

The *Third Parties (Rights Against Insurers) Act 1930* transfers the rights of the policyholder to third parties to whom the policyholder is liable on the bankruptcy or insolvency of the policyholder. It is not necessary for that liability to be established at the time of bankruptcy or insolvency, but the rights can only transfer if liability is established. Once liability is proven, the third party can then enforce the policy as if they were the policyholder. Technically the third party must obtain the permission of the court to sue the insolvent or bankrupt policyholder, win their case and then seek to enforce the award against the insurer. In practice, insurers will generally investigate the case before proceedings commence, with a view to settling out of court if liability is not in dispute or defending the action if it is.

If a company is actually defunct having been wound up, s651 *Companies Act 1985* permits the courts to 'resurrect' the company for the purpose of allowing a third party to make a personal injury claim. Again, however, insurers would not insist upon this if liability was not disputed and there was no need for court proceedings.

The third party cannot obtain any greater rights than the policyholder possessed at the time of transfer. Therefore if the insurer could have avoided the policy or the individual claim for non-disclosure, breach of conditions or suchlike prior to transfer, they can avoid any liability to the third party as well. The exception to this rule is where the insolvency itself makes it impossible to comply. Similarly the policy limits of indemnity will apply and the third party cannot recover any more than the policyholder could have done. As the courts cannot know how many third parties will emerge in the future or even if any will, claims are made on a first come, first served basis. If the policy is exhausted, latecomers will get nothing. Any policy term which attempts to exclude the insurer's liability under the act in the event of the policyholder's insolvency will be ineffective.

Reform of the Act is widely considered to be long overdue and the Law Commission has recommended change. In particular, while it is accepted that the intent of the Act is not to put the third party in a better position than the policyholder, it was not the intent that their position be any worse. Policy conditions that the policyholder could meet without difficulty, might be impossible for the third party to satisfy. It does not seem reasonable that the third party should be denied a claim because they are unable to provide records or other information as specified by the policy, which are not in their possession.

Contract (Rights of Third Parties) Act 1999

This has the potential to benefit third parties, however in practice rarely does. Its intent was to bypass the doctrine of privity of contract, the principle that only the parties to a contract may bring an action under it. The Act permits third parties to enforce a contract where either the contract expressly states that they may or alternatively the contract confers a benefit on them. There can be no question that a life policy confers a benefit on the beneficiary, equally, liability policies can be said to confer a benefit on third parties. However, the Act specifies that where a contract does confer a benefit on a third party, the right to sue will not exist if the parties to the contract do not intend such rights to be created. Insurers invariably insert a clause in the policy stating that the policy is not intended to create rights under the Act, effectively removing any potential influence the Act may have on the policy.

The Motor Insurers Bureau (MIB)

Compulsory motor insurance covering liability to third parties was introduced in the UK by the *Road Traffic Act 1930*, since superseded by the *Road Traffic Act 1988*. At a time when the number of cars and therefore road deaths and injuries was rising, the government was concerned that many motorists would be unable to compensate road accident victims from their own resources. Compulsory insurance would ensure that compensation was paid. It was immediately realised that this would not always be effective. Some drivers would in defiance of the law not take out insurance. Others, having effected insurance, would invalidate their cover due to non-disclosure or breach of policy conditions. There was of course no guarantee that the insurer would be able to meet the claims.

Coming into effect in 1946, the Motor Insurers Bureau (MIB) was set up by the motor insurers following discussions with the government. The existence of such a body subsequently became a requirement under European Union law in any event. The MIB is not a statutory body, it is a private company and is controlled by the motor insurers themselves. The majority of the Board of Directors are non-executive representatives of member insurers. All insurers (including Lloyd's syndicates) who are authorised to write motor insurance in the UK must be members of the MIB.

Technically, where a judgement is obtained against a driver and the damages remain wholly or partly unpaid after seven days, the MIB pays the unrecovered damages. In practice, the MIB is likely to step in before the matter proceeds to court and will negotiate the claim. The MIB is funded by a levy on its membership, in proportion to their premium income.

The MIB is only concerned with situations where compulsory insurance is required. Therefore if the accident occurred in a situation where insurance would not be required by law, the MIB is not required to offer compensation. For example, accidents occurring on private property which does not constitute a 'road' within the meaning of the Road Traffic Act.

Two agreements exist. The uninsured drivers agreement and the untraced drivers agreement.

Uninsured drivers agreement

Drivers may be identified but uninsured because of three problems:

1   There is policy of insurance but it is invalid. In this instance the insurer who insures the driver meets the claim as the 'insurer concerned'. The *EU 2nd Motor Directive* requires the insurer of a vehicle to meet third party claims irrespective of whether the driver is covered by the insurance. Although member states could elect to exclude cover for drivers of stolen vehicles, the UK does not permit this exclusion. The insurer will handle the claim as normal, but can pass the costs to the MIB if the driver was not entitled to an indemnity under the policy. The amount can be recovered from the driver and also the policyholder if they knowingly permitted the driver to use their vehicle without insurance. Obviously if the vehicle has been stolen, the policyholder will not be required to pay.

2   There is no policy in force. In this case, a claim is made directly to the MIB. The MIB will settle the claim if liability exists. The MIB can then recover the cost from the driver and owner of the vehicle if different, again only if they knowingly permitted the vehicle to be used without insurance.

3   The insurer is insolvent. The MIB handles the claim and settles where liability exists. The MIB are then entitled to any recoveries made from the Financial Services Compensation Scheme. As motor insurance is compulsory, this will be 100 per cent of the claim. In this situation obviously no right of recovery against the driver exists, they have purchased valid cover and are not responsible for the failure of their insurer.

Under this agreement, the MIB will provide compensation against both personal injury and property damage claims. The maximum liability follows the legal requirement to insure. Personal injury claims are compensated without limit but property damage claims are restricted to a maximum of £1 million. Property damage claims are subject to an excess of £300.

Exclusions

There are some exclusions applied. As mentioned, the MIB are only responsible in situations where compulsory insurance ought to have been in force. A vehicle must be insured not only if it is used on a public road, but in a public place. Therefore private roads and car parks would be 'highways' within the meaning of the law if the public have access. Injury or damage caused by vehicles lawfully uninsured will not be covered by the MIB. This is most likely to involve agricultural vehicles or mobile construction plant that would not be used on the public roads. Another example would be motor racing. As incidents involving such vehicles would generally be covered by public liability insurance, compensation is usually available anyway.

The conduct of the claimant may affect their right to claim. There is a well-established principle of law *ex turpi causa non oritur actio* (from a base act no action results). The uninsured drivers agreement states clearly that claims from injured passengers will not be accepted if they knew or ought to have known the driver was uninsured, the vehicle was stolen or the vehicle was being used for the commission of a criminal offence.

The MIB will not accept claims where the property damaged is adequately insured. Neither will they accept subrogated claims from the insurers of such property. Therefore if a person's car is damaged by an uninsured driver, they must claim for the damage from their own insurers if possible, who then have no right to recover the indemnity settlement from the MIB. This would not affect the right of the policyholder to claim for any uninsured losses. In the event of personal injury claims, the existence of life or accident policies would be ignored, entitling the claimant to recover in full from the MIB, as subrogation rights would not be created in any event on such policies.

Central government does not purchase insurance and vehicles owned by the Crown are exempted from compulsory insurance requirements, as are certain other public bodies such as metropolitan or county councils and police authorities. The MIB are not required to compensate claimants involved in accidents with such vehicles, unless insurance has in fact been purchased and is ineffective due to breach of policy conditions or insolvency. In practice, councils and police authorities usually do purchase insurance.

Recoveries

The MIB will seek to recover their outlay where possible and offset this recovery against the levy charged to the member insurers. All claimants are required to assign their rights to the MIB as a condition of receiving compensation. The MIB will then use this assignment to subrogate where possible. The uninsured driver and possibly the owner of the vehicle will be the obvious target if culpable. However, the right is often worthless as uninsured drivers do not tend to be wealthy. Young drivers are particularly likely to be uninsured, in part due to the high cost of insurance for young and inexperienced drivers. A teenager is unlikely to have much in the way of assets that the MIB can seize and will not normally be a homeowner. They are likely to be lowly paid, if they have a job at all. In many cases the recovery the MIB can expect to make will be less than costs incurred in pursuing it. As mentioned above, in the event of insurer insolvency, the MIB can recover from the FSCS.

Untraced drivers agreement

The uninsured drivers agreement can only operate where it is known that the driver is uninsured. If the driver does not stop and is not subsequently traced (a 'hit and run' accident), the existence or otherwise of valid insurance cannot be ascertained.

Surprisingly, this type of accident fell outside the scope of the MIB's duties for many years, although they did have a discretionary power to award compensation. It was not until 1969 that this anomaly was rectified.

The MIB is now responsible where the driver causing an accident cannot be traced. Where it is apparent on the balance of probabilities that had the driver been traced, they would have been held legally liable for the accident compensation will be payable. However, this compensation is limited to personal injury only, damage to property is not compensated under this agreement unless significant personal injury is also caused in the same incident. Full compensation is available for personal injury on the same basis as under the uninsured drivers agreement. Again compensation is limited to situations where compulsory insurance would have been required.

Although the lack of cover for property damage may do the owner of the property an injustice, it would be very difficult for the MIB to determine whether the alleged incident had actually occurred as described. Therefore, covering property damage would lead to fraudulent claims where motorists who had crashed themselves might blame a fictitious 'hit and run' driver for the loss. The property most likely to be damaged would be motor vehicles or buildings adjoining the road. Both risks are freely insurable and the MIB justifiably takes the view that if the claimant is not prepared to insure their property, why should the MIB? If significant injury is caused, they must also compensate for property damage as a matter of EU law. The risk of fraud is much reduced as it may be presumed that the police and ambulance service will attend the accident.

If having settled a claim, the driver is subsequently identified, the MIB would have a right of recovery against them. This would be a rare occurrence as the police would take a hit and run accident very seriously if injury is caused and if the initial investigation does not identify the driver responsible, the truth is unlikely to emerge later.

Other functions: accidents abroad

The MIB is responsible for policing the *EU 4th Motor Directive*. This requires all EU insurers to appoint an agent in every EU state who is authorised to handle claims on their behalf. The purpose of this measure is to allow an EU national to bring a claim in their own state (and own language) if they are involved in an accident in another EU state. The directive further provides that an action may be commenced directly against the insurer rather than the driver responsible.

The MIB's role is twofold. First, they maintain a register allowing the insurer of a vehicle to be identified on production of the registration number. Once this is known, the MIB can direct the claimant to the UK agent for that insurer. Second, the MIB can intervene if a 'reasoned reply' to the claim is not made within three months. If they deem it necessary, the MIB can take over the handling of the claim, settle the third party claim where appropriate and then recover from the insurer concerned.

If the driver was uninsured or untraced, the MIB will provide compensation as appropriate, acting as the agent of the equivalent body to the MIB in the EU state concerned. The costs will be ultimately be met by the overseas fund.

Other functions: the Motor Insurance Database

The maintenance of a database holding the insurance details of all UK vehicles is a requirement of the *EU 4th Motor Directive*. The MIB has to be able to provide details to their European equivalents where an EU national is involved in an accident in the UK. It has also been used as a major weapon in the fight to reduce the number of uninsured vehicles.

It used to be the case that the police had to give a driver seven days to produce insurance documents at a police station. This allowed time for forged or backdated certificates to be arranged. Alternatively some motorists would take out cover, pay only the first instalment of the premium and after allowing the policy to lapse, fail to return the certificate. They could then produce an apparently genuine certificate to the police.

The police have now have access to the Motor Insurance Database and can check at the roadside whether the vehicle they have stopped is insured. If it is not, they can arrange for the vehicle to be towed away on the spot and they do not have to offer the driver a lift home. They may even be permitted to have the vehicle destroyed. In 2008, the police seized 180,000 uninsured vehicles. This is a significant step forward in the detection of uninsured driving and of course the MIB have a vested interest in minimising the number of such offences. Vehicle owners can check their vehicle is on the database online free of charge via the MIB website. A charge is made for checking whether vehicles owned by other persons are insured and this will disclose the name of the insurer and the policy number.

The *Road Safety Act 2006* will soon allow action to be taken from the record. The Act states that it is an offence to keep a vehicle if insurance is not in force, so the police do not have to prove that it has been used on the roads. Note that this section has not at the time of writing come into force. If the vehicle is genuinely laid up out of use, on private property, the keeper of the vehicle can by making a declaration to that effect, lawfully leaving the vehicle uninsured. The regulations governing this action are going through the consultation process at present with the intent that Continuous Insurance Enforcement, as it is known, will be introduced in 2011.

The MIB: facts and figures

The MIB raised a levy of £407 million from its membership in 2009. As can be seen in Figure 12.2, costs have risen alarmingly in recent years. There are, however, encouraging signs that the campaign against uninsured driving is beginning to produce results. Although £417 million was levied in 2008, the MIB were able to return £40 million to their members as the cost of losses was below expectations.

The problem remains significant and although the motor insurers initially bear the cost, this is subsequently recovered from policyholders. The MIB estimates that as much as £30 on average is added to the cost of the premium for the honest, insured motorist.

There will be a time lag between MIB and police initiatives producing a reduction in claims and then again before the reduced number of claims brings about a reduction in levy. Nonetheless, if the corner has been turned, the levy should be falling noticeably over the next couple of years.

Conclusion

Policyholder and third party protection is a complex area as the protection is offered directly and indirectly via numerous pieces of legislation, statutory bodies and industry initiatives.

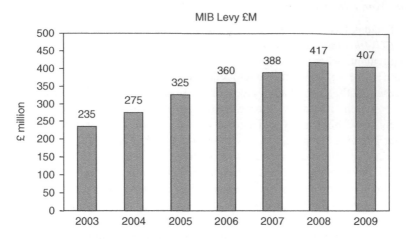

Figure 12.2 MIB levy, 2003–2009.

Nonetheless the protection offered to consumers is, if not quite all-embracing, very good. Recent changes have included small businesses within the protective umbrella; however, while well protected against insurer insolvency, the approach of the FOS towards the application of the strict law of insurance really needs clarification. Alternatively this can be brought about by reform of the law (see Chapters 2 and 3). Larger businesses have been left to fend for themselves; however, they can reasonably be expected to obtain the necessary advice and in any event as the size of a company increases, so the relative importance of insurance as a means to finance risk tends to decrease.

The MIB provides third parties with an effective guarantee as regards road traffic injuries, but of course their remit extends no further. It is worth noting that in the case of the other major compulsory class, employers' liability, no equivalent body to the MIB exists. If an employer neglects to purchase insurance, invalidates the cover or the employer has gone into liquidation and the identity of their insurer cannot be ascertained, no protection exists. Although such incidents will be few in number in comparison to uninsured driving, the injured employees will often be suffering from serious, perhaps terminal illnesses. The liability should by law have been insured, as it is not the fault of the employee that the liability either wasn't insured or if it was, the insurer cannot be traced. There is certainly an argument that the employees' position should be protected, perhaps as a part of the FSCS as it probably would not be cost-effective to establish a separate body.

13 Alternative insurance systems

The ability of the private insurance market to assume risk is limited, but the fact that insurers are unable or unwilling to cover a risk in no way means that a demand for risk transfer does not exist. There is also the question of whether the use of private insurance to handle a particular area of risk is the most efficient method. This question is considered by government and insurance buyers alike. Finally, in recent years, the buyers have begun to consider whether there may be alternatives to traditional insurance, given that 250 years of legal decisions have imposed a degree of inflexibility on the insurance contract and that these decisions are largely products of US and Western European courts and arise from the application of common law and civil law systems.

Government: the division of responsibility

State insurance

By far the largest 'insurer' in the UK is Her Majesty's Government. The 'premium income' of the National Insurance scheme alone is £100 billion. This funds a range of insurable events such as the state pension, unemployment and disability benefits. All of these could be covered by private insurance. The approach taken is, however, slightly different. National Insurance works on the basis of a set percentage of income being contributed as premium (including contributions from the employer). There is a different equitable premium concept as contributions are based not on the risk brought to the pool, but on ability to pay. This is certainly fair but not in the same way as private insurance. Benefits, however, are the same for all contributors, as high earners do not receive any greater pension or unemployment benefit despite their greater contributions. As payment of National Insurance is compulsory, the government does not have to consider the distorting effect of flat rate premiums or benefits. All must join, regardless of whether they believe that the scheme offers good value for money or not. There is then a social effect in that the wealthy subsidise the poor.

However, the largest 'insurance' scheme offered by the UK government is the National Health Service. Total NHS spending is presently over £100 billion, funded from general taxation. Although private sector health insurance is available, total premiums amount to around £4 billion, meaning that the risk of ill health is overwhelmingly 'insured' by the state. In a further departure from normal insurance arrangements, in the case of the NHS, benefits can be secured without the payment of 'premium'. All are covered irrespective of whether they pay tax, although the VAT levied on purchases means that almost the entire population does in fact pay tax. The unemployed would not have the means to pay private premiums, likewise private cover would be unaffordable for most pensioners due to the risk that they would bring to a private insurance pool. In the absence of a government scheme, such individuals might be excluded from healthcare provision.

Clearly there is no link whatsoever between tax contribution and entitlement to treatment. Although individuals are free to make private arrangements, they cannot avoid paying a 'premium' for NHS cover via general taxation, therefore the pool is again free from distorting factors. The UK approach can be contrasted to systems operating in other countries, most notably the United States, where the majority of health provision is funded via private insurance.

Other government services could be funded by insurance where they provide protection against a risk rather than a requirement for service. By way of example, the Fire Brigade began as a private service operated and paid for by the insurance industry. On the other hand, it is not possible to insure against the need for education, street lighting or refuse collection. There is no element of uncertainty about the requirement for the service and therefore no risk that is capable of being insured.

There are therefore a number of potentially insurable risks that the UK government has taken responsibility for. These are all areas where, if left to the private sector, there would be a risk of less than universal coverage as not everyone would be able to pay the required premiums. Government would in any event be considered to have a moral obligation to intervene to ensure that the sick receive treatment and the unemployed have the means to buy basic necessities. The concept of collective responsibility, as opposed to allowing the loss to fall where it will, lies at the heart of the insurance concept. The government is merely engaging in a degree of social engineering by modifying the principle of equitability of contribution from one based upon risk to one based upon ability to pay.

The counter-argument is that as government involvement increases, so does the danger that it will promote a culture of dependence rather than self-reliance. People will expect government to intervene and relieve them in the case of misfortune. In a variation on the theme of moral hazard, this may also mean that they consider that they are relieved of any responsibility to minimise the risk of loss or to mitigate the loss once it has occurred. It is arguable that if private health insurance was the norm in the UK, rates of smoking would decline as this would be reflected in the premium. Certainly a higher percentage of Britons smoke than Americans, although it cannot be said that this is solely due to different approaches to healthcare in the two countries. Health and liability insurers are well aware of the problem of malingering as the compensation offered removes some of the incentive to return to work. Government schemes often fail to link payment of benefits to risk management, with the result that the total loss is not minimised and the cost duly escalates. This problem can be exacerbated by political gerrymandering, for example, easing the criteria for disability benefit to reduce the apparent rate of unemployment.

It can also be noted that government schemes rarely offer an indemnity, often providing no more than a basic safety net. This is the case regardless of whether an individual's contribution has been at a level to justify full indemnity. Of course, once government offers cover for 'free', it is very difficult to establish private sector insurance solutions. A lack of full indemnity is a valuable marketing tool for the private sector if they can offer a more valuable benefit.

Compulsory insurance schemes

In other areas, government has chosen to use the private insurance sector in support of its objectives. Often, but not always, in situations where they would be required to meet the cost in the absence of private insurance cover. The obvious examples are the compulsory insurance of third party motor risks and employers' liability. Coming into force in 1930 and 1972 respectively, these require that those injured in road accidents or suffer accidents or illness in the workplace have a more or less guaranteed route of compensation recovery backed by the financial resources of the insurance industry, augmented by the Financial Services Compensation Scheme and the Motor Insurer's Bureau (see Chapter 12). In the absence of such legislation, the burden of caring for the injured would fall on the government. The thinking is that it is fairer for motorists and employers to pay these costs via insurance rather than the taxpayer who may or may not drive and probably does not run a business. It is also the case that compulsory insurance only covers situations where the motorist or employer is legally required to compensate, albeit that in many cases they would be unable to afford to do so in the absence of insurance. It is of course arguable that the existence of compulsory insurance has affected judicial decisions, leading to more adventurous, some might say claimant friendly, decisions, extending the boundaries of liability. This in itself is not problematic, indeed it is arguable that it is in the wider interests of society. The caveat would be that such judgments should not be so adventurous that the financial position of the insurance industry is endangered.

There are also numerous examples of 'compulsory' insurance being introduced as a requirement for permission to follow a profession. Some come into being as a result of legislation, for example, the FSA require that insurance intermediaries hold professional indemnity cover. In other cases, such insurance is required by the rules of the relevant professional body, solicitors and architects being examples. As such cover does not insure personal injury, the argument for compulsion is less persuasive. It is, however, an example of a growing number of consumer protection measures. As the government has assumed greater regulatory responsibility, so the expectation has arisen that the government will take responsibility for the failure of such regulation. This is illustrated by the long-running argument over whether the government should compensate the policyholders of Equitable Life (see Chapter 5). The government does not currently accept that such a responsibility exists, but the use of compulsory insurance can conveniently relieve them of any need to become involved in many cases.

In the UK, as in all developed countries, there is a shifting boundary of responsibility between the state and the private sector as regards the provision of cover against insurable risks. Where that boundary is drawn is matter of political policy. This can entail the full nationalisation of the insurance industry as seen in the Soviet bloc up until 1991 and in China until 1980. In a truly communist system the limited private ownership of property means that demand for insurance is in turn limited. Nationalisation has been tried in non-communist countries. For example, Indian life assurers were nationalised in 1956 and general insurers followed suit in 1972. This ended in 1999 when private insurance companies (and limited foreign investment) were once again permitted and the government stake in the nationalised companies was reduced to 50 per cent. Note this was not a matter of seizing control of British-run insurers post independence, as the life assurance market was, by 1956, dominated by Indian companies. At the other end of spectrum are the *laissez-faire* policies, throwing responsibility onto the private sector wherever possible. The United States is the largest proponent of this approach. In the developed world, most governments steer a path between the two extremes, generally seeking to take responsibility in areas that are particularly politically sensitive, such as health and pensions.

The manner in which nationalised insurers operate is not distinct. The equitable premium concept was in place, although it is arguable in the case of general insurance that the calculation was cruder than might have been the case in a competitive market. In a competitive environment, companies often seek to 'cherry pick'. This involves identifying low risk groups who are contributing more to their present pool than their individual risk truly warrants. Lower cost cover is then marketed to this group secure in the knowledge that the reduced premium is based on sound actuarial calculation. Nationalised life assurers constructed mortality tables and charged premiums in exactly the same way as their counterparts operating in a free market. Being state-owned, nationalised insurers are very secure, but it is questionable as to how strongly motivated they would be to keep premium levels to a minimum. Certainly, when India de-nationalised insurance, poor marketing, lack of innovation and excessive bureaucracy in the nationalised companies were cited as reasons to move to a free market system.

Government: the insurer of last resort

Government does have a further role. In a similar way to which central banks act as a lender of last resort to maintain liquidity in the banking system, governments also on occasions act either as the reinsurer of last resort, in partnership with private insurers or even as the sole insurer. This is not the same as making a policy decision to provide a government scheme in preference to private insurance. This occurs when there is a full or partial failure of private insurance to provide cover for a risk that would ordinarily be in their sphere of responsibility.

This in turn occurs when a risk is or becomes so fundamental in nature, that insurers cannot safely cover the risk and are unable to purchase reinsurance to cover the potentially excessive levels of risk. It can also arise in circumstances where the risk ought to be insurable, but due to a failure of risk management by both policyholders and insurers, cover cannot be maintained. If the reasonably foreseeable consequences of risk would be beyond the resources of the insurer, then no prudent insurer can provide cover. If cover is to be provided, it requires the far greater resources of government. This can arise in a number of situations.

A localised risk of natural disaster is unacceptable to private insurers

In response to the near unavailability of flood insurance in flood-prone areas of the United States (the Mississippi valley being one example), the US government passed the *National Flood Insurance Act 1968*. This Act established the National Flood Insurance Program (NFIP), a Federal insurance scheme for policyholders in areas unable to obtain flood cover. If the State government adopted a flood management programme designed to reduce flood risk to acceptable proportions, home and contents cover would be made available to private individuals in the affected areas.

Administered by the Federal Emergency Management Agency (FEMA), the Act was adopted as an alternative to Federal emergency aid in the aftermath of catastrophe losses. Take-up of the scheme was slow, due in part to continued reliance on Federal funds being made freely available post disaster. The result was the passing of the Flood Disaster Protection Act 1973 which prohibited Federal funds being used to relieve flood-prone areas which did not join the scheme. The result has been the creation of a large insurance fund, managed entirely by government. While the government does not go so far as to guarantee the fund, NFIP have a line of credit of up to $1.5 billion from the US Treasury. It seems likely that that borrowing facility would be extended if necessary. It is also noteworthy that much of the work of the NFIP is in the area of risk control, using the availability or otherwise of insurance to generate action at a local level. Unless the risk is reduced to acceptable levels, the NFIP will not offer cover. Insurance cover is often offered via insurance companies, but the company in this instance acts as an agent for NFIP who bear the risk.

This government as insurer solution is one means of handling risks that could be considered fundamental and which cannot be adequately spread in the international reinsurance markets.

A localised risk of natural disaster becomes unacceptable to private insurers

Hurricane Andrew in 1992 produced record losses for the insurance industry. Causing widespread damage across Florida, reinsurance cover for Floridian insurers was unsurprisingly hard to come by in its aftermath. In a bid to maintain the availability of insurance, the Florida State Legislature set up the Florida Hurricane Catastrophe Fund (FHCF) in 1993. A state-controlled reinsurance fund, it was designed to provide reinsurance capacity to allow insurers to continue to write property insurance without resorting to excluding hurricane damage. Augmenting rather than replacing the reinsurance coverage available from the private sector, nonetheless it is fair to say that it assisted in maintaining insurance rates below the level that they might have risen to. The intent appears to have been that the capacity of FHCF would be eroded over time as the private sector recovered from the shock of Andrew and resumed offering reinsurance in Florida. The fund, however, continues to this day, albeit that it is planned to slowly reduce the capacity offered with a view to withdrawing state support altogether by 2014. This of course depends upon benign weather as should a serious loss occur before that date, Florida may find itself in the same position as it was in 1993.

There are occasions where government simply sponsors a solution, rather than taking responsibility. The cover of earthquake risks in California is one such example. Sitting as it does astride the San Andreas Fault, California has over the last century or so suffered a number of major earthquakes. The 1906 San Francisco quake led to the failure of a number of US insurers, yet surprisingly the risk continued to be insured. But in 1994 the Northridge earthquake struck causing around $12.5 billion of insured damage (and considerably greater uninsured damage). The resultant losses led to the many insurers restricting or refusing earthquake cover in the State. In response, the California State Legislature created the California Earthquake Authority (CEA), a publicly run but privately funded earthquake insurance pool. Earthquake cover is mandatory on all domestic home insurance policies in California, however insurers can elect to participate in the CEA scheme.

A separate policy is issued for earthquake cover alongside the main home insurance policy. The premium for this cover is passed to the CEA. The insurer is then relieved of liability for earthquake losses. The CEA have the responsibility to build and maintain a suitable fund to meet the cost of the earthquake risk and to arrange reinsurance where appropriate (and available). The State government is not required to make good any shortfall, however, if the CEA funds are insufficient. The scheme does not cover commercial property.

The long-running argument between the UK government and the ABI over the provision of flood cover in the UK may yet see a not dissimilar scheme established in the UK to provide cover to 'at risk' properties should there be further repetitions of the major losses sustained in 2000 and 2007.

Other risks become unacceptable

In the UK, if an employee is injured at work, they are free to sue the employer for negligence or breach of statutory duty. The process is ultimately controlled by the courts, although in practice most claims are settled without the need for a hearing. The compulsory insurance system is intended to ensure that should the employee establish negligence, then compensation will be forthcoming. The United States (along with a number of other countries) takes a different approach. Under the Workers' Compensation system, the right of an employee to sue in tort is traded for a no fault compensation scheme. The employee does not have to prove fault, but neither can they bring the matter before the courts. Medical costs are paid and prescribed benefits are offered for a range of injuries and disabilities. Naturally, employers are required to purchase compulsory workers compensation insurance.

The problem with compulsory insurance purchase is that if insurance is unavailable, the unsuccessful proposer is forced to cease the activity giving rise to the insured risk. In the case of motor insurance this is not too controversial. If a motorist's prior conduct has been so poor that they are uninsurable, then they can take the bus and few would have much sympathy for them. Where compulsory workers compensation insurance is required by a business, there are other factors to consider. A refusal of cover will usually be due to prior conduct, but equally it may be that the business engages in high risk areas (asbestos removal specialists perhaps) that the private insurance industry is unwilling to cover. Even if the refusal of cover is due to prior claims, the effect of an inability to obtain cover might be to force the closure of the business, probably meaning that all the employees lose their jobs.

In a number of states in the USA, underwriting losses became so heavy that private insurers refused to provide cover, either to certain trades or at all. The result has been the development of a number state-owned workers compensation insurers. Some operate as an insurer of last resort alongside private insurers, while others operate as state monopolies. This has avoided the problem of firms either trading illegally or closing down, although premiums may still be prohibitively expensive.

The argument against this approach is that it does not address the root cause of the problem, that the level of claims is too high and needs to be reduced. The incentive to properly manage the risk may be diminished if an insurer can simply turn down any risk it does not like, passing it on to the state insurance company. Similarly, policyholders may not take steps to control risk secure in the knowledge that the state insurer of last resort is available. One reason why NFIP has so far successfully handled flood risks, is that the offer of cover is tied to a commitment to improve the risk. If a state workers compensation company does not take a similar approach, there is the danger that either premiums continue to rise or taxpayers' subsidies will be needed. It is worth noting that workers compensation is not a fundamental risk and there is no particular reason why it should not be successfully insured.

Increasing political risk causes a withdrawal of cover

An unpleasant recent development has been the string of terrorist attacks between 2001 and 2005 on New York, Madrid and London. This has led to a degree of government involvement in the insurance of terrorism risks. In the UK this was unfortunately not a novelty. The 'Troubles' in Northern Ireland saw the government step in to assume responsibility for property damage caused by acts of terrorism, initially with the *Criminal Injuries to Properties (Compensation) Act 1971*, subsequently replaced by the *Criminal Damage (Compensation) (Northern Ireland) Order 1977*. This offered full cover, effectively replacing the role of private insurance and remains in force today.

In 1992, the IRA campaign in the UK caused the government to intervene once more. In the aftermath of the London Baltic Exchange bomb in April 1992, insurers began to encounter difficulties in obtaining reinsurance. As a result, UK insurers announced that with effect from

1st January 1993, terrorism was to be excluded from the property damage and consequential loss sections of commercial policies. For political reasons as much as economic, the UK government was forced to intervene and working with the insurance industry established Pool Reinsurance Company Ltd, commonly known as Pool Re. Pool Re can be viewed as mutual reinsurer, owned as it is by its member insurance companies. Separate terrorism cover was made available on a very crude dual rate premium structure, one rate for city centres and a second rate for all other areas. Subsequently new rates were issued, one higher rate for outer London and other city centres and another lower rate for Cornwall and Scotland. The premiums were passed to Pool Re who was then responsible for all claims above £100,000 for each policy section. As commercial policies usually note buildings, plant and machinery, stock and consequential loss as separate items, up to £400,000 of cover was available from the main policy. Initially the insurers had to contribute a further 10 per cent to Pool Re funds if necessary, but this has now been discontinued. The government was required to meet the loss if Pool Re's funds were exhausted. Despite several large claims in the following years, government intervention was not in fact required.

After the World Trade Center attack, Pool Re was reformed. Cover was extended to an All Risks basis (but excluding acts of war) rather than limited to fire and explosion. This includes nuclear, biological or chemical attack. The members collectively must accept an industry-wide deductible of £100 million per event, limited to £200 million in aggregate per annum. Each member then has an individual retention limit within the collective limit in proportion to their participation in Pool Re. The more business they reinsure with Pool Re, the higher their individual retention will be. The scheme remains voluntary for insurers who may, if they wish, find alternative reinsurance. It is semi-compulsory for policyholders who may elect not to insure at all or to insure the property damage but not consequential loss. Having elected to insure property, they must insure all their property and cannot simply select high risk buildings for cover.

Although membership of the scheme is voluntary for insurers, once they have joined, they cannot refuse to offer terrorism cover and must cede any terrorism risk to Pool Re above their individual retention limit. They are free to set their own premium rates, but in practice most follow the Pool Re rates, perhaps adding a margin if the insured property is at particular risk. When introduced, Pool Re was at the time seen as unusual, only South Africa having a comparable scheme in place. But following the World Trade Center attack in 2001, this approach has become commonplace.

In the United States, the *Terrorism Reinsurance Insurance Act 2002* was passed. A temporary measure, it has been extended in 2007 for a further seven years. This requires insurers to offer cover against terrorism on all property and casualty policies. Initially limited to foreign acts of terrorism, the 2007 version now includes domestic acts. If an act of terrorism causes loss greater than $100 million, Federal assistance may be available. The insurer must bear a deductible for any loss equal to 20 per cent of their previous year's direct earned premium income from property and casualty insurance. The US Treasury will then pay 85 per cent of the balance. The total liability of the US government is capped at $100 billion. Note that in 2002 the relevant figures were a $5 million trigger, 1 per cent of premium as a deductible and 90 per cent of the balance was then paid. The present scheme is then markedly less generous. AIG, the largest US insurer with total US commercial premiums of £22 billion (not all of which will be property and casualty) might have to contribute up to $4.4 billion before receiving any Federal aid. Indeed, had the 2007 Act been in force in September 2001 it is possible that the US government's liability would have been minimal.

In the Netherlands, NHT, a joint insurer, reinsurer and government scheme provides up to €1 billion of reinsurance cover. Reinsurance of terrorism risk into the scheme is compulsory. Similarly in France, GAREAT, a reinsurance pool provides cover for losses above €6 million with no upper limit. This is structured as conventional reinsurance, but with state involvement and compulsory membership and reinsurance. The state reinsurance cover is triggered when losses exceed €2.2 billion. In Germany, Extremus was established along similar lines to Pool Re, a reinsurance mutual backed by government guarantees.

The question then arises as to why these schemes could not have been achieved by private insurance alone. Clearly in the immediate aftermath of a major attack, a degree of panic is to be expected, not just in the insurance market but in the reinsurance market. This can lead to a withdrawal of cover as seen in 1992 after the Baltic Exchange bomb, while the availability of cover is reassessed. The huge problem faced is that as terrorism risk is not evenly spread, it cannot then be said that all owners of property face a similar risk. Terrorist attacks are usually concentrated on high profile targets, either to maximise publicity or to maximise economic damage. Financial centres, the aviation and transportation sector and tourism have been targeted in the past, although new terrorist strategies should not be ruled out. The risk is therefore very high or almost non-existent, dependent on the business activities or location of the policyholder. If an equitable premium is charged, the premium for a high risk activity or location is so high it may be unaffordable, while the premium in a low risk location would be trivial. No pool is likely to succeed if it only attracts a small percentage of prospective policyholders. Constructing a common pool on this basis is extremely difficult. Government involvement allows an element of compulsion to be introduced and has often but not always led to a state or state-sponsored monopoly of such cover. Premiums charged are often inequitable. For example, the original Pool Re rate for inner London was five times the rate in a small provincial town. The equitable premium for inner London should have been considerably higher and the rate in the provinces much lower. Even within inner London, wide differences in exposure exist which are not differentiated.

A combination of heavy concentration of risk and highly unpredictable, almost random patterns of loss would make it very difficult for private sector insurance to construct and operate a successful insurance pool. Compulsion and limited inequitable rating bands may be considered crude, but when backed by government and broadly supported by the insurance industry, they can be made to work.

Takaful: Islamic insurance

It has long been recognised by Western banks that Western banking practice is in conflict with Islamic beliefs. Clearly the Western banking system operates on the principle of banks acting as intermediaries between lenders (depositors) and borrowers. The bank assumes the credit risk on behalf of the lender and the liquidity risk on behalf of the borrower.

Risk assumption is a valuable service and as such will cost the transferor. This cost is known as the risk premium. In a banking transaction this cost materialises as the interest payable. The interest payable on a deposit account is lower than the interest charged to borrowers. The difference represents the risk premium. The payment of interest lies at the heart of Western banking.

This concept is relatively modern. The charging of interest (or usury) has attracted considerable religious opposition. It is well known that Islam prohibits the activity. What is less well known is that the Catholic Church also prohibited the activity for many centuries.

In the fourth century the clergy was prohibited from engaging in the practice and this was extended to the laity in the fifth century. Although not strictly adhered to, the Church continued to oppose the practice. In 1311, Pope Clement V issued an outright prohibition and even declared void any secular law to the contrary. Usurers were effectively excommunicated for much of the twelfth to the fourteenth centuries. The prohibition was only definitively lifted in 1830.

Islam followed this doctrine of disapproval. Viewing money purely as a medium of exchange rather than a commodity, Islam prohibits charging money for its use, hence the view that *riba* (interest) is *haram* (prohibited). This view has remained fairly constant through the centuries although the lack of economic development in many Islamic countries meant that this was not a significant issue. Other Islamic countries such as Malaysia and Indonesia were a part of Western empires and Western banking practices were imported.

However, while money lending was an established practice when Islam emerged in the seventh century, insurance was not. This is not to say that early forms of insurance were not practised, but they were not in widespread use. For this reason, Islamic attitudes to insurance are far from clear as such attitudes are based upon interpretation of other Koranic strictures.

There is little evidence that Christianity even considered the religious status of insurance. This is perhaps not surprising as insurance only developed as a significant economic force in the late seventeenth century by which time the modern banking practices were well established. It is also noteworthy that many of the early insurance centres were in Protestant countries and Protestantism never seems to have taken issue with usury. Given the tacit acceptance of bank interest, the Catholic Church was never likely to intervene in other financial areas. This was particularly the case given that governments were beginning to regulate financial practices, usurping the moralistic role the Church had previously undertaken.

Islam, on the other hand, has considered insurance transactions, as economic development in the Middle East and independence in the Far East in the late twentieth century have led to the emergence of locally owned companies, run by Muslims and serving a predominantly Muslim clientele.

Islamic objections to insurance

Given that financial services markets are beginning to develop in Islamic countries, the migration of Muslims to Western countries and the export of Western business methods to Islamic countries, Islamic scholars have increasingly considered the status of insurance within *Shari'a* (Islamic law). The range of opinion is bewildering, from cautious approval to outright prohibition. The balance of opinion appears to tend towards prohibition due to three main objections: *gharar*; *maisir*; and *riba*.

Gharar

Although at root, this refers to deception, the literal translation is 'uncertainty':

> It is not permissible to sell an article without making everything (about it) clear, nor it is permissible for anyone who knows (about its defects) to refrain from mentioning them.
>
> (Al-Hakim and Al-Bayhaqi)

Gharar may arise due to uncertainty as to the nature and attributes of the subject matter or its availability, existence or quantity. Alternatively, uncertainty as to the price and/or terms of payment or delivery (and perhaps performance) is not allowed. It is worth noting that this jurisprudence arises from a time when contracts tended to involve tangible products.

Examining the insurance contract, some Islamic scholars have declared that *gharar* is present as insurance is an aleatory contract. When the contract is entered into, neither party can know whether the risks insured against will occur and therefore whether any claims will be made. Furthermore, the extent of loss should the risk occur cannot be known and therefore neither can the amount of any claim. The ultimate financial positions of the two parties could be viewed as being uncertain.

In some contracts, the amount of premium is unknown. Many commercial insurance premiums are based upon the turnover or wage roll of a company. This cannot be ascertained in advance, therefore a deposit premium is paid and adjusted once the true figures are available (almost certainly after the contract has expired). It should be noted that the percentage rate to be charged is specified in advance.

If the subject matter of the contract is considered to be the occurrence of a specified risk, this is clearly uncertain. This uncertainty extends to include whether it occurs at all, the timing and the extent of the consequences.

Finally, there is the question of the duration of the contract (i.e. delivery). Under the established principles of Islamic *mu'amalah* (commercial transactions), if a contract involves deferred performance, it is void if the period is not specified. Most insurance contracts are for a specified period (generally one year) and therefore do not fall foul of this principle. Life and marine policies are often issued for the duration of a life or a voyage and it is argued that this period is uncertain.

The most extreme objections are based upon the belief that whatever occurs is ordained by the will of God.

> If God wills any hardship for any people, no force can stop it. For they have none beside Him as Lord and Master.
>
> (A.L.M.R 13:11)

It is argued that purchasing insurance is an attempt to circumvent the will of God and implies a failure to place trust in God. It should be noted that this cannot be considered mainstream opinion.

Maisir

Wagering is clearly regarded as *haram* within Islam.

> O Believers! Intoxicants and gambling and divining arrows are an abomination of Satan's handiwork. Leave it aside in order that you may prosper.
>
> (Al-Maidah 5:90)

Some Islamic commentators have stated that insurance is a form of wagering, based on the fact that the policyholder may collect a far greater sum by way of a claim payment than they paid in the form of premium. From the perspective of the insurer, they retain the premium if the risk does not occur. This, it is argued, is no different from the relationship between a bookmaker and a gambler.

Riba

Again there is a clear prohibition against the charging of interest in the Koran.

> O you who believe, devour not usury, doubling and quadrupling, the sum lent. Fear Allah and observe your duty to Him, that you may really prosper.
>
> (Al-Imran 3:130)

Although this creates greater problems for bankers, modern insurance operates on the principle of profit via investment income. Claims and operating expenses often equal (and sometimes exceed) the premiums collected. The insurer relies upon the period of delay between collecting the premium and the claim first arising and then being settled to earn investment income on the premium. It is this investment income that often provides the profit in the transaction for the insurer.

Insurers invest a proportion of the premium funds in bonds, indeed, they are often forced to do so due to market regulation. Many insurers act as banks, entering into direct loans. Their liquid cash is placed on short-term deposit earning interest.

Another common practice in general insurance is offering instalment plans to the policyholders, whereby premiums can be paid in monthly instalments. This usually attracts an interest charge.

Some Islamic commentators have focused on the insurance transaction itself. Most life assurance companies operate a system of bonuses as a part of their 'with profits' policies whereby the policyholder receives a variable percentage of their fund value each year. This, it has been argued, is a form of *riba* if the policyholder is viewed as 'charging' the life assurer for the use of the money in their fund, in other words, receiving interest for money on deposit.

A more extreme view considers payment of a specified sum and acceptance of a smaller or larger sum to constitute *al riba*. This is a possible outcome of an insurance contract. This is based upon the opinion that the concept of riba can be divided into *Riba An-Nasiah* (interest on borrowed money) and *Riba Al-Fadl* (exchanging goods for a larger quantity of inferior quality goods of the same kind). It has been argued that the money paid in premium is exchanged for a larger quantity of money paid as a claim. It relies upon money paid as a claim payment being regarded as inferior in quality to the money received as a premium.

This argument is based upon the opportunity cost of the delay between premium payment and claim payment. The present value of £1 of premium is greater than the present value of £1 of claim payment and therefore it could be argued that the claim payment is of inferior quality. It is suggested that most Islamic scholars would consider this to be an erroneous interpretation, not least because the objection to *riba* is based upon the view that money is not a commodity or good.

However, Muslims living in Western countries clearly do buy insurance and there are insurance companies in the Islamic world. Leaving aside the undeniable fact that religious observance is far from absolute and the differing attitudes to insurance exist within Islam, how can this be explained?

Even if insurance is *haram*, many Islamic scholars feel that the duty to avoid insurance purchase is overridden by the duty to obey the law. Therefore, if insurance purchase is a legal requirement, such purchase is *halal* (acceptable) as there is compulsion and to break the law would be a greater sin.

The validity of Islamic objections to insurance

There are therefore a number of objections to insurance based on interpretation of Koranic strictures. Accepting that Muslims are required to follow the clear injunctions contained within the Koran, does this mean that *Shari'a* law and modern insurance practice are fundamentally incompatible? Given a perfect understanding of both *Shari'a* and insurance on the part of Islamic scholars, this may indeed be the case. Although it may be presumed that Islamic scholars possess expert knowledge of the Koran, do they properly understand insurance theory?

Gharar *(uncertainty) in insurance contracts*

There is no doubt that uncertainty lies at the heart of an insurance contract. By definition, the policy is designed to cover uncertain future events. It is worth noting that there are, however, different uncertainties. The uncertainty insured against might be uncertainty as to occurrence. However, in the case of whole life assurance occurrence is certain, it is the timing of the occurrence that is insured.

In the case of commercial liability policies issued to major organisations, the possibility of no occurrence is so low that it can be discounted as an outcome worthy of consideration. Such policies are insuring against the uncertainty as to the number of occurrences. Such policies generally contain a large deductible which means that the majority of occurrences are not insured, as the cost would fall within the deductible. In this instance the uncertainty is not as to the occurrence of risk, but rather the quantum. The concept of uncertainty is therefore flexible from the perspective of insurers, but must be present to form the basis of the contract.

However, this uncertainty is pre-existing and is not brought about by the insurance contract. Insurance is the response to the uncertainty:

(a) *Uncertainty from the perspective of the policyholder* – If the insurance contract is viewed as the sale by the insurer of cover to a policyholder, it is arguable that *gharar* exists if there is uncertainty in the policyholder's mind as to how the contract will turn out.

The amount of premium is almost always certain as it is a fixed sum. However, in the case of certain commercial policies (a small percentage of the total number of policies issued by the insurance market), a fixed rate may be quoted where the degree of exposure (amount of turnover, quantity of goods shipped, etc.) cannot be determined in advance, with a later adjustment based upon this fixed rate when the true figures are known. The policyholder knows with certainty the unit cost, however, but does not know the actual premium that will be paid.

The question then is whether the prohibition on *gharar* is a prohibition on uncertainty as to the contract terms or uncertainty as to the contractual outcome. If the former is the case, then there is no uncertainty. If the latter is the case, then *gharar* exists in a huge range of contracts where contractual clauses are inserted to cover future contingencies and not just insurance contracts.

However, premium payment is only one part of the financial transaction, so surely *gharar* exists in relation to claim payments? It is not known whether a claim will be made, it is not known what the amount of the claim will be, should it arise, and it is not known when a claim might arise. The policyholder does not know the amount, if any, that may be recovered under the policy.

This is true, but is based on a very narrow view of the transaction. The promise made by the insurer is not to pay a specific sum (except in life assurance) but rather to indemnify the policyholder against certain specified losses. The true construction of the policy is that the policyholder elects to make a small certain loss (the premium) in order that future losses are indemnified.

Under the contract after the premium has been paid, the policyholder's position in respect of the risks insured is financially neutral. If the risk does not occur, their financial position is unchanged. If the risk does occur, the policyholder will be indemnified and their financial position is still unchanged. The purpose of insurance is to offer certainty in the face of uncertainty. To declare that the policy is *haram* due to *gharar* is to fail to understand the whole insurance concept.

(b) *Uncertainty from the perspective of the insurer* – While the policyholder is being offered a certain, financially neutral outcome, this it could be argued is not the case for the insurer. They cannot know in advance whether claims will be made on a particular policy and therefore the outcome of an individual contract must be uncertain.

Given that the prohibition on *gharar* is based upon the avoidance of deception in contracts, it is questionable as to whether or not this is a problem. The insurer is offering to sell the policy; if the contract contains uncertainties for them, it could be argued that this is acceptable so long as it does not contain uncertainty for the purchaser. Should they be prohibited from deceiving themselves?

But to what extent is the insurer's position uncertain? Examining a single contract, uncertainty does exist. However, this is not how insurance companies operate. A well-managed insurance company will be indifferent as to the outcome of any single policy. They rely upon the operation of the law of large numbers. Therefore, a large motor insurer can predict the overall outcome with a considerable degree of accuracy even if individual policies are uncertain.

What is more, insurers will consider the longer term. They are well aware that claims experience may fluctuate to an extent from year to year. Hence the existence of reinsurance, to enable these fluctuations to be smoothed out over a number of accounting periods.

There is therefore limited uncertainty from the perspective of the insurer. It has been argued by some Islamic scholars that no contract of any description can be entirely free of uncertainty and that *gharar* is permitted so long as it is not excessive.

Finally, there is the question of whether the purchase of insurance is an attempt to circumvent the will of God. The obvious counter-argument is that God helps those that help themselves, a philosophy that exists in both Christianity and Islam. 'Trust in God but tie up your camel', as the Arab proverb goes. A more mainstream opinion would be that rather than pray for freedom from danger, one ought to take reasonable steps to safeguard oneself first and then start praying. Otherwise wearing a seat belt or buying a fire extinguisher might be considered *haram*. It is also the case that purchasing insurance does not in any way prevent the occurrence of the loss, clearly the purchase of life assurance does not invoke immortality! Insurance exists to spread the financial costs of loss among a group rather than permit the loss to fall on one unfortunate. It is difficult to see how this aim is in conflict with Islamic principles.

Maisir *(gambling) in insurance contracts*

Are insurers and bookmakers one and the same? Most insurers would be outraged at the very suggestion, but looking behind perceptions can an insurance contract be distinguished from a wager? The *Oxford English Dictionary* defines a bet as to 'risk one's money ... against another's on the result of doubtful event'. Put another way, each party states an opinion as to the outcome of an unknown future event, both parties stake a sum of money and whoever is correct recovers their stake and receives the other party's stake.

Is this analogous to an insurance contract? Examined closely, there are a number of significant differences:

(a) *Source of risk* – Insurance responds to a pre-existing risk faced by a policyholder while a wager actually creates a risk for both parties.

(b) *Nature of risk* – An insurable risk may be physical while the risk created by a wager is purely financial. Note that the occurrence of physical risk must have financially measurable consequences in order to be insured by what is by definition a financial contract.

(c) *Interest* – The policyholder is required to have a financial interest in the subject matter of an insurance contract while a gambler faces no such restriction.

(d) *Premium/stake* – An insurance premium once paid cannot be recovered. The winning gambler recovers their stake. The premium is therefore a charge made by the insurer rather than a returnable deposit.

(e) *Claim/winnings* – Claim payments are not pre-determined but depend upon the loss sustained (although invariably subject to a maximum limit). The winnings in a wager are determined when the wager is made. Payments under an insurance policy are determined *a posteriori*. Payments under a wager are determined *a priori*. An indemnity insurer does not therefore pledge a specified sum.

(f) *Contractual negotiations* – Full disclosure of information by both parties is required prior to conclusion of an insurance contract under the principle of uberrima fides. No such disclosure is required in a wager which is not even subject to the scrutiny of the courts.

The sceptics might say that this is all very well, but the policyholder still pays a small sum and if the event occurs, stands to receive a much larger sum.

However, the state of mind of the two parties is very different from that in a wager. This is an important point when making a moral judgement. Gambling is condemned because it performs no vital social or economic function and in the case of compulsive gamblers can be harmful to society. Is the behaviour of the parties to an insurance contract such that they deserve similar condemnation?

It is to be presumed that when you place a bet you wish the particular outcome that will lead you to win the wager to occur. It is unlikely that a wager would be accepted if the outcome could be brought about by one of the gamblers, as the future event would cease to be uncertain.

Compare this to the state of mind of the policyholder. Although many people take out life assurance, it can be presumed that they do so not in the hope that they die. Up to a point it could even be said that they will do everything they can to avoid this particular outcome. It is for this reason that life assurers are happy to offer such cover even though control of the event lies in the hands of the policyholder. The crucial difference is that the policyholder has entered into the contract to gain protection against an unwelcome occurrence rather than for a welcomed gain.

The next point to consider is whether the policyholder actually 'gains' at all. The element of gain lies at the heart of a wager. At the point of claim payment, the policyholder undoubtedly gains financially, but to limit examination of an insurance contract to the premium payment and claim settlement and ignore what has occurred in between is to ignore the whole purpose of insurance.

Almost all insurance policies are governed by the principle of indemnity. In order to claim under a policy, the policyholder must first lose the equivalent sum due to the operation of an insured risk. They are then entitled to recover their loss, but are not entitled to recover more than they have lost. Irrespective of whether the risk occurs, after the initial loss is incurred (the premium), the policyholder's financial position remains neutral. The critical prospect of gain is not present. Even though the amount of the claim is likely to exceed the premium paid, as an equivalent amount must first be lost, the policyholder always makes a small certain loss.

It is also important to consider the co-operative nature of the insurance contract. It is easy to view a single transaction in isolation, but this ignores the central principle of insurance, the common pool. Insurers do not offer cover in isolation. They provide a facility whereby a large number of policyholders who all face a common risk can pool their collective resources to fund the collective loss. All make a small certain loss in order that the collective are relieved of the possibility of a larger loss.

It could be argued that bookmakers also pool the wagers of a large number of people, however there is a critical difference. The bookmaker's pool operates so as to provide a gain to the fortunate few. An insurance pool provides compensation to the *unfortunate* few.

Finally, it is worth contemplating exactly what difference exists between investment, speculation and gambling. In all cases, a sum of money is risked in the hope or expectation that a larger sum will be received in the future. Any distinction between the three is a function of the degree of risk, the potential return and the duration. An investment is comparatively low risk and low return and of extended duration. A gamble is a high risk, high return arrangement, often determined in a very short space of time. Speculation falls between the two, but there are no clear dividing lines. It is not the basic structure of an arrangement that makes it a gamble, it is a subjective assessment made on the basis of these three variables. If the same thinking that has been applied to insurance is applied to investment, surely investment should be judged *al-maisir* and therefore *haram*? This, however, is clearly not a view that would gain any noteworthy support among Islamic theologians. Why should insurance not be judged by the same standard?

Riba *in insurance contracts*

In general, insurance contracts are not interest-bearing. Many life contracts do have an investment element, however they do not offer a fixed rate of return. Percentage bonuses are commonly paid to participating or 'with profits' policies. These, however, represent a share of the assurer's profits and are not fixed, indeed they may not be paid at all. This is analogous to the *halal* practice of *mudharabah*, whereby one party provides the capital and the other the expertise and the profits are then divided between them with a risk of capital loss falling on the provider of the capital (in the case of life assurance, the policyholder).

It is, however, undeniable that a proportion of the premiums received will be invested in interest-bearing investments. The funds belong in law to the insurer even if held in premium trust funds and therefore investment decisions are made by the insurer and cannot be controlled by the policyholder beyond the decision as to whether to participate in the fund in the first place. Although the policyholder does not directly participate in an interest-bearing contract, a proportion of the premium paid will be invested in this manner.

It is worth noting that it may well be that the insurer has little choice. First, a proportion of the premium fund must be kept in a readily liquidated form to meet current claims. Of course, interest could be foregone, but at the cost of higher premiums. Second, market regulation will force an insurer to hold a proportion of funds in gilts to prevent an overly speculative investment strategy which could leave the insurer unable to meet claims due to investment losses.

Conclusion

Many of the objections raised by Islamic scholars appear to have no or questionable validity. It would seem that in some cases scholars, although expert theologians, do not properly understand insurance. The one clear problem, however, is *riba*. Although the policyholder does not directly pay or receive interest, investment income is fundamental to the process. Given the nature of the investment opportunities available to insurers, it is inevitable that in most territories a proportion of the funds will be invested in interest-bearing financial assets. Even if they only benefit indirectly, a Muslim purchasing insurance will be permitting their premium to be invested in interest-bearing investments.

Takaful insurance companies

Generally speaking, insurance purchase is a function of wealth. Insurance is essentially a luxury rather than a necessity. As an economy develops and the population becomes wealthier, so they become able to pay a proportion of earnings to protect their financial position in the form of insurance premiums. It is relevant that as they become wealthier, they acquire more assets and enjoy enhanced earning potential which forms the basis for most insurance contracts.

Therefore, the most underdeveloped countries in the world purchase very little insurance. Most cannot afford the premiums and they have little to insure anyway. However, as GDP grows, so the proportion of GDP that is paid in premiums will almost always tend to increase, what is termed insurance penetration. It is Islamic countries that are the exception to this rule.

In 2008, according to Swiss Re Sigma Research Report, *World Insurance in 2008 (sigma No. (3/2009))* and IMF figures on GDP per capita, the insurance penetration in selected countries was as shown in Table 13.1.

This is the profile that might be expected, with a strong correlation between increasing GDP per capita and increasing insurance penetration. The correlation will not be absolute as the level of risk, sophistication of the insurance industry and political environment will

Table 13.1 Non-life insurance expenditure as a percentage of GDP, 2008

Country	GDP per capita ($)	Insurance as a % of GDP
USA	46,859	4.6
UK	45,785	2.9
Japan	38,559	2.2
Slovakia	17,630	1.7
China	3,315	1.0

Table 13.2 Non-life insurance expenditure as a percentage of GDP, Islamic
         countries, 2008

Country	GDP per capita ($)	Insurance as a % of GDP
Kuwait	45,920	0.46
Saudi Arabia	19,345	0.58
Turkey	10,472	1.02
Malaysia	8,141	1.47
Algeria	4,588	0.56
Egypt	2,161	0.47

differ from country to country. The position in the Islamic world is though markedly different (Table 13.2).

Here there is no correlation at all. In the case of Islamic countries, wealth is not so much an inaccurate predictor of insurance spending, it is not a predictor at all. It could be argued that secularisation is the true determinate, with secular Turkey seeing relatively high penetration and countries like Saudi Arabia, governed by *Shari'a* law, seeing surprisingly low penetration in comparison to GDP per capita. Malaysia not only has a large non-Muslim minority, but was of course a part of the British Empire and inherited an established insurance industry at the time of independence.

On the strength of these figures it would be easy to predict a bleak future for Middle Eastern insurers. This might indeed be the case if religious objections were ignored. Insurers have, however, been working with Islamic scholars to produce a *Shari'a*-compliant insurance product. The result is known as *Takaful* insurance.

The principles of Takaful *insurance*

First appearing in Sudan in 1979, *Takaful* can be translated from the Arabic as meaning 'mutual guarantee'. This is a form of insurance governed by three main principles:

(a)   a co-operative system;
(b)   payments made under *Tabarru* (charitable donation) principles;
(c)   compliance with *Shari'a*.

The relationship between the insurer and policyholder also has to be determined.

Co-operative system

In its purest form, this is essentially the well-established mutual concept. The concept being that a group facing a common risk form a collective pool which takes collective responsibility for that risk. The collective (or common) pool is owned by its participants. This indeed was the model on which many early forms of insurance were based.

Such companies may be termed co-operatives or mutuals. There is no substantive difference. A co-operative can be defined as 'an enterprise or organisation that is owned by and operated for the benefit of those using its services'. A mutual clearly meets this criterion.

Co-operation lies at the heart of the insurance contract, whether the insurer is operating on a commercial or mutual basis. Without this collective approach, insurance cannot function and all insurers regardless of motivation follow this model. What is perhaps surprising is that mutuality is not a prerequisite of *Takaful* insurance.

Tabarru

This is best explained as a form of charitable donation. This donation is made by the policyholder to the pool with the implicit recognition that this donation will be used to compensate pool members who are unfortunate enough to suffer a loss due to a risk covered by the pool. As it is a donation, it cannot be recovered.

With respect, this is an exercise in semantics. It does not matter whether the payment is termed a 'donation', a 'contribution' or a 'premium'. It does not matter whether the payment is made to a *Takaful* company, a mutual or a proprietary insurer. The effect is identical. It is a fundamental principle of insurance that the policyholder is electing to make a small certain loss to avoid the uncertainty of a possibly much larger loss. It is an equally fundamental principle that these payments are pooled and used to meet the collective loss in respect of the risk insured against. *Takaful* stresses that the 'donation' is made in order that others who may suffer misfortune will be aided. It is hard to accept, however, that those making the 'donation' do so for any other motivation than to receive financial assistance in the event that *they* suffer misfortune.

However, this allows the payment of premium to be described in terms that are clearly *halal* and assists in overcoming the objection of *al-maisir*. No gambler could be described as 'donating' money to a bookmaker. If the bet is won, the stakes are returned with the winnings. Of course in practice, all too many gamblers do end up 'donating' their stakes to the bookies!

Shari'a *compliant*

Even if the co-operative structure and *Tabarru* system eliminate *al-gharar* and *al-maisir* or reduce them to acceptable levels, the issue of *riba* remains. The investment of premiums is a critical part of the insurance process and operates to reduce the cost of premiums and/or provide a profit/surplus for the insurer. However, these investments need not necessarily involve fixed income securities or equity investments in companies that are engaged in activities incompatible with Islam (brewers spring immediately to mind).

When investing in equities, this is not actually that difficult. There are a large number of Islamic stock market indices, offering global, regional or sector-specific investments. These exclude equities in the areas of alcohol, tobacco, pork-related products, financial services, armaments and entertainment.

Islamic bonds, known as *Sukuk*, are also available. These can be zero coupons (to avoid the payment of interest) but with an enhanced redemption price. Alternatively, this may involve the leasing of assets to provide a cash flow for the duration of the loan. Until recently they were of marginal importance globally due to the lack of any noteworthy secondary market. This has now changed and such securities are now more liquid, a crucial factor for an insurer who might need to liquidate a position relatively quickly.

This investment strategy is not in itself sufficient. The operation has to be supervised by a *Shari'a* advisory board who will issue a fatwa confirming that the operation conforms to

Shari'a principles and is therefore acceptable under *Shari'a* law. This would be subject to an annual audit.

Principles of insurance law in **Takaful**

Takaful accepts the core insurance principles of insurable interest, utmost good faith and indemnity as being fundamental to a contract based upon ethics. It is arguable that this is not so much an importation of Western insurance thinking, but rather an acceptance that the insurance concept cannot function properly in the absence of such principles.

Takaful *insurance companies in operation*

Given the clear distinction between what *Shari'a* advisory boards term 'commercial' insurers and the co-operative or mutual vision of *Takaful* insurance, it might be expected therefore that all *Takaful* insurers would be mutuals. In reality, very few of them are mutuals and three distinct variations exist.

1 *Social insurance model* – Government-owned, ostensibly on a non-profit basis. Although technically a mutual, the organisation is essentially state-owned with the government meeting the operating cost, retaining surpluses and meeting deficits.
2 Al-mudharabah model – Given modern regulatory constraints it would be almost impossible to establish a mutual to write personal lines insurances (and extremely difficult in the commercial sector). Base capital requirements and the need to maintain solvency margins would require a considerable amount of initial capital. A pure mutual would intend to return surplus to policyholders, thus eliminating the possibility of returns for shareholders. Loan capital would be difficult to raise and service in the early vulnerable years before reserves had been established. Most *Takaful* insurers are therefore run by a *Takaful* operator, a commercial, proprietary company. They may be hybrids containing elements of both mutualisation and commercialisation, although they are more commonly purely commercial.

     This draws on the established Islamic principle of *mudharabah* or profit sharing. The *Takaful* operator and the policyholders (who technically own the premium funds) enter into a contract specifying how any underwriting profits will be divided between them. Usually this will be after allowing operating costs, but not always. This is akin to the with profits funds offered by UK life assurers where a proportion of profits are allocated to the policyholder via the with profits fund, but is not a model that is used in UK general insurance, which are either mutual or proprietary, not a mixture of the two. Certainly the relationship between operator and policyholders is more formalised than would be the case with a proprietary life assurer operating a with profits fund.

     Some *Shari'a* advisory boards might not approve such contracts for general insurance as the surplus is what remains in the participants' funds and is not a profit on capital employed. There would be no difficulty in a *mudharabah* contract on an investment-based life assurance cover, where the investment profits were split on pre-determined percentages. Nonetheless many such general insurance operations exist.
3 Al-wakala model – In this example the *Takaful* operator is not an underwriting participant but rather provides an underwriting, claims and investment service for a fee (although not at cost, these are profit-orientated organisations). Any surplus would belong to the policyholders.

Takaful companies offer both general insurance products and life and pensions (usually known as family *Takaful*).

Treatment of deficits

Of course, the nature of insurance is such that there will be years in which the premiums plus investment income are insufficient to meet the claims arising and the fund will be in deficit. Early mutuals operated on the basis that the initial premium was essentially a deposit. In the event of a shortfall, the mutual could call upon its members for further contributions. In the modern era this cash call is usually limited (often to a nominal sum).

One answer is to create contingency reserves from surpluses, which can be released to balance the books in deficit years. The erosion to the reserves can be corrected by increasing premiums in future years. This was the normal approach taken by mutuals/co-operatives around the world.

If the policy is to distribute all surpluses to participants, such reserves cannot be established. *Takaful* insurers overcome this problem by offering the policyholders an interest-free loan to meet deficits. This will then be recovered in the traditional manner by increasing future premiums.

Re-Takaful

Takaful companies are by definition recently established and are therefore small-scale and under-capitalised by the standards of the large Western and Japanese insurers which have been developing for far longer. There is then a considerable need for reinsurance. There is no reason why *Takaful* principles, the co-operative system, *Tabarru* payments and compliance with *Shari'a*, should not extend to reinsurance as well as insurance.

In practice, this has not happened to any noteworthy degree. Raising the capital to launch an insurer is not easy. The capital requirements of a reinsurer are significantly greater. For this reason *Re-Takaful* companies are somewhat thin on the ground and the few that do exist have limited capacity. There is also the question of the international nature of reinsurance. A regionally based reinsurer of any description would be vulnerable if it attempted to retain the risk of a local natural disaster, particularly if the reinsurer concerned was relatively small-scale. Limited capacity for such coverage is available and such risks are better spread within the international reinsurance markets.

Shari'a advisory boards have therefore given permission to *Takaful* insurers to reinsure in the conventional market subject to three criteria:

1 No *Re-Takaful* coverage is available.
2 Commissions are not accepted from reinsurers.
3 Profit shares are not permitted, as such profit accrues from non-*Shari'a*-compliant investment.

Quite why there is a prohibition on commission is hard to see as the commission element in reinsurance is intended to make the contract fairer by compensating the insurer for the extra costs they incur. In practice, this effect could be achieved by a modification to the rate charged by the reinsurer, therefore this is not of crucial importance. The reality, therefore, is that a significant percentage of premiums paid in Islamic countries are ceded to Western reinsurers.

The future of **Takaful**

Some commentators have waxed lyrical over the future prospects of *Takaful* insurance in the Islamic world. There have even been predictions that *Takaful* insurers will become a force in global insurance markets.

It is possible that the startlingly low rates of insurance penetration in the Middle East have a solely religious base and if this objection is removed, the market will grow quickly. Alternatively, it could be argued that as few have the insurance buying habit, it will take time to establish the product and that therefore growth will be slow.

In non-Muslim countries, *Takaful* products are likely to hold a religious observance advantage among Muslims. However, in the longer term, premium and performance may determine success or failure. It would appear that distinguishing between *Takaful* and Western insurance is largely an exercise in semantics. The semi-mutual, semi-proprietary model of many general *Takaful* companies is distinctive, however it is not apparent whether this in fact offers any noticeable advantage to the policyholder. If *Takaful* is to spread beyond Islamic countries, some incentive will be required in order to convince policyholders to insure with *Takaful* companies rather than the established insurers they presently use.

There are a small number of *Takaful* companies operating outside of the Islamic world. However, it is difficult to see how *Takaful* is a genuinely alternative insurance system, operating as it does so closely to established insurance models.

Alternative risk financing

There are, however, some genuinely alternative (and some not so alternative) means of providing risk finance in the aftermath of an insurable loss. This has been a rapidly expanding area in recent decades. This is more properly considered as a part of risk management, discussed in Chapter 14.

14 The role of insurance in risk management

These days, large organisations are far more likely to talk in terms of risk management than insurance. Insurance companies and intermediaries are increasingly likely to promote themselves as risk management consultants. What then is the relationship between risk management and insurance?

The first point to consider is whether risk management is to be viewed as a technical process or a management discipline. The former considers the practical process by which the overall cost of risk to the organisation can be effectively minimised. The latter, also referred to as enterprise risk management, concentrates on the strategy by which this can be achieved and includes aspects such as corporate governance and culture, systems and audit. Both are equally valid approaches, however as this book concerns insurance, risk management will be discussed from the technical process perspective.

Risk management from the technical perspective involves a three-pillar process whereby risk analysis, risk control and risk financing together support the overall risk management aim of effective risk cost minimisation (Figure 14.1).

Risk analysis

This is a two-stage process. Risk management begins with the identification of risk. This goes beyond a mere perception of risk as its aim is to prepare the ground for the second stage. It can be broken down into five steps as follows:

1 *Risk perception* – an awareness of the possibility of a particular risk.
2 *Risk confirmation* – Is there actually a threat? Alternatively, has it already been effectively managed?
3 *Risk causation* – What could go wrong? What perils would be involved? How would it come about?
4 *Risk consequences* – What is likely to happen? What will it cost? Is it of significance?
5 *Hazard factors* – Which hazards increase/decrease the probability of occurrence or affect the amount of loss?

The aim of the process is not merely to identify risks, it is also to eliminate risks from the investigation process because their occurrence is so remote or their impact so trivial that to investigate further would be a waste of scarce resources. Of course, such assumptions have been known to be wrong!

Once the risk is identified, it must be measured or quantified. The degree of difficulty inherent in this exercise varies according to the nature of the risk. If the risk occurs frequently

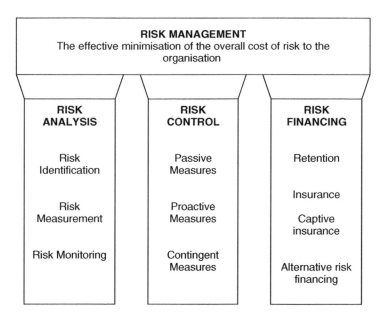

Figure 14.1 The three pillars of risk management.

data should be available or can be collected; if the risk occurs very rarely, data will in all probability be hard to come by and possibly out of date even if available. This is due to the nature of most insurable risks, so the tendency is for the frequency of a risk to be inversely proportionate to its severity. This can be shown diagrammatically by the Heinrich triangle devised by H.W. Heinrich in his 1931 work *Industrial Accident Prevention* (Figure 14.2).

The four categories of loss in the Heinrich triangle can be defined as:

1   *Catastrophic* – This magnitude of loss is likely to cause the financial collapse of the organisation or at least have a significant effect on solvency, cash flow, balance sheet and profitability for a significant period (three or more years).
2   *Severe* – This is survivable, but the loss will have a significant effect on cash flow, balance sheet and profitability in the short term (up to three years).
3   *Minor* – There is a short-term, localised effect on cash flow. In isolation, would not affect profitability or balance sheet to a noticeable degree, but an accumulation of such losses might have a severe or even catastrophic effect.
4   *Trivial* – In isolation, this would have no visible effect but again accumulations of loss might be more problematic.

Note that Heinrich's analysis was based upon a study of industrial accidents and does not necessarily hold good for all types of loss. Nonetheless the basic concept has been shown to be sound in many applications. Heinrich's suggested ratio was 300 incidents to 29 minor injuries and one serious injury. This is still cited today by Health and Safety specialists, although it is worth noting that Frank Bird produced an alternative triangle in 1969 showing a different ratio of 600 near misses to 30 incidents involving property damage to 10 minor

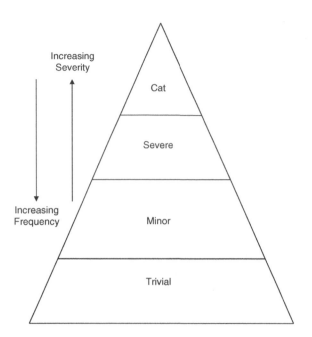

Figure 14.2 The Heinrich triangle.

injuries and one serious injury. The ratios may then vary, but there is often an observable correlation between the numbers of minor incidents and major incidents. The problem is that while major incidents will be reported and remembered, minor incidents (particularly near misses) may not.

An analysis of past losses will for any large organisation show a number of minor losses. This might even reveal the occasional severe loss. It is highly improbable that any catastrophe losses would be on record. The cost of minor losses can be estimated by statistical analysis of the relative frequency and cost of past losses, although care would need to be taken that there had not been a change in the hazard factor which might suggest future losses would not follow the same pattern. The theory of correlation between minor and major incidents may be of some assistance in predicting major losses, however this is dependent on a reliable system of recording the minor incidents which is often not the case. Predicting catastrophe tends then to rely on subjective probability estimates rather than objective statistical calculation. A greater margin of error is to be expected.

The risk measurement process is not just concerned with predicting the frequency of loss, it is designed to estimate the total cost of loss. The total cost of loss will be its frequency multiplied by its severity, for example, the total number of motor accidents expected multiplied by the average cost for a motor accident. The next question then is, what should be recorded as a cost?

For insurance companies, the cost of loss is limited by the policy wording. The insurer's promise to indemnify is not open-ended, it is constrained both by the policy's description of the events insured and the sum insured or limit of indemnity. Furthermore, insurance usually only covers direct measurable losses stemming from the insured event (consequential loss insurance or business interruption are obvious exceptions). This is not to say that there are not indirect losses, some of which may not be capable of precise measurement. The risk-managed organisation has to consider all loss, not merely those losses that happen to be covered by an insurance policy. Even a simple motor accident has indirect costs. The insurance policy pays for the cost of the repair, but a claim form must be completed, arrangements must be made to take the vehicle to the garage, estimates must be arranged and all the while the firm is losing the benefit of the use of the vehicle. A standard policy will, however, not meet any of these losses other than the repair cost. In other examples the direct insurable cost can be trivial in comparison to the indirect costs.

Suppose a motor manufacturer launches a new model at a cost of several billion pounds in development, a reworking of the manufacturing process and marketing. Also suppose that three months after the launch they are informed by a customer that they have been in a minor accident after the brakes failed. Their investigation reveals that there is a defect in the brakes and that they have to be redesigned and all the cars already manufactured must be modified. The costs to the manufacturer of this incident can be broken down as follows:

1   *Direct costs* – This would be the cost of repairing the customer's vehicle and the third party vehicle they collided with.
2   *Indirect measurable costs* – The manufacturer must redesign the braking system. They must then change the manufacturing process to incorporate the redesign, possibly modifying machinery. Vehicle stocks awaiting sale must be modified. The vehicles sold must be recalled (there may be many thousands) and the necessary modification carried out, very possibly involving the fitting of new parts.
3   *Indirect immeasurable costs* – It is almost certain that the problem will have come to the attention of the media and the resultant bad publicity may cause a reduction in sales, not just of this model but possibly across all models as the manufacturer's reputation is damaged. The huge marketing cost of launching a new model may be wasted and additional advertising costs will be incurred in an attempt to limit the damage. However, even if a drop in sales is noted, the brake defect problem is not necessarily the cause. Customers may simply prefer a competitor's model and this incident may disguise the fact that the new model simply is not good enough to compete.

A standard product liability insurance policy will only cover the direct costs and would certainly fall within the excess (which is likely to be significant in the case of a motor manufacturer). Some of the additional costs can be insured via a policy covering the costs of product recall, again, large excesses would be expected. A general loss of confidence in the firm's products would, though, be uninsurable. Risk analysis in the business organisation must of necessity go far beyond the underwriting process which considers insured loss only.

Risk control

Having identified and measured risk, the organisation will next consider how risk may be reduced. This is the area that insurance companies sometimes tend to identify (erroneously) as the risk management process. It is not, it is but one part of the process.

Losses can be prevented/minimised by three methods:

(a) *Risk elimination* – Also known as risk avoidance, the only reliable method of achieving risk elimination is to stop doing whatever it is that creates the risk. Often this is not possible, as this will not only eliminate the risk of loss, but the rewards of running the risk as well. Nonetheless, a firm may decide that the risk of loss posed by one part of their activities is greater than the potential reward and cease that particular business activity. This ought to reduce revenue, but boost profitability.

(b) *Risk transfer* – Transfer the responsibility for risk to another party (other than via insurance or similar contracts which do not actually affect the loss sustained by the firm but pass the financial consequences after the event). This would be achieved in practice by entering into contractual agreements to pass responsibility. An example would be property owners passing the risk of damage to the buildings to the tenants via the lease. This is rarely possible in practice unless there is a common interest in the risk as in the case of a landlord and tenant situation. Otherwise the other party is unlikely to be willing to accept the transfer.

(c) *Risk reduction* – This involves carrying out the activity or process in such a manner that frequency and severity of losses are at the lowest level economically possible and is the dominant form of risk control.

The motivation for risk control is threefold:

(a) *Economic* – Accidents and/or errors cost money and such cost comes straight off the bottom line profit. The occurrence of loss will not increase revenue, however, it will have to be added to costs. It makes sense therefore to allocate resources to minimise the cost of risk, if the cost is less than the benefit. This is why risk measurement is so important, as if the anticipated cost of risk is not known, the level of risk control spending that can be economically made cannot be calculated. This leads to variable levels of risk control according to the degree of risk. The aim is not to minimise risk to the maximum extent possible but to seek to reduce risk to acceptable levels. For this reason security at airports is much tighter than at railway stations. Indeed, employing the same level of security at a station would create such delays that it would be likely to defeat the entire object of running a train service in the first place.

(b) *Legal* – Legislation, particularly Health and Safety legislation, may demand risk control measures are undertaken. Market regulation is another example of risk control expenditure being demanded by government. A company will have to comply with the law, irrespective of whether the expenditure is economically justified. It must, however, be noted that a failure to follow the law is likely to result in fines and the fact that these fines are effective must exceed the cost of legal compliance. Most companies would also wish to avoid the reputational damage that can result from having been found to be breaking the law, as this can of course lead to indirect immeasurable losses. The spending can probably be justified economically in any event.

(c) *Moral* – Killing employees, customers or members of the public due to lax safety standards is generally viewed as unacceptable on moral grounds. Environmental pollution will similarly lead to public disapproval. There is then an argument for spending more than the amount economically justified, if by doing so the risk of serious harm is reduced. Again there can be hidden benefits as the possibility of reputational damage is also reduced.

Commercial organisations clearly exist in order to deliver profit and it is therefore easy to be lured into considering decisions in purely financial terms. Legal and moral issues may indicate that loss control expenditure is undertaken that cannot be justified in purely financial terms. Perhaps a more suitable way of considering loss control decisions is not in terms of cost benefits but in terms of utility benefits. Unfortunately this becomes a subjective rather

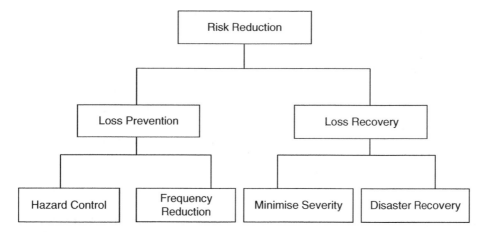

Figure 14.3 The objectives of risk control.

than an objective exercise. What is the utility of peace of mind? What is the utility of a clear conscience? Justifying decisions on economic grounds is inherently easier, but this does not mean that other justifications should be ignored.

Risk control is achieved in a number of ways, concentrating either on preventing the loss in the first place or alternatively reducing the impact of the loss should it occur (Figure 14.3):

1 *Loss prevention* – This involves modifying the overall hazard factor, which in turn concerns eliminating or reducing negative hazards while introducing or enhancing positive hazards. Hence the reason for the risk analysis process, as proper risk identification ought to have identified these hazards. First, this will concentrate on minimising the risk that individual loss events will occur. Second, this will seek to reduce the number of losses stemming from an event by seeking to ensure that losses are independent as far as possible.

2 *Loss reduction* – With the best will in the world the risk will not be eliminated and losses will still occur. Even after the event giving rise to the loss has occurred, it may still be possible to reduce the severity of the loss. Effective disaster recovery will minimise the consequential losses stemming from the direct loss.

Risk control measures can be subdivided as to when they take effect relative to the event or incident giving rise to the occurrence of a loss.

3 *Passive measures* – These are hazard control measures introduced with the aim of preventing the incident occurring or if this is not possible, reducing the severity of the incident. Examples would be the use of non-combustible materials in building construction to reduce the risk of fire or fitting good quality locks to doors and windows to deter theft.

4 *Proactive measures* – These come into play after the incident has occurred but before serious loss has taken place, with the aim that the size of the loss is restricted to minor or even trivial proportions. Examples would be sprinkler systems or fire doors to extinguish or restrict the spread of fire or burglar alarms to alert the police and minimise the amount of time the thieves have to make off with goods.

5   *Contingent measures* – These measures are effective after the initial loss has occurred and are designed to minimise the indirect losses arising in consequence. Disaster recovery plans, the outsourcing of production or hire of alternative premises are all examples.

The role of insurers in risk control

Risk control can and should be carried out irrespective of whether the risk is insured or not. Insurers do though have a role to play. The underwriting requirements indirectly promote risk control by making cover more expensive or unobtainable in the absence of risk control. This is a feature even in personal insurances. Discounts are offered on home insurance premiums for improved security and on motor premiums for fitting approved security devices. It could even be argued that the premium loadings imposed by life assurers for policyholders who smoke or who are overweight also promote risk control, although it is perhaps debatable whether this is truly influential.

The involvement of insurers in commercial insurance is far more direct. It would be normal for quotations for small commercial policies to be made subject to survey. If the quote is accepted, the insurer's surveyor will visit, prepare a report and often require risk control improvements. The policyholder will then have a specified period of time to make the required improvements if cover is to continue.

This controls risk from the perspective of the insurer as the intention is to reduce the probability of an insurance claim. It is not, however, risk control as the risk manager might understand it. The requirements are not the product of a cost/benefit analysis but rather standardised requirements imposed by the insurer, sometimes without regard to the actual risk. This methodology can be controversial, as the cost of improvements is the responsibility of the policyholder, but the benefit accrues to the insurer. This can lead to the problem that as the improvement comes cost free to the insurer, they may impose requirements that provide minimal risk reduction at significant cost to the policyholder. The author can cite the example of the insurers of a computer policy who required window locks to be fitted to all windows. This might seem reasonable except that the insured premises were on the eighth floor of a large office block! Policyholders can also legitimately complain that this makes the process of comparing quotations difficult. If an alternative insurer quotes a more competitive premium than their existing insurer and they accept the quote, will they subsequently find that the costs imposed by the survey make the new cover more expensive than the previous insurer's policy? As the survey follows acceptance, they cannot know the true cost when making their decision.

Both insurers and intermediaries do offer pure consultancy services in the area of both risk analysis and control. Not necessarily linked to any kind of insurance purchase, such service is available on a fee basis.

Insurers are in a position to make a more positive contribution to risk control. They do have vast experience in the field of risk analysis, and their long-term survival depends upon being able to judge the applicable hazards pertaining to a risk and to place a value on the probable outcome of that risk. This knowledge has the potential to be immensely valuable to risk control. The problem, however, is that this knowledge is commercially sensitive. An insurer that is better able to predict risk outcomes has a natural competitive advantage and will seek to protect this advantage by keeping such information confidential.

Nonetheless there are examples of the insurance industry as a whole promoting risk control. The Motor Insurance Repair Research Centre at Thatcham was established by the insurance industry in 1969 to provide a research facility aimed at improving vehicle safety and security. Reports from Thatcham affect the determination of insurance grouping and therefore the cost of insuring particular models. Their research is then influential in improvements in car design as manufacturers take note of their findings, seeking cheaper insurance rates for their customers. This is not to suggest that motor manufacturers are not already fully aware of the benefit of a reputation for making safe cars, however the Thatcham findings are freely available while the manufacturer's own research will usually be jealously guarded as they seek competitive advantage.

The ABI has the necessary authority within the industry to promote joint ventures with the aim of reducing loss for the benefit of all. An example is the Arson Prevention Bureau, established by the ABI in conjunction with the Home Office to research and disseminate strategies to reduce the incidence of arson.

Risk financing

At the end of the risk control process, no matter how thorough, there will remain a residue of risk. The next risk management process is to determine how the occurrence of such residual risk will be financed.

There are effectively only two methods of risk financing (although numerous sub-divisions exist):

1 The organisation can retain financial responsibility for the risk. The theory is that only a percentage of the premium paid is the pure risk premium. The rest, perhaps 30 per cent or more, goes to cover the insurer's costs (and possibly underwriting profit). If the loss is likely to be minor, the organisation can retain the risk and as long as their costs are no greater than the insurers would have been, obtain a financial advantage. The insurance of small value, predictable loss can be viewed as analogous to playing a fruit machine. The insurer will estimate the likely cost of such predictable loss and charges the pure risk premium plus a margin for costs. They will then charge a further amount to cover the unpredictable severe or catastrophic losses that may arise. For every pound put in, the organisation can expect to receive back about 70 pence. This is a process known as 'pound swapping', although in fact as noted, less than a pound is generally received back from the insurer. Crucially, when risk is retained, the organisation benefits from the investment income earned on any funds prior to the settlement of losses.

2 Alternatively, the organisation can transfer financial responsibility for the risk via a financial instrument or contract. The purchase of insurance is common, but other kinds of instruments or contract exist, dealing with both pure and speculative risk.

In most cases, a mix of these two methods is used. The skill in risk financing is arriving at the optimum mix.

This in turn involves two financial functions:

1 *Investment* – The application of funds in order to do the following:

    (a) prevent or reduce loss (actually part of the risk control function);
    (b) replace or repair lost or damaged assets (internal deployment);
    (c) obtain a return from funds prior to loss (external deployment).

2   *Financing* – Sourcing and cost of funds required for investment. Including:

   (a) arranging insurance or other financial contracts;
   (b) borrowing from banks or other sources;
   (c) redeployment of own resources (in other words, retention).

For individuals and small businesses, insurance is the dominant form of risk financing. Their retention capacity is so low and their risk so concentrated there is no realistic alternative. Although small losses may be retained (and the excess on most insurance policies would require this), the point at which such losses become unacceptable is not sufficiently high that more imaginative solutions are viable.

As the size of a company increases, so the relative importance of insurance tends to reduce. This is not to say that the amount spent on insurance reduces in absolute terms, as clearly large companies spend more than small companies. However, insurance expenditure as percentage of revenue and perhaps more pertinently the percentage of overall risk financing that insurance represents, will usually decline. This is in part due to the greater capacity to retain risk, but also because as a firm grows in size so its risks tend to become more widely spread. Multinational conglomerates can reach a size where certain forms of conventional insurance offer them no real benefit. An oil rig, for example, may cost more than $1 billion and could be totally destroyed by a single fire. A clear case for fire insurance one might suppose. However, BP's revenue in 2008 was $361 billion. Applying the Heinrich triangle definitions, a $1 billion loss would be no more than a minor loss, certainly not even close to being a catastrophic event. Scaled down, it would the equivalent of the average individual losing £100 or so, less than the excess on many private motor policies. Therefore the risk financing decision depends less on the amount that might potentially be lost, but rather on the impact that loss might have on the risk bearer.

The anticipated response to differing levels of risk can be mapped (Table 14.1):

   (a) *Trivial* – Retain and ignore. The loss can be met as an operating expense and indeed the cost of more complex forms of finance would probably outweigh any benefit. Insurance will probably not be available for such losses in any event as the cost would be within the policy excess.
   (b) *Minor* – Retain and fund. The loss is within the retention capacity of the organisation, but some prior planning of financing is required if such losses are not to cause cash flow difficulties. Any attempt to insure such risks would probably result in a pound-swapping exercise, to the financial detriment of the policyholder.

Table 14.1 Risk financing – anticipated response to risk

Type of loss	Frequency	Severity	Predictability	Impact	Decision
Trivial	Very high	Very low	Easily	Negligible	Retain and ignore
Minor	High	Low	Fairly in the short term	Insignificant	Retain and self-fund
Severe	Low	High	Difficult in the short term	Measurable in the accounts	Transfer but partially self-fund
Catastrophe	Very low	Very high	Very difficult in any period	Crippling	Transfer

(c) *Severe* – Although survivable, the impact would be such that the loss would be unacceptable. External financing via insurance or alternative means of risk transfer would be recommended.

(d) *Catastrophic* – By definition, the organisation cannot survive without some external source of financing. Insurance or alternative risk transfer is an absolute necessity.

The severe or catastrophic losses faced by individuals or small businesses are, in isolation, comfortably within the capacity of insurers. Where there is a risk of a large accumulation of such losses arising out of a single event, the position is not so clear. The severe or catastrophic losses of very large firms become progressively harder for insurers to handle as the size of the firm increases. These types of risk-managed organisations also seek to retain significant quantities of risk. There is then a need for more innovative approaches than those offered by conventional insurance. These solutions are known as alternative risk financing.

Alternative risk financing and alternative risk transfer

Alternative risk financing can be categorised in two ways. Alternative risk *financing* itself implies the sourcing of funds to meet the cost of loss. Either the funds will have been set aside in advance or will be borrowed post loss. These types of arrangements are not related to insurance as commonly understood, even though they may have the insurance label attached to them.

Then there is alternative risk *transfer*, which requires the transfer of the financial consequences of loss to another party, generally prior to the loss occurring. This category includes quasi-insurance contracts, although there are clear differences in approach. This is self-evident as they could not be termed 'alternative' if this were not the case.

Alternative risk financing: captive insurance companies

A captive is essentially a retention vehicle. Once an organisation decides to retain risk to any significant degree, they must consider how the occurrence of such risk will be financed. In the absence of any prior planning the sudden demand for cash could provoke a liquidity crisis, therefore it would be normal practice to create a special internal fund to finance loss. A captive insurance company takes the concept of such internal retention fund to the ultimate expression. However, by separating the funds within a wholly owned subsidiary, with contributions labelled as 'premiums', a captive should be able to operate if not quite at arm's length from the parent, at least with a degree of objectivity.

A true captive can be distinguished by three primary characteristics:

1   It is a wholly owned subsidiary.
2   Its parent company is not *primarily* engaged in insurance.
3   Its primary function is to cover the risks of its parent company.

There are two main reasons for forming a captive. First, it is to allow premium contributions to the captive by group companies to be tax deductible. Second, it allows the captive to purchase reinsurance. Reinsurance rates will be lower than the rates for insurance due to the commission payable on reinsurance contracts (see Chapter 7). It could be seen as the organisation buying their cover at wholesale rather than retail prices. This of course would constitute risk transfer as financial responsibility for the risk would pass outside the group companies. As an alternative, using a captive would enable the organisation to access financial reinsurance solutions.

It has to be said that the great majority of captives are located in offshore locations. Bermuda is particularly popular, but many British captives are based in the Channel Islands or the Isle of Man. There are also some onshore locations with special captive regimes such as Dublin or Vermont. On the one hand, it can be said that special regulatory rules applicable to captives in such territories are a part of the motivation for location. It must also be recognised that advantageous tax rates are also a part of the attraction, although such benefits are being continually eroded by amendments to taxation law in the major economies.

Financial reinsurance

Rather than concentrating on the risk that economic loss will be caused by the occurrence of a specified peril, financial reinsurance concentrates on the risk that a given financial target is or is not met. The risk transferred is then the risk of an unacceptable overall financial result, what may be described as *financial* risk not an *underwriting* risk.

Of course, there is an overlap between the two risks. For an insurance company, the most common cause of a disappointing financial result will be underwriting loss and therefore traditional reinsurance can to an extent perform the financial reinsurance function. This is not, however, the only possible cause, for example, the investment of insurer's funds is a crucial factor in the overall result and investment returns can vary. In the case of risks in general and long tail risks in particular, the speed of settlement has a financial impact even though the underlying underwriting loss is unaltered.

Therefore, financial reinsurance can provide protection against the following:

(a) losses resulting from lower than anticipated investment returns (or even a negative result);
(b) losses resulting from changes to the settlement pattern.

This can be achieved by breaking the link between an indemnity under the underlying policy and indemnity under the reinsurance policy. Instead of reinsuring individual losses or clearly defined accumulations of such losses, the reinsurance policy can be used to reinsure the overall result.

Traditional reinsurance however, respects the indemnity principle. It would appear at first glance that excess of loss ratio or stop loss reinsurance provides protection for the full financial result by reinsuring losses above a certain ratio within specified classes of business (see Chapter 7). However, the ratio reinsured is the ratio of losses to premium. It does not usually take account of the investment income earned on this premium or the discounted cash flow resulting from the claim settlement pattern (see Chapter 4).

Insurance is a cyclical business. In part, this is due to imbalances in supply and demand for the product leading to pricing fluctuations, the 'hard' and 'soft' market conditions familiar to all in the market. However, fluctuations in the level of insured loss can also be expected due a variety of factors, such as economic conditions, weather patterns, political upheaval and innovations/errors in risk control. Unfortunately these factors affecting revenue and cost are not always correlated and an insurer cannot rely upon an increase in losses being balanced by an increase in premiums.

Of course, an increasing trend in underlying loss will theoretically lead to premium increases. However, there will be a lag while the trend is identified during which period the original (inadequate) premium level will continue to be charged. In a particularly competitive market, it may not be possible to increase premiums without loss of market share. The result of all these factors is that even if the mean result for the insurer in the long term is an acceptable level of profit, there will be fluctuations in results leading to disappointing years, perhaps even serious losses on occasions. This can cause short-term damage to the creditworthiness of the business and investor confidence. It may also cause regulatory difficulties. There are therefore advantages in seeking to reduce the impact of the "poor" years financed by the excess profits of the "good" years.

The obvious answer to this would be to simply set aside a reserve in a year when results exceeded targets and use this reserve to meet targets in future years when results fall short of expectations. The age-old practice of setting aside funds for a rainy day. Unfortunately, the Inland Revenue forecasters apparently believe the skies are always blue. Such reserves will be treated as profits and taxed accordingly. This requires the insurer to set aside larger sums than necessary to meet future claims to enable the tax bill to be paid while still leaving sufficient sum to meet such future claims.

Traditional reinsurance will only produce proceeds following underlying insured losses. There is no guarantee that these will coincide with weaknesses in the profit and loss account or balance sheet. However, a reinsurance premium is an allowable expense for taxation purposes, hence the role of financial reinsurance. The required loss-spreading effect can be created without the inefficiencies created by taxation, if instead of setting aside a cash reserve the funds are used to purchase reinsurance, the proceeds of which can then be used to bolster funds when required.

As a general rule the Inland Revenue consider that insurance takes place when 'a risk is transferred to the insurer, in return for payment of a sum of money, and relief is obtained from uncertainty'. It is clear therefore that transactions will be closely scrutinised and the tax deductibility of premiums will be challenged where the 'insurance' is deemed a fiction as no risk has been transferred or the risk transfer is without substance.

Banking policy or banker

As the name implies, this is a hybrid of banking and insurance principles. The essence of the contract is that the 'premium' is deposited with a 'reinsurer'. The 'premium' is then retrieved at a later date to meet the cost of losses as they arise (clearly an insurance contract). The 'premium' will, however, be returned at a later date (in full or in part) whether these losses arise or not (clearly a banking contract).

If this is treated as a reinsurance policy for tax purposes, the 'premium' set aside would be less than if a simple reserve was set aside as it would not be assessed for tax purposes. The problem is that in order for this to be allowed, the Inland Revenue need to be convinced that this is truly an insurance contract.

The problem arises where there is no risk transfer. If there is a guarantee that the 'premium' will be returned irrespective of the occurrence of loss or as is commonly the case, a 'profit commission' ensures the return of a sum equivalent to the premium, no transfer has occurred. To constitute true risk transfer, the reinsurance should potentially return more than the amount of the premium plus investment earnings.

However, by considering the problem in the longer term, a valid reinsurance contract may emerge. If a contract is entered into on the basis of five annual 'premiums' of £1m, but with a five-year aggregate limit of £5m (or £5m plus investment earnings), this could constitute valid reinsurance as a sum greater than the premium could be recovered in an individual year even if over the longer term the recoveries are limited to the contributions.

Rollers or roll up policies

These are a variation on the banker policy, as under this contract, the premium less losses (i.e. the profit) is added to the indemnity for the following year, hence the term 'roll up'. This may be used as a reward for the reinsured, for example, a relatively low stop loss offered to a recently formed insurer or captive can be incrementally increased as the quality of the reinsured's underwriting is proven. More commonly, however, it will be used as a banker policy with profits from a good year stored in the next year which may see a worsening loss experience. It may be that in the first year, no risk transfer occurs as the policy limit will be limited to the premium. Assuming profit, however, the future limit will exceed the premium, creating a valid reinsurance contract.

Time and distance policies

These policies are so named because the indemnity increases over time and distance. Usually the indemnity is limited to the premium paid plus accrued interest. As time passes, the investment income will increase and therefore the indemnity will increase. This is a popular method of dealing with the financing of long tail liabilities as the discounted value of the claims can provide the basis for the premium while the accrued interest will theoretically ensure that funds are available as claims are settled, often many years into the future.

A common theme with many of these policies is that there is no effective risk transfer. Such 'policies' are often no more than a tax efficient method of setting aside reserves to pay future losses (and in particular IBNRs). They are then subject to challenge by the Inland Revenue.

Although called reinsurance, all these arrangements are designed to provide financing facilities rather than risk transfer, as would be expected with conventional reinsurance. As such, they may fairly be described as alternative risk financing, but not as alternative risk transfer. They can be used either by insurers or captive insurance companies, but either way, their purpose is to fund retained risk.

Borrowing as an alternative to insurance

Once the decision has been taken to retain, the organisation is consciously deciding not to transfer risk. It then makes commercial sense to select the most cost advantageous method of financing loss. It is generally considered that the maximum retention should not exceed an amount that the organisation could afford to meet in the short term without significant effect on normal trading activities. It is, however, possible to consider retaining risk even into the severe loss category. The insurance market can be bypassed altogether and the loss can be funded by long-term borrowing. As stated in Chapter 1, one way of looking at insurance is that it is a means of spreading the long-term cost of risk via relatively stable annual payments. It could be argued that there is little practical difference between arranging the necessary risk financing pre-loss via an insurance policy and arranging it post-loss via a loan. Indeed, given that the pure risk premium may be no more than 65–70 per cent of the total premium, the interest charged is likely to be less than paying the insurer's administrative costs, making the loan a more efficient means of financing.

There are often clear problems with this approach. It cannot be an adequate response to the possibility of catastrophe loss as it is highly improbable that a sufficiently large sum could be borrowed to cover losses of this magnitude. Similarly, the loans to cover multiple severe losses might be unobtainable or raise borrowing costs to unacceptable levels. There is also the possibility that where the risk is that property will be damaged, the collateral necessary to secure a loan will be destroyed at the time the loan is sought, making lenders reluctant to lend. It would also be crucial that the finance was available in the immediate aftermath of a loss to minimise the consequential losses that might arise. Contingency loans can be arranged in advance, so this need not be an issue.

If, however, an organisation owns a large number of properties, none worth more than a very small percentage of total assets (a maximum probable loss equivalent to no more than a low end severe loss), and if these assets are also geographically well spread to ensure independence, the methodology is sound.

Alternative risk transfer

Large though the global insurance industry is, its financial muscle is dwarfed by the capital markets. The global non-life premium income is presently about $1.8 trillion per annum. This would indicate that the assets available to insurers would be somewhere in the range of $800–900 billion based on what would generally be accepted as an adequate solvency margin. The assets of the life assurers are harder to estimate as a high percentage of their funds properly belong to the policyholder. The market capitalisation of the global stock markets as at August 2009 is $41.6 *trillion* according to the World Federation of Exchanges. This does not include securities and other forms of financial instrument. The capital markets therefore have vastly greater capacity to absorb loss.

By way of example, between May 2008 and May 2009, the total market capitalisation of the global stock markets fell from $57 trillion to $37 trillion (again according to the World Federation of Exchanges). The losses equate to 395 Hurricane Katrinas. Alternatively, the $144 billion of damage caused by Katrina was equivalent to a fall of considerably less than 1 per cent in the global stock markets, an event that would pass almost unnoticed outside the pages of the *Financial Times*. The potential to fund catastrophe loss is significant, but the problem is how to access these funds.

Catastrophe bonds

This 'new' approach is actually derived from an idea used thousands of years ago. An early risk transfer method used in Ancient Greece (and very likely by the Phoenicians as well) was bottomry. Loans were taken out on marine ventures that did not have to be repaid in the event that the ship was lost. Enhanced interest was paid if the venture succeeded. The even older code of Hammurabi (see Chapter 5) states at clause 48 that where a farmer's crop is destroyed by storm, he 'washes his debt-tablet in water'.

The concept then slumbered for over two thousand years before being resurrected in the aftermath of Hurricane Andrew in 1992. A shortage of available reinsurance cover led to a demand for more imaginative solutions designed to increase capacity. The result was the emergence of the catastrophe bond (or cat bond as it is more commonly known). The problem with conventional reinsurance is that it has the effect of concentrating catastrophe risk in a small number of reinsurers, who are understandably reluctant to accept the possibility of large-scale loss. As reinsurance and retrocession became more difficult to come by, insurers and reinsurers sought to spread this risk into the capital markets via securitisation.

The issuer raises capital from investors through a traditional bond. The bond will offer above average interest, almost certainly on a floating interest basis (i.e. a specified number of basis points above LIBOR). If the catastrophe protection covered by the bond is triggered, no interest is paid. It may even be that the principal need not be repaid. The issuer can either divert investment income earned on the principal to cover loss or use the principal itself. Obviously the greater the risk to the investor, the higher the interest that will need to be offered. If the investor stands to lose their capital rather than merely the return on that capital, they will require considerable compensation for running such a risk. Investors will typically be hedge or private equity funds, seeking high returns and a diversified investment portfolio. The 'risk thermometer' of such funds will be set at a considerably higher level than pension funds, for example.

As this is not an insurance contract, it is not bound by principles of insurance law and a variety of triggers can be used. Many do use an indemnity trigger whereby the bond is liable to pay insured losses as would be the case in traditional reinsurance. This may be estimated by modelling the loss in advance and triggering payments based upon applying the event to the model rather than waiting to see whether the actual loss follows the estimate. The advantage is that payments are triggered immediately and the issuer does not have to deal with the problem of finding the necessary liquidity to meet claims. This may result in a payment that is more or less than the actual loss, but is analogous to an agreed value policy.

Alternatively, the payments may be triggered by industry losses. Therefore, if total insured losses arising out of a defined event exceed a specified sum, the issuer has the right to call upon the bond. This assumes that the issuer is proportionately exposed to loss, which may or may not be the case and stretches the indemnity principle to breaking point.

In some cases, the principle of indemnity may be dispensed with altogether, with set payments made, dependent on the magnitude and location of the event. Therefore, in the case of an earthquake, a formula will be devised to determine payments based upon the strength of the quake as per the Richter scale and its epicentre. The stronger the quake and the closer it is to the risk, the higher the payout. The argument for the indemnity principle is one of moral hazard, that if the policyholder is allowed to speculate, they may seek to influence the occurrence of the risk. In the case of earthquake, such moral hazard does not exist as the occurrence is wholly outside the control of the policyholder. These parametric triggers, as they are known, will often be combined with modelling to ensure that the sums paid do bear some resemblance to likely loss.

Although a high risk investment, the attraction for investors is that the cat bond risk is not correlated to market risk. Normally, in times of economic recession, all investments are likely to perform poorly as stock markets fall and defaults on bonds rise. Diversifying investments does not help to reduce risk if they all fall in value simultaneously. As natural disasters occur irrespective of economic conditions, the investor can spread their risk to a degree. It must, however, be said that at present the cat bond market is significantly smaller than the traditional reinsurance market. It is also hampered by a close correlation with reinsurance pricing. In hard market conditions (usually following the occurrence of major catastrophe losses), the number of issues increases. As the market softens, so the reliance on cat bonds decreases. The costs of issuing a bond are significant, therefore if reinsurance prices fall, cat bonds can become comparatively uncompetitive. Unless a longer-term view is taken whereby the costs are averaged over a number of years, this may hamper the development of this form of risk financing.

Reinsurance sidecars

These are analogous to quota share reinsurance or retrocession. They are so called because they sit alongside the main insurance/reinsurance venture and provide additional capital. Structured as separate but associated companies, rather than specifically covering individual risk, they are designed to provide additional capacity at a time when capital is hard to come by. Unlike cat bonds which come pre-packaged and can involve relatively low investments, sidecars are individually negotiated and will tend to require significant financial commitment, albeit on a fairly short-term basis. Losses or profits are shared between the insurance company and the sidecar in pre-determined proportions (hence they can be viewed as a form of quota share reinsurance). Typical investors will again be hedge or private equity funds.

The question then arises, why not simply invest in the insurer or reinsurer directly? A return will be generated that should closely follow the fortunes of that company. The answer is that the sidecar allows an investment in the outcome of only one part of the insurer's business, usually the volatile property catastrophe risk associated with natural disasters. The period is finite, possibly one year but not necessarily, and there will only be a single cedant. In addition, the investor can influence the investment strategy of the sidecar. The advantage to the insurer is that the ceded risks are collateralised. The funds are actually handed over and controlled by the ceding insurer and are therefore to hand if called upon. In the case of traditional reinsurance, the claims would have to be met first before a claim could then be made upon the reinsurer. There would be a credit risk as the reinsurer's solvency cannot be guaranteed.

The problem, however, is that so far these arrangements have only proved attractive to investors when a hard or hardening market is anticipated and the investors wish to benefit from the supernormal profits that such market conditions generally produce. In a softening market, capital is likely to desert the sidecars. Admittedly a soft market is indicative of over-capacity and the loss of capital is not critical, but catastrophe insurance should be viewed as a long-term investment due to the extreme volatility that may be experienced.

Conclusion

In Chapter 1, it was argued that insurers can only really be comfortable covering particular risks and that the occurrence of a truly fundamental risk has the potential to bring down the insurer if fully covered. Nonetheless there remains a demand for cover which the insurance industry will always be under pressure to provide. It is financially inefficient for insurers to permanently maintain capital to meet the cost of occasional catastrophe losses, hence the existence of reinsurers who are used as the repositories of such long-term capital.

As has been seen, even the reinsurers struggle to provide the capacity to fully cover catastrophe events with the result that much of the loss is uninsured. There is no reason, however, why the financial consequences of the largest disaster reasonably foreseeable should not be adequately spread. This after all is what insurance is supposed to do. However, in order to achieve this, the greater resources of the capital markets and possibly governments need to be utilised.

At present, an ad hoc system manages to provide inconsistent coverage against fundamental risks to a minority of policyholders through primary insurance, backed by a mixture of reinsurance, capital market solutions and government initiatives (Figure 14.4). The capital markets have yet to demonstrate a commitment to long-term, permanent risk-financing

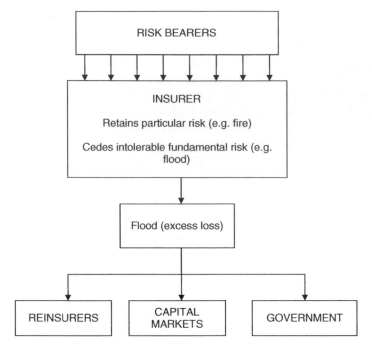

Figure 14.4 The source of finance for fundamental risks.

solutions, tending only to participate when short-term supranormal returns are potentially on offer. Governments tend to be unwilling participants.

There are examples of this structure in operation. Pool Re's terrorism cover follows this model, as does the National Flood Insurance Protection scheme in the United States. What has not been fully evolved is the capital market option. Perhaps the next stage of evolution in risk financing is capital market solutions, whether on the cat bond or reinsurance sidecar model, to provide long-term financing of catastrophe loss.

Insurers have for centuries dealt efficiently with particular risks and there is no reason to suppose that they will not continue to do so. This is due to the experience they have gained as administrators of risk pools. They have the necessary systems in place to market insurance products, price risk and collect premiums and negotiate claims settlements. This experience and the administrative structures that have been established, form a part of the solution to the handling of fundamental risk even if the potential losses are beyond the capacity of the insurers. There is no reason why this should not permit catastrophe events to be insured and administered by a standard insurance policy.

As regards fundamental risks, the insurers could then be viewed as an intermediary, collecting premium contributions from huge numbers of policyholders and passing them on to reinsurers. The reinsurers can then in turn use their expertise in risk modelling to construct retrocessional products, backed by the capital markets (Figure 14.5). The capital markets have the financial ability to bear the risk and expertise in managing financial risk, but lack the structures to use this financial muscle to market risk assumption products to the millions of potential customers. They certainly do not have the ability to handle the large

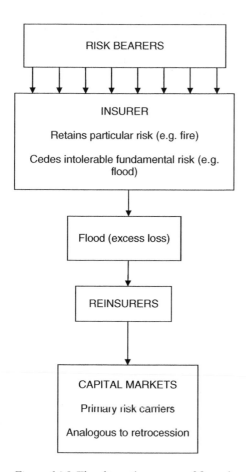

Figure 14.5 The alternative means of financing fundamental risk.

number of claims that will emanate from a major disaster. This is a role that insurers are uniquely equipped to fulfil.

Although there are some signs that this model is beginning to emerge, for example, the involvement of some reinsurance companies in the development of cat bonds, it is far from being the standard approach to fundamental risk. The position is distorted by the involvement of governments, however unwillingly, as the insurer of last resort. While such coverage is in place, there is reduced incentive on the part of the private sector to cultivate their own solutions. If the loss bearing capacity of the capital markets is properly utilised, governments should not need to be involved. However, it may be difficult for them to withdraw unless private sector solutions are in place, but their involvement hinders the development of such solutions.

Such solutions need to be long term and, within the limitations of insurance transactions, reasonably stable. Whether the hedge funds which make up much of the alternative risk transfer market in this area are prepared to invest in the medium to long term is open to question. A short-term involvement in a reinsurance sidecar is one thing, managing catastrophe risk over a period of ten to fifteen years is quite another. The potential is there for financial markets to use their various strengths and abilities to provide wide-ranging catastrophe protection. The development of such products remains in its infancy. However, perhaps in future, should another event such as Hurricane Katrina occur, maybe the majority of the loss will be covered rather than less than half.

Appendix I The major classes of personal lines insurance

Private motor

Since the original *Road Traffic Act 1930*, some degree of liability cover has, for the great majority of road users, been compulsory. The original Act has gone through various incarnations over the years, however this basic compulsion has remained constant.

Compulsory insurance

The *Road Traffic Act 1988* s143(1) states:

> [A]person must not use a motor vehicle on the road unless there is in force in relation to the use of the vehicle by that person such a policy of insurance … in respect of third party risks as complies with the requirements … of this Act.

It is also an offence to 'cause or permit any other person to use a motor vehicle' unless valid insurance is in force. Certain bodies are exempt. For example central government, county or metropolitan councils and police authorities do not have to insure (although many choose to do so).

To be valid, a motor policy must be issued by an insurer authorised to write motor insurance under the terms of the *Financial Services & Markets Act 2000* and that insurer must be a member of the Motor Insurers Bureau (see Chapter 12). The policy must insure against legal liability for death or injury to an unlimited amount and for damage to property to a minimum of £250,000 (in practice, private policies usually offer unlimited cover against property damage claims). A certificate of insurance must be delivered by the insurer to the policyholder (or their agent).

Since 1973, a further dimension has been added to the UK law as a result of membership of the EU. A fundamental principle of the Treaty of Rome is that there is free movement of goods and services within the EU. Differing compulsory motor insurance laws could prevent the free movement of vehicles and therefore the free movement of goods. The only answer is to have a European wide standard.

1   *The 1st EU Directive* – As a first step towards harmonisation of the law across Europe, this introduced the requirement that all motor insurance policies issued within the EU provide the minimum legal cover in all other member states. Several non-EU states have also joined the agreement, such as Switzerland and Norway. This automatic cover could vary according to differing minimum requirements.

2   *The 2nd EU Directive* – This introduced provisions concerning compulsory insurance and uninsured injury and damage. Third Party property damage must be included within the minimum required cover, however a maximum limit is permitted (£250,000 in the UK). The insurer of a vehicle must pay personal injury claims arising out of the use of that vehicle regardless of whether the loss is actually insured and irrespective of who is driving the vehicle. Compensation schemes must be introduced for injury and damage caused by uninsured or unidentified drivers, although property damage may be excluded or limited.

3   *The 3rd EU Directive* – The directive required that any motor policy issued in the EU provided minimum legal cover or normal policy cover (whichever was higher) in any member state without additional premium. It also extended compulsory insurance requirements to include liability to all passengers.

4   *The 4th EU Directive* – This concentrated on cross-border claims, allowing motorists to sue the insurer directly. The insurer must have a local office or agent in each EU state to handle such claims. The compensation body (the MIB in the UK) is liable to settle claims if no such representation exists or they settle too slowly. The claim will then be passed to their counterpart in the state of domicile of the insurer who will then seek reimbursement from the insurer.

5   *The 5th EU Directive* – This amended existing directives, but several requirements are significant. For example, the minimum level of third party property damage cover was raised to €1 million. This has yet to be incorporated into UK law, although as stated above, in the case of private motor policies, such cover is generally offered on an unlimited basis. The directive also required that the compensatory body (the MIB) provide cover for property damage caused by untraced drivers if the accident also caused 'significant' injury.

Cover available

Third party only

This covers the legal minimum and little more. Therefore, it covers against third party claims for personal injury and property damage as required by law, but would not provide any cover in respect of loss of or damage to the vehicle itself. This would include legal costs incurred in defending a claim and would usually also pay for the cost of representation at an inquest or fatal accident enquiry (but not usually for general criminal proceedings).

Third party, fire and theft

This covers third party risks as above, but with the inclusion of cover for fire and theft, in other word, limited property damage cover. Theft in the sense of motor vehicles has its own meaning. Usually an element of theft is an intention to permanently deprive. s12 of the *RTA 1988* makes the taking of a vehicle without authorisation a separate offence and this unauthorised use would fall within the definition of theft for insurance purposes. This would include cover not only for the total disappearance of the vehicle, but also for damage caused prior to recovery. Note, however, the vehicle must actually be stolen; repairing damage due to an attempted break-in is not usually covered under motor theft cover, neither is the theft of parts or accessories where the vehicle itself is not stolen.

Comprehensive

This extends the limited cover on a TPF & T policy to include cover against accidental or malicious damage to the vehicle. Note that this approach does not limit how the damage might occur, it is sufficient to establish that it is unintended on the part of the policyholder. There may also be a modicum of cover in respect of contents of vehicles, but limits will be low (say, £100) and valuables will be excluded. Anything actually attached to the vehicle, however, (stereo system, for example) is usually covered.

Laid up cover

If a vehicle is not in use and kept on private land where compulsory insurance would not be required, it is possible to insure the vehicle against physical damage. This might be on a fire and theft basis or a comprehensive basis.

Types of policy

Private car

Obviously this is the most common policy issued, and all the above cover options are widely available (dependent upon insurance history and risk, of course). The policy covers identified vehicles (usually one per policy although multi-vehicle policies are available). It is also usual to offer policyholders over the age of 25 third party only cover while driving other vehicles.

The premium is based upon a factor of type of car, age of driver, driving history and location, less a no claims discount (NCD) calculated on the number of claim-free years up to a maximum of 60–65 per cent. Cars are allocated to a 'group' numbered from 1 to 20. The higher the value and/or performance of the car, the higher the group and therefore base premium will tend to be. This is not absolute as factors such as vehicle security, likely cost of repair and passenger safety are all relevant and are not necessarily correlated to the purchase price of the car.

Cover is always offered for social, domestic and pleasure use, but it is usual to include personal business use. This would allow the vehicle to be used for commuting but would exclude commercial travelling. The carriage of goods or persons for hire or reward is a standard exclusion (but car sharing with no element of profit is not deemed to be 'hire or reward').

Motorcycles

Whereas once it was normal to cover the rider to ride any motorcycle up to a certain size, now a group rating is applied in the same way as for car insurance. The same criteria as regards driver age and history and location apply and NCD is also a standard feature.

Home insurance

Home insurance covers physical, tangible property against various perils causing loss of or damage to the property. This usually constitutes either buildings or the contents of buildings, although moveable property can also be covered outside the home.

Modern policies are, however, usually hybrid policies as they almost always cover the legal liability associated with the ownership and/or occupation of buildings. Contents policies almost always cover the personal liability of the policyholder.

The standard home insurance policy originally covered fire, lightning and explosion, although such restrictive cover is unlikely to be encountered today and cover is usually modified by the addition of cover for additional perils. Common examples are:

Aircraft (including 'aerial devices')
Earthquake
Storm and Flood
Riot & Civil Commotion
Burst Pipes
Malicious Damage
Impact (Various options)
Subsidence
Accidental Damage

The property insured is covered under three headings:

1   Buildings
2   Contents
3   Personal Possessions

Buildings cover

This cover is important as it underpins the entire mortgage system. The existence of buildings cover is a requirement of any mortgage and it follows that mortgage lenders have been influential in developing cover in this area. A good example of this is subsidence cover, introduced at the behest of the mortgage lenders. Cover is usually on a fire and special perils basis, however accidental damage cover is widely available. A standard feature of cover is the cost of alternative accommodation if the property is uninhabitable following insured damage (or loss of rent if the property is rented out).

The definition of 'building' is drawn wider than most people assume. In law, anything permanently attached to a structure becomes a part of that structure. Therefore a buildings policy would cover the replacement of wallpaper following insured damage, but not the cost of carpets or curtains, which can be removed and therefore are not considered to be attached to the structure. In addition, outbuildings, walls and fences would also be considered 'buildings' although cover may be reduced.

Contents cover

The cover offered is on a similar basis to a buildings policy, but is more likely to cover accidental damage. The policy only covers moveable contents while in the home and not fixtures and fittings, i.e. the kind of property that might be taken in a house move. Cover will generally extend to the contents of garages and outbuildings although possibly on a more restrictive basis. Property which should be insured by other classes of policy will be excluded, therefore motor vehicles or boats kept in a garage will not be covered as these, although personal property, should be covered by a motor or marine policy. Contents policies usually offer a number of extensions often offering cover for personal possessions outside the home, cover for bicycles and other classes of insurance as part of a package or combined policy.

All Risks cover and accidental damage cover

The average consumer tends to view these variations on fire and perils cover as one and the same. There is though a subtle but possibly important difference. Accidental Damage is an extension to a Fire & Perils policy, if you like, the peril of unspecified accidental damage. Sudden and unforeseen damage to property is covered but gradual deterioration is not. The nature of the damage is not specified in advance, which is a departure from the normal principle of a perils policy. Although this cover is derived from the standard fire policy, the difference is that instead of the insured having to demonstrate that a particular peril has operated and that it caused the damage, the insured has the easier task of showing that the damage was fortuitous and not excluded.

An All Risks wording has no specified perils. The policy covers sudden and unforeseen loss, subject to an exclusion of gradual deterioration. This appears to be one and the same, however, accidental damage extensions do not override the provisions of clauses covering specified perils. If a loss clearly caused by fire is not covered due to the terms of the clause covering fire, the policyholder cannot turn to the accidental damage clause and attempt to claim under that.

Household cover is very rarely offered on an All Risks basis, but accidental damage extensions are widely available. The exception is personal possessions cover. Usually a contents policy only provides cover while the property is at the insured address. Personal possessions cover provides cover anywhere in the UK (perhaps even extended to provide cover overseas). This is usually issued on an All Risks basis. Originally this was designed to cover jewelry and other valuables, each item being identified and valued in advance. These days, unspecified items are covered, although a limit on any one item is imposed.

There is a basic presumption that an All Risks insurance policy covers sudden unanticipated losses, while a perils policy will specify cover. All policies exclude wear and tear, gradual deterioration, moths and vermin. The mechanical or electrical breakdown of property is not covered, although separate specialist policies are available, usually marketed as extended warranties. The general insurance exclusions apply, war-related and nuclear risks being the common examples.

Travel

Travel insurance is widely purchased, generally for minimal premiums and for many years most sales were largely unregulated. This is surprising as it is actually a rather complex policy. Travel cover usually offers multiple categories of cover, with the added complication that it is often purchased well in advance of the trip.

The main sections would be:

Medical expenses (including repatriation)
Baggage and personal possessions
Money, tickets and travellers cheques
Personal accident
Cancellation and curtailment

Personal liability
Legal expenses

The policy is then a hybrid of life, health, property, liability and contingency insurance.

Cover is offered according to geographical areas, with premiums for North American holidays being more expensive due to the high costs of health care. Standard cover will exclude a number of activities likely to result in injury, with specialist policies available for skiing and other higher risk sports.

Personal accident and sickness

Although a variation on life assurance, covering as it does life and limb, personal accident insurance is offered by general insurers. The policy provides a set benefit in the event of accidental death or specified injuries (loss of limb, eye, permanent disablement, etc.). No cover is provided for death or injury arising from natural causes.

In addition, policies may provide a weekly benefit while policyholders are unable to work due to illness or injury. Unlike Permanent Health (see Chapter 10), the benefits will only be payable for a limited period, usually a maximum of one year for sickness and two years for accident and will be subject to an excess period of not less than one week during which no benefit will be paid.

A variation on this type of cover is mortgage protection or payment protection insurance which undertakes to meet the cost of the loan while the policyholder is unable to work due to accident or illness. The policy will, however, often cover other contingencies such as losing one's job due to redundancy, which moves cover outside the personal accident class.

Private marine and aviation

Although marine and aviation are primarily known as commercial insurance classes, private yachts and aircraft are of course insured. The basis of cover is broadly similar to the commercial cover, albeit generally in a simplified form. Cover would usually extend to cover the hull as well as legal liabilities (indeed, the existence of such cover would often be a prerequisite for entry to harbours or airports). Quasi-commercial cover exists for commercial charter of private yachts and aircraft.

Appendix II The major classes of commercial insurance

Commercial property

Cover is usually divided into three categories, although variations may exist according to the nature of the business:

1   *Buildings* – Generally covered for the full rebuilding cost, the principle is similar to the insurance of domestic buildings. The variety of buildings insured is wide, and cover may be limited in the case of particularly vulnerable structures, for example, an exclusion of storm cover for open sided structures.
2   *Plant, machinery and other contents* – The permanent physical assets of the firm, again almost always insured on a reinstatement cost basis (the cost of replacing the item with a new item of similar quality and specification). This can include machinery used for manufacturing or processing, furniture, office equipment and items of mobile plant.
3   *Stock* – This section covers consumables used in the business and includes raw materials, finished goods, stock held for sale and stationery. Such property is insured on a replacement cost basis, so the policy does not cover expected profit margins on the sale of such items.

Standard fire policy

The starting point for all commercial property insurance is the standard fire policy for the simple reason that when the cover originated, fire was the only peril covered. In its modern incarnation, cover is offered for losses arising out of fire, lightning and explosion. However, in order that the policy cannot be confused with policies offering wider perils cover, fire resulting from other commonly insured perils (earthquake or riot) is excluded. In addition, explosion cover is limited to explosion of domestic-type boilers or gas supplies for lighting or heating the building, although other explosions caused by a fire would be covered (fire would in this event be the proximate cause).

Fire and special perils

Over time, additional perils have been added to the cover offered by the standard fire policy, either due to policyholder demands or possibly as a marketing tool for insurers. They are commonly subdivided into 'wet' perils (i.e involving water) and dry perils. Alternatively, perils can be subdivided according to their nature.

Chemical perils

1   *Explosion* – This widens the cover offered by the standard fire policy (SFP) to include the risk of explosion caused by materials used by the business. Obvious examples include petroleum products or liquefied gas. Less obvious is the explosion risk presented by dust, for example, flour or sugar. What is not covered is explosion of the insured's own pressure plant (industrial boilers or compressors). This is to avoid overlap with engineering policies.

2   *Spontaneous combustions* – Rare in practice, but bulk storage of coal or coke and certain fertilisers can cause this peril to occur. Vegetable matter can spontaneously combust as well, however this is actually a biological problem rather than chemical.

Social perils

1   *Riot and civil commotion* – Arson caused by the firm's own workforce as a result of a labour dispute is covered under the SFP, arson by rioters is excluded. Such cover is available and the extension would cover not just fire, but other forms of physical damage inflicted in the course of a riot.

2   *Malicious damage* – Related to riot cover, but the definition of riot requires at least three persons to be throwing bricks. This extension covers the possibility that one or two persons might cause damage. In practice, malice is not required (although usually present), and criminal damage as defined by the *Criminal Damage Act 1971* suffices. The difference being that under this Act reckless behaviour is included, the crime being one of basic intent. Again, such damage must be physical.

Perils of nature

1   *Storm and tempest* – The issue here is what constitutes 'storm'. In *Oddy v Phoenix Assurance (1966)*, storm was held to mean 'some form of violent wind usually accompanied by rain or hail or snow'. Tempest was held to mean merely a severe storm and the wording is in fact unnecessary. In practice, a hailstorm would probably be considered to be storm damage even though wind is rarely a factor. Even heavy rain or snow might constitute storm damage if the weight of water/snow was the cause of damage. Freezing temperatures, on the other hand, are not considered 'storms' and frost damage is excluded.

2   *Flood* – The escape of water from lakes, rivers or canals is clearly covered, as is inundation by the sea in many cases. Floods caused by the run off of ground water are not covered by many wordings.

3   *Earthquake* – The SFP excludes fire caused by earthquake; the cover can however, be extended by including this peril. Severe structural damage from this cause is rare in the UK, although mild tremors do occur occasionally. Subterranean fire is a further derivation, often covered as a separate peril.

4   *Subsidence* – Although a standard feature of domestic property insurance, this peril is not a standard commercial peril. It is, however, insurable and can be included.

5   *Burst pipes* – Although an internal risk, this is essentially a weather-related risk normally brought about by extremely cold weather (although accidental damage to pipes and the overflowing of tanks is normally included). Cover may also be offered for sprinkler leakage following accidental damage.

Impact perils

1   *Aircraft* – Although predominantly referring to aircraft as commonly understood, this would include all 'aerial devices or articles dropped therefrom'. This could be anything from a space station to a couple of kilos of yellow ice ejected from a passing aeroplane. In fact this has given rise to a modified form of the SFP, known as the FLEA (fire, lightning, explosion and aircraft). The possibility of loss is remote but the consequences are catastrophic. It is also worth noting that such losses would be likely to give rise to a subrogated claim against the aircraft's insurers.
2   *Impact* – Impacts caused by road vehicles or animals are covered. This commonly excludes damage caused by the policyholder's vehicles, but an extension of cover is generally possible. Again, subrogation is probable in the event of damage caused by vehicles.

Commercial All Risks

A modern development has been to extend cover to include damage caused by most accidental means. Originally this was achieved by adding a further clause covering unspecified accidental damage. It was, however, realised that all the previously mentioned perils could fall under this heading and new wordings appeared on the now commonplace Commercial All Risks basis. This is a new approach. Instead of saying what the policy does cover, such wordings concentrate on what is *not* covered. Therefore, so long as the damage is accidental and does not fall foul of policy exclusions it should be covered. Standard exclusions include:

   Fundamental risks – war, nuclear risks, sonic bangs
   Political risks – confiscation or detention by government
   Non-fortuitous risks – wear and tear, gradual deterioration, action of pests and vermin
   Unproved loss – unexplained inventory shortage
   Internal derangement – electrical or mechanical breakdown.

Cover is undoubtedly wider than that offered by the Fire and Special Perils wording. The title 'All Risks' is misleading, however, as no insurance policy ever provides cover against *all* risks to the subject matter.

Theft

Theft cover is normally granted separately from the main property insurance (although usually as a separate section of a single policy rather than a separate contract). This is due to differences in the approach taken towards such cover in comparison to consumer policies. Commercial theft cover is limited to theft following forcible and/or violent entry or exit to or from the premises. The policy does not therefore cover pilferage or shoplifting. Theft by employees is excluded as are thefts involving the collusion of employees. Collusion is likely to be present if non-forcible entry has occurred, as it is not unheard of for copies of keys to be provided to the thieves.

Pecuniary loss

Such insurances cover purely financial losses. This may be the loss of the financial assets of the firm, but can also constitute the loss of expected future financial assets.

Money

This covers physical loss or damage to cash and negotiable instruments (cheques, money orders, etc.) at the firm's premises and in transit. Although theft is the main risk, such policies would also cover against damage on an All Risks basis. Theft cover would exclude theft by the firm's own employees.

Fidelity guarantee

Such policies insure against dishonesty by employees. This can cover named individuals, any employee holding a designated position or all employees. Although primarily designed to protect against the risk of financial frauds, cover can be extended to include the theft of company property which is not strictly a pecuniary insurance. Although less widely purchased than theft insurance, the risk of significant loss is usually greater. Not only do employees have free access to accounts and goods, they also have the opportunity to cover their tracks. Such dishonesty can be hidden for an extended period, increasing the risk that large sums will be lost.

Credit

This insures against the risk of bad debts. Where credit is extended to buyers, the insurer will settle the invoice if the debt proves unrecoverable due to the insolvency (or possibly fraud) of the debtor. In order to encourage sound credit control, insurers would insist upon a substantial co-insurance clause under which the policyholder would be liable for 10 per cent or more of the debt. Given the close correlation between economic recession and a rise in the level of bad debts, it could be argued that this is a fundamental risk. Certainly insurers can expect to see significant variation in their annual loss ratios based upon underlying economic factors.

Business interruption

The largest and perhaps most critical form of pecuniary insurance is business interruption insurance, also known as consequential loss or loss profits insurance. This form of cover compensates the business for the loss of expected future profits following damage to the insured premises and possibly due to other defined events.

The basic intent of the cover is to provide the necessary compensation to allow a business to survive while physical damage to its assets is put right. In the absence of such cover, the availability of insurance against serious property damage would be irrelevant as the business would probably fail due to cash flow problems in any event. This is not an insurance against the basic risks of the business environment; however, with the exception of certain defined extensions, cover is only operative following material damage to property insured under an underlying policy, almost certainly, but not necessarily, insured by the business interruption insurer. The extent of cover would therefore be determined by the underlying property damage policy.

The cover is often extended to cover damage occurring other than at the insured premises which causes interruption to the business. This would include damage causing denial of access to the premises, damage to the premises of public utilities and suppliers' or customers' premises.

Policy cover does not simply operate until the damage has been repaired, it operates during the period of interruption and is designed to compensate for loss of income arising from the original physical damage. It can be anticipated that even once the firm is back in full production, it will take time to recover market share and the policy should continue to compensate until the business is back in the position it was prior to the incident.

Property policies contain a specific exclusion of any consequential loss, requiring separate cover, commonly insured as an additional section on a combined policy. Nonetheless, loss of profits is insured by a material damage policy, but only where the goods have been sold and are awaiting delivery. In such cases the loss of profit is factual rather than based on expectancy and therefore forms a part of the insured's proprietary interest.

The compensation paid will be based upon the turnover of the business for the equivalent period in the year prior to the loss. This will then be adjusted to reflect known trends such as inflation, an observed rise or fall in turnover or changes in the business. Any cost savings resulting from the cessation or reduction in business activity will then be deducted from the turnover figure in order to indemnify the policyholder for their actual loss, it being the gross profit rather than the turnover. Known as specified working expenses, this would include items such as purchases, light heat and power, business rates and rent (if the business is no longer liable to pay). Wage costs would normally be insured. Although the business can elect not to insure the wages, the cost of laying off the workforce, subsequent recruitment costs and the poor industrial relations that will result, mean that this is not likely to be cost effective.

The sum insured is based on the expected gross profit, often covered on a declaration basis. The policyholder estimates the figure and a deposit premium is paid. At the end of the period, the actual figure is declared and the premium is adjusted accordingly. The policyholder selects the maximum period for which an indemnity will be provided. This would normally be between 12 and 24 months from the date of loss, although longer and shorter periods may be covered according to circumstances.

Liability

These policies are designed to cover compensatory awards made against the insured business together with the associated legal costs, usually following personal injury or property damage, but including pure financial loss in some circumstances. Cover is provided via a number of distinct policies.

Public liability

These policies cover the general liability of the policyholder to members of the public, including customers, suppliers and persons on or in the vicinity of the firm's premises. The insurer will indemnify the policyholder against legal liability to pay compensation and claimants' costs and expenses in respect of:

(a) bodily injury to any person;
(b) loss of or damage to material property;
(c) nuisance, trespass, obstruction or interference with any right of way, light, air or water resulting in financial loss.

Such liability must occur within the geographical limits specified during the period of insurance in connection with the business. The policy will, however, exclude personal injury to employees or claims arising from the sale or supply of products. The property damage cover will not operate in respect of property in the custody or control of the policyholder (this should be insured under a property insurance policy). Liability arising out of the use of motor vehicles is excluded, however it is possible to cover vehicles used off the road as a tool of trade.

Although pollution claims are covered, this cover is limited to sudden and accidental pollution. Claims caused by long-term emissions would not be indemnified, whether intended or not.

The policy will be subject to a maximum limit of indemnity which will need to be sufficient to meet compensation costs and the third parties' legal fees arising from incidents occurring during the period of insurance. The policyholder's legal fees will be met in addition to the limit of indemnity. It is common to arrange excess of loss insurance over and above the primary policy to ensure that a prudent level of cover is available.

Product liability

The policy is intended to pay compensation for sums the policyholder is legally liable to pay to third parties in respect of accidental bodily injury or accidental damage to property caused by the policyholder's products. The wording will be broadly similar to that of a public liability policy from which it is derived. Indeed, it is rare for product liability cover to be issued in isolation, it is almost always provided as a package with public liability.

Limits of indemnity operate in the same way as public liability policy. Even greater care is required in selecting an adequate limit, as a manufacturing defect can affect multiple products and therefore give rise to multiple claims. Certain industries are particularly exposed, for example, drugs companies who face vast claims if a drug is found to cause harmful side affects, thalidomide being a notorious example. Geographical limitations are also more important due to the possibility that goods may be exported. It would be normal to exclude products exported to North America and while such cover may be available by special arrangement, it will be expensive due to the high cost of legal settlements. Similarly, products supplied to the aviation industry are excluded. Such cover is provided by aviation insurers due to its specialised nature.

Employers' liability

Under the terms of the *Employers' Liability (Compulsory Insurance) Act 1969*, all employers carrying on business in the UK must insure against liability for bodily injury and disease sustained by employees in the course of employment. The *Employers Liability (Compulsory Insurance) Regulations 1971* specified a minimum cover of £2 million per occurrence (raised to £5 million in January 1999). Certificates of insurance must be displayed at every place of employment. The intent of this legislation is to ensure that employees injured at work due to the fault of their employers are guaranteed that financial compensation will be forthcoming.

Cover is limited to personal injury claims made by employees and arising out of the course of their employment. Although it was once standard practice to provide unlimited cover, as a reaction to the huge claims received in the aftermath of the Piper Alpha oil rig disaster in 1988, all policies are now subject to a limit of indemnity. A minimum level of £10 million would be normal, although again excess of loss cover can be purchased to provide higher levels of protection. In the same way as public liability, this would cover compensation and claimant's legal costs, with defence costs paid in addition.

Note that there is no reason why a claim from an employee in a situation other that the course of employment should not be met by a public liability policy or if appropriate a product liability policy.

Professional indemnity

Public/product liability policies exclude cover for advice, design or specification provided for a fee. They generally only cover personal injury and property damage and not claims for pure financial loss. Professional indemnity (PI) insurance is available to cover these eventualities. Although derived to cover the legal liabilities of recognised professions (lawyers, accountants, surveyors, architects, etc.), the scope is now far broader, covering a wide variety of consultancy, broking and design roles. The policy covers legal liabilities arising from errors or omissions by the policyholder and indeed is often abbreviated as 'E & O' insurance.

As with other forms of liability insurance, PI coverage is subject to a limit of indemnity. Unlike other forms of liability insurance, this is almost always an aggregate limit rather than a limit on any one claim or event (although product liability policies in particular will often have an aggregate limit as well). They are also distinct as they are the only UK liability policies issued on a claims made basis. Most liability insurance is on an occurrence basis, covering incidents occurring during the period of insurance irrespective of when the claim is notified to the policyholder (which may of course be many years later). A claims made policy only covers claims actually made during the period of insurance. When the policy expires, no further cover is available, unless the policy is renewed.

A variation of professional indemnity is Directors & Officers cover. Operating on much the same basis as PI, this covers the directors and senior officers against sums they may be legally obliged to pay due to the negligent performance of their duties. Such liability may be towards shareholders, creditors or employees, but such cover cannot indemnify any individual against the consequences of their own fraud or personal fines.

Commercial motor

The commercial motor sector is divided into two parts. First, there is the motor fleet market, comprising the private cars owned and operated by firms. Second, there is the insurance of commercial vehicles, being vehicles designed for commercial purpose.

Fleet insurance

Clearly it is nonsensical for companies operating perhaps hundreds of vehicles to purchase individual policies. In such cases all the vehicles are covered by a single policy and certificate. The certificate, instead of identifying a particular vehicle, only identifies a class of vehicle and covers all vehicles owned or operated by the policyholder within that class. If both private cars and commercial vehicles are included, then separate certificates would be needed as the wording of each certificate differs. The policyholder will then make periodic declarations of the number of vehicles in the fleet and the premium will be adjusted accordingly.

In the case of small fleets (less than 10 vehicles) an individual rating based on the vehicle may be used. Instead of the NCD system used in private motor insurance, a fleet discount is applied based upon previous claims experience. This is much more flexible than NCD which is based upon set increments. For larger fleets, instead of rating vehicles individually, a fleet policy will charge a flat premium for every vehicle. This minimises underwriting cost and maximises the economies of scale the fleet policy is designed to generate. There will be a clear correlation between claims experience and subsequent premium, encouraging good risk management.

Commercial vehicles

There are four main types of policy:

1   *Goods-carrying vehicles* – Cover can be issued either purely for the carriage of own goods or to include haulage work. The policy would exclude damage to goods being carried. This could cover any vehicle from a light van to an articulated lorry.
2   *Passenger-carrying vehicles* – This is a specialised area as there is a risk of heavy liability claims due to the number of passengers carried. This might include a variety of vehicles from taxis up to coaches and buses.
3   *Agricultural and forestry vehicles*.
4   *'Special types'* – Working vehicles such as construction plant when registered for road use. Cover will often include 'working risk' (liability associated with the use of the vehicle as a tool of trade). Also included in this category would be the weird and wonderful: ice cream vans, mobile chip vans, ambulances, hearses, etc.

Certificates of insurance will make it clear which of these use categories the policy is covering. Note that use is not determined by the type of vehicle, but on the basis of the policyholder's declaration regarding the use the vehicle will be put to. So, for example, multi-purpose vehicles like Landrovers may be insured as private cars, goods-carrying vehicles or agricultural vehicles. Where the use is commercial, it is usual to include cover for private use as many commercial vehicles are occasionally used for private purposes.

The cover issued to the motor trade forms an area of insurance all of its own. Motor traders have trade plates (registration plates that can be fitted to any vehicle). They also drive customer's vehicles, have their own demonstration vehicles and may also run courtesy or even hire cars. A single certificate is issued to cover all these possibilities, however the underwriting is complex due to the need to assess all these variables.

All motor policies would cover any third party liability associated with a trailer while it is being towed behind an insured vehicle (subject to restrictions on use). This cover can be extended on commercial policies to include accidental damage to the trailer, sometimes including damage while detached.

Engineering

This class of insurance is designed to cover against sudden and unforeseen damage and breakdown to items of machinery and plant. Rather than covering against external damage (largely the province of property insurance), engineering insurance covers risks such as explosion, breakdown or collapse. This may be extended to include operator error, damage to surrounding property or collision and, if required, the business interruption arising in consequence. Most engineering insurers also provide an inspection service providing the periodic surveys of pressure and lifting plant required by law.

Computer insurance is considered an engineering risk by some insurers. Cover is provided on an All Risks basis, which causes significant overlap with property insurance. Nonetheless risks such as the recompilation of lost data and the increased costs of working manually following breakdown or malicious viruses would fall into the natural province of engineering.

Construction

Construction insurances are hybrids of elements of property, liability and sometimes engineering covers. They are also noteworthy because they are in most cases insuring liabilities arising out of standard form contracts, allocating responsibility between contractor and employer.

The property element is covered by a contract works policy, covering the works in the course of construction, together with unfixed materials and construction plant and equipment. The policy is usually issued on an All Risks basis and indemnifies the policyholder against the cost of restoring the works to their pre-loss condition. It follows then that the insurer's exposure increases as the contract progresses until the point is reached close to completion when the value at risk is close to the full contract price. A variation is Erection All Risks, an engineering cover, which insures the risks associated with the erection or installation of major items of plant and machinery. Contract works cover can be extended to insure consequential losses such as a delay in receiving expected profits or increased interest charges on loans.

Any building contract would require the contractor to take out and maintain public and employer's liability insurance, including a requirement to indemnify the employer against sums they are legally liable to pay as a result of the contractors' work. Building contractors do not purchase product liability cover as this risk is not excluded from the public liability coverage. If the contractor is involved in the design of the works, a professional indemnity policy will be required as well, as public liability will only cover personal injury or property damage arising in consequence of defect design, materials or workmanship. There will be limited cover for damage to the works themselves and no cover for pure financial losses (where no physical damage occurs).

MAT (Marine, Aviation & Transportation)

Known generically by the acronym MAT, these are three independent but related market sectors. All cover the risks associated with the carriage of goods and/or persons, including the means of transport, the goods themselves and liabilities owed to passengers.

Marine

One of the oldest forms of insurance, the marine market is split into three main segments: hull, cargo and protection & indemnity (P & I) clubs. Policies may be time policies (issued for specified period, commonly 12 months), voyage policies (issued for the duration of a voyage) or open policies (open-ended coverage valid until determined by one of the parties, sometimes issued in respect of cargo risks). Marine hull and cargo policies are often valued polices, with the maximum indemnity agreed by policyholder and insurer in advance rather than determined after a loss. This is due to the practical difficulties involved in valuing property that may, after the loss, be at the bottom of the sea.

Hull

Hull insurers cover the ships themselves, cargo-carrying vessels, passenger ships and special cases such as dredgers and tugs. In addition to the hull proper, such policies will cover machinery and freight or hire charges. A variety of policies are available from different marine insurance markets around the world, mostly developments of the now defunct Lloyd's SG form, first used in 1779. Cover might be expected to include Marine Risks, such as the perils of the sea (storm, stranding, collision, etc.), fire, lightning and explosion, earthquake, aircraft, violent (but not clandestine) theft or piracy and earthquake. In addition, cover will be provided against damage to the hull caused by the explosion or failure of its own machinery, known as Inchmaree clauses. The Inchmaree clause also covers barratry (fraud by the master and/or crew). Limited liability cover is provided in the event of collision with another vessel, normally up to 75 per cent of the insured value, but only for damage to the vessel and/or its cargo. While damage to the vessel itself caused in an attempt to limit pollution, liability for discharge of pollutants is not itself covered.

As might be expected, the risk of war is excluded from a standard hull policy. Unusually war risks can be insured in marine insurance, by means of a special discord or war and strikes cover. As the vessels insured are widely distributed, war is not necessarily a fundamental risk to marine insurers as only a small percentage of risks are likely to be within a conflict zone at any one time. Only if warfare becomes more general (for example, the First and Second World Wars) will a marine insurer be unable to consider offering cover. Dependent upon the level of risk, cover can be purchased against the risks of war, strikes and in the modern era, terrorism.

Cargo

The goods carried on insured vessels are separately insured, by either the buyer or the seller of the goods, depending upon the contract between them. The cover offered can again vary from market to market. The most common form in the London market would be the Institute Cargo Clauses. First introduced in 1982, there are three levels of cover offered by the 'C' clauses, the 'B' clauses and the 'A' clauses.

The most basic cover is provided by the 'C' clauses, insuring against fire and explosion, sinking, capsizing or stranding, overturning or derailment, collision, discharge of cargo at port of distress and sacrifice or jettison. The 'B' clauses provide the same cover but add protection against earthquake, volcanic eruption or lightning, entry of sea, lake or river water into the vessel, conveyance, container or place of storage, the total loss of a package overboard or dropped during loading or unloading of a vessel and accidental jettison or washing overboard. The 'A' clauses provide cover on an All Risks basis.

It will be noted that, although termed marine cargo, the policy potentially provides cover for the entire journey and includes the risk of loss or damage while being conveyed or temporarily stored on land. A related version of the cover is goods in transit insurance, which insures, in a similar fashion to marine cargo, goods being transported by road or rail within a single country.

P & I clubs

These are mutual associations, established to meet the legal liabilities not covered by hull insurance. This would include the removal of or disposal of obstructions, wrecks or cargoes, liability for damage to property other than other vessels and property on such vessels, liability for damage to cargo or other property on the insured vessel. Liability for loss of life, personal injury or illness, including crew members and passengers, is insured. Cover for pollution or contamination may be included as well. Finally, the policy will meet the remaining collision liability not insured by the hull policy.

Aviation

Aviation insurance is in many ways similar to marine. This is unsurprising as both are international markets concerned with the carriage of goods and passengers. The first aviation covers were offered by Lloyd's marine syndicates and were based upon marine policies. Cover is therefore offered separately on hulls, cargo and liabilities, although it should be noted that air freight may be insured by a marine cargo policy which is not limited to sea voyages.

Aviation hull policies insure the hull, machinery, instruments and equipment of the aircraft on an All Risks basis. This would include parts or machinery temporarily removed. As in marine, war risks are excluded, but can be purchased separately, including strikes, terrorism and hijacking.

Aviation liability polices cover two major risks. First, the liability of the operator to passengers or goods being carried. This is usually limited by international convention. Second, their liability in respect of collision with other planes or impact with property on the ground. Aviation insurers also provide liability coverage to operators of airports and manufacturers of products intended for use on aircraft.

Energy

This is a specialised area of insurance which due to the nature of the risks insured provides a mix of marine and property insurance. The market sector insures the energy industry, including oil and gas production and refining, electricity generation and distribution and petrochemicals. These risks may be categorised as upstream (the supply of fuel to power stations or refineries) and downstream (the distribution of fuel or electricity). Although such risks have been insured for many years, the emergence of a defined energy insurance sector is a relatively new development and, it can be argued, is a response to demand for a more sophisticated approach to a high risk enterprise.

Policies may cover marine type risks such as offshore drilling rigs and undersea pipelines. Once ashore, fuel storage facilities and refineries are covered in a similar fashion to other commercial property. The insurance of electricity generation is particularly specialised, including as it does the requirement to cover nuclear power stations as well as those burning fossil fuels.

Index

Alternative risk financing (see also financial
  reinsurance) 295–301
  captive insurance 169, 287, 295–296
  catastrophe bonds 299–300
  reinsurance sidecars 301
Association of British Insurers (ABI)
  code of conduct 194–195
  statements of insurance practice 55–59, 76,
    251, 256–258

British Insurance Brokers Association (BIBA)
  196–197, 201
Broker (see intermediaries)

Claims 203–211
  Claims & Underwriting Exchange 208
  loss adjusters 209–212
  loss assessors 210–211
  fraud 206–209
Chartered Institute of Loss Adjusters (CILA)
  (see loss adjusters)
Compulsory insurance 205, 242–243, 259–262,
  266–267, 270, 305–307, 316–317
Contribution 51–55

Financial Ombudsman Service (FOS)
  252–258
  analysis 255
  criticism 255–258
  determination 254
  establishment 252–253
  funding 254–255
  jurisdiction 253–254
Financial reinsurance
  bankers 297–298
  rollers 298
  time and distance policies 298
Financial Services Authority (FSA)
  high level standards 117
  ICOBS 55, 58–60, 74, 76–77, 198–199,
    210, 251–252, 257–258
  prudential standards 117–122

role in the failure of Equitable Life
  129–135
solvency II 123–128
**Financial Services Compensation Scheme
  (FSCS)** 245–248
  compensation 245
  excluded policies 247–248
  operation 245–246
  levy funding 246–247

Government insurance schemes 265–272
  natural disasters 268–269
  terrorism 270–272
Indemnity 42–47
Institute of Insurance Brokers (IIB) 196–197,
  200–201
Insurable interest 25–32

Insurance accounting 89–97
  balance sheet 94–96
  insurance premium tax 97
  profit and loss 91–94
  ratios 90
  technical accounts 89–91
Insurance companies 103–106
  mutuals 104–105
  proprietary 105–106
Insurance concept 10–19
  Common pool 10–11
  equitable premium 11–12
  insurability of risk 15–18
  risk transfer 10
  role of insurers 12–13
Insurance contracts 64–76
  cancellation clause 73–74
  conditions 68, 71–73
  exclusions 67–68
  interpretation 74–75
  operative clause 66
  proposal forms 64–65
  recital clause 66
  renewal 75–76
  schedule 66–67

Insurance contracts (*Cont'd*)
  warranties 68–73
  Insurance Fraud Bureau 208
Insurance Ombudsman Bureau (IOB)
  (See also Financial Ombudsman Service)
  approach 249–250
  establishment 250–251
Intermediaries 185–202
  agency 187–190
  duties 191–193
  regulation 193–200

Life assurance 213–224
  legal aspects 218–219
  policies 216–218, 220
Lloyd's of London 136–163
  crisis 149–160
  corporate capital 161–162
  Equitas 157–159
  financing 138–142
  regulation 144–149

Motor Insurers Bureau (MIB) 259–264
  exclusions 261
  other functions 262–263
  recoveries 261
  uninsured drivers agreement 260–261
  untraced drivers agreement 262

Pensions 225–240
  annuities 228–229
  Equitable life and guaranteed annuity
    rates 232–234
  mis-selling 229–231
  occupational schemes 227–228
  state provision 225–227
Personal Insurance Arbitration Service (PIAS)
  251–252
Policies (see also life assurance)
  all risks 309
  aviation 321
  business interruption 314–315
  commercial motor 317–318
  commercial property 311–313
  construction 319
  employers liability 316–317
  energy 321
  engineering 318–319

  fidelity guarantee 314
  home 307–309
  marine 319–321
  personal accident 310
  product liability 316
  public liability 315–316
  private motor 305–307
  professional indemnity 317
  travel 309–310
Proximate cause 39–42

Risk 4–9
  definition 4
  fundamental 5–6
  hazard 5
  particular 5–6
  peril 5
  pure 5–6
  speculative 5–6
Regulation (see also Financial Services
    Authority) 106–129
  approaches 106–110
  developments in government supervision
    111–114
  Financial Services & Markets Act 2000
    117–118
  INSPRU 118–122
  insurer failure 127–129
  solvency II 123–128
Reinsurance 164–184
  market 180–181
  methods 169–173
  policies 173–180
  purpose 165–167
  systemic risk 181–183
Risk Management 286–304
  Heinrich triangle 287–288
  risk analysis 286–289
  risk control 289–293
  risk financing (see also alternative risk
    financing 293–301
Takaful (Islamic) insurance 272–285
Subrogation 47–51

Utmost good faith 32–39, 55–63
  materiality 34–37
  remedies 38–39
  law reform recommendations 55–63

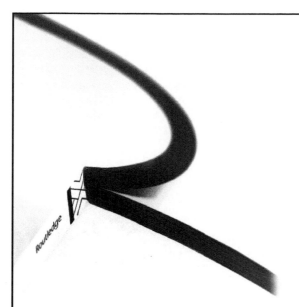